PICTURE PERFECT FLASH

Using Portable Strobes and Hot Shoe Flash
to Master Lighting and Create Extraordinary Portraits

ROBERTO VALENZUELA

rockynook

PICTURE PERFECT FLASH
Using Portable Strobes and Hot Shoe Flash
to Master Lighting and Create Extraordinary Portraits

Roberto Valenzuela
www.robertovalenzuela.com

Editors: Christina Borchers Leung and Ted Waitt
Project manager: Lisa Brazieal
Marketing coordinator: Katie Walker
Interior design and composition: Kim Scott/Bumpy Design
Front cover design: Aren Straiger
Cover production: Aren Straiger
Cover photograph: Roberto Valenzuela
Cover photo retoucher: Lana Polic
Proofreader: Linda Laflamme
Indexer: James Minkin

ISBN: 978-1-68198-973-0
1st Edition (1st printing, March 2024)
© 2024 Roberto Valenzuela
All images © Roberto Valenzuela except author photo on page vii and back cover by Peter Hurley
and R'Bonney Nola Gabriel photo on page xiv (photographer unknown)
Lighting diagrams and studio renderings were created with ellixier's set.a.light 3D software

Rocky Nook Inc.
1010 B Street, Suite 350
San Rafael, CA 94901
USA

www.rockynook.com

Distributed in the UK and Europe by Publishers Group UK
Distributed in the U.S. and all other territories by Publishers Group West

Library of Congress Control Number: 2022950236

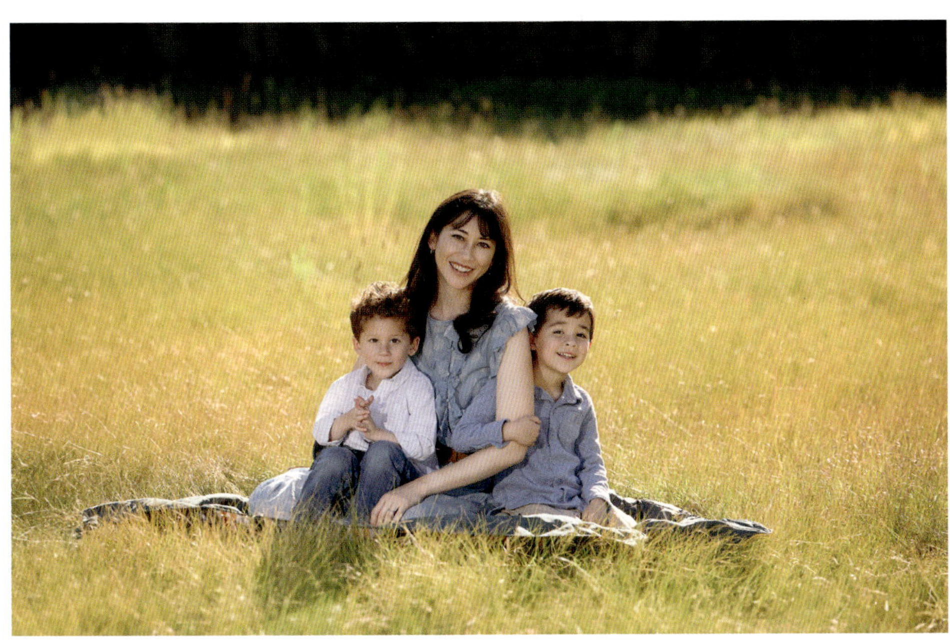

Acknowledgments

It is so rare these days to have an incredible relationship with industry friends for well over a decade now! For this reason, I have so much appreciation for my great publisher Rocky Nook's Scott Cowlin and Ted Waitt. Not only are we great friends, but we have the most fun working relationship. Like I have said before, writing a book is a huge undertaking; without the support of Scott and Ted, this book and any other book I have written would simply not be possible. To Ted and Scott, thank you both so much for your friendship and everything you have done for me as an author! I love you both very much.

To my beautiful mom, I love you so much, Mutti! You have always inspired me to have an enormous work ethic and hunger to succeed. Also my big brother Antonio, my sister Blanca, and my little sister Susana, and my awesome brother-in-law Daniel Yu. I would also like to thank my brother-in-law Kent for always being a great listener and advisor in personal and business matters. To my awesome nephew Ethan. It's been so fun seeing you become an adult and staying as cool as you have always been! I have always been so proud of you Ethan. To my little nephew Caleb, I'm so glad we have been able to see more of you during your trips to California for your parkour competitions! But what's even more impressive is the dedication you have shown to master the double bass! And to my always amazing, energetic, and sassy niece Ellie. You are almost done with your film education at Baylor! How crazy is that? You have grown to become a beautiful, intelligent, and very capable young woman. I hope you show Steven Spielberg how it's done! To my little nephew Miles and my new nieces Hanna and Lily, I love spending time with you and seeing you blossom as well as discover your personalities! Lily, welcome to the world! You are the last of the little ones to be born, and you are a huge blessing!

To my mother-in-law, Christina: Christina! I can't believe we have worked on another book together! This book is number seven now! Every time I write a book, I feel so incredibly lucky to have you be the first editor. I know I send you documents with more grammatical mistakes than there are pages in this book, but you always take care of me and make me look like I can actually write well! LOL! I know how much work you put in page by page, so meticulously looking for the perfect way to correct my run-on sentences or choose the perfect word that describes what I'm trying to say. Thank you again so much, Christina! I also want to thank my father-in-law, Peter! Peter, you are such an incredible father figure to me! I'm truly blessed to have you be my father-in-law. Thank you for printing out all the chapters and making sure they make it back to me. I love you, Peter! To Amy, Sarah, Neal, and Ryan, we have so much fun together everywhere we go. I truly feel so loved by all of you. It's great to have such a good group of sisters and brothers you can rely on. To Wendy Wong: Wendy, I love you to pieces. I always look forward to your visits to Los Angeles. You introduced me to the finest foods in the world, and I became addicted. Thank you for your love and support! Can't wait for the next adventures.

To Arlene Evans: Arlene, you are a rock! I can't believe after almost 20 years, we are still working together. I know I can be a pain sometimes, but no one is more patient with me than you. I promise I'll do my very best to not be the last or almost last person to submit my talk for WPPI. LOL! I got this! But on a serious note, I really appreciate you, Arlene! I'm so happy you are still here in this crazy industry of ours. Remember to never consider retiring.

To Tyler Austin and Andre Plummer. You guys are my best friends! I'm so lucky to have friends like you. We have had so many unforgettable moments and memories throughout all of our world travels! Thank you for your friendship and for putting up with me!

To Mandy Krause and Candice Godwin-Brown: You guys are incredible! There are no words to describe my appreciation for everything you do for The Photo Creators Conference! I have never met two people who work as hard as you do. Your attention to detail is unmatched. I love how we got to know each through my workshops, and we have grown together to become great friends. I love you both very much! Awesome memories in NYC!

To the incredible people I am so blessed to be able to call friends, real friends! You guys have been with me for many years! Enough time to know that our friendship is solid. Many "friendships" in this industry are so brittle that they seem to stand on a wet paper towel, but you have all been as solid as a rock! Alphabetical order: Rocco Ancora, Assa, Tyler Austin, Carol Boss, Anna Cantu, Michele Celentano, Joe Cogliandro, Skip Cohen, Tony Corbell, Mike Corrado, Gregory Daniel, Lou Desiderio, Laurel DeWitt, Dixie Dixon, Lan Doan, Ivan Duran, Andreina Duven, Marian Duven, David Edmonson, Luke Edmonson, Susan Ely, Brent Eysler, Andrew Funderburg, Jerry Ghionis, Melissa Ghionis, Cami Grudzinski, Cliff Hausner, Scott Heath, Michael Hollender, Laretta Houston, Scott Kelby, Noëmi Kocher, Brad Levin, Joey Lopez, Mary Ellen McBee, Dave Moser, Mario Munoz, Tom Munoz, Paul Neal, Maureen Neises, R'Bonney Nola Gabriel, Kristi Odom, Dylan Quigg, Luis Quiroz, Jessica Raab, Laken Romine, Griselle Rosario, Sara Strid, Sarah Tierney, Hiram Trillo, Justine Ungaro, Luis Urtaza, George Varanakis, Robert Vanelli, Jason Vinson, Remi Vision, and Tanya Wilson. Everyone in my Camera Craftsmen family, and all the great folks over at The Tanque Verde Guest Ranch.

To my good friends at Canon USA: Kevin McCarthy, Len Musmeci, Linda Milano, Taylor Nicole Bueti, Mike Larson, and Jim Booth: I feel so blessed to work with all of you and call you friends! I consider our Canon EOL team part of my extended family. We go on all of these great adventures together, and work on the exciting new product campaigns! Thank you all so much for having me be a part of this amazing program. I love being an EOL, and I appreciate the trust you put in me very much!

To all the incredible fashion designers: Laurell Dewitt, RMINÉ, and Son Jung Wan.

To Lisa Smith Craig: Lisa, you have been an imperative part of my success in this crazy world of fashion and editorial photography. I have learned so much from you. Every time I have been hired for a major campaign, you have always been there. Not only do you find the most incredible pieces of clothing from all over the country, but you bring my wildest fashion visions to life, time after time! We have had so much fun shooting together. From happy mistakes to publishing photos in major fashion magazines, we always have fun and you always come through. From the bottom of my heart, thank you for what you do! You make a real difference.

And finally, to my awesome wife, Kim, and our two beautiful sons, Lucas and Evan: I do this for you! Your beautiful faces, hugs, and kisses are everything to me. All I want is to make you proud of me, just like I am eternally proud of each of you! Daddy loves you unconditionally every second of the day. You are the greatest blessings of my life! Kim, thank you for putting up with me! I know it's not easy! But we are team V, and together we are unstoppable. Love you so much!

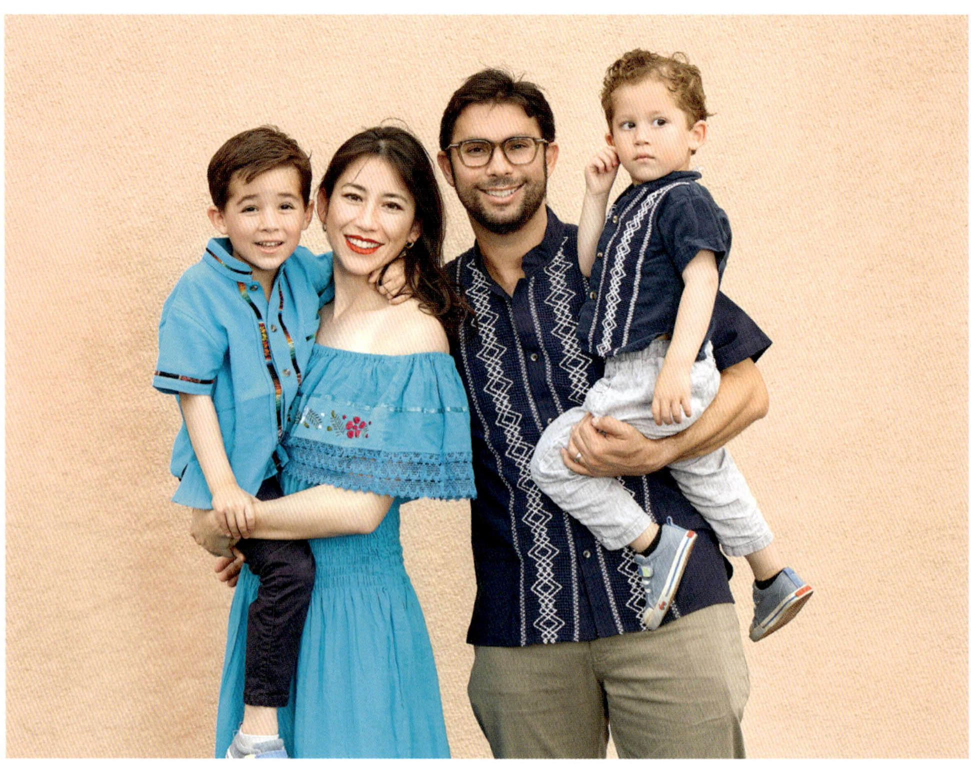

About the Author

Roberto Valenzuela is a photographer, author, and educator based in Beverly Hills, California. As a member of the prestigious Canon Explorers of Light group, he is considered to be one of the most influential photographers in the world.

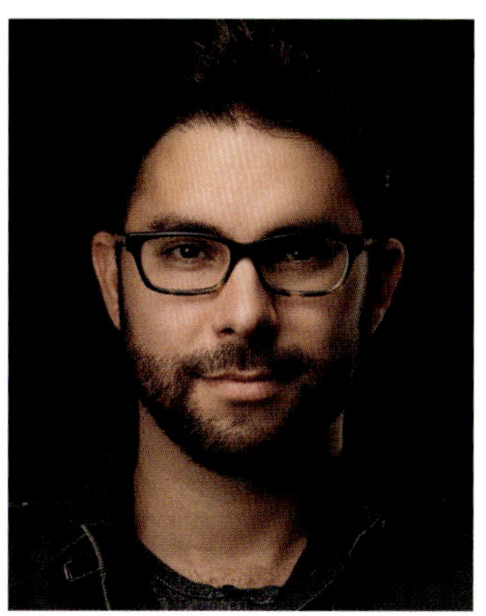

Roberto developed his unique teaching style by following the same rigorous regimen he developed as a professional concert classical guitarist and educator before becoming a photographer. He believes that it is not talent but deliberate practice that is at the core of skill and achievement. He has traveled to every area of the world, motivating photographers to practice their craft as musicians practice their instruments before performing on stage.

Roberto is one of the most well-known photography authors globally. His books *Picture Perfect Practice*, *Picture Perfect Posing*, and *Picture Perfect Lighting* have become staples in the photography industry and in academic photography departments. The books have been translated into numerous languages, including German, Chinese, Indonesian, Spanish, Portuguese, and Korean.

His book series *Wedding Storyteller, Volumes 1 and 2*, are the top selling wedding photography books in history. And his book *The Successful Professional Photographer* applies his college degree in Marketing and Consumer Behavior to help photographers be recognized, hired, and maximize potential sales.

Roberto serves as a chairman and judge for some of the largest photography competitions in the United States, Europe, Mexico, and South America. He is an avid educator and has been the keynote speaker at some of the largest photography conventions and events worldwide. He also teaches private workshops on posing, lighting, and wedding photography.

Roberto has been nominated by his peers as one of the ten most influential photographers and educators in the world. He has photographed major campaigns for Canon USA for the 5D Mark IV. Recently, Roberto was commissioned by Canon to photograph the global campaigns for Canon's top mirrorless cameras, the Canon EOS R5 and EOS R6, as well as the long-awaited Canon RF 100mm-300mm f/2.8 IS USM lens. He has also been published in several fashion magazines such as *L'Officiel*, among many others.

Aside from photography, Roberto is a long-distance runner. His goal is to run as many experienced-based half and full marathons as possible in the world, including some of the marathon majors. Roberto believes there is a strong parallel between marathon training and the journey he has experienced pushing the limits of what's possible in photography.

Contents

PART ONE
THE FLASH ADVANTAGE 1

CHAPTER 6

Sculpt the Light   137

CHAPTER 7

NAME: Your Game Plan   155

FLASH BASICS EXPLAINED — 175

Foreword

By R'Bonney Nola Gabriel, Miss Universe 2022

I remember when I first heard Roberto give a speech. We were in India, and he had this incredible talent for providing educational information in a hilarious way, and he somehow made an analogy to bananas. Although I don't remember how the heck bananas had anything to do with his teaching, I do remember how inspired I felt after that speech.

For many years now, he has been a great mentor in my life. When I first set out to begin training to become Miss Universe, I was fearful of the unknown. However, Roberto has always had a way of pushing me past my comfort zone, and he never hesitates to tell me when he knows I can do better. When I won the title of Miss Universe, he was one of the first people I called to thank for encouraging me to step fully in my talents.

I have witnessed Roberto's obsession with his craft. He can dissect any location, subject, or situation, and transform it into a magical photograph. He has committed years to sharing his knowledge of photography all over the world through workshops,

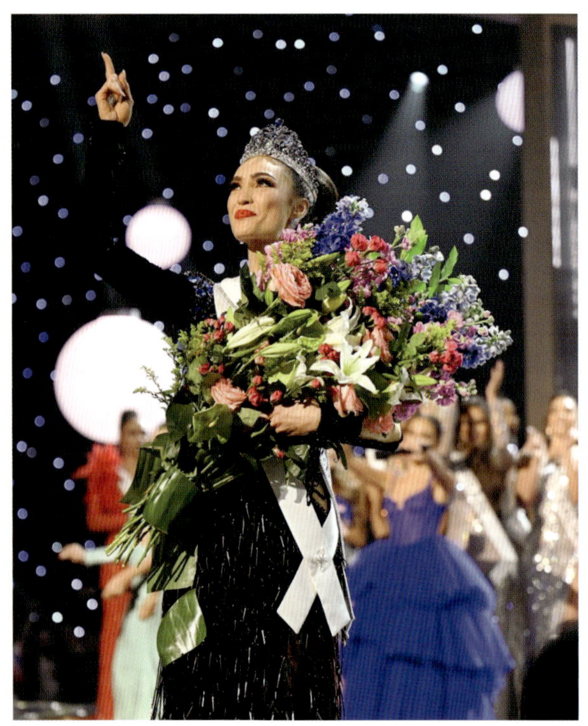

conferences, and books. My favorite thing is seeing him communicate and connect with people from any background or walk of life and making his educational material understandable to all.

In the pages that follow, I hope you experience a world of inspiration full of insight and growth, just as I have experienced with my dear friend.

—R'Bonney Nola Gabriel, Miss Universe 2022

Introduction

Before I write another word, I want to make this very clear: This book was written for photographers who photograph people. Portrait photographers, family photographers, fashion photographers, high school senior photographers, wedding photographers, and event photographers, etc.: *This book is for you!* More knowledge and skill with flashes and portable strobes will always work in your favor, regardless of your style. I believe that, for anyone who is determined, skill and practice will make you unstoppable.

When I decided to write this book, I thought long and hard about all the times when I was on photo assignments and portable strobes or hot shoe flashes saved my butt time and time again! I thought, "What would I do without these lights?" I also worked my memory backward: I started thinking about the reaction people had when looking at a final photograph, and then worked my way back to when I was setting up the lights to create that portrait. When you hold a print of the final photo in your hands and you go back to the BTS (behind the scenes) footage of the shoot, you would not believe how incredibly different the reality of the shoot was when compared with the final photograph. It's unbelievable to many people, and it brings the biggest smile to their faces! They say, "Wow, wow, wow!" so many times without even noticing it. The printed photo looks like a work of art, and the reality of the shoot was an ordinary place filled with mixed lighting that was not flattering from any angle. This large difference between reality and the final photograph can only be achieved with these hot shoe flashes and portable strobes. They help you transform a mundane scene from boring to "Wow, wow, wow!"

With clever use of strobes, no photographer is limited on where and what time to shoot. You become the captain of the ship, instead of being helpless and succumbing to the waves taking your ship wherever the current is moving.

There is no reason to keep comparing natural light to flash. I strongly believe it's time to move past that. A well-rounded photographer doesn't even see the difference. Strobes can look like natural light, and natural light can look like flash. But use both together, and there will be no problem that you can't solve or vision that you can't bring to life.

This book was written to help you have a vision and become aware of the photographic possibilities all around you. Light can do it all! So why limit ourselves? I know very well that it is difficult to imagine what's possible with lighting wherever you are, indoors or outdoors. You see what is in front of you, and maybe you can imagine one change you could make with flash to improve the photograph. But with The Picture Perfect Flash System, you will be able to see not just the obvious change, but every possible change you could make to either fix the light, add light to bring attention to a specific area, create a different mood if the mood is boring, add some special effects if your vision calls for that, or even sculpt light on your subject's face to create something more dramatic and interesting. It's so liberating to know that everything is possible with these lighting tools.

This is not a book you read on a plane and call it a day. That would be nice, wouldn't it? This is a book you have to work through. Chapter by chapter, the skills you acquire will compound, making you a fine-tuned creative lighting machine…but only if you work through the chapters and exercises. Skills cannot be acquired by only reading pages in a book or watching a video. You must experience it for yourself. You must act. You want to know through experience what failed and why, and then find out what works and why. Reading is just the first step; by no means will it ever be a proper substitute for rolling up your sleeves and doing it yourself. By reading this book and working through the techniques and exercises, you will become a photographer who has no limits!

This book is split into three major parts.

Part One

Part One covers The Picture Perfect Flash System. This is the meat of the entire book. Part One goes over the creative and practical uses of hot shoe flashes and portable strobes. Depending on how you use this book, you will keep improving your skillset for each of the elements that make up The Picture Perfect Flash System, regardless of what skill level you feel you are at. From beginners to the most advanced users of flashes, this is a unique system that will stimulate your brain in ways you might have never thought of when using flash in your work.

Part One is meant to help you open up your creative mind to the great possibilities that using flashes can provide to any scene, inside or outside. We can't just buy a strobe, point it toward our subject, and call it a day, right? There is so much more to these tools that make photography more interesting and far more fun! Part One is the gift that keeps on giving, because no matter how good you are at flashes/strobes, you can always get faster, better, and more versatile at each of the elements that make up Part One.

Part Two

Part Two was written for those of you who want to understand the ins and outs of how different flash features work. If you feel comfortable with these common flash concepts, feel free to skip Part Two. But if you feel there are gaps in your understanding of how these different flash functions work and it's affecting your decision making, then this section is for you. If I were you, I would not skip Part Two. If anything, it can be a quick read to freshen up your understanding of the most popular settings on your flashes or portable strobes. There may be some nuggets of information that could prove very useful in the heat of the moment during a photo shoot.

Part Three

Part Three is very important! This section is meant to be a very time-consuming part of working through this book the correct way. Part Three consists of highly involved lighting exercises to strengthen your first-hand experience using lights, modifiers, and quick problem-solving skills. I would carve out an hour or so for each of these exercises in a place where you can really concentrate on the process and note taking. These exercises play a pivotal role in making your knowledge of lighting and modifiers become second nature to you. Having the freedom to concentrate on your vision instead of how to make that vision happen technically will be a liberating experience. It is at this point when photography becomes a lot of fun! Your work will improve drastically when you are having fun creating it.

The Goal

Let's make the confusion of flashes and strobes go away. Let's make it simple to understand. I want you to feel so comfortable with artificial portable light that you always want to embrace it and feel 100% comfortable implementing it. Before we get too excited, though, you should understand that knowing how to use these types of lights does not mean you are able to use them creatively. That's a different skillset. Think of it like buying ingredients at a grocery store. Knowing the name and flavor of the ingredients does not mean you can put them all together, transform the ingredients through a cooking process, and make a delicious, cohesive meal out of them.

The good news is that, for creativity to spark, you must feel comfortable with the technical aspects of any lights such as their features, power, and functions in order to think creatively. How could you expect to be creative with tools when you don't even know what they do? It's just not going to happen. Know your tools—then and only then will creative thinking come to you. One step at a time, right?

I have been a photographer for about 20 years now, and in all my world travels talking with other photographers, the topic of flashes and strobes always leaves people feeling overwhelmed or confused by it all. We all seem to understand natural light. We are comfortable with the exposure triangle, and we feel at ease making a proper exposure in natural light. But as soon as we decide to add that little device called a flash to our exposure, our heads start spinning, and we go down a spiral of confusion. We feel a loss of control over the exposure, so we start guessing and hoping for the best with our flash. That's a horrible feeling, so let's fix that! Together, through this book, we will once again feel like we are in complete control of our exposure whether we are using one flash, two flashes, or ten flashes.

The Reason

Writing a book is a monumental amount of work. The project requires not just the writing part, but the organizing and thinking parts that go on all day, every day, when writing a book. So why do this? Because I like self-inflicted torture? I took on this project because I think it is very doable to explain flashes and strobes in an easy-to-understand way. I'm honored to be able to write a book when I want to explain a subject, and this subject has been on my to-do list for years.

One of the aspects of photography that makes it so exciting is light. When the light is flat and says nothing, the photo is just that: a photo. But when the lighting jumps out at you, when it draws you in in such a way that you can't look away, that's amazing! I call this type of lighting "spicy lighting" because it awakens your senses when you experience it.

To make another food analogy, seasoning food is essential for flavor. You can't make a meal without salt and maybe some pepper, right? But to me, adding a spice or chili to a dish takes it to a whole other level beyond basic seasoning. It takes it to the kind of level that, when you experience the chili on your tastebuds, you can't ignore it. In fact, you must focus on cooling your tongue as fast as possible. You don't care what anyone is saying, and you can't concentrate on anything other than resolving the burning feeling in your mouth. That is what spicy lighting is all about! I want light to be used in such a way that it communicates something so strong that the viewer can't ignore the photo. They can't look away, and they can't stop staring at it.

Focus on Simplicity

Let's keep it simple! My first and foremost goal for this book is to teach everything I can about these incredible lights with the simplest approach possible. With this approach, you will not feel overwhelmed. I'm going to embrace the power of simplicity to maximize your understanding of the material in these pages. This is not to say that I don't think you can handle complex topics or that we won't touch on more advanced techniques, because we definitely will! But I have been a teacher my entire adult life. And I know that people learn best when the topic at hand is taught in bite-sized pieces in a simple way. Once your understanding of the key features of the lights is solid, we can explore more difficult or advanced techniques, and you will have no problem keeping up.

This book focuses on flashes and portable strobes. Any strobe that has a portable battery qualifies as a portable strobe. This book is written for those of you who want to feel 100% comfortable with using lights to either complement the existing natural light or create your vision completely from scratch using only flashes and strobes. This book is for those of you who don't want to be afraid of using these amazing tools, but instead wish to take full advantage of their power, flexibility, adaptability, and portability to give your photos some spice. I believe that by breaking down the features of these lights one by one, and helping you understand how each feature can be used practically and artistically, you will embrace them.

As noted earlier, to achieve this level of skill and comfort requires more than just read-ing the book. I have put a great deal of effort into developing and creating the exercises that you should complete. Do the work and it will pay off tenfold. I know it's not sexy to say this, but it's reality: A person who is considered a master at something has worked incredibly hard at building that skill. There are no shortcuts to mastering a skill. If you want to be good at something, you have to be okay with experimenting with techniques that are outside your comfort zone, possibly failing at them, and then learning from those mistakes in order to do it again with success. Repeat this process to keep expand-ing your skillset and enlarging your comfort zone.

There is no question that learning artificial portable lighting will present its fair share of challenges. Learning this skill can be confusing at times. Once you get it, though, you will be able to do anything! Flashes and strobes can make a stale scene look exciting. They can take an otherwise boring photo and bring it to life. But most importantly, these lights will bring *consistency* to your work. And that is a powerful word. People like to have a photographer who they can rely on, rain or shine. If you can produce consis-tent, high-quality results for your clients, you are the person they will want to work with. And if photography is just a hobby for you, learning this skill will help you expand your creative interpretation of anything you photograph, and thus you will have more fun than ever with your photography. Let's get started!

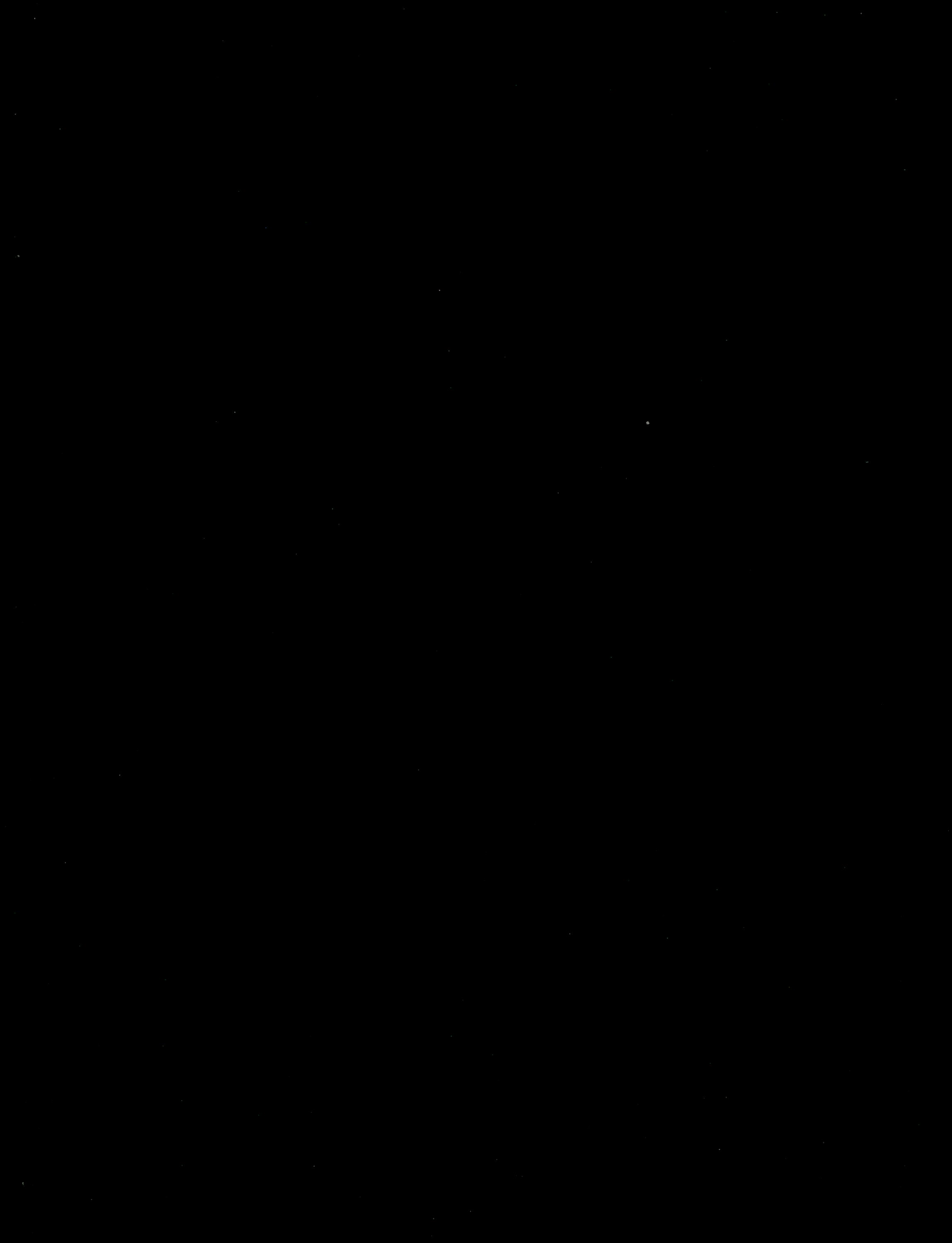

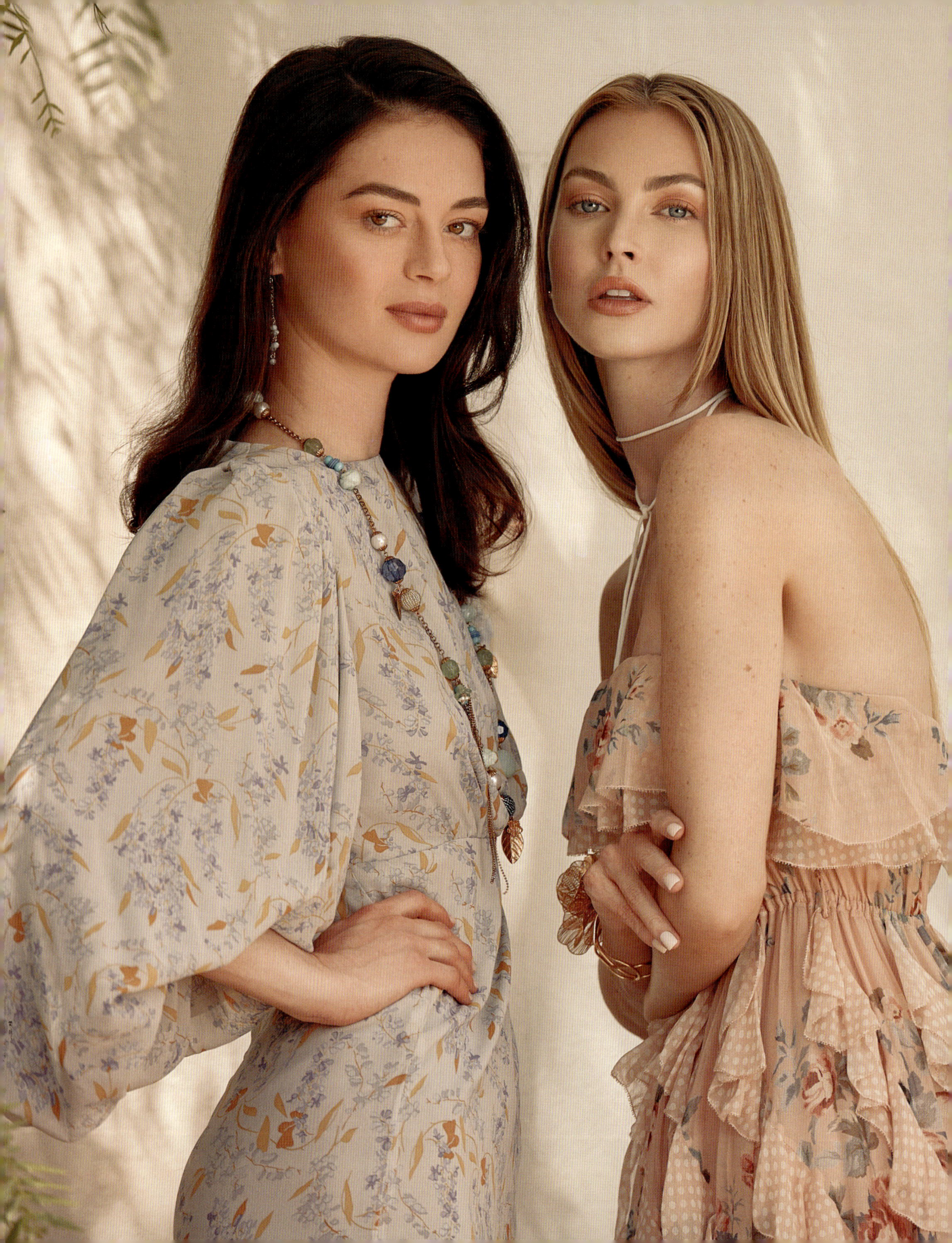

Chapter 1

The Picture Perfect Flash System

Strap on your seatbelt, and let's get ready to discover the wonderful world of flash. Once you gain the ability to control the quality, quantity, and direction of light, you will be able to truly communicate with light, not just illuminate with it. With flashes or portable strobes, you will no longer be at the mercy of the elements. You will not need to look out the window or at the weather app on your phone to check the weather on the day of the shoot. It won't matter. You will be able to produce what's expected of you in any weather.

No longer will you have to schedule shoots at sunset because the light is softer. You won't have to raise your camera's ISO to some absurd number because you are working with a low quality (and quantity) of light. In fact, for the most part, you will live between ISO 100–400. With the power of flashes and portable strobes, you will have the capability to change an ordinary, mundane location into something inspiring! You won't have to depend on the ambient light to provide you with mood. Instead, you will be able to create any mood you wish.

Best of all, you will be able to draw the viewer's eyes to precisely where you want them to go in your photographs. The days when everything in a scene is lit by the same light and your viewer doesn't know who or what the main subject is supposed to be will become a thing of the past.

There is nothing more exciting to me than talking about great lighting in photography! When I began my journey in photography, it was this subject that first consumed every minute of my waking hours to better understand it. Lighting is what makes photography exciting! Yes, you need other elements to make a photograph work, such as posing, composition, and storytelling; however, after 20 years of being a full-time professional photographer and educator, I will stand by the fact that lighting is, indeed, the most exciting part of a photograph.

The Challenge with This Book

I know that, to many people, talking about flash is like asking them to get out of bed and run a marathon without any prior training. The concept is laughable, and it can trigger a lot of perceptions and thoughts in your head: tons of equipment, math, something not working the way you envisioned, the flashes not firing, the flash looks flashy, you can't control the flash and it looks terrible, people look washed out, the batteries on the flash die too quickly, flashes stop communicating with each other. It's difficult to carry all the necessary modifiers to make flash work. Why is TTL flash so bright or so dark all the time? Manual flash can be scary, so let's forget it! I don't know how to blend flash with natural light so that it looks natural. Did I miss something? The list goes on and on.

I can't blame people for feeling this way. Flash does add a certain level of complexity to making a photograph, and some knowledge is, in fact, needed to be able to harness its seemingly mysterious powers. My challenge with this book is to address all of these possible situations and help you see the incredible benefits of using flash.

But flash *is* easy to use. That's the truth, and there is not much to it. It's the mental block photographers have against flash that is the biggest challenge to overcome.

To get the most out of this book, you need to ask yourself a question: Are you the kind of photographer who is ready to take control and become the lighting craftsman you want to be, or are you more interested in copying other photographers' lighting recipes so you don't have to think for yourself? In other words, do you want to copy the masters, or do you want to become a master yourself?

I wrote this book for those who wish to become masters themselves. You will not find lighting recipes in this book that you can just copy. What you will find is a book that guides you through each and every step, one by one, to awaken the learning monster inside you! The contents of this book will grow as you grow. I'm still growing my lighting skillset myself. But you have to work through this book, not just passively read it on a couch or a plane. I wrote this book for the disciplined side of you.

I don't have anything against lighting recipes, by the way. They have a place in photography education, and it's a valid approach for many. And you'll see in this book that I use lighting diagrams as visual aids. But looking back at my own career, I realize that I had to wean myself away from predetermined and prescriptive recipes because they were not actually helping me. They only gave me the illusion of help. But when it came down to the particular situation I was in, these recipes didn't match what I was doing or where I was having a shoot, so they didn't work. What made the biggest impact in my lighting skills was being able to understand the principles and techniques myself so well that I could decide what was the best choice for my situation. The most important phrase here is "best choice for *my situation*."

This book is all about opening your eyes to the incredible lighting possibilities you have in any and every situation you are in. You will become the photographer who has both the vision and the skill to execute that vision. We can all write lighting recipes. They are easy to do, and they seem to help, but in your day-to-day reality, you are going to have to learn to be independent and learn to think for yourself. Once you do, you will be unstoppable!

The Solution This Book Offers

Of course, I once had the same challenges as you do with flash. So it is very exciting to be able to write a book about how I not only overcame my fears, but I mastered flash to levels I would never have imagined. As a direct result of my using flash in portraiture, weddings, fashion, and editorial photography, I have photographed some of the most influential people in the world.

I love gaining all the benefits from flash without any of the problems or the "flash" aesthetic we have etched in our minds. Instead, the portraits I create look completely natural, just like the one on the cover of this book, featuring R'Bonney, the current reigning Miss Universe as I write this. Photos with flash can have soul! And I am truly delighted to pass my excitement on to you!

My solution is to walk you through the process I use, which is entirely responsible for the success I have had using flash in my work. The process involves three steps. These steps guide you through the maze of trying to figure out what to do and what the possibilities are in any given situation. We will go into each of these steps in great detail later, but for now I just want to give you a lay of the land or bird's eye view of what The Picture Perfect Flash System is all about. Here is a brief description.

Step 1: Scenario

Everything starts with the situation you are in, right? This step will make you keenly aware of your surroundings. It trains your eye to see, not just to look. That means you will *see* the possibilities.

For example, a trained photographer can see a couch beneath a large window and think of 10 or more possibilities he or she can use in such a scenario. Furthermore, a trained photographer can visualize the final photo simply by looking at the scene in front of him or her. A well-trained photographer sees the objects in a room as possible light modifiers, props, or compositional elements, whereas a novice photographer will only see what that object is: a chair is a chair. That's it. A novice photographer will look at the same exact scenario and go straight to the most obvious photo a person could possibly make there.

The power behind the first step of The Picture Perfect Flash System is that you'll become very skilled at assessing any location, in any situation.

Step 2: FACES

FACES is where the magic happens. This acronym categorizes the options you have in your approach to lighting:

- **F**ix the Light
- **A**dd Light
- **C**reate a Mood
- **E**ffects with Flash
- **S**culpt the Light

In this step, you are able to walk yourself through all the lighting possibilities. You are no longer on your own, wondering what to do. During this process, it is like having someone hold your hand and guide you through the lighting options. FACES trains you to see what's possible in your current scenario. This is a skill that's a million times better than copying someone else's lighting recipe.

Why? Because lighting recipes are only effective if the scenario is the exact same or you are in a completely controlled environment where you can replicate the conditions in which the lighting recipe was created. But with FACES, you can think for yourself and create the most remarkable photographs using flashes creatively to fit *your* vision, not someone else's vision.

You don't have to use every aspect of FACES, but it's all there for you to challenge yourself, to get you out of automatic mode, and to push the boundaries of your skillset.

Furthermore, each part of FACES can be achieved at higher and higher levels of mastery. So, if you think you are good at one of the FACES elements, guess what? You can focus on it and then completely surprise yourself with how much better you can understand that specific element. Each letter in FACES represents an entire world of skills and knowledge that will grow as your skills grow. How high will you go?

Step 3: NAME

This final part of The Picture Perfect Flash System is about the technical steps you must take for your vision to become reality. This step will help you question or confirm the decisions that you make, and it will help you to remember them. NAME stands for:

- Number of Flashes
- Angle of Flashes
- Modifiers for Flashes
- Energy of Flashes

Eventually, by going through this process repeatedly, you will develop incredible speed, because your brain will learn to go through each of these steps automatically. You will not have to think about each element one by one; instead, your brain will scan through the scenario and implement FACES and NAME as if it were second nature. If you stay with the program, you will experience this, and when you do, it is the most beautiful thing!

I developed this process to help me with my goal of becoming a true lighting master. I didn't want to just scratch the surface of lighting skills. I wanted to conquer lighting! Lighting makes all the difference in a photograph of any genre. This subject is far too important and fun to just be okay at it. I know that if you work on each of these elements with the dedication and respect they deserve, you will experience a higher level of understanding and mastery of lighting that is hard to imagine now.

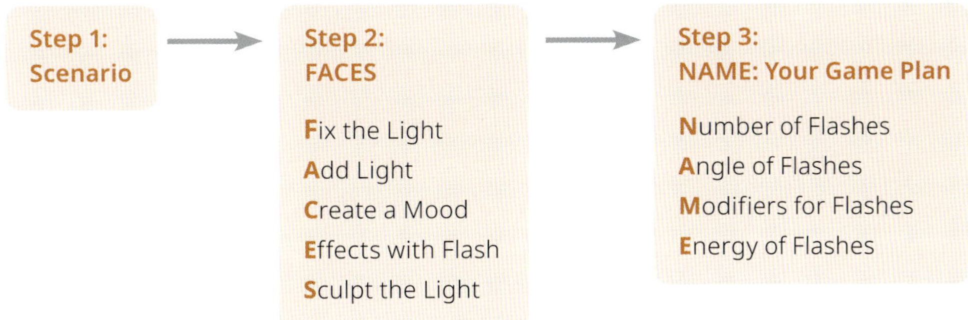

A Note about Flash, Strobe, and Portable Strobe Terminology

I will mention this a few times throughout the book, but I want to start by making this very clear! In this book, when I mention the words "flash," "strobe," or "portable strobe," they mean the same thing. Most people think "flash" strictly denotes a hot shoe flash that goes on top of your camera. And a strobe is a more powerful monolight with no hot shoe, but it has a clamp to attach to a light stand instead. And a monolight is a strobe with a battery attached instead of a studio strobe, which requires the light to be plugged into an outlet.

In this book, we are not going to discuss plug-in studio strobes. This book is only about hot shoe flashes and portable strobes. Remember this: If I want to specifically discuss a hot shoe flash, I will say "hot shoe flash." But if I write "flash" or "strobe," please think of them as the same thing. I often use the word "flash" generally to describe a piece of equipment that flashes a very fast pulse of light energy when triggered. That description fits both hot shoe flashes and portable strobes.

This has to be very clear before we go on. In order to save time and make this book more enjoyable to read, I didn't want to always write something like "flash, or strobe, or portable strobe." That would take way too long and annoy many readers having to read that combination of words over and over. To simplify, I use both words, "flash" and "strobe," interchangeably.

Scenario

Learning about flash by reading stories of photos or looking at a photographer's lighting recipes is definitely not going to put *you* in control of your flash decisions. Why not? Reading stories about photos is interesting, but unfortunately, your situation will always be different from the photo you are reading about.

The scenario is key! That is the first challenge every photographer confronts. The way you would decide how to use flashes at a beach shoot, in the middle of the day, is 180 degrees different from what you would do in a hotel room at a wedding, or at a moody library at a Victorian home. Therefore, every decision you make begins with what scenario you are in.

Think of the scenario as a situation that you draw inspiration from. The scenario gives you a host of possibilities based on its architecture, the objects in the room, the materials around you, and the surfaces that could become light modifiers. Your job is to recognize those possibilities and act to achieve your vision. Mastering the scenario or situation you are in is the first step to lighting greatness.

If you only see the obvious, you are not growing. If you see the possibilities, you are making progress. But if, when you simply walk into any location, you can visualize the end result and know what you need to do with finesse, you, my friend, are becoming a master. The scenario you are in dictates the rest of your decisions within this system. It's like the key to the ignition.

Figure 1.1: The way I see it, every location—from professional studios to parks to city streets to hotels to homes—has hidden gems lurking all around you. However, our human eyes are trained to be drawn to what we know. That's the easiest path. Our brains do this to filter out distractions and conserve energy, which is a precious resource. However, by doing this in scenarios where we are photographing, we are preventing ourselves from growing.

In this example with the ice cream, we have a visual representation of what goes on inside our heads. We walk into any location, and we go straight to what we know. This is represented by the vanilla ice cream. All these amazing and exciting flavors are right there in that same location, but we don't even see them. We only see the vanilla ice cream. So, what do we do? We go for the vanilla flavor. That's not a bad choice. Vanilla is fine, but it's boring, standard, bland, and unexciting. What we missed is the abundance of incredible ice cream flavors that were right in front of us, but we didn't see them.

Figure 1.2: With a little effort, our world will open up to the incredible opportunities that each location has to offer. However, these gifts are only visible to the trained eye. This book was written with every intention to have you become one of those photographers who can see all the flavors of ice cream when you walk into any location—not just the obvious one.

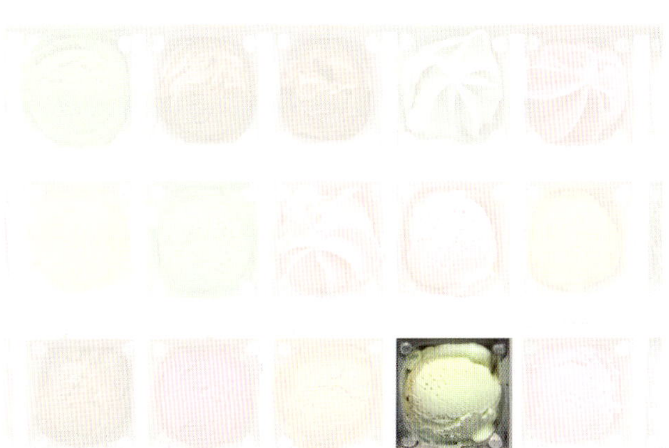

FIGURE 1.1

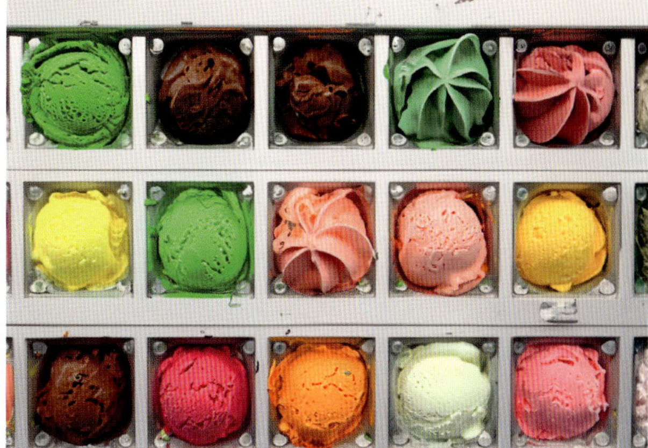

FIGURE 1.2

FACES of What's Possible

With flashes or strobes, you can implement a variety of techniques that are simply not possible using just natural light. For example, you can use flashes to:

- **Fix the Light:** Fix a low light problem, color cast, or poor quality of light.

- **Add Light:** Add light to boost existing available light to enhance or create separation.

- **Create a Mood:** Create your desired mood for any location or subject.

- **Effects with Flash:** Create visual special effects.

- **Sculpt the Light:** Sculpt light strategically to add drama, shape, and contouring.

To easily remember what you can do with flash, remember the acronym FACES. These five categories of techniques can be used on their own or in combination with each other. For example, you could both *fix* a low light problem and *create* mood in a scene. If used skillfully, these techniques will make your photography come alive, and they can turn an ordinary shoot into something truly special.

I'm going to show you some examples when flash is the hidden hero behind the magic of photos. The key word here is "hidden." You want your work to benefit from the use of flash, but you do not want to show that it was obviously flashed. That is the key! Of course, photography is an art, and therefore every suggestion is subjective to the artist's vision.

Later in this book, we will go over each of these five FACES techniques in more detail. But for now, since this is the first chapter, let's keep it light and fun and show you some photo examples of each of these techniques.

Fix the Light

Figure 1.3 (ISO 100, f/2, 1/200): This is one of the best examples I could find to show how flash can produce magic in any photograph. I was photographing my two children for a Mother's Day present for my wife. However, I had seen this scenario before: Natural light from the window would be completely blown out and only the sides of my sons' faces closest to the window would be well lit. The other sides would be in shadow. But I knew that, with the help of flash, I could do much better.

Next, we have a lighting problem to fix. When shooting in natural light, strong light comes in through the window, but it quickly dies down within inches of entering the room. My boys are sitting too far away from the light, and the small tent is also blocking any light that could have reached them. I'm photographing the sides of their faces furthest from the window. The dark wood floor doesn't help reflect the light, either. And, to make matters worse, the rug absorbs a great deal of light.

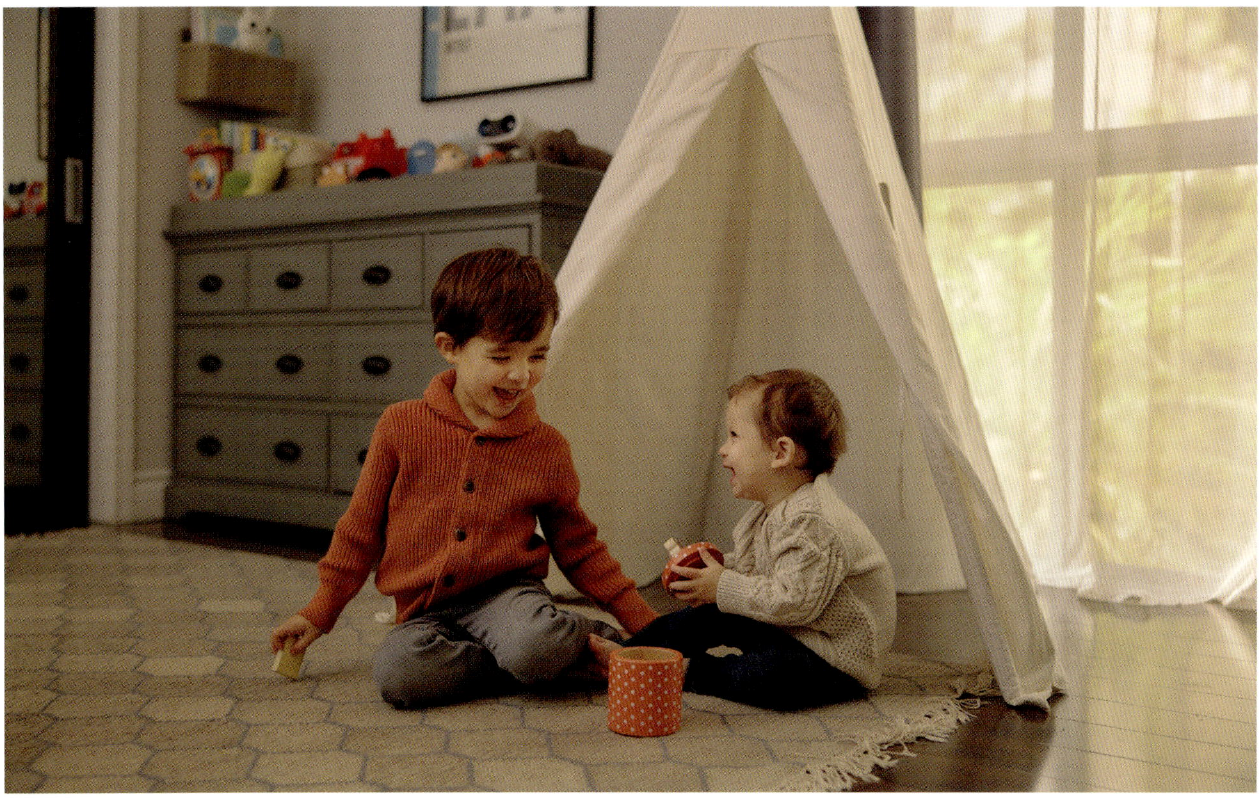

But with the addition of flash, this photo looks a bit more like a painting. Thanks to the flash, I could expose for the window to show the beautiful garden outside and even show the soft texture of the sheer curtain. The exposure on both boys is spot on and soft. The photo almost looks three-dimensional.

The best part is that when looking at this photo, there is no evidence that flash was ever used. The flash is working its magic without being seen. That's awesome! And by using flash for this photo, I reaped another benefit when printing this photograph: I'm talking about the incredible clarity you have when shooting at a low ISO. In this case, I could get the maximum quality out of the file by shooting this at ISO 100. The flash provided enough power to achieve this photo at ISO 100 while still managing a shutter speed of 1/200, which is fast enough to freeze most motion of the boys playing. These high-quality settings would have been impossible using only natural light.

By fixing the light with flash, I could greatly improve the quality of light illuminating the entire scene without being stuck by the window, which is how most window-lit photographs are taken.

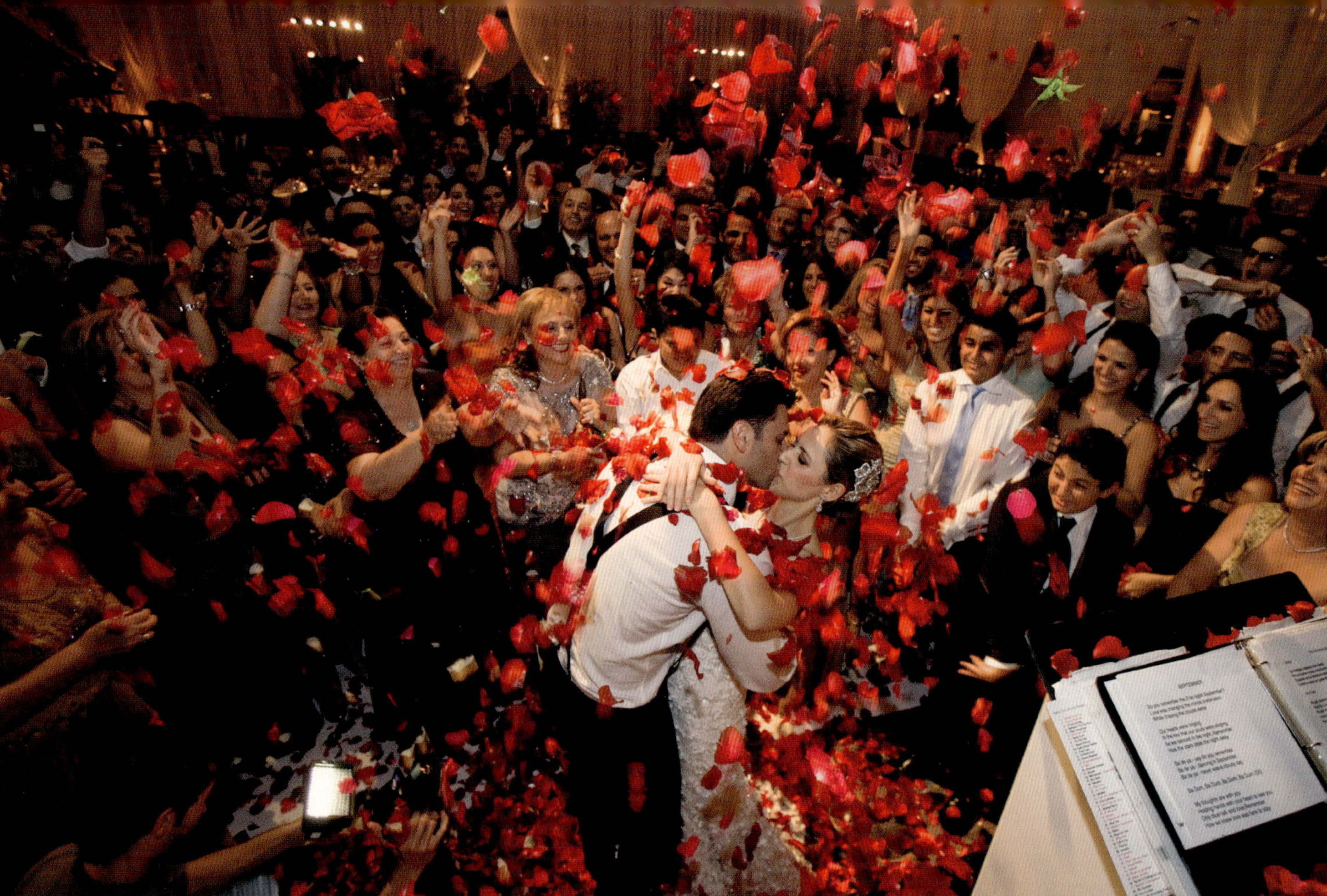

Figure 1.4 (ISO 640, f/3.5, 1/60): This is a perfect example to use to demonstrate the Fix the Light technique. Here we are in a dark room during a Persian wedding reception. There is not much light other than available mood lighting. At a Persian wedding, when the couple is showered with rose petals, it is a key moment that must be captured properly.

This moment is full of emotion, fast movements, and priceless expressions. The only way to capture this type of unpredictable movement is by using the help of flash to freeze the moment. Notice that my ISO speed is still relatively low. My ISO is only 640, yet everyone in the scene is frozen, even though my shutter speed is only 1/60. That's the power of flash! In this case, I had to use flash to do two things: fix the low light situation and allow me to freeze all the movement happening around me.

Without flash, I would have had to push my camera to ISO 12,500, and the cost would have been an image with low quality, a lack of sharpness, and a great deal of noise.

Add Light

Figure 1.5 (ISO 100, f/3.5, 1/250): This is an example of where we need to add light to an outdoor garden. The key to implementing this technique correctly is to add light to a decent amount of natural light. The key word is "decent." What does that mean?

This Add Light technique is meant to be used as a small extra boost of light to an already decently lit subject or scene. The photographer should be skilled enough to find decent available light to work with as a starting point. He or she then adds artificial light onto the subject or background to increase the quality of light to superb levels.

Looking at this photo, you notice how the model, Alisha, is sitting on the grass under open shade. Flashes were used with modifiers to give Alisha a much-needed boost of light to separate her from the background. They also give her beautiful catchlights and achieve phenomenal lighting on her face, dress, and hair. Without flash and under shade, this portrait would have looked flat and lifeless.

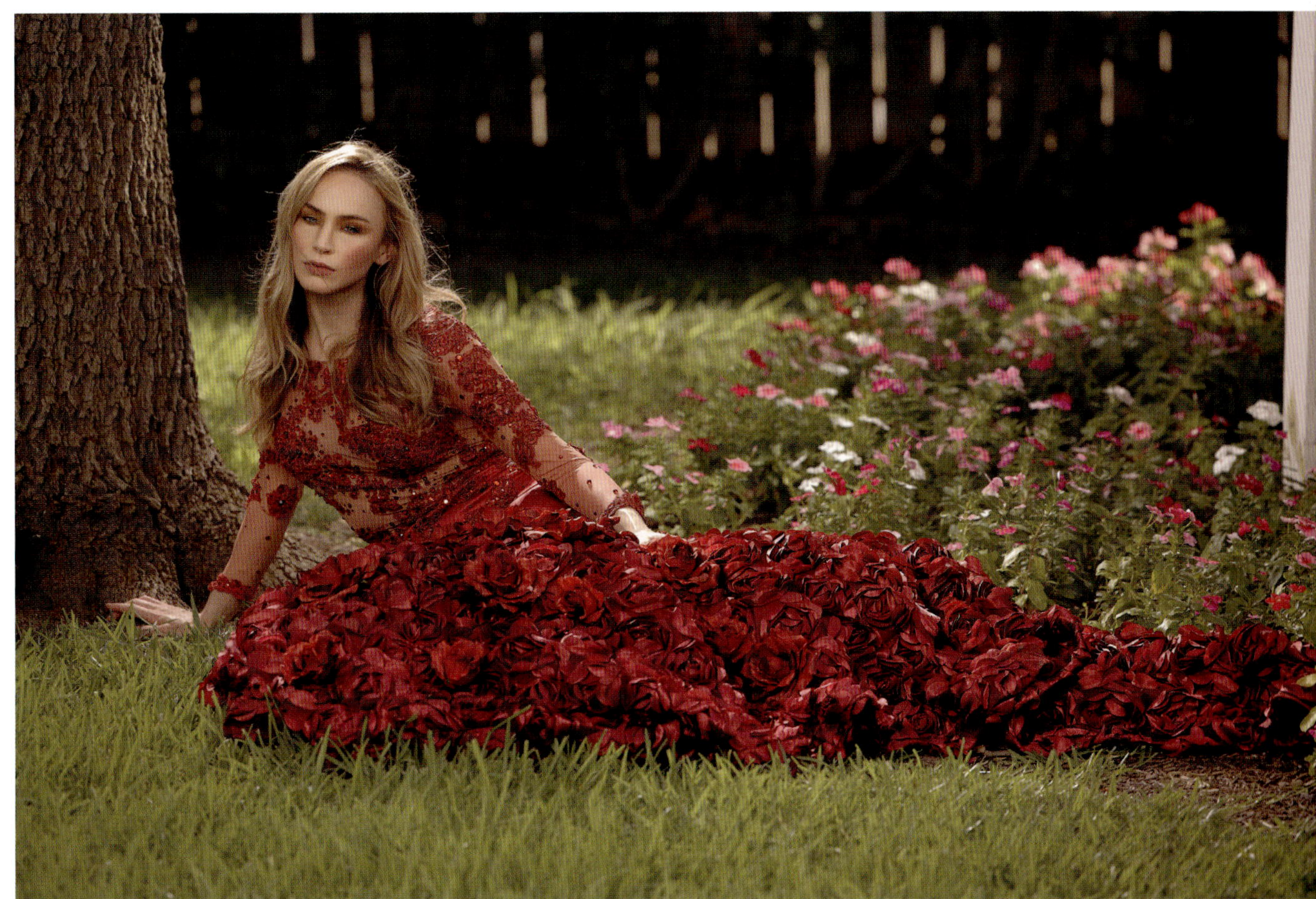

FIGURE 1.5

Figure 1.6 (ISO 50, f/4, 1/640): In this photograph, we have a similar situation as in the previous example with Alisha. However, this time, cowgirl Hope is not in the shade. Instead, this photo was taken in the middle of the afternoon under very harsh sunlight conditions in Tucson, Arizona. I purposely chose this location and perspective to take this portrait because the sun was directly behind Hope, giving her clean light on her face. However, the sun was so strong that, to take this photo without flash, I would have had to expose for Hope and the horse. That would have completely blown out the sky, rendering it pure white. Since she is wearing a hat, Hope's face would have been completely in the shade, and chances are, you wouldn't even be able to see her eyes.

With a flash fitted with a modifier, I could expose for the sky and use the modified flash to illuminate Hope and the horse in a very flattering way, without the obvious signs that flash was used. My favorite thing about the photo is how soft and beautiful the light looks on her face under her hat. It is very impressive how much more you can achieve with your photographs by introducing artificial light into your work.

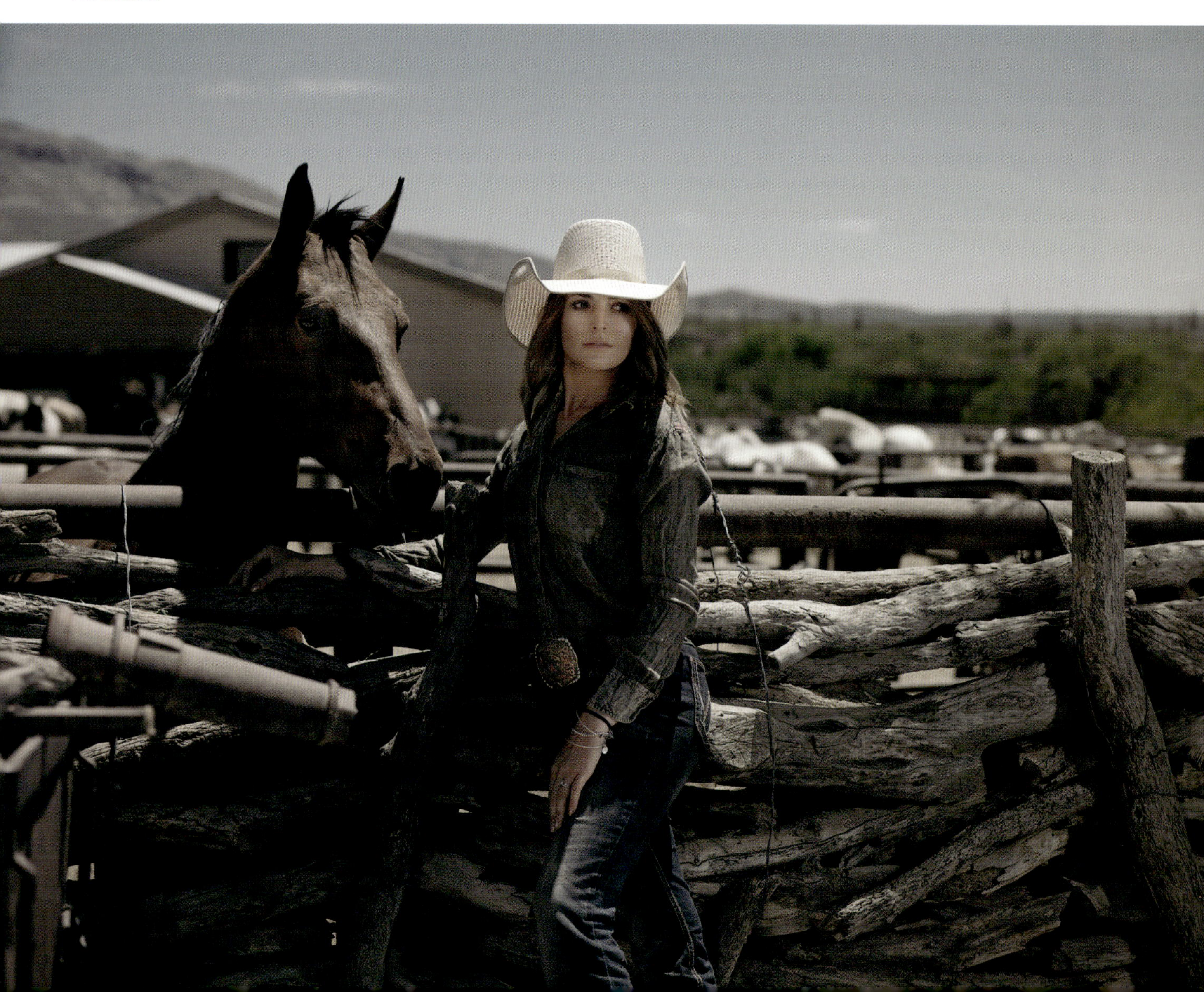

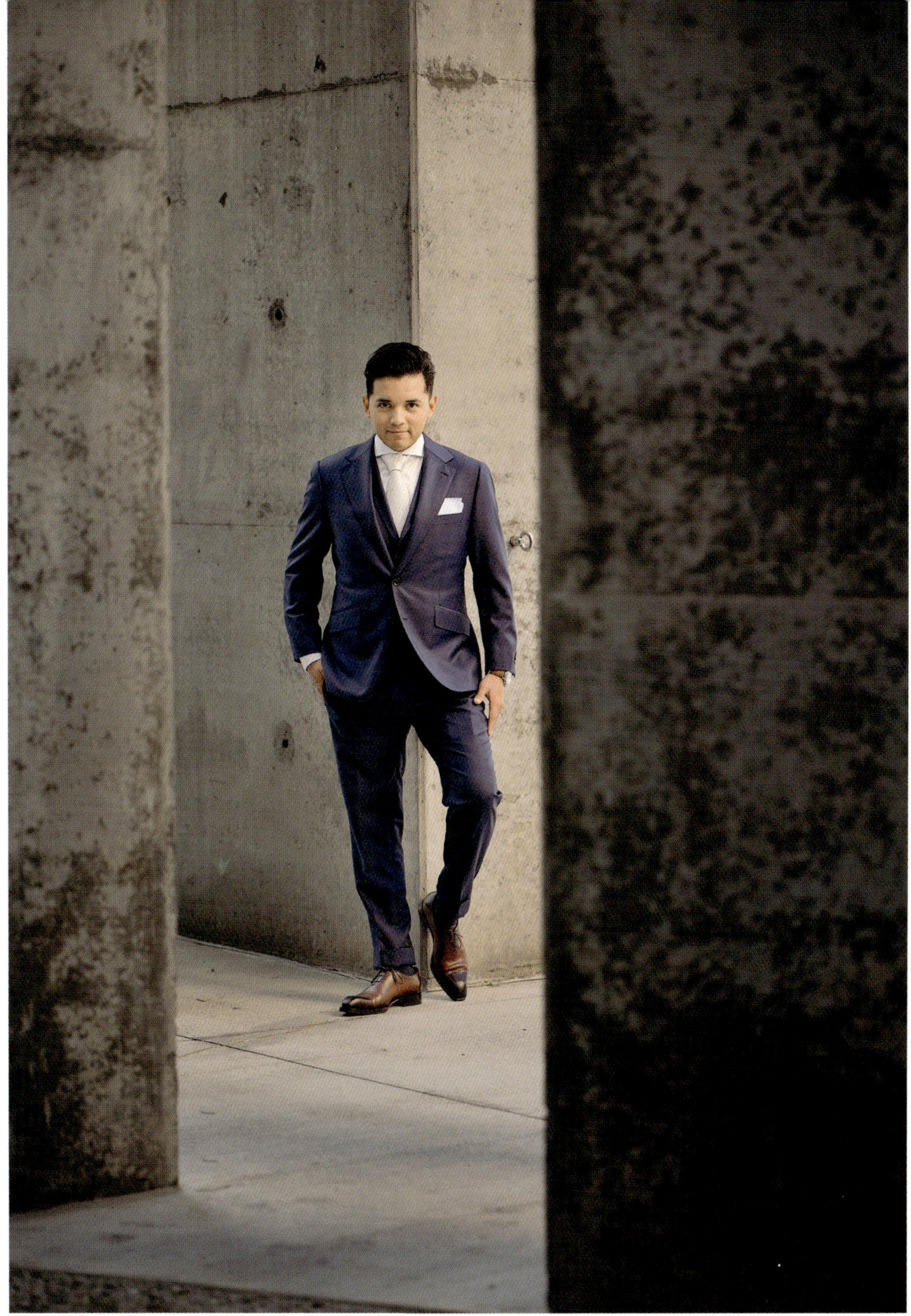

Figure 1.7 (ISO 100, f/1.2, 1/500): For this photo of photographer Ivan Duran, I used an indirect "Add Light" method: We used the existing architecture around him to bounce light to one of the columns from a flash (the column at camera right). This creates a soft light on Ivan, making it almost impossible to tell that flash was used. However, you can see that one side of his face has more light than the other side. Without the flash, both sides of Ivan's face would have been lit much the same, and therefore the photo would have looked flat.

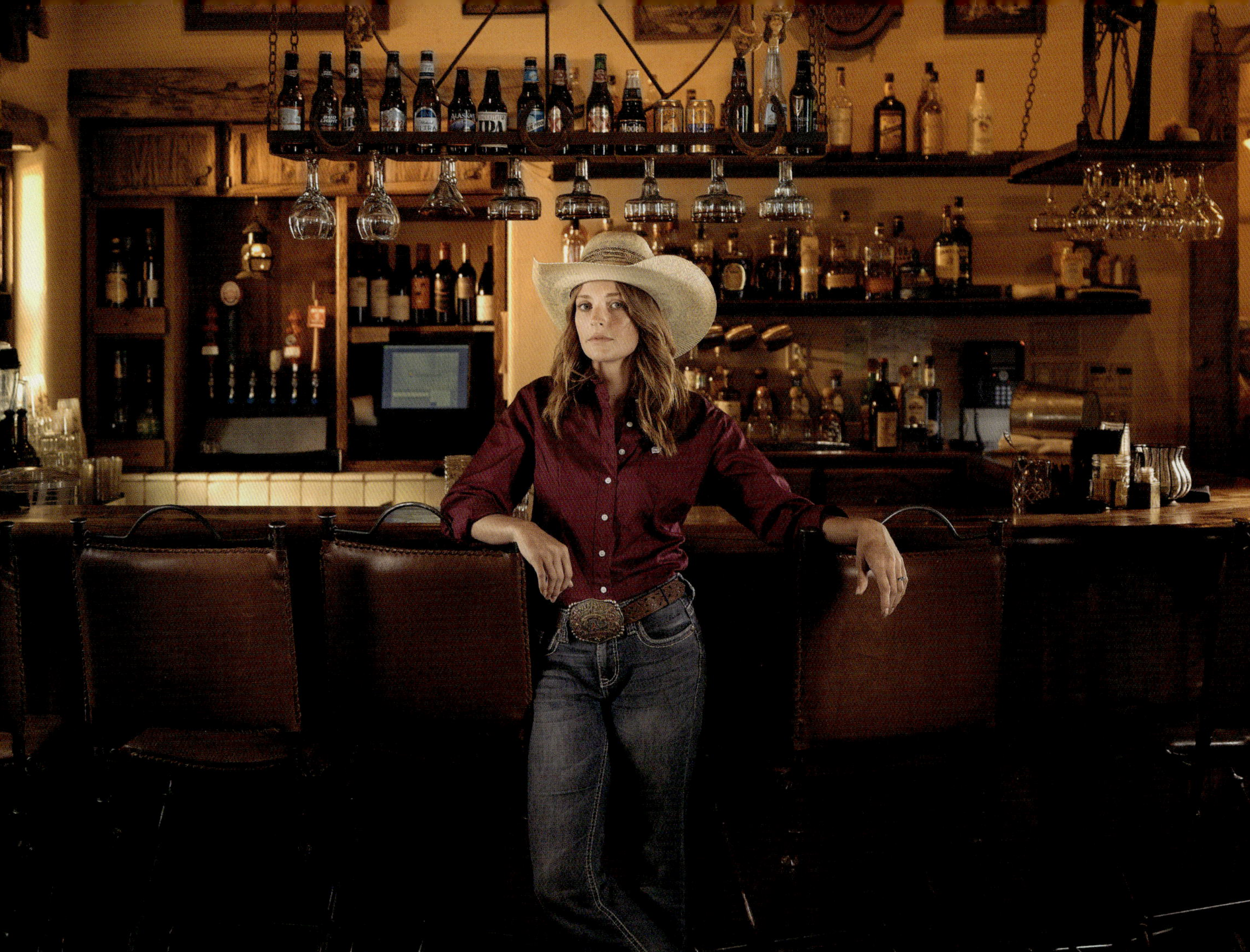

Create a Mood

Figure 1.8 (ISO 250, f/4.5, 1/50): This portrait of Hope is a perfect example of the Create a Mood technique because everything you see in this photo was lit by my flashes. When we took this photo, the bar was not open. The owner let us in, but all the lights were off except for the bathroom light, at camera right. It looked quite dark inside.

However, instead of running away from such a place, I decided to create the light myself. The light entering from the window at camera left was created by shooting a portable strobe with an orange gel from the outside through the window. This creates the feeling of a setting sun shining warm light through the windows. Creating the light from scratch is not necessarily easy, but it is fun! Once you have good control over your lights, it isn't any more difficult to use three lights or ten. More lights are not more complicated. They are simply illuminating other parts of the scene. That's all.

For this photo, it was quite fun figuring out how to modify the flashes and how to keep them hidden from the camera's view. This was incredibly exciting to do, and I love the results. As soon as I had the chance, I printed this photo myself and had it framed by Levin Frames to give to Hope. We used quite a few flashes and portable strobes to create this photograph. I will go over in detail how this photo was created in Chapter 4.

Figure 1.9 (ISO 50, f/5.6, 1/250): This photo of my beautiful, pregnant wife Kim was taken indoors. I used the Create a Mood technique because the image was taken indoors without any decent natural light coming into the room.

For this photo, I used a large modifier on a portable strobe directly behind me to illuminate the entire scene with the same light. Next, I added a second portable strobe with a smaller modifier to just illuminate Kim. The reason for the second light on Kim was simply to create a very elegant separation between her and the background. Creating separation is one of the key reasons why I use flash so much in my work. Without flash, everything from the scene to the background to the main subject would be illuminated by the same light source; therefore, nothing would stand out because everything would be similarly lit.

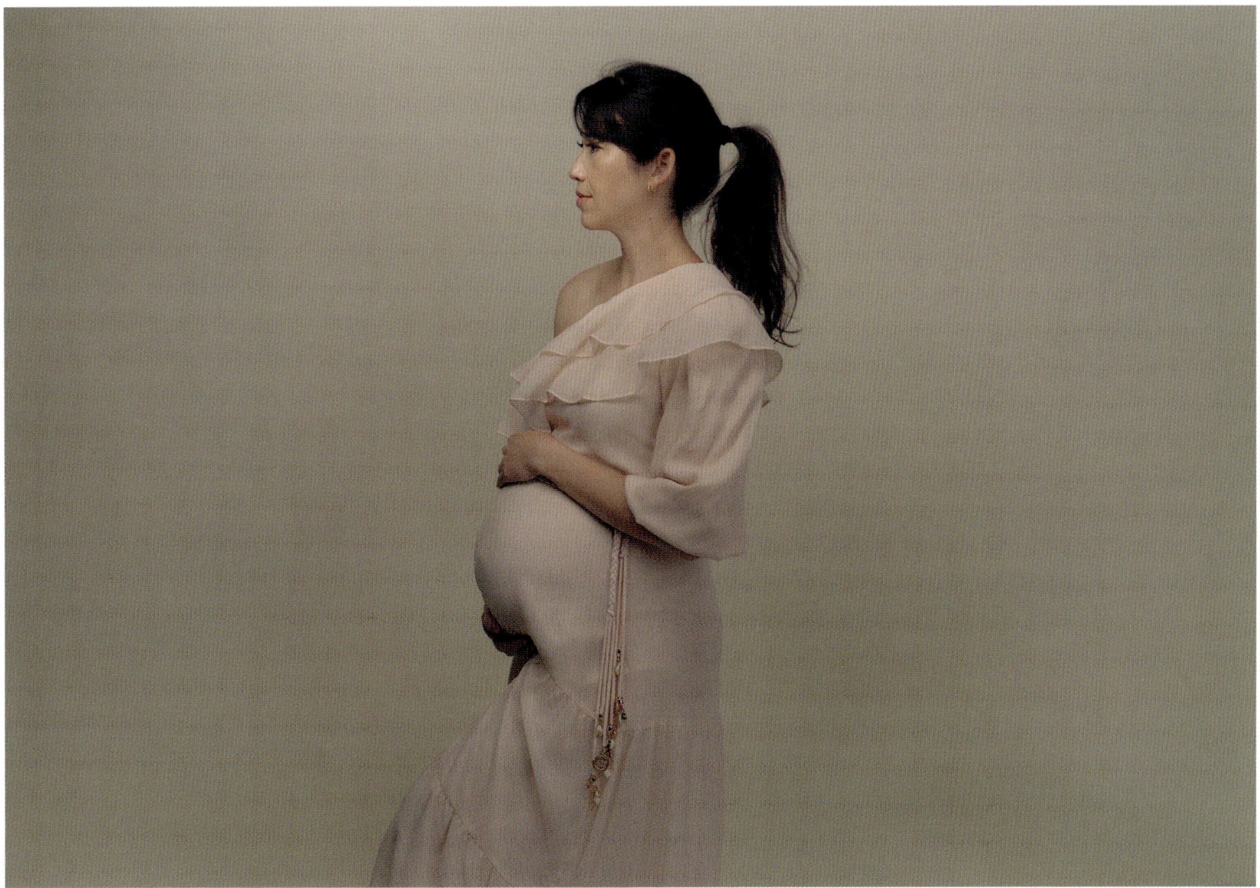

Well, let's stop the presses for a bit, because the entire room was dark, and there was no sun. In fact, the sky was turning quite dark from a rainstorm that was beginning to form. To take a photo in these conditions using just natural light would have been an undeniable disaster. Out of curiosity, I tested out a picture using just the ambient light. I had to use an ISO of 1600 to obtain any kind of decent shutter speed that wouldn't blur the model, Sarah—not a great approach. Of course, the actual quality of the light was also not good.

The solution was to use the Create a Mood technique and create a sunrise from scratch using flashes. It's hard to believe, but the entire mood of this photo was created with only one flash located outside the room. The flash was directed toward the room, and I used a full CTO gel on the flash to give the light a nice orange color, imitating sunrise.

I used a second flash on top of my camera, at a low power and pointed toward the ceiling. This helped reduce contrast and slightly lift the shadow detail. It is incredible how much mood one can achieve with a simple flash used creatively. More on how this photo was envisioned and created later in the book.

FIGURE 1.11

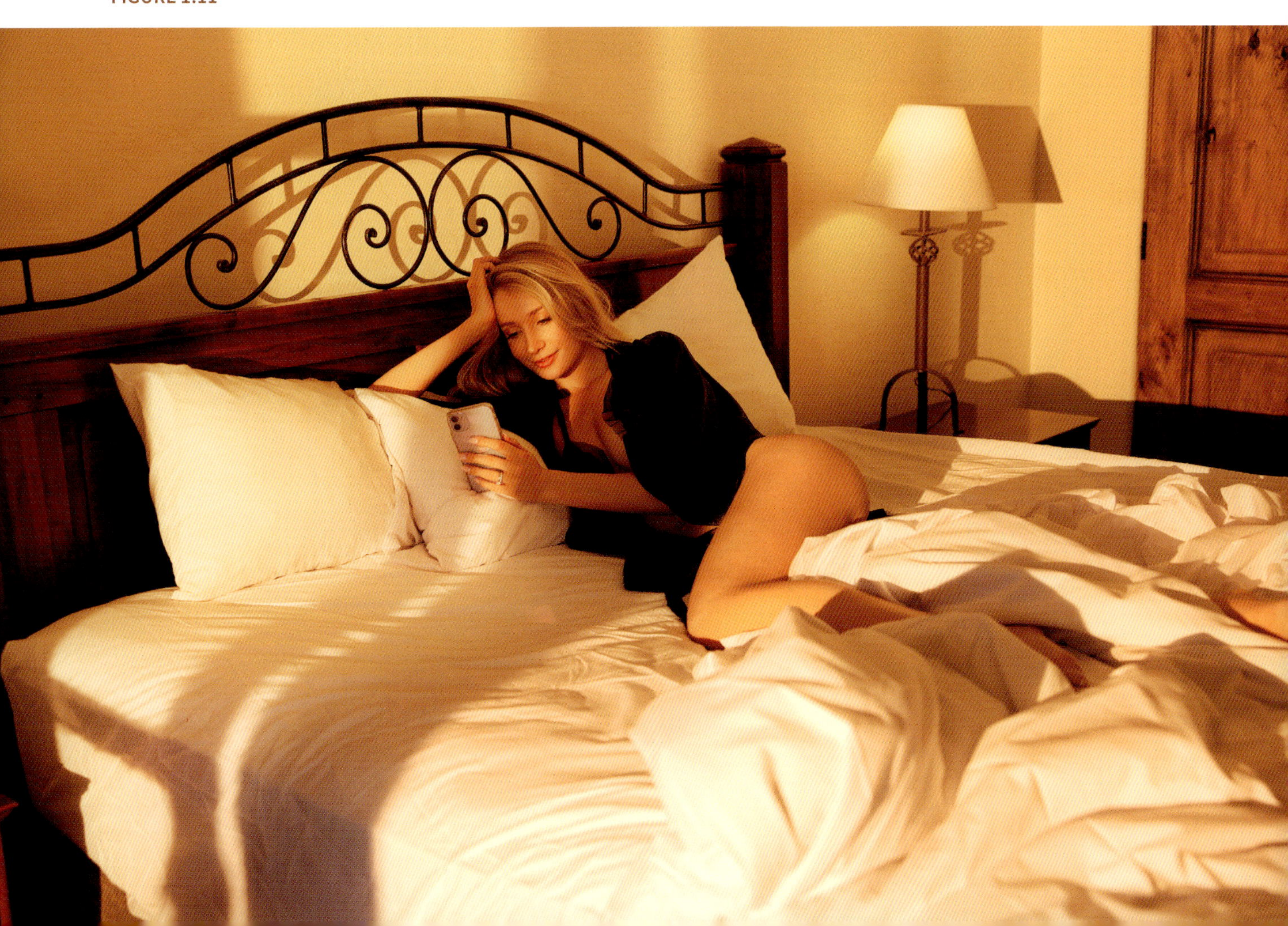

Effects with Flash

Figure 1.12 (ISO 100, f/8, 1/2): Let's continue and discuss another technique that you can use to spice up your work. This is the Effects with Flash technique, and this is also when lighting becomes quite exciting!

Since this was a high contrast scene with a dark background, it was the perfect opportunity for a fun special effect called "dragged shutter." I put my camera on a very slow shutter speed and had the model move in a specific way that we agreed upon beforehand. I put my portable strobes on 2nd Curtain Sync (which I explain later in the book) to freeze her motion with the flash at the end of the exposure.

I absolutely loved the drama this effect created. It is so much more interesting than a normal exposure without the special effects.

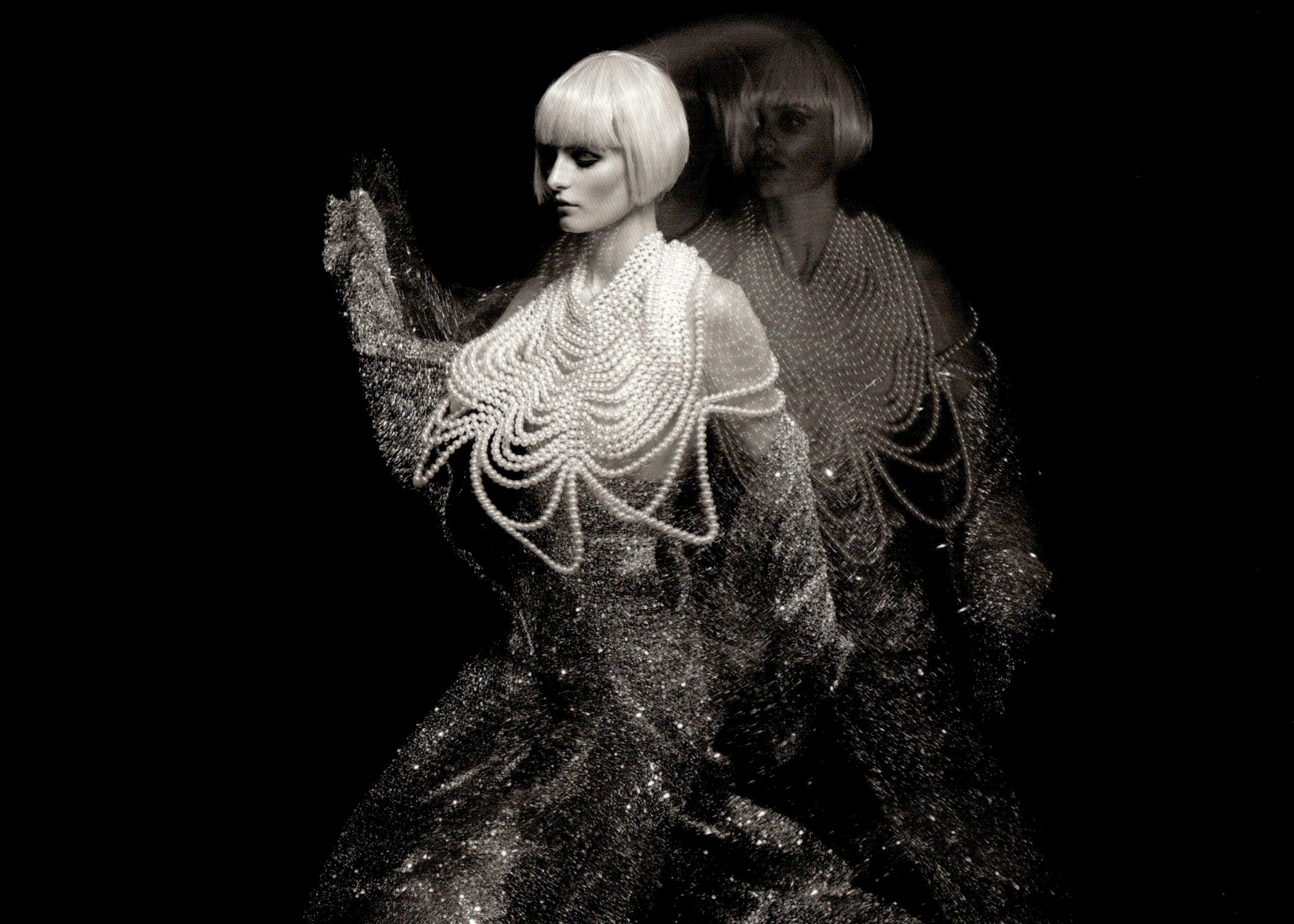

FIGURE 1.12

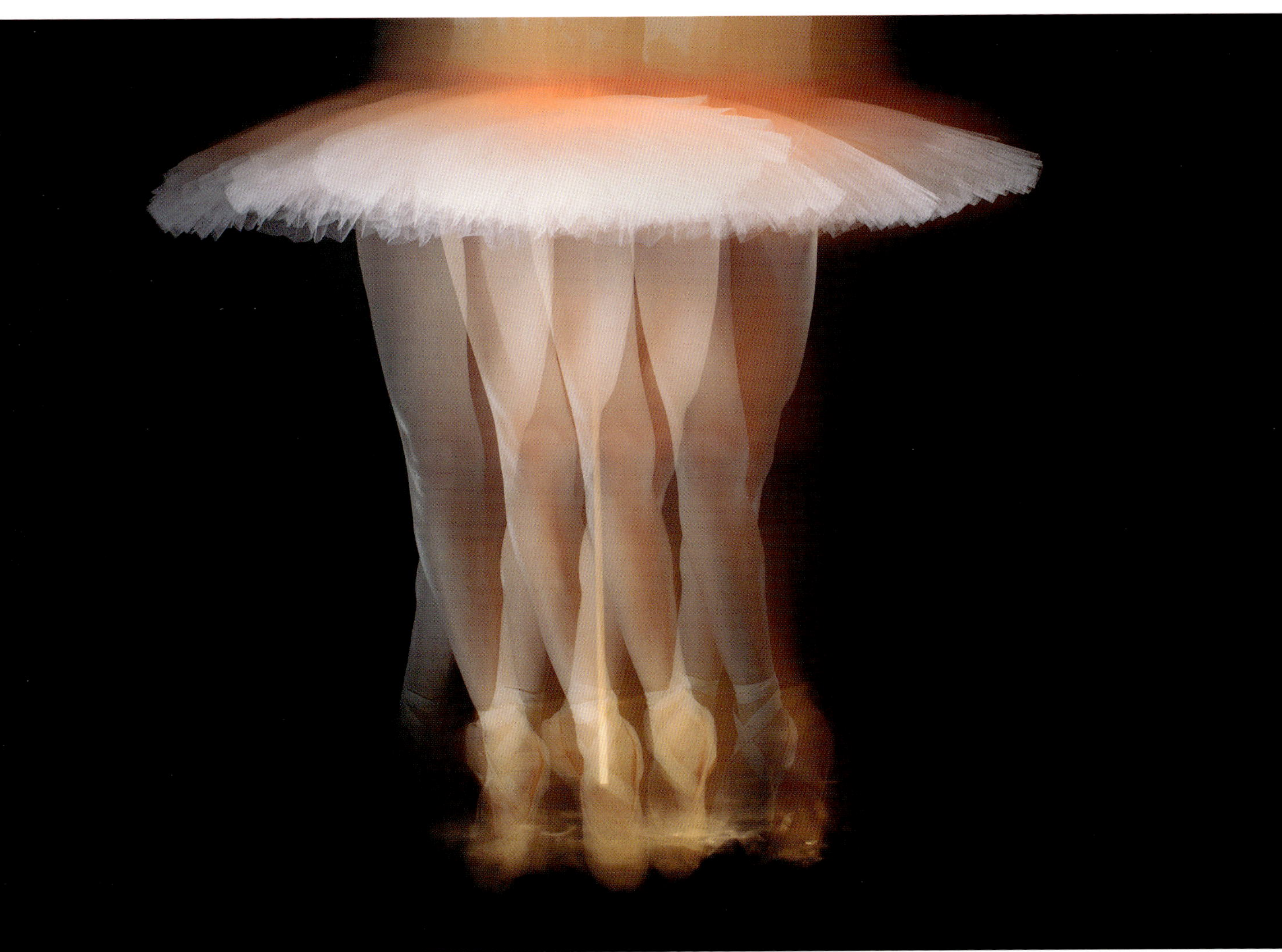

Figure 1.13 (ISO 160, f/7.2, 1/3): How unique is this? What a great way to showcase the graceful foot movements of a trained ballerina! This is Ellie, a former ballerina. I have always been mesmerized by the incredible precision of the foot movements of a balle-rina. To show this movement to the viewer, I used the Effects with Flash technique. More specifically, I used a multi-stroboscopic flash technique, which I explain in further detail later in the book.

The point is that, by using this underappreciated technique, I created something truly special that people would not expect to see. Everything is possible with the power and versatility of flash/portable strobes.

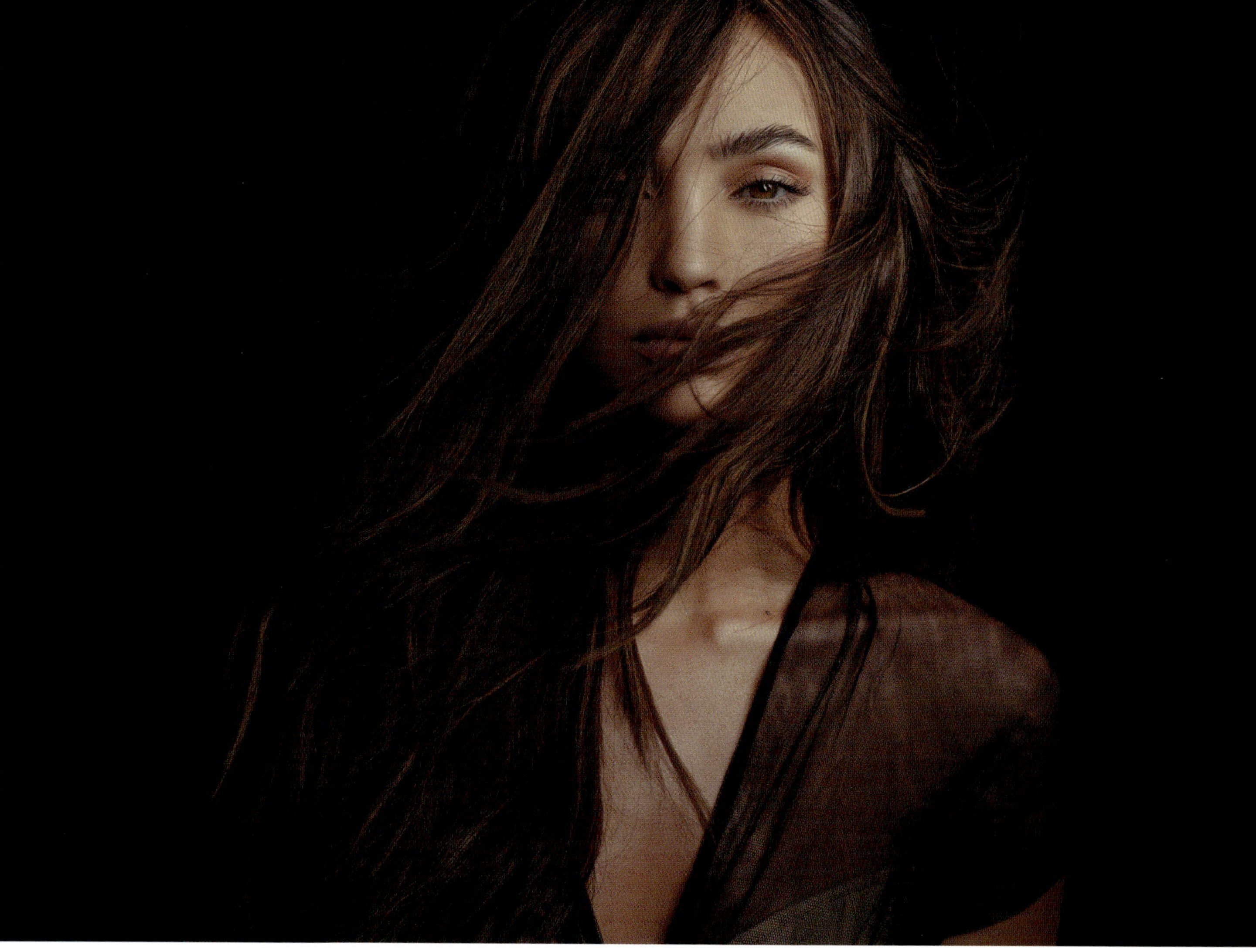

Sculpt the Light

Strategically sculpting light in a portrait is the key to making your photos stand out and provide mood. In my opinion, masterful subtraction and precise addition of light is what separates a great photographer from an average one.

If you are not sure how sculpting light applies to a photograph, just imagine a portrait in which the middle of the person's face from forehead to chin is in light, but both sides of the face are in soft shadow. The effects of this light and shadow on a person's face will give their face some shape. In this case, the shadows elongate the face and make the person look thinner.

Most portraits you make will have some automatic subtraction of light happen naturally, but I'm not talking about happy accidents. I'm talking about you visualizing where exactly you want less light, and knowing how to do it! Subtracting light is an advanced technique, but don't let that scare you. That's why you bought this book—to become a better photographer, correct?

When a portrait artist strategically subtracts light from a desired area of the photograph, that's sculpting. And this skill is what puts photographers on the map. A portrait with dark areas and bright areas gives it shape, contrast, dynamics, contouring, drama, dimensionality, and mood. But most importantly, it makes the portrait far more interesting! Anyone can create a portrait with just natural light or a simple flash aimed at the ceiling, but you cannot stop looking at a portrait with visually compelling contrast!

Figure 1.14: This photo is of R'Bonney Nola Gabriel, the current Miss Universe (as of the writing of this book). It was taken at my studio in Los Angeles. When planning this portrait, I knew I wanted to sculpt the light with R'Bonney in order to create something that had soul and feeling—an expression that makes you look, and keep looking. The only way to achieve this was through light sculpting. Imagine just putting R'Bonney directly in front of a couple of softboxes and firing my lights. What would that look like? It would look like every other photo most people take, just a well-exposed photo. That's it. No feeling, no vibe, no soul. Learn to sculpt light, and you will acquire an enormous ability to create thought-provoking portraiture.

Note: You might have noticed that I included the camera settings for most of the photos in this chapter. However, moving forward, I will only include or discuss the camera settings if they pertain to the lesson at hand. If not, I will omit the camera settings—not to deprive you of this information, but to maintain your focus on the material covered in that lesson. For many years, I too was a victim of thinking that the camera settings were the secret to success. *But they are not.* Instead, they serve only as a distraction that will prohibit you from learning the material. For this reason, I can tell you this: If the camera settings are important in order for you to understand the technique being covered, I will include and discuss the settings, such as ISO, shutter speed, and aperture. Otherwise, I will not include them. I wanted you to know that this is intentional for your benefit. Let's move forward.

Are You Getting Excited?

I hope you now recognize the possibilities of using The Picture Perfect Flash System. With this approach, you can be in any situation, indoors or outdoors, and create amazing photographs. Through practice and experience, you will be able to walk into any room or location and quickly determine which of the FACES techniques is best suited for that situation.

Your artistic vision and your ability to make that vision a reality will become a faster and faster process for you to execute. This method will become second nature to you, and when it does, *that's* when you will be unstoppable and a true master of your craft. Let's begin!

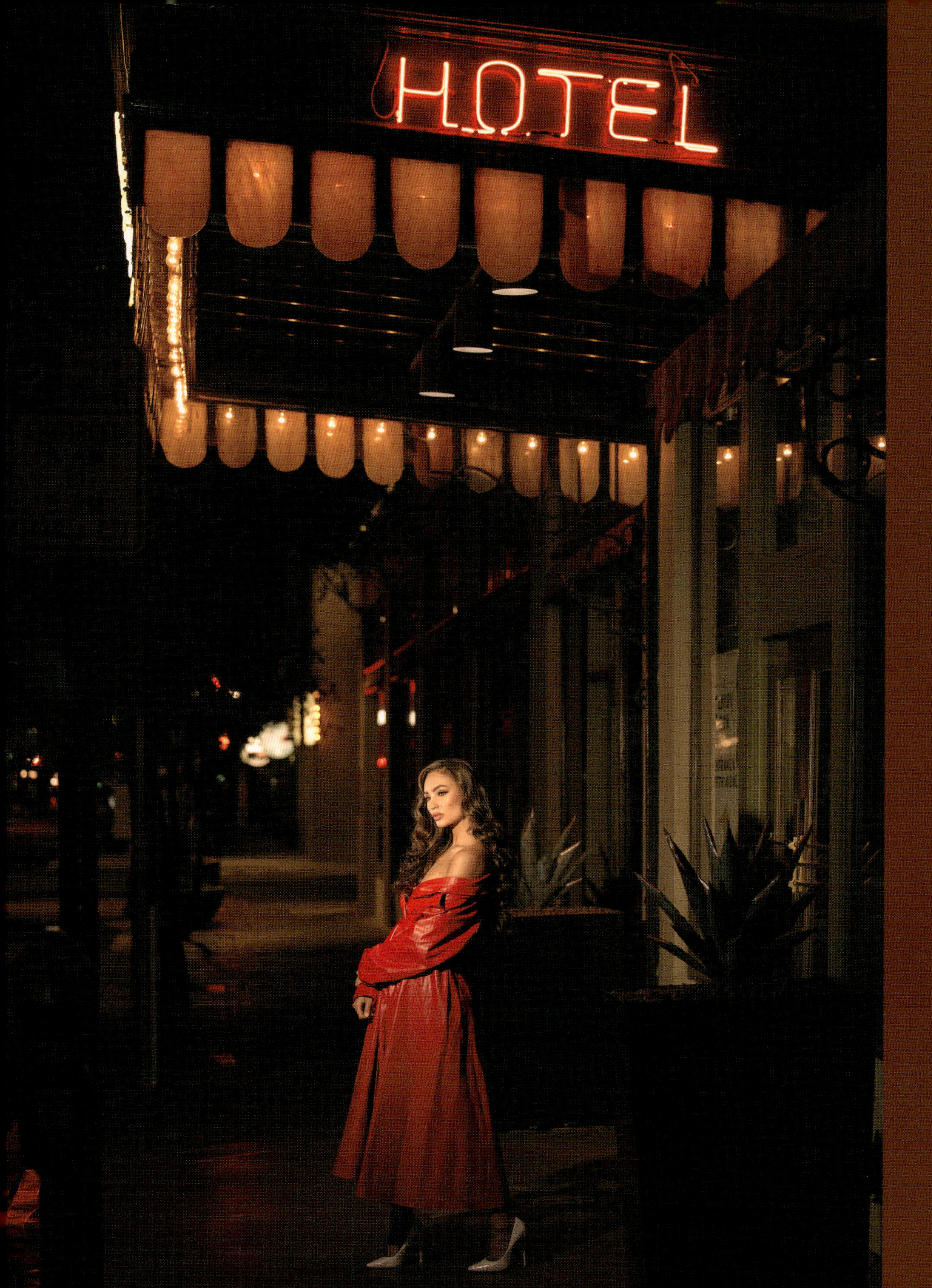
HOTEL

Chapter 2

Fix the Light

A
C
E
S

It is said that the first step to fixing a problem is to recognize that there is a problem. Simple? Well, no. When it involves lighting, realizing that there is a problem to fix is not as easy as it sounds. Some problems are obvious, but others are not. It took me considerable time to figure out all the types of lighting problems that I face on a daily basis. For this reason, I want to make it easier for you, so in this chapter I give you a precise list of lighting problems. I also provide you with a list of solutions that you can choose from to solve each problem.

To simplify, there are two top-level problem categories: "exposure based" problems and "unflattering light" problems. If you take a person outside at almost any time of the day and take a quick photo of them, chances are the lighting is going to look quite unflattering. Regardless of the angle or the position of the sun, your normal everyday lighting almost always needs to be fixed for proper portraiture. Keep this in mind. Fix the light first, and then you can add light or do whatever you want to create a stand-out portrait.

An easy-to-follow list of potential lighting problems that need to be fixed can be extremely helpful.

Whenever you encounter any of these problems, you must fix some lighting.

Photographers mean well. They want to use gorgeous light for their portraits, but under the pressure of a photo shoot, it's difficult to focus on the quality of light. The first step is to stop for a quick second, look around you, and ask yourself, "Is there a lighting problem here?" Trust me, it will be very much appreciated by your clients when they see the results.

Since this question can be so broad, my hope is that, by listing the categories of lighting problems, it makes it a lot easier to recognize that you have a lighting problem to fix. If you are indeed in a lighting situation that requires attention, fixing the light is the very first step you must take to turn a bad lighting situation into something beautiful.

Not Enough Light

A Not Enough Light problem means that the situation is dark or nearly dark, such as a photo shoot occurring at night on a city street. There is not much light except for the small lights of the city, restaurants, bars, and maybe the small streetlights above. Another example of Not Enough Light could be when doing a shoot around sunset when you cannot see the sun because it is blocked by a building or some other structure. A situation like that can be quite dark. If you find yourself indoors in a room without much window light coming in, that would also be considered a Not Enough Light problem. Yet another example would be a moody bar that's generally dark, but it's lit ever so faintly by the small amber lights to give the bar its cozy mood. Simply put, a Not Enough Light problem stems from darkness, indoors or outdoors.

But why not just raise the camera's ISO to deal with the darkness?

Because our goal when we are trying to improve our photography skillset is not to simply be able to get a proper exposure, but to achieve a high quality and robust file right out of camera. Regardless of a camera's technology, raising the ISO to compensate for low light will always result in introducing noise to a file, and most importantly, it will weaken your ability to make adjustments in post-production without damaging the file. Higher ISO settings weaken the robustness of the file. Simple as that! You might not see the damage on the back of your screen, but you will definitely see it when you try to process the file and print the photo. The bigger the print, the more apparent the damage will be.

Figure 2.1: This photograph is obviously too dark, and therefore we have a Not Enough Light problem. I photographed this at my studio as an example for this book. I had to block most of the light to make the place as dark as possible with just a bit of spill light coming in from other parts of the studio.

Remember that Not Enough Light is a different problem than Poor Quality of Light. Not Enough Light means there is just not enough light to work with; you are working, more or less, in darkness. When dealing with a Not Enough Light problem, you have minimal light contamination on your subject because there is not enough light to begin with. Keep this in mind as you continue reading. Many headshot and portrait photographers create a Not Enough Light problem on purpose to have a blank slate to work with as a starting point. Dealing with unwanted light pollution can be very frustrating for some photographers.

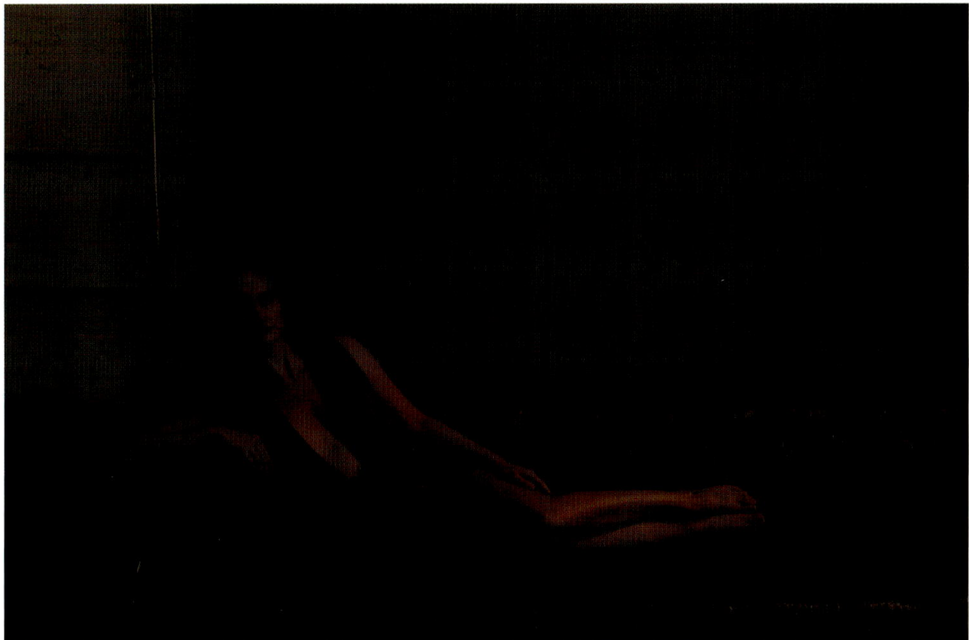

FIGURE 2.1

Fixing a Not Enough Light Problem

As in many aspects of life, opportunities always originate from problems. This book is about teaching you how to achieve amazing results with your flashes, so what's a better starting point to paint with light than a dark canvas? With darkness as your starting point, anything you light up will be clearly visible, and any place where the light doesn't reach will remain dark. This means that you are in complete control!

The opportunity that darkness offers is so beneficial that sometimes studio photographers remove as much light from their studios as possible to avoid any light contamination in their photos. The only light captured in the photo is the light that was carefully placed by the photographer. This is a remarkable opportunity when working on a headshot of a portrait, fashion, or glamour client. Naturally, you wouldn't want to take a traditional family portrait in the dark, but it wouldn't be so strange to do a much more creative group portrait starting from darkness.

If you want to be a much better photographer, think about the possibilities you could take advantage of that stem from any problem, such as a lack of light. An average photographer, faced with a Not Enough Light problem, would probably say, "Well, I can't do anything here! It's far too dark." Don't let the problem defeat you; turn it into an opportunity instead.

Of course, you won't always have the ability or the equipment to craft light and create shadows in the perfect spot on a person's face. So, then what? Well, the next option is to add a flash to illuminate the subject from the darkness. This is the option most photographers choose, and there is nothing wrong with that. But just realize that simply lighting a dark scene with your flash is not the only option; it is just one of the options.

Another option you can try in the dark is to play with the Multi or Stroboscopic flash technique. If you are not familiar with this, most modern flashes offer this special effect. The effect outputs a series of flashes within a single exposure. You determine the number of flashes and the strength of each flash per exposure. For this special effect technique to work, you need darkness.

A final option would be to implement a light painting effect with a slow shutter.

Let's take a closer look at these options.

Options for Working with a Not Enough Light Problem

Illuminate the Subject at a Basic Level Using Basic Flash Functions

Figures 2.2 & 2.3: This is as basic as it gets when it involves fixing a darkness problem. In this example, we used a simple setup with an on-camera flash aimed straight at the subject on TTL mode, or Automatic mode. I would never use this technique myself, because direct flash on camera directed at the subject is about as unflattering a light

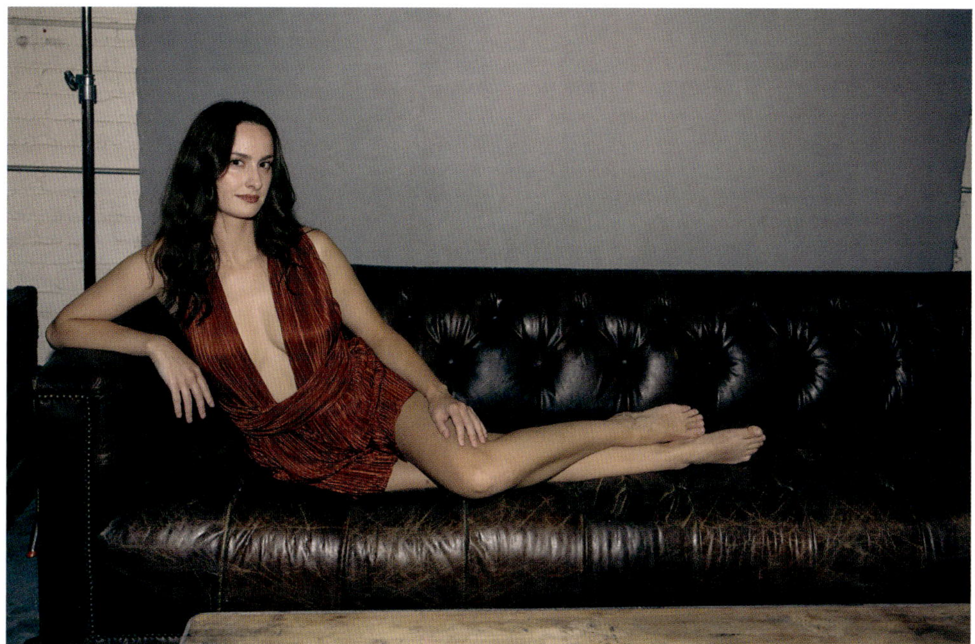

FIGURE 2.2

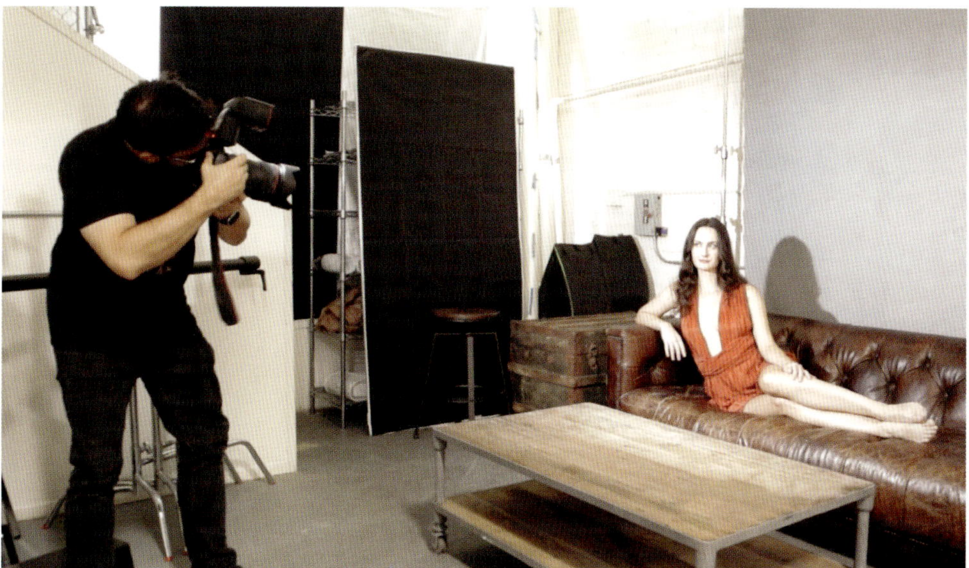

FIGURE 2.3

as you can get. It creates hot spots all over the face and hard shadows that can be very distracting. However, this does fix the problem. You had no light; now you have light. You can make a proper exposure that viewers can see. Good! But now it's time to refine our approach.

Figures 2.4 & 2.5: What an enormous difference it makes when you tilt the flash head up and pull the white bounce card out from the flash. This time, the light is indirect. The ceiling, walls, white card, and any objects in the room are lit from the light modifiers of the little flash head. The light that hits Dylan is no longer directly from the flash, but it comes from the bounced light all around her. Notice how soft her skin looks now with such a small change in the flash direction.

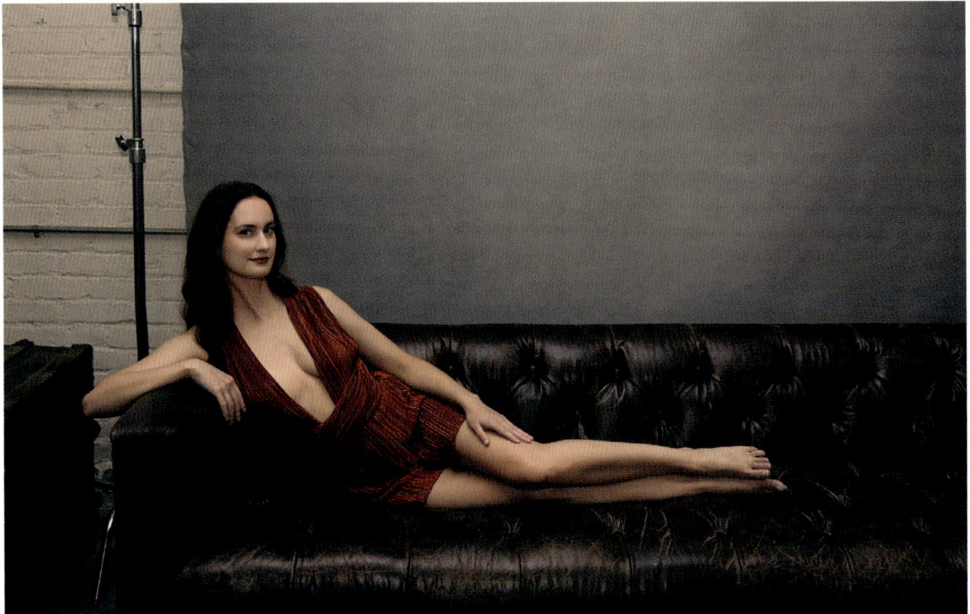

FIGURE 2.4

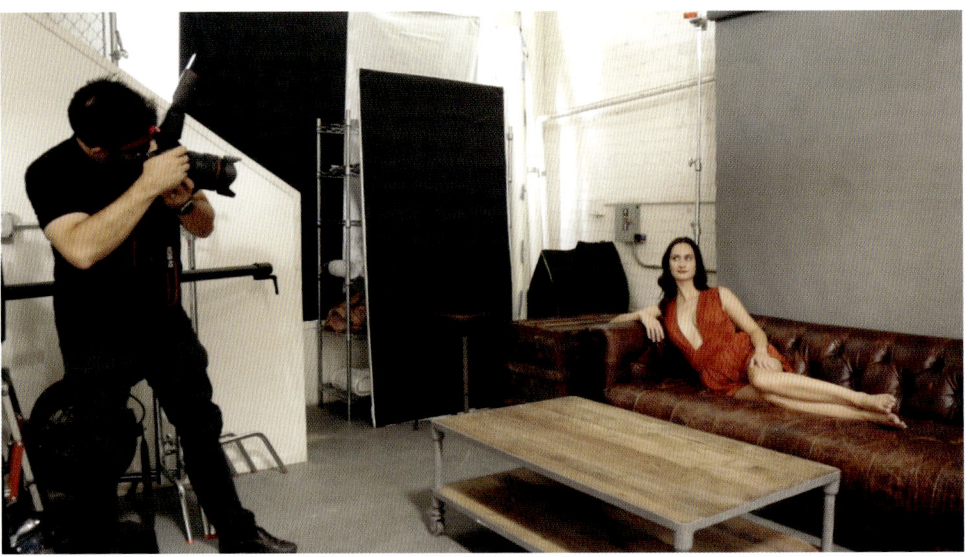

FIGURE 2.5

Add Light to a Specific Place to Carefully Craft the Lighting on a Person's Face to Create Drama, Contouring, and a Fashionable Look

Figures 2.6 & 2.7: This photo of Dylan was taken with the studio as dark as possible. Yes, there was a small amount of light spill here and there, but for the most part, the room was very dark. However, this photo was taken at ISO 100, because all of the light that reached the sensor was created by the beauty dish you see in the BTS (behind-the-scenes) photo. Because there is no other light on her face or body, you can see the beautiful shadows contouring her face. Dylan's cheekbones are defined, and her jawline looks great! This is all possible because we turned the problem of darkness into an opportunity. Make a mental connection between darkness and total light control.

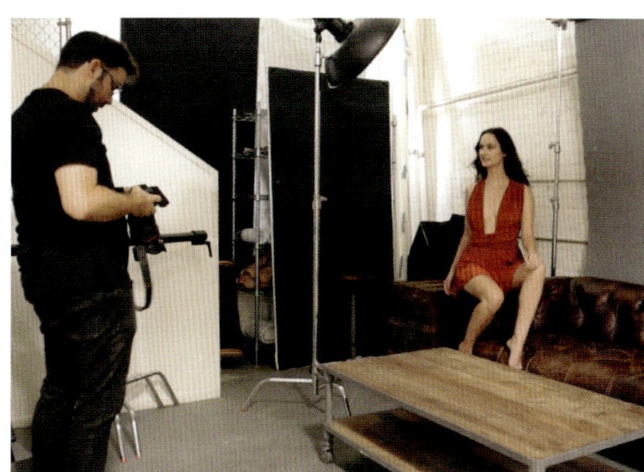

FIGURE 2.7

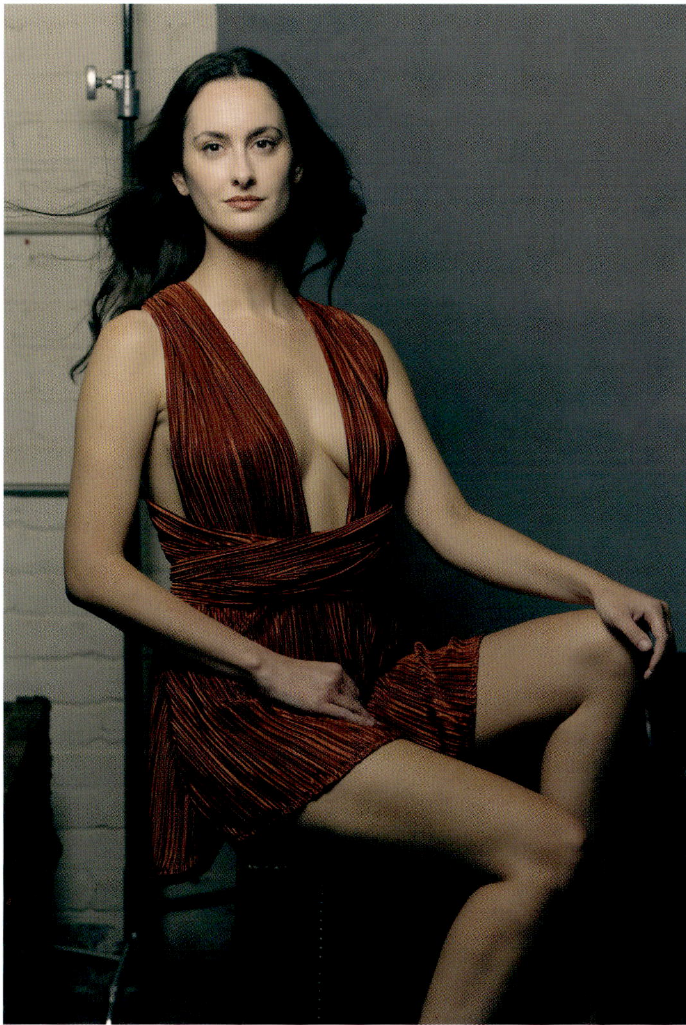

FIGURE 2.6

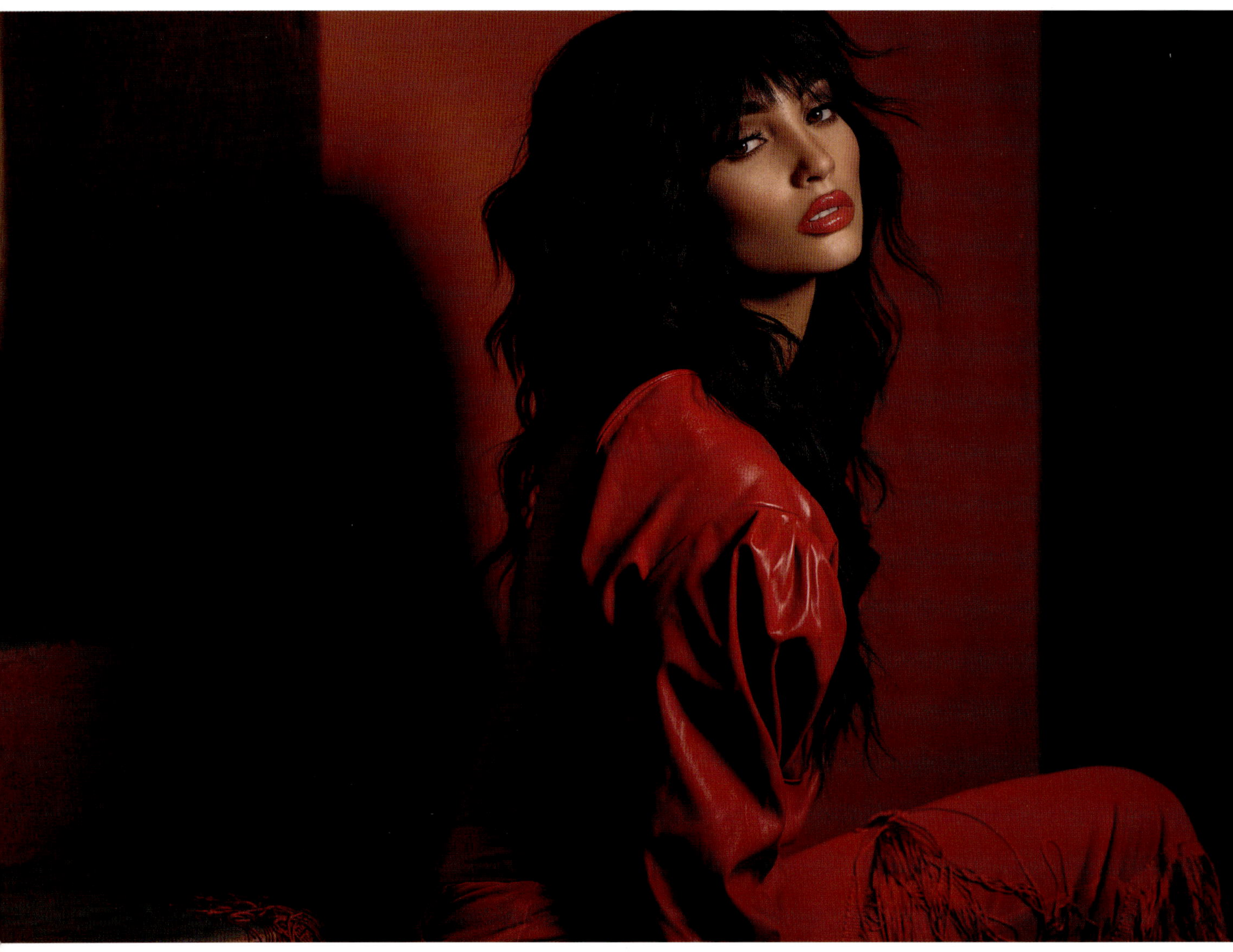

Figure 2.8: This photo of model and friend R'Bonney was taken at 3:00 a.m. in downtown Tucson, Arizona. The street was so dark I couldn't even see her very well. We had to use a small LED light just to see her and to help the camera's autofocus sensor track her eye. For this photo, we used a Profoto strobe with a gridded beauty dish to control the spread of light. The shadows on her cheekbones and jawline look absolutely stunning, giving her a high-fashion look. You don't see many on-location photos that look like this. It is all possible by turning the darkness of the night into flattering, controlled light.

Stroboscopic Flash Effects

Figure 2.9: One of the most interesting and rarely used flash techniques you can try when dealing with a dark room inside or at nighttime outside is the Multi or Stroboscopic flash technique to bring attention to movement. In this case, I asked the ballerina to create the movement of walking on the tips of her toes. That movement is graceful and impressive, but it's hard to appreciate because it all happens so quickly.

Therefore, I used the Multi flash technique. I turned off all the lights in the room and pulsed her legs moving across the floor with light. This flash technique is so unique, because it almost plays the movement back to you in slow motion; the viewer can really appreciate the highly technical footwork. Remember that almost complete darkness was needed to make this creative technique work.

In this chapter, I am just showing you what is possible when working with darkness, but in the Effects chapter (Chapter 5), I will discuss these special effects photos one more time, with a detailed explanation of my flash settings, flash positions, and overall strategy.

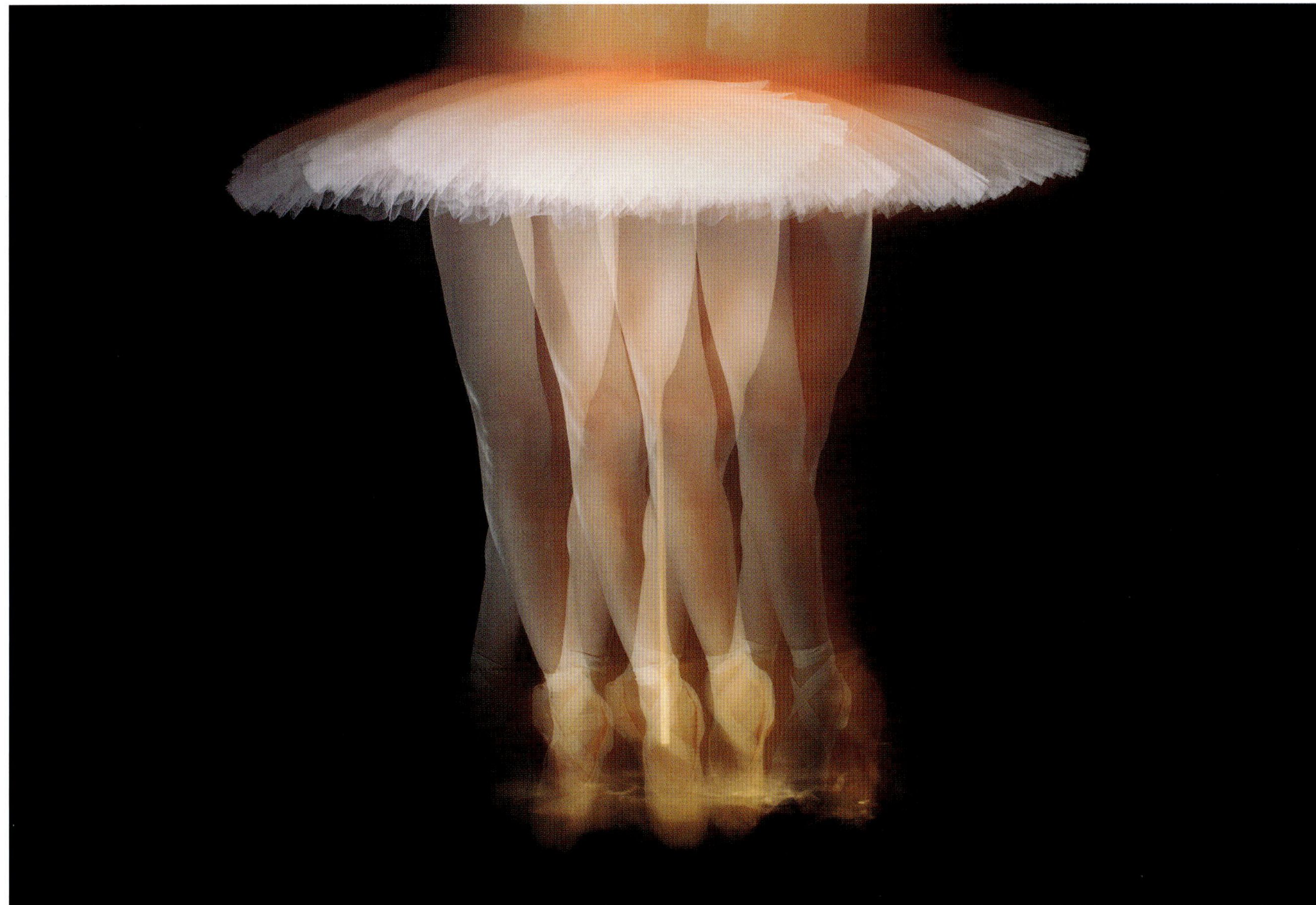

FIGURE 2.9

Light Painting Effects Using a Slow Shutter

Figure 2.10: It is easy to see how this flash technique can help you create a very painterly feel in your photograph. Again, this technique starts with a dark room. Have a long shutter speed on the camera—around 1 second or longer—and set the flash to fire at the end of the exposure. When the flash fires at the end of the exposure, it's called 2nd Curtain Sync. Because this was done in darkness, when the flash fires, it freezes the movement at the end of the exposure.

Note: Keep in mind that for these effects to take place using a slow shutter speed, there must be some amount of ambient light that is still reaching your subject. This ambient light gives you the light drag you see in the final photo. It is the ambient light that creates the sense of movement. The burst from your flash is responsible for freezing that movement at the end of the exposure if you are using 2nd Curtain Sync.

Figure 2.11: For this fashion shoot example, again I used a slow shutter speed with 2nd Curtain Sync flash to create a trail of movement. To make the trail more interesting, I always start with the subject's eyes open and have them close their eyes at the end of the exposure, or vice versa. More on this in the Effects chapter later.

Creating a Moody Painterly Look

I normally would not recommend this technique to most photographers. However, since this book might be read by more advanced photographers, I would like to address this more advanced technique in case it sparks your curiosity. For certain genres of photography, such as boudoir or fine-art nudes, you can use this technique that gives your photos a distinctive painterly look.

You work in very low light conditions with a subject who is not moving at all! A boudoir portrait is perfect for this. The photographer takes a full resolution RAW photo (never JPEGs) with a relatively low ISO but with a slower shutter speed. The low ISO is the key! Try to stay at or

FIGURE 2.10

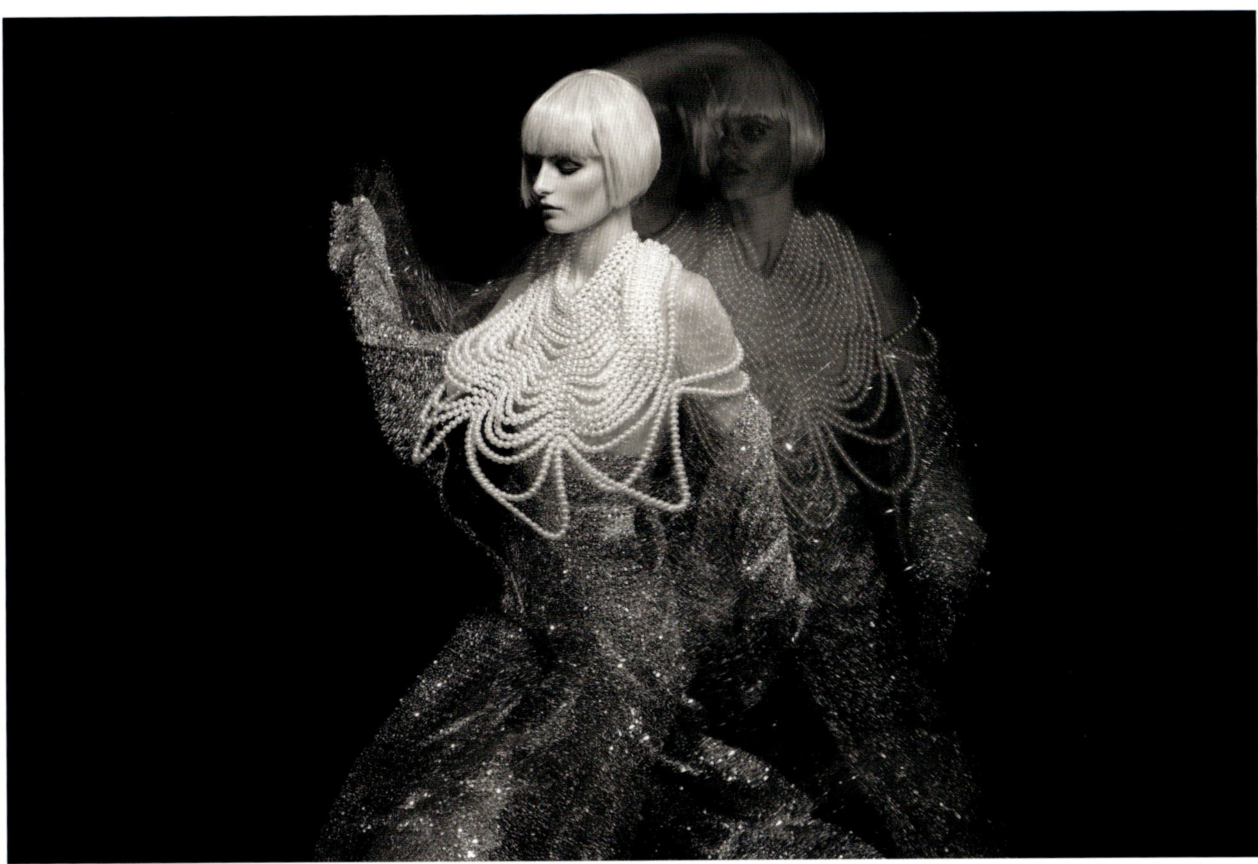

below ISO 400. You will need to use a tripod for this! Do not try to hand-hold your camera when using this technique.

Take the photo. If you did it correctly, the camera's screen should be mostly dark. You should be able to see the person on the screen, but it should not be easy to do so. The person should be faint but still visible. The magic happens when you import the RAW photo into a processor like Capture One or Adobe Lightroom. Because you took the photo with a low ISO, you should be able to recover the shadows beautifully using the shadow recovery slider in combination with the brightness slider. The low ISO allows you to push the shadow recovery slider all the way up without introducing much noise. If done correctly, the result is a moody photo that, after post-processing, looks like a painting. When I see photos like this done well, I can't help but feel a strong emotional response to the photograph. Its low-key nature is truly beautiful. So, in a way, since this is the Fix the Light chapter, you are in essence fixing the portrait created in low light with RAW editing software.

Figure 2.12: Here is an example of this technique I used on a bridal portrait in Switzerland. The interior of this ancient building provided the perfect reason to use this painterly technique. My settings for this photo were: ISO 400, f/2.4, 1/30. I wanted to use ISO 200, but my shutter speed would have dropped too far, certainly resulting in a blurry photo.

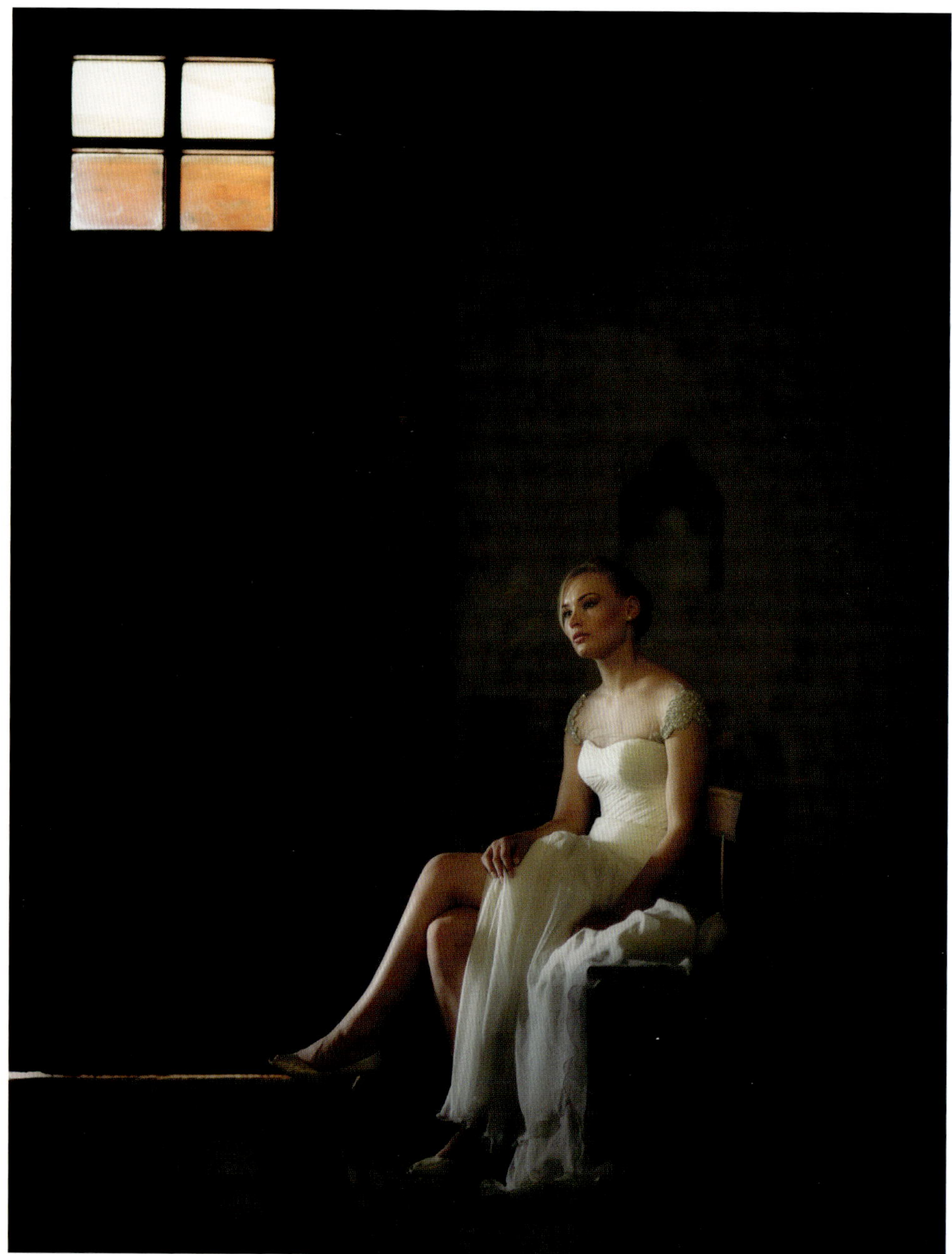

FIGURE 2.12

It is my hope that after reading these examples, you will see darkness as the great opportunity that it is. When used properly, darkness can give you a blank (dark) canvas to make something creative, unique, unexpected, and compelling! When working with darkness, you have the opportunity to put light exactly where you want it with no risk of light contamination from anywhere else. You are in control! Now, it's up to you to actually try these techniques on your own. One by one, you will learn how to execute these techniques faster and more effectively.

Figure 2.13: For this example, I decided to go with the moody painterly technique. The difference here is that I forced the darkness with my camera settings in the studio and used a couple of Profoto studio strobes to create the contrast on her muscles. So I created an exposure that was dark enough to barely see the photo on the camera's screen, but then I was able to recover the shadows and highlights in post.

Again, the key for this technique is to shoot with the lowest ISO possible, but still have a sharp photo. In summary, you can either work in a dark environment or create a dark exposure with the camera settings. It's a cool technique. Try it!

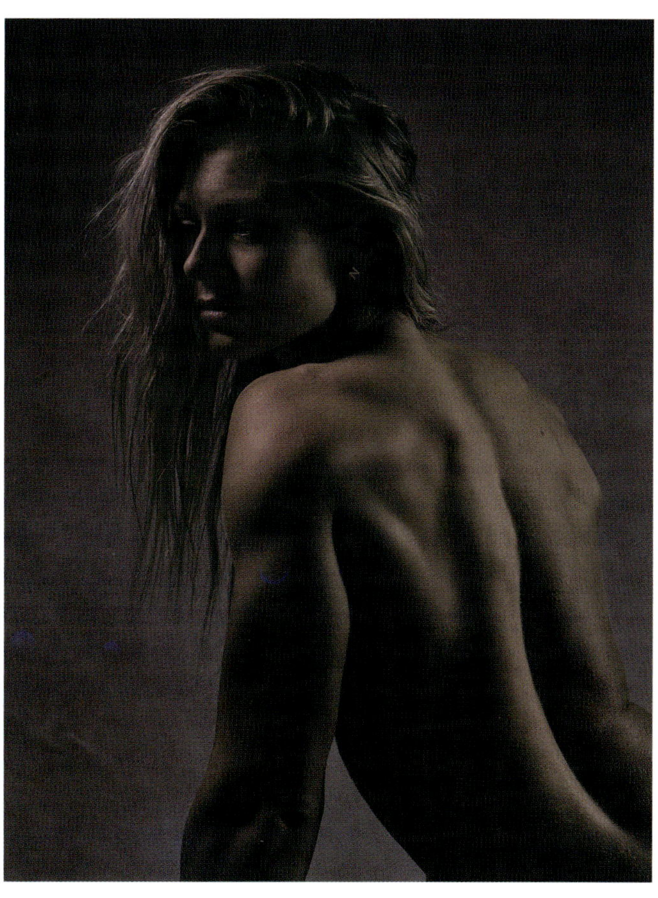

Too Much Light

Too much light seems like it would be a good problem to have, right? And it is actually good, for the most part. But when you have too much light, you must tame the light so it looks flattering on a subject. We have all seen that straight sunlight on people's faces. They look as if they are being tortured.

THE THREE MAIN PROBLEMS YOU WILL FACE WITH TOO MUCH LIGHT

- Blown-Out Light
- Splotchy Light Caused by Unwanted Hard Shadows on the Face or Body
- Uncomfortable Facial Expression with Heavy Squinting

Blown-Out Light

Actually, too much light is a worse problem than not enough light. When you are dealing with too much light, it is usually from clear skies and direct sunlight on the face. Far too often, I see photographers taking photos of clients outdoors. If the photographer isn't paying attention, the subject can easily turn their head left or right and become hit directly on one side of their face by direct sunlight. Due to the shape of the face, there would be very unflattering hard shadows all over the subject's face.

Another common occurrence is blowing out the top of someone's head. This issue is most likely to happen when photographing people with light-colored hair. It doesn't look very professional to take a portrait or family photo and leave the back or top of clients' heads blown out. That's very amateurish, and it looks sloppy. With a flash or even a diffuser, you can easily address this problem and produce more professional results.

Quick Fixes to Solve Blown-Out Light

Here are a few great ways to quickly tackle blown-out light.

Shadow Direction Technique

Good news! Transforming direct natural light on a face into clean light on a face is a simple fix. All there is to do is to turn your subject's face in the same direction as their own shadow. By doing this, you have the sun directly behind the back of their head and not on their face. Now the subject's face is lit purely by fill light instead of harsh direct light. Using this shadow technique, you can also use a reflector (or some sort of object acting as one) very efficiently, since the sun is hitting your reflector directly. By adding this reflected light, you improve how flattering the light is on your subject. When people are lit with flattering and robust light, they seem to glow.

Figures 2.14 & 2.15: This is what it looks like when the hard light from the sun is hitting the subject directly. Notice that the direction of her shadow is going away from me. When the subject's shadow is facing away from the photographer, the sun is hitting the person's face directly. Direct sun is a very harsh light source, producing a high contrast and unflattering light, as you can see.

Figures 2.16 & 2.17: Look closely at the shadow in Figure 2.17. Here, I simply turned Dylan around and moved to the other side of her, until the top of her shadow was pointed directly at me. With the shadow pointed at the photographer, the sun is precisely behind the subject's head, which is out of camera view. What you are left with is clean, soft light on the subject's face.

Please note that clean light does not necessarily mean good quality of light. But at least it is much more flattering and usable. From here, you could easily add a reflector or a modified flash to add a slightly softer light to the face. This will highly improve the quality and intensity of light on your subject.

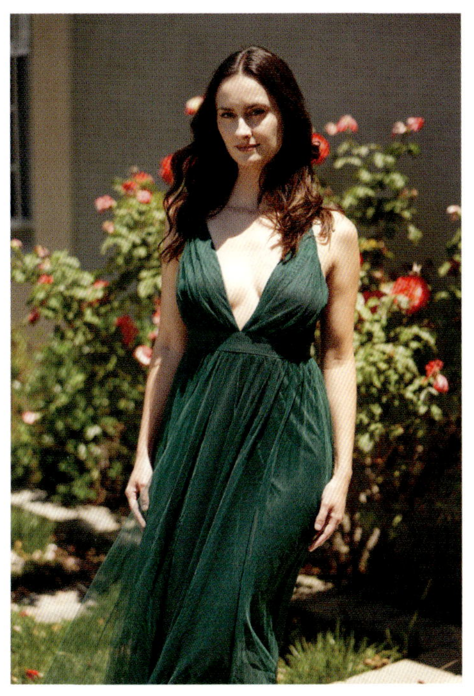

FIGURE 2.14

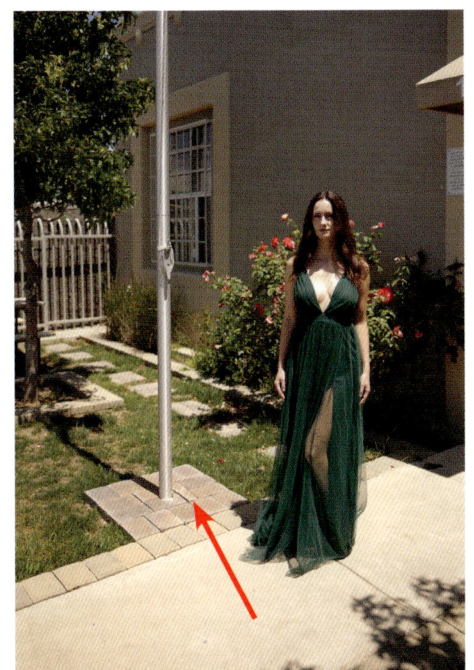

FIGURE 2.15

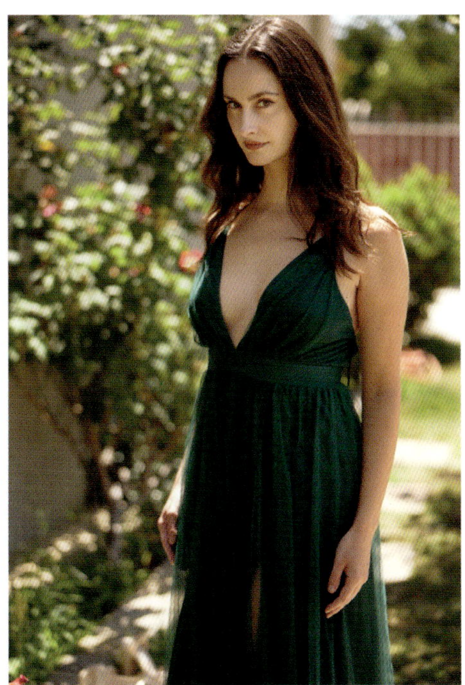

FIGURE 2.16

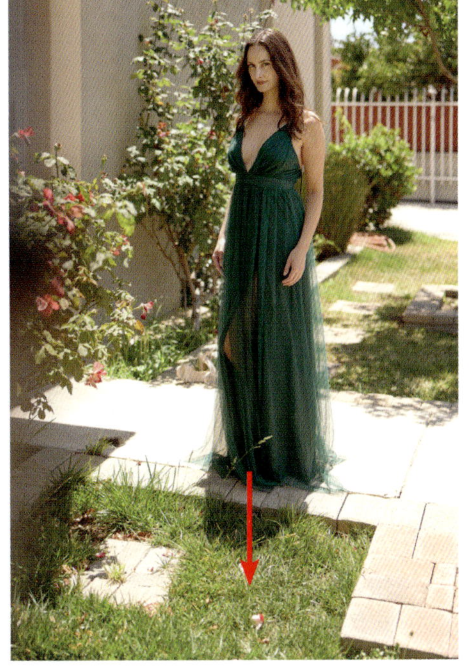

FIGURE 2.17

This is a very useful and quick technique, because it allows you to do a photo shoot at any time of the day without worry. By having the sun directly behind the subject's head, you can always count on a more flattering light on your subject's face than with direct sun hitting them from the front. There are many times at jobs, such as outdoor fashion shoots or weddings, when I don't have time to set up overhead diffusers, lighting, etc. So I quickly turn to this technique, knowing that it will always look presentable, and it gives the photos a nice lifestyle feel.

Figure 2.18: This is an example of a commercial shoot for Canon where I was in a major rush, but I had to get this look in to complete the required set. My lighting team had already walked back to the rental property, so I was left with just my camera and the model, Chanel. I quickly glanced at the ground and found the shadows created by the bushes. I positioned myself and Chanel so that the shadows were pointed at me, as discussed above. The ground provided enough bounce light to illuminate her face very well! I had Chanel keep her chin down so that the bounce light from the ground would illuminate her face in a more flattering way. Without doing so, her neck would be brighter than her face.

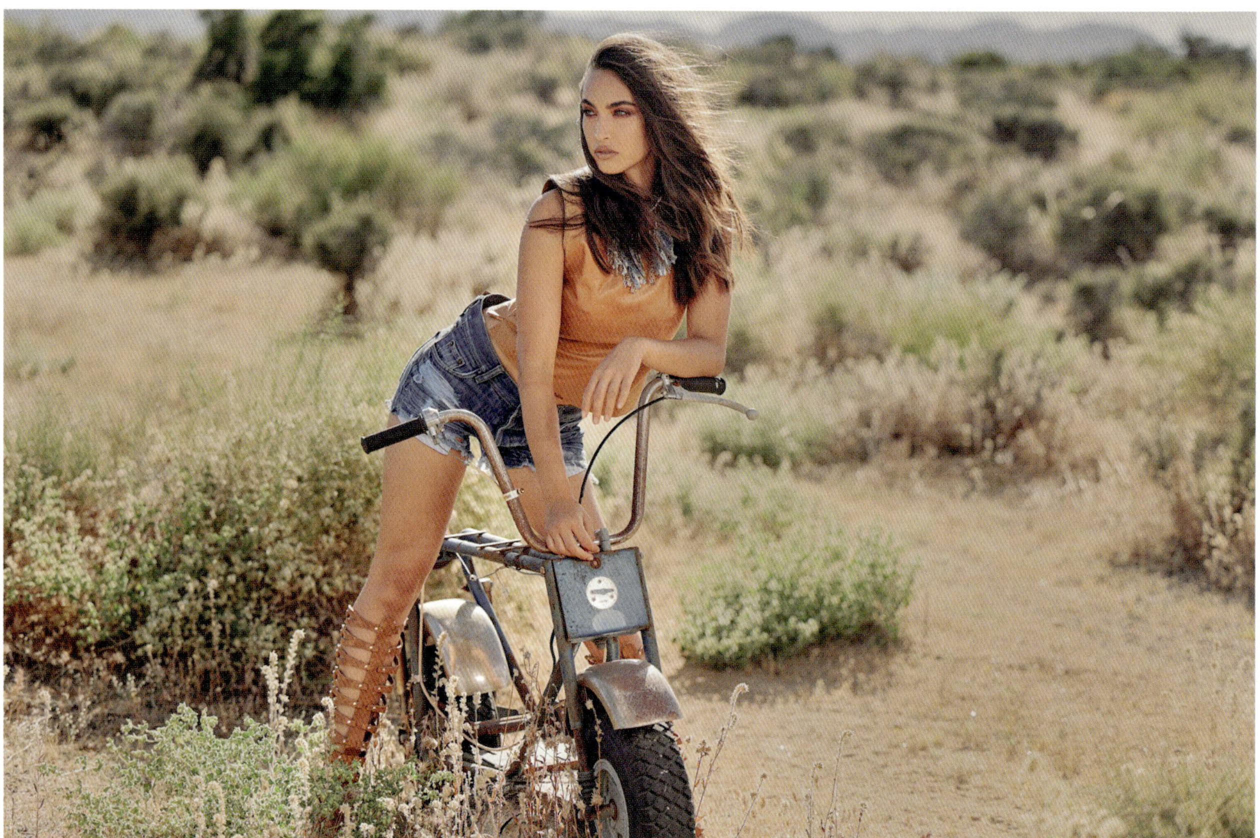

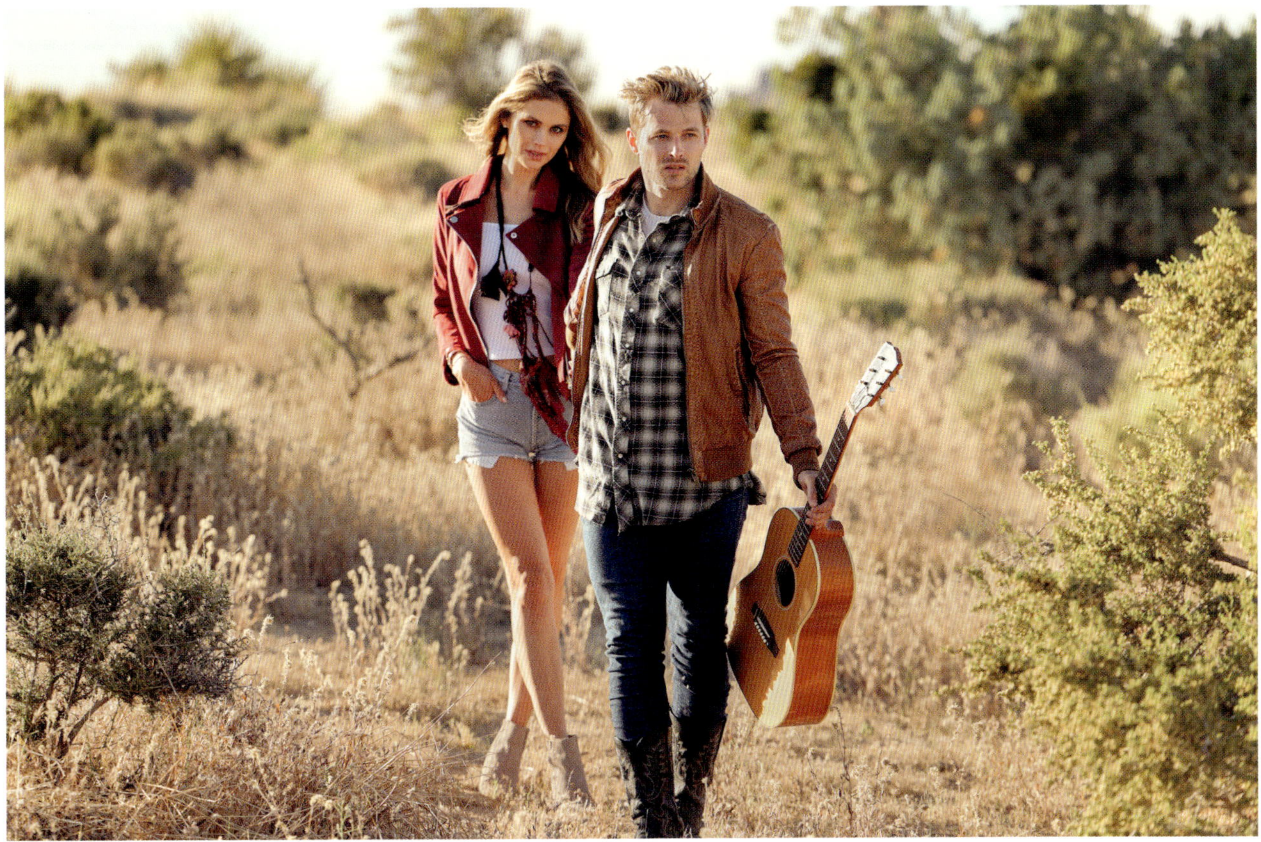

This photo turned out great without the use of any equipment. If I had a flash with me, I would have used it to create a pop of light and a little kicker to add some dimensionality to her face.

Figure 2.19: This is a very cool technique but it's risky! For this photo, taken during the same commercial shoot I was on, I stood a few steps to the left of the shadow direction. Moving your position relative to your subjects' shadows like this exposes part of your subjects' faces to the sun. As long as those rays of light don't actually hit the front of the subjects' faces, it will look like the faces are lit by clean light, while just the sides of their faces have that natural direct sun kicker. I love that!

Diffuser Overhead Technique

A collapsible diffuser is one of the most inexpensive and effective tools a photographer can buy. I have so many of them that I have lost count. One thing I do need my diffusers to have are handles to hold them. Profoto makes some great collapsible reflectors and diffusers with handles, and those are the ones I use.

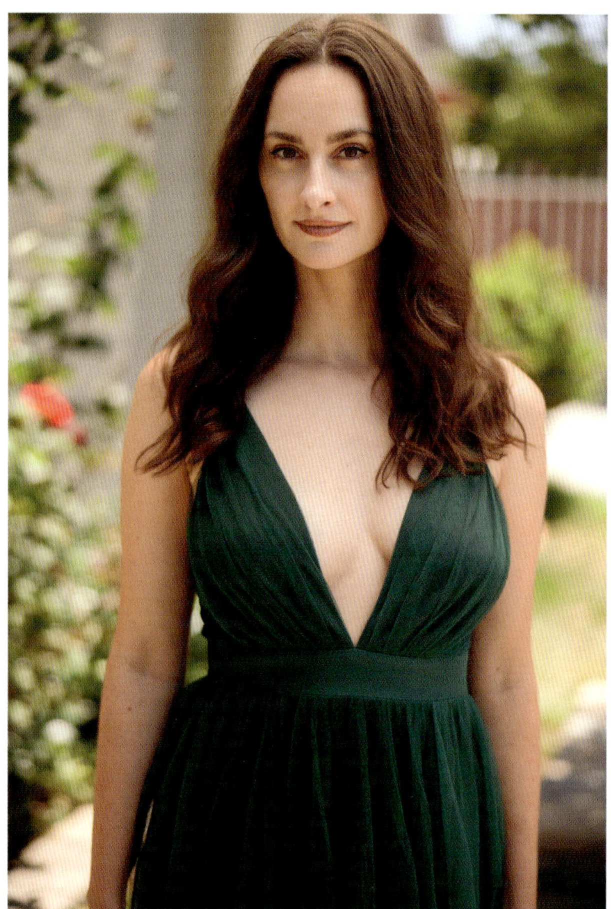

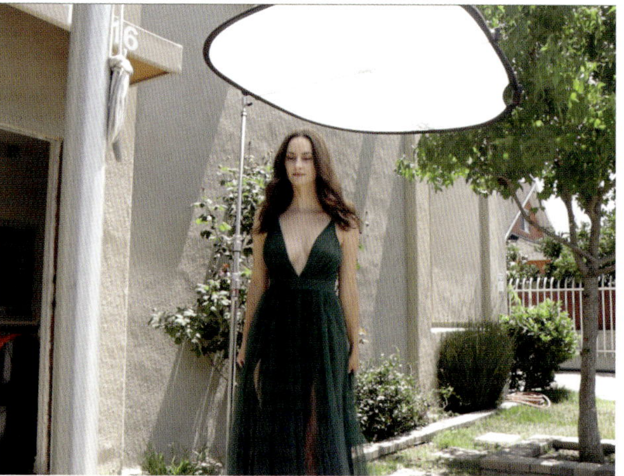

By using a diffuser over your subject's head to fix the light, you can shoot at any time of the day. And most importantly, with a diffuser overhead, you don't have to rely on the Shadow Direction technique explained above. With a diffuser, you can turn your subject's body and face in any direction you wish in order to attain the desired background. A diffuser overhead also eliminates the blown-out-top-of-the-head situation that you can get with the Shadow Direction technique, when the sun hits the back or top of the subject's head.

Figures 2.20 & 2.21: For this photo, the sun is directly illuminating the back of Dylan's head. So you can tell I'm using the Shadow Direction technique. With the addition of a diffuser overhead, it quickly becomes apparent how soft and beautiful this combination is. Look at the top of Dylan's head and the sides of her hair. The lighting is soft and diffused. This almost gives you a dreamy feel. I love it! Not a single strand of her hair is blown out by the sun, thanks to the overhead diffuser taking care of it all.

Figures 2.22 & 2.23: By turning Dylan's face directly toward the sun but then diffusing or fixing the harsh light with an overhead diffuser, what results is a still soft but much punchier photo. This combination of direct light and a diffuser gives you a higher-contrast photograph. Everyone is different, but I usually use this diffused direct sun approach when the subject has short hair or has hair pulled back, and has stronger facial features. I use the previous technique in Figure 2.20 when a person has long hair and I'm trying to achieve a more soft and dreamy effect. Experiment to figure out what you like.

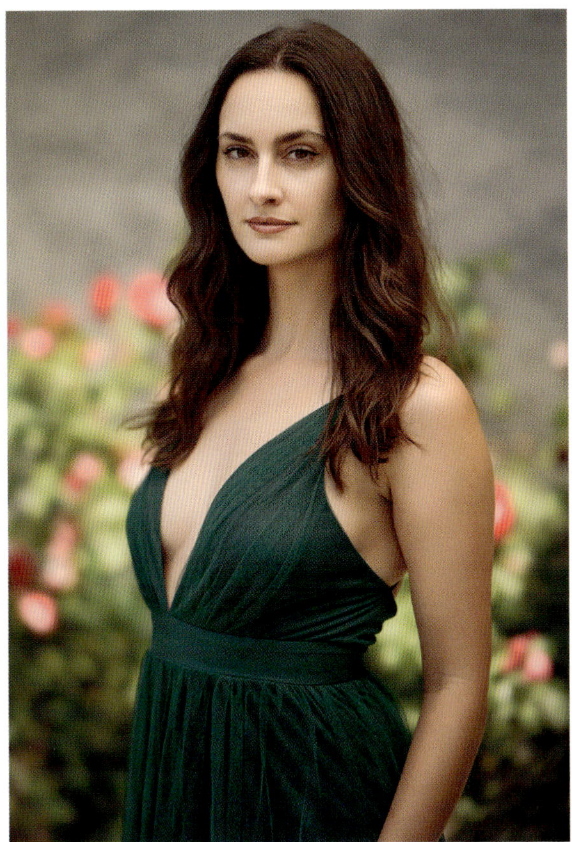

FIGURE 2.22

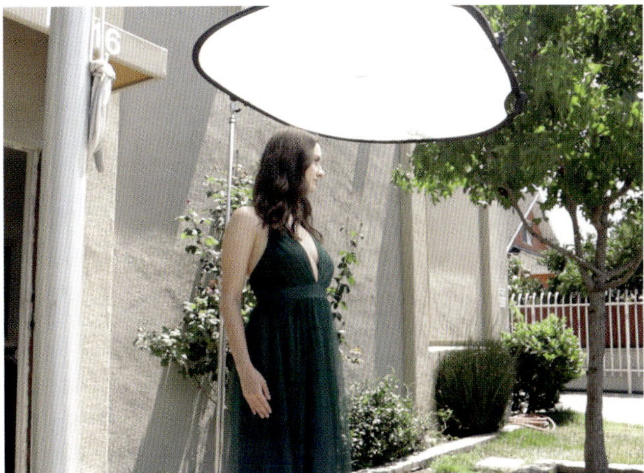

FIGURE 2.23

Combining the Shadow Direction Technique with Fill Flash

This is one of the most useful combinations to employ in your work. Think about it. The Shadow Direction technique fixes the splotchy harsh light hitting the subject's face and leaves you with a clean light canvas for you to add any light you want. For example, you could easily use bounced light from nearby buildings to add some light onto the subject's face, or you could add a reflector to give the light a little pop.

However, using a flash in this situation will give you by far the most options and control. The advantage of using a flash instead of a reflector is that with the flash you can dial in exactly how much light you want to add to the fill light, and you have more options for modifying that light. Furthermore, using a flash will result in a crisper photo. Reflectors are far too harsh on a clear sunny day and not very effective on an overcast day, which is why I rarely use them. (More on this later in the book.) But since this chapter is about fixing the light, our goal here with flashes or reflectors is not to be overly creative with lighting but to fix bad light on a subject. We will discuss how to add and create beautiful light in the next chapter, but for now we just want to fix bad light to have a fighting chance.

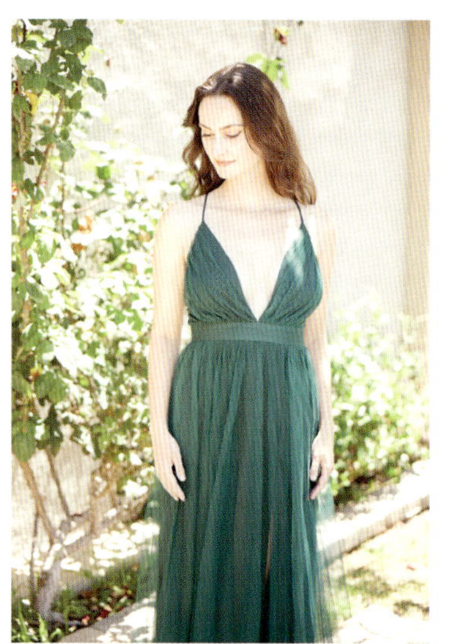

Figures 2.24–2.26: This is why people usually dislike the look of flash. They think it always looks like this first photo (Figure 2.24), which is totally unnatural and harsh. Well, they are right! Flash on its own with no modification is ugly. For this photo, we used the Shadow Direction technique to achieve clean light on Dylan's face. Next, we used a bare off-camera flash propped up on a lightstand. I turned it on, put the flash on Manual mode and just guessed at a power setting. Clearly, I guessed wrong! The flash was far too powerful and harsh.

But that's okay because this gives me a starting point. Now I know that I'm about two stops too hot. From there, I grabbed a simple and quick flash modifier called the MagBounce and lowered the flash power by two stops. Look at Figure 2.26. It looks great now, doesn't it? What a simple and easy way to make the harsh light from a flash look completely natural and perfectly blended with the natural light around Dylan.

The key here is not to panic when the light from the flash initially looks bad. It just needs a little TLC to reel it in and make the photograph look gorgeous. Not to mention, because you can put the flash exactly where you want it, fill light from a modified flash will illuminate the subject's face at a more flattering angle. That's a huge advantage!

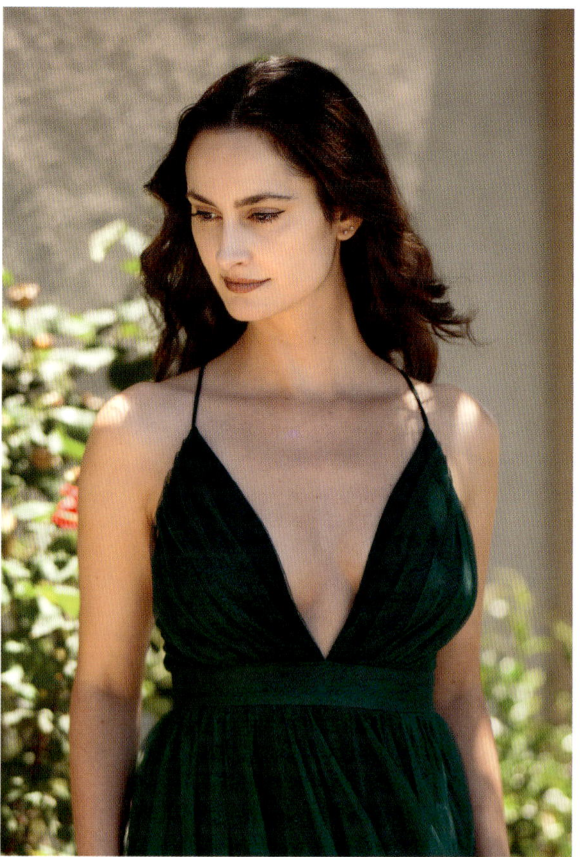

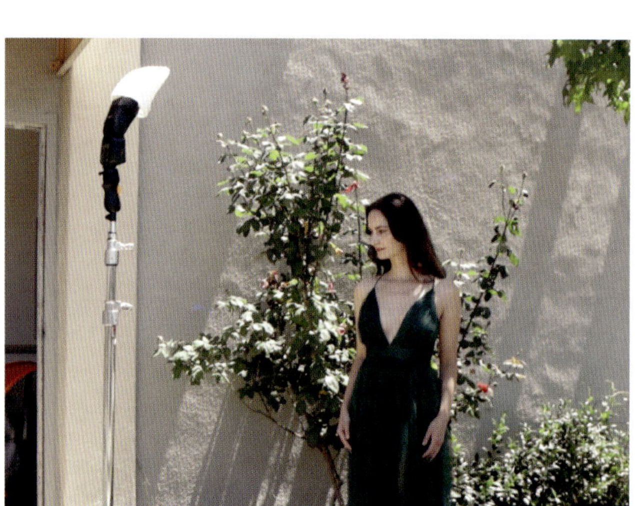

Adapting the Pose to the Sun Technique

Yet another method to deal with direct sunlight hitting your subject's face is to adapt the pose to the light. By positioning one of the person's upper cheekbones directly toward the sun, you will achieve a high-contrast dramatic lighting.

Keep in mind that for a pose such as this, the person's eyes must be looking down or must be completely closed to maintain a flattering look. You could take a photo of the person looking directly at the sun, but you would have to do it in a fraction of a second. Start with their eyes closed, then give them a countdown to the exact moment they should open their eyes with clear direction where to look. Otherwise, you will be burning the person's eyes when they're looking directly at the sun.

Another point to make about this pose is that it really looks best with a fashion style, single person photo shoot. Imagine a family of five all pointing one of their cheekbones to the sun. That would look very silly. But a young model in a fashion style shoot can definitely pull this off. This technique is helpful to have in your back pocket because if you are in a situation where you don't have a flash or a diffuser, you can always bring the subject's chin up to the sun so that one of his or her cheekbones is aligned with the sun. This looks exciting, dynamic, and alive. Be sure that the expression matches the dynamics of the pose.

Figure 2.27: This terrible lighting is a perfect scenario for the Adapting the Pose to the Sun technique.

Figure 2.28: This is the perfect application of this technique. Since this technique really works best with just one person, I decided to have this couple hug but feature the woman as the main subject. I kept asking her to raise her chin a bit more until the hard shadow under her nose disappeared. Finally, I worked on her expression so it felt like a passionate moment with this gorgeous dynamic lighting. This photo was taken just minutes after the badly lit photo in Figure 2.27.

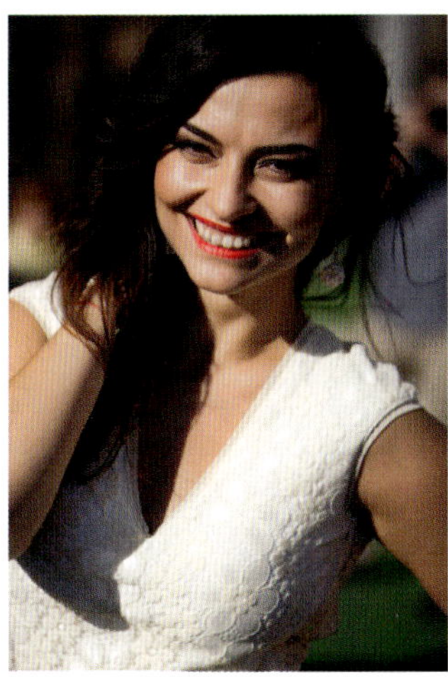

FIGURE 2.27

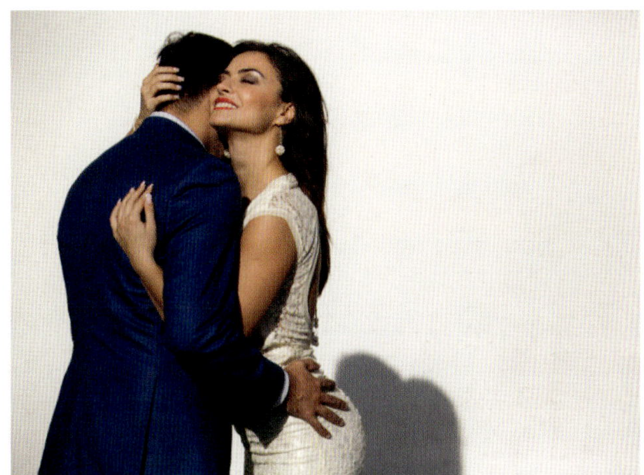

FIGURE 2.28

Splotchy Light

Splotchy light is a byproduct of hard light combined with objects such as tree branches that create unflattering shadows on a person's face or body. Splotchy light is easy to detect and correct. Most outdoor light without any modification is unflattering to the human face, and a photograph highlights how unflattering it can look. The reason for this is that our faces have bones that are meant to protect our eyes from the sun. With the sun above us, this leaves deep shadows in our eye sockets and all sorts of splotchy light on our faces. None of this looks good. This means that, by default, regular everyday outdoor light doesn't look good, and it should almost always be modified to make it look great on a human face.

I know this sounds a bit pessimistic, but thinking about outdoor light like this has worked well for me. When working outdoors in natural light, I assume the worst and know that I must modify the light somehow to make it look flattering. I can count very few times when the ambient light was phenomenal and required no modification whatsoever. Therefore, I come ready to deal with whatever mother nature throws at me.

Figure 2.29: As I mentioned earlier, splotchy light is easy to detect. It is the result of harsh sun, which is a small light source, combined with the wrong angle of the sunlight relative to the subject. When you see patches of sun and hard-edged shadows all over the face, you have a Splotchy Light problem. The good news is splotchy light is very easy to fix.

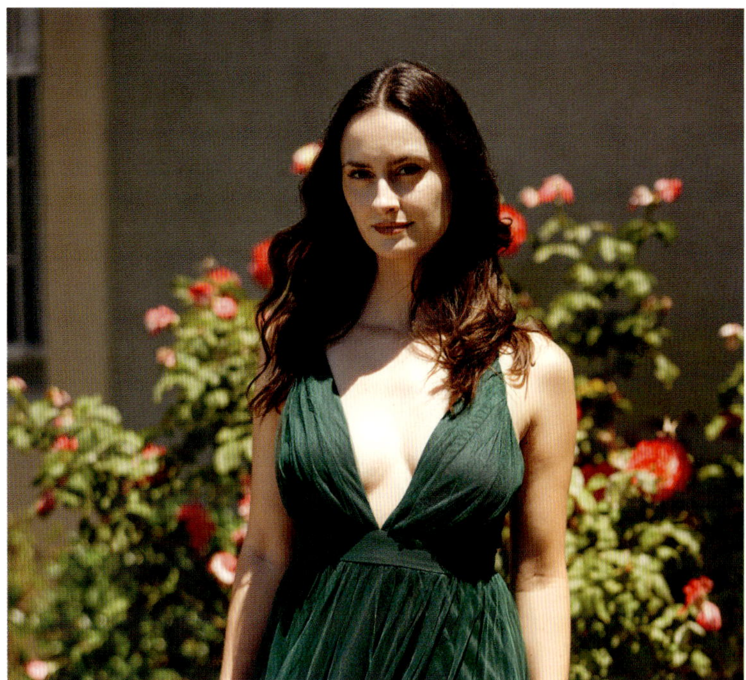

FIGURE 2.29

Shadow Direction Technique

Once again, the simplest method to deal with splotchy light is to turn the subject's face toward the direction of their own shadow.

Diffuser Overhead Technique

This technique allows the photographer to work with any direction the subject's face is pointing. By placing a diffuser overhead, the light will spread evenly across the subject's face. This technique works best when the person's face is directly pointed toward the sun.

Pocket of Clean Light Technique

This is my favorite solution to solving a Splotchy Light problem. You need some sort of a wall for this, but walls are everywhere, so it shouldn't be too hard to find one. This is a simple technique. On a wall lit by splotchy light, find a large enough pocket of clean light and place your subject's face in that pocket.

Figure 2.30: This wall was lit by splotchy light from a large palo verde tree in Tucson. Between the trunk's shadow and the branches' shadows, I found a clean pocket of light. Perfect! I placed Kenzie within that pocket and slightly angled her face toward the sun to eliminate any unwanted shadows on her face. Notice how cleanly and beautifully the sunlight illuminates Kenzie's face. Furthermore, notice how the shadows to her right and left create a natural frame for her. Note that this solution is for one or two people max. You wouldn't take a family portrait like this, but you can get away with using pockets of clean light on a single person or two.

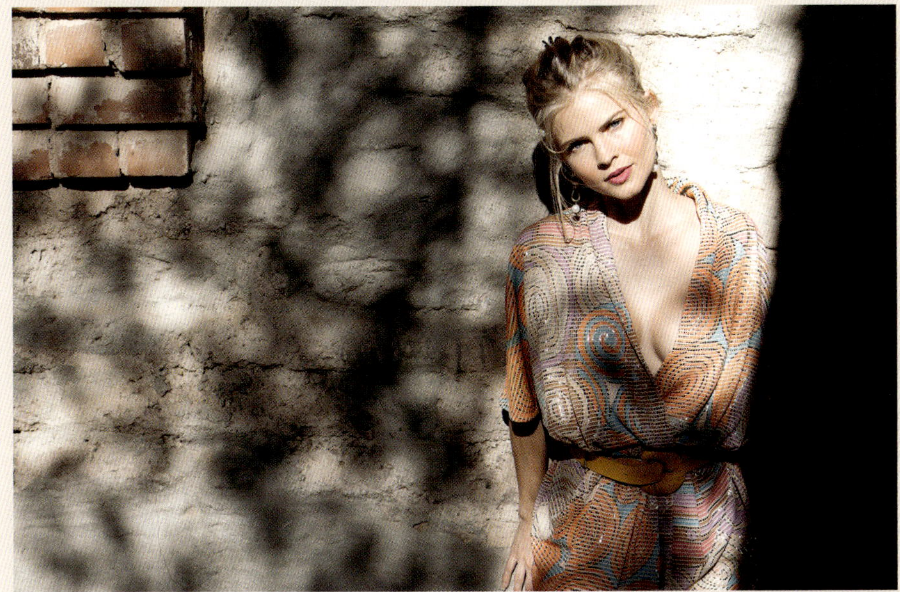

FIGURE 2.30

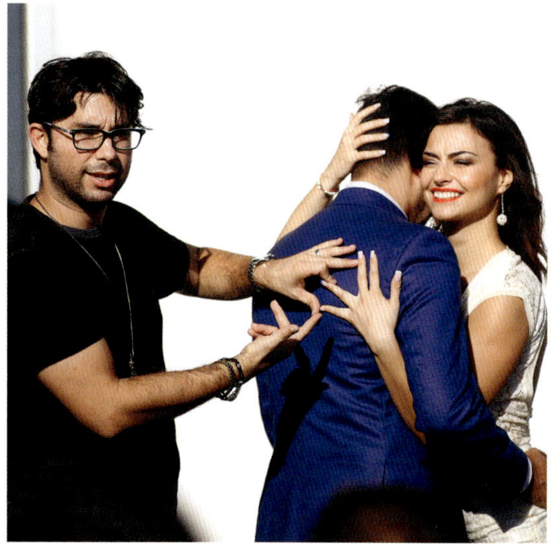

FIGURE 2.31

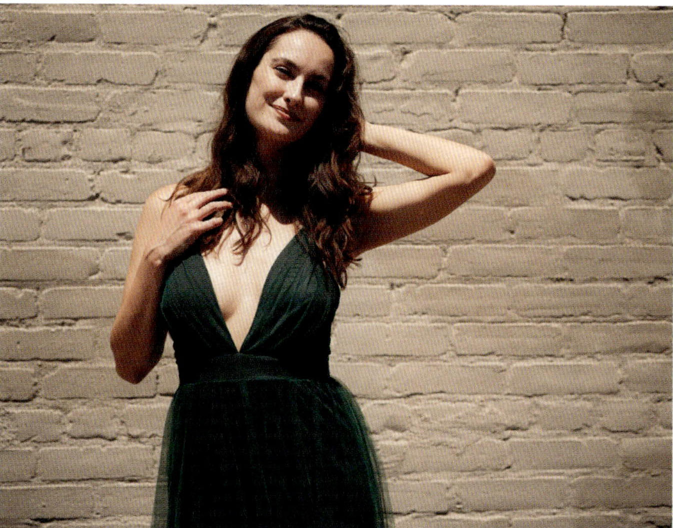

FIGURE 2.32

Uncomfortable Facial Expression with Heavy Squinting

The best part about this problem is that we can all relate to it. When the sun is directly hitting our eyes on a clear sunny day, it's going to cause the most comical facial expressions around! While it can be funny, these expressions are definitely not flattering!

Figures 2.31 & 2.32: During this class I was teaching, I couldn't keep a straight face for a second. The female model was having the hardest time trying to keep her face calm. Just look at how strained our foreheads are. And Figure 2.32 shows Dylan trying to smile with direct sun in her face, and it's nearly impossible to do so without looking tortured.

The good news about someone squinting is that it means you have strong light to work with. That's a great start if you can control it. If you place a diffuser between the sun and the subject's face, as close to the subject's face as possible, you will get the most incredible glowing light. Try it!

Unflattering Light Problems

Now let's tackle the four kinds of Unflattering Light problems you will encounter.

THE FOUR MAIN PROBLEMS YOU WILL FACE WITH UNFLATTERING LIGHT

- Poor Quality of Light
- Unwanted Color Cast
- Wrong Direction and Size of Light Source Relative to the Subject
- Clashing Moods Between the Ambient Light and Artificial Light

Poor Quality of Light

First let's discuss the obvious question that's probably on your mind right now: "What is the difference between a Not Enough Light problem and a Poor Quality of Light problem?" A Not Enough Light situation is when the photographer has a hard time seeing the subject because it is dark. A Poor Quality of Light situation is when there is plenty of light for the photographer to easily see the subject, but the light is weak. It is as simple as that. But because a person's eyes adjust to poor light, it makes it much trickier to spot when you are in a Poor Quality of Light situation.

Here is the odd part. Most photos taken on location are usually taken with a less-than-ideal quality of light. The reasons for this are that our cameras are so good at working well with high ISO settings, and our post-production tools such as Lightroom, Capture One, and Photoshop are so incredible at handling this kind of problem that people have simply grown accustomed to not worrying about it. Many photographers often think that the problem can simply be fixed later.

I'm going to be perfectly honest. You can certainly do "professional" photo shoots with mediocre light and fix it later. But you can also very easily turn that mediocre quality of light into gorgeous quality of light. I recommend the latter! Polishing a turd all day will never ever look as eye-catching as a polished diamond.

So, is there a way to know definitively if you are dealing with a Poor Quality of Light problem? Well, yes there is. In my book *Picture Perfect Lighting*, I wrote about a Lighting Benchmark that you can use as a guide to gauge the quality of light on your subject. If you haven't read that book, I highly suggest you do. It will really help you on your journey to becoming a master of light for photography. In the meantime, here is the essence of what you need to know in case you haven't read the book.

THE LIGHTING BENCHMARK FOR POOR OUTDOOR QUALITY OF LIGHT

For an outdoor situation, set your camera to the following ISO, aperture, and shutter speed: ISO 100, f/4, 1/60.

These settings are exactly three stops lower than my ultimate outdoor Lighting Benchmark settings, which are ISO 100, f/4, 1/500 (as written in my book *Picture Perfect Lighting*).

So what does this mean? Set your camera to these settings (ISO 100, f/4, 1/60), point your camera at your subject, and take a test photo. If you get a proper exposure on your subject's face at those settings, you definitely have a Poor Quality of Light problem. If you need even more light—for example, you have to go slower on your shutter speed (1/30), more open on your aperture (f/2.8), or higher on your ISO (ISO 200 or 400)—to get a proper exposure on your subject's face, then your subject is standing in absolutely terrible light!

This test of the quality of light is very important and extremely helpful, because without it, you have no reference to go by. Unless you have a trained eye for determining quality of light, you wouldn't know how to determine what kind of light you are dealing with. Now you have an easy, clear, and exact way of determining how good or bad the light you are dealing with is. The way I see it, three stops below my optimal Lighting Benchmark is bad light, and four or more stops below it is horrible light.

When I was first learning about light, it wasn't so easy to determine when I was dealing with a Poor Quality of Light situation. It's often easy to read about this subject matter and think you understand the concept, but under the pressures of a photo shoot with a client on location, reality sets in and you find yourself wondering about the true quality of the light illuminating your subjects.

Figure 2.33 & 2.34: Both of these photos were taken outside under the same sunny conditions just a few minutes apart. The darker photo represents approximately three stops under my ideal Lighting Benchmark mentioned above, which means this is an example of Poor Quality of Light. For the brighter photo, I spotted a location that qualified for my ideal Lighting Benchmark. Now, you can see the difference between ideal natural light on a subject and poor quality of light on the same subject, just minutes apart. And what a difference it makes!

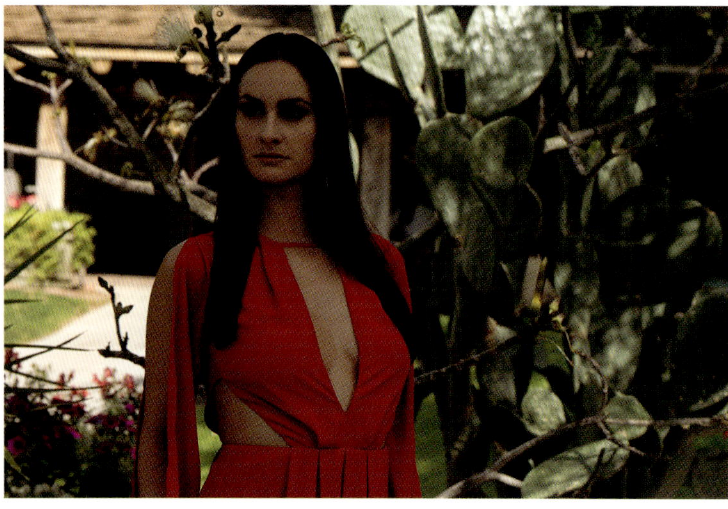

FIGURE 2.33

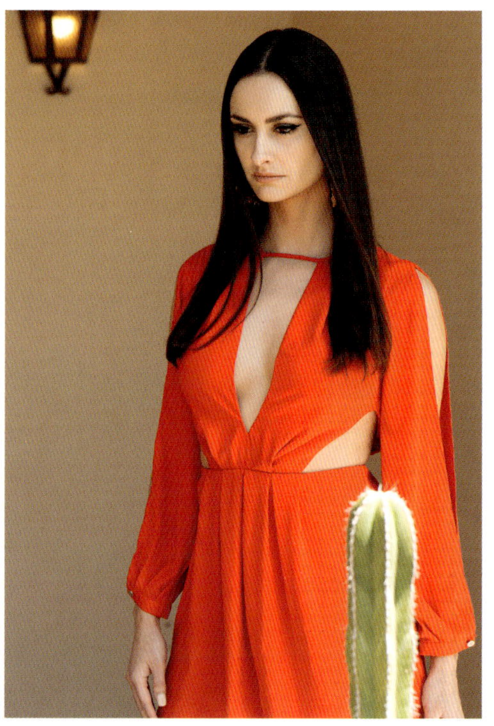

FIGURE 2.34

When you are in a Poor Quality of Light situation, you can address it in one of two ways: you either "fix" the light by moving to a location that passes the Lighting Benchmark test and thus has a better quality of light, or you can add light (which we'll cover in the next chapter).

Unwanted Color Cast

Another infamous problem photographers deal with is using light that is heavily contaminated by a strong unwanted color cast. The most common example of an Unwanted Color Cast problem is when photographers go to parks to do photo shoots and place their subjects on green grass or next to green leaves or plants. In this situation, the photographer is using green light bouncing from the grass or plants to illuminate their subjects. That's not a good idea! Most likely, you will not notice the heavy light contamination on the small screen on the back of the camera. But when you open the photo in Adobe Lightroom or Capture One, or when you print it out, you will be shocked at how much green appears on your subjects' faces.

Many family photographers fall into this trap of taking the family to a park for their photos. A park is fine, and it can be a great setting, but you need to be aware of light color contamination from all the nearby greenery. The same problem occurs when placing people near something that is black or dark. Black absorbs light, so if, for example, you place a subject near a black wall, you will see that the side of the face closest to the black wall will be much darker than it otherwise would be; that dark wall absorbs so much of the light.

Most of the time, an Unwanted Color Cast problem is indeed an undesired effect. However, if you think outside the box, a strong color cast could be used to your advantage. Around my neighborhood in Beverly Hills, California, there are so many beautiful retail stores with brightly colored walls to draw your attention. Walls can be bright red, pink, yellow—it's all there to be used creatively. Light will always take on the color of the surface it bounces off of. Keep that in mind and be more aware of your surroundings. A skilled photographer on location will notice this very easily; an average photographer will not.

Usually an unnatural color cast on your client's face is not going to go well. Unless you are working on some sort of creative experimental project, I highly recommend that you become aware of colorful objects that could be adding color contamination to your subjects, and you fix it.

Figures 2.35 & 2.36: Both of these photos suffer from a strong and unflattering color cast from the environment. The first photo, where the model is wearing an orange dress, has a green color cast on the model's face. This comes from being surrounded by green cacti. When the sunlight hits the cacti, the bounced light becomes green.

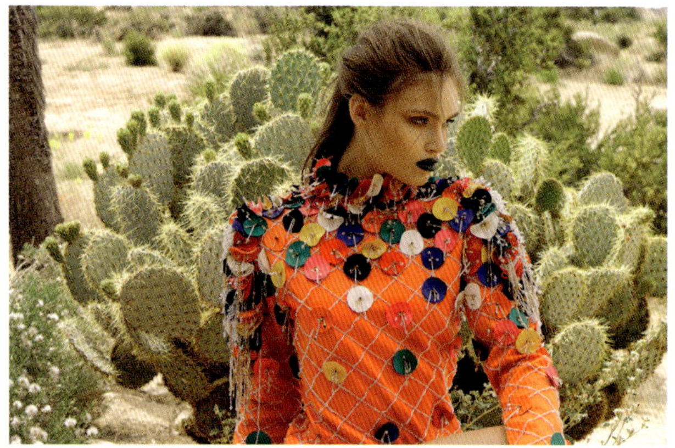

FIGURE 2.35

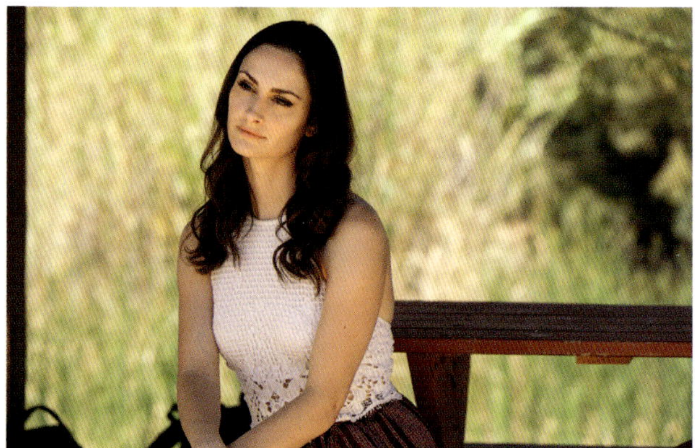

FIGURE 2.36

Look carefully to see how much green you can detect on her face (minus the lipstick, of course, which was green on purpose). The second photo has an evident yellow/green color cast. The desert plants surrounding Dylan were yellow and green. All this foliage affects the light on her face, turning it very yellow/green. Be careful with color casts. They sneak up on you!

OPTIONS FOR WORKING WITH AN UNWANTED COLOR CAST PROBLEM

Clean White Light from a Flash Technique

Any color cast can be remedied by overpowering the color-contaminated light with clean white light such as the light from a flash. A family portrait over grass will have a green cast on everyone's faces. However, if you add the light from a flash, which is daylight balanced, it will overpower the green light. By combining that light with a large modifier, such as a large umbrella or a large softbox, you have not only clean white light on everyone, but you also have a soft and flattering light illuminating your family portrait. Take the extra steps to correct for color casts; it will go a long way in your success as a professional photographer.

Reflector on the Ground, Floor, or Wall Technique

The second most effective technique is to use the white or silver side of a reflector and put it over the object that is causing the light color contamination. For example, if you are working at a park, place the reflector or reflectors on the ground, as close to your subjects as possible but still out of frame. If the reflector(s) must be in the camera frame, that's totally okay, because an object such as a reflector placed over green grass can easily be singled out in post-production and removed digitally.

If your subject is close to a wall that has a strong color, you can place the reflector against a colored wall next to your subject's face. This will clean up the light that is illuminating your subject's face.

Wrong Direction and Size of Light Source Relative to Subject

On a clear sunny day, the sun illuminating a subject on earth is a very small light source. Direct sunlight is a small and strong light source. This can lead to splotchy light, which we discussed earlier in the chapter. But, to keep things organized, we'll discuss the wrong direction and size of light on a subject here, as it is indeed better categorized as an Unflattering Light problem.

Figure 2.37: The problem is that the sun is too high in the sky, so it's illuminating Dylan's head too harshly. Simply turning her head to one side or the other will improve the light on her face, but it won't fix the top of her head.

Figure 2.38: This is a perfect example of the wrong size and direction of light. We have a small pocket of light but it's in the wrong place. No one wants to illuminate a person's neck like this, correct? However, even in difficult situations like this, there is a way out of it with surprisingly beautiful results.

Solutions to the Wrong Direction and Size of Light Problem

Your quickest solutions here are:

- Turn the head little by little to one side or the other until the face is lit with clean light.

- Use a diffuser overhead to diffuse the harsh light on the top of the head and face.

- Feature a part of the face with a small pocket of light for a creative portrait.

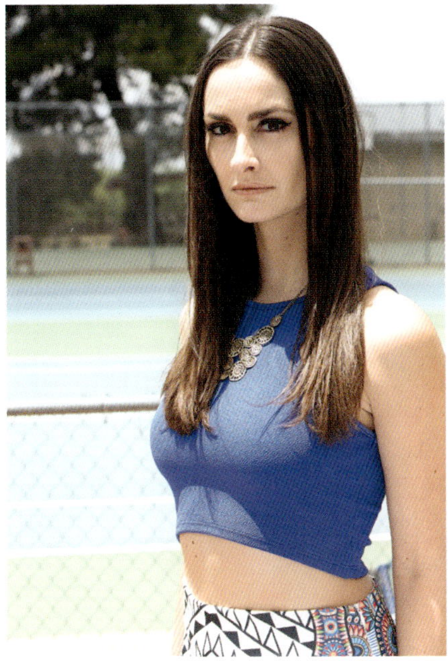

FIGURE 2.37

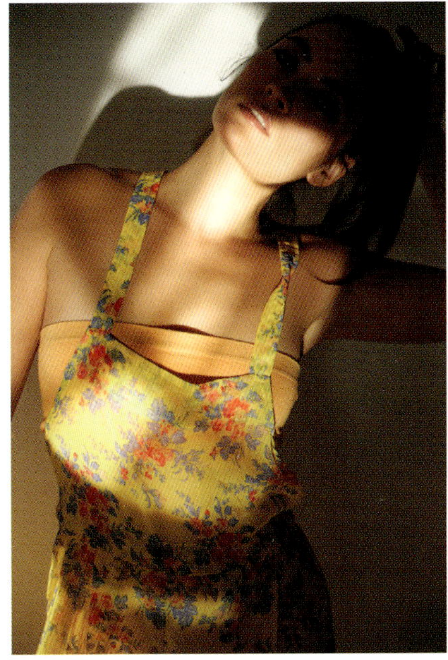

FIGURE 2.38

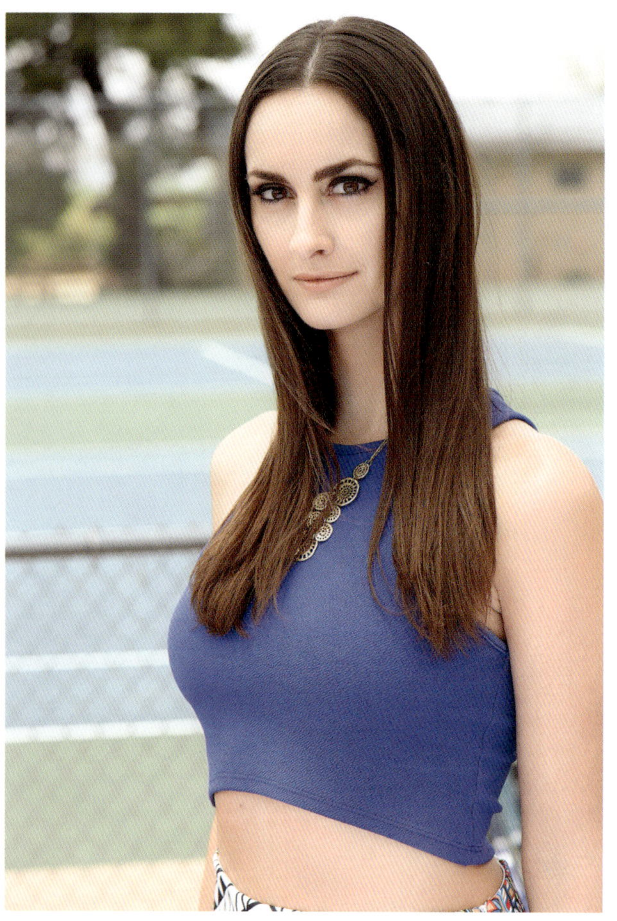

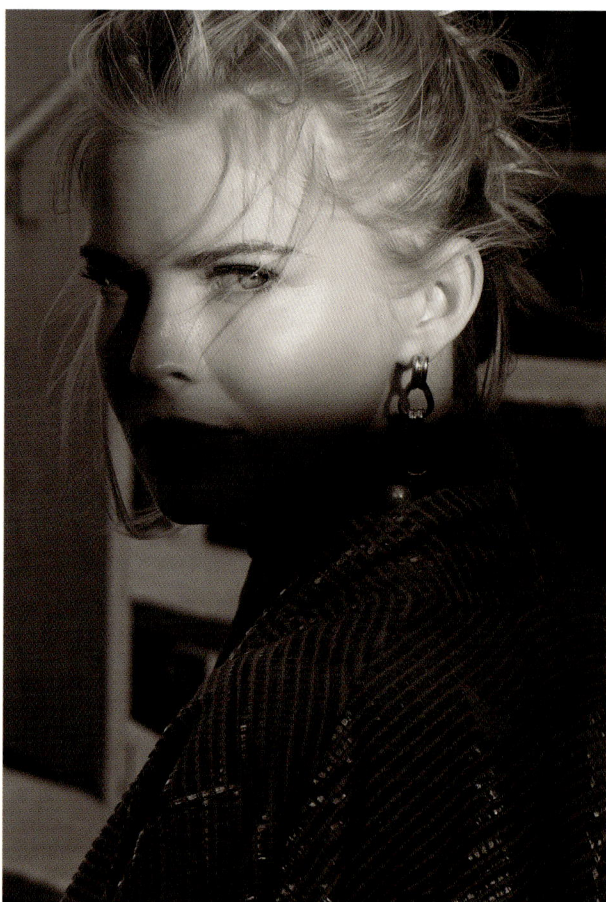

Figure 2.39: In this case, I had no choice but to use the diffuser technique, because I wanted to address the light on the top of Dylan's head. That was the only way. But how much better does this look?! It's impressive how much of a difference a simple diffuser and paying attention can make.

Figure 2.40: Here we have another pocket of strong light in the wrong place, similar to Figure 2.38. The solution is to use this pocket of light and turn it into a creative portrait. For this photo, I had to ask Kenzie to sit down so that the pocket of light reached her face. Next, I asked her to turn her face toward me with her eyes closed, until she felt the sun's heat on her closed eyes. Finally, I counted to three to prompt her to open her eyes in the direct path of the sunlight for just an instant while I took the photo. This is a creative portrait made possible as a solution to a difficult lighting problem.

Clashing Moods Between the Ambient Light and Artificial Light

This is a biggie! Unfortunately, I see this far too often. The problem with mixed lighting is that the light from the sun is constantly changing throughout the day in intensity, direction, and color. But the light from our flashes is always consistent in color and size. We usually think to change the energy or power of our flash, but nothing else.

The most popular example I can think of for this problem is the photo shoots that take place at the beach during sunsets with the ocean and sun behind our clients. During this time of day, the sun is large, a bit softer, and very orange. But what many photographers do is turn on their on-camera flashes and aim the flash head right at the subject(s) to correct the exposure. That is the biggest clash of mixed light I have come across. Without modification, the light from the flash is white, small, and harsh. These attributes do not blend well with sunset photos at the beach. Quite the opposite.

Figure 2.41: This beautiful building in Heidelberg, Germany, was moody and quaint. The room had big windows and light-colored walls that bounced the light relatively well. But the bare bulb flash on camera completely destroyed the mood of the room. This is a Clashing Moods problem. We need to fix it before we can create something special.

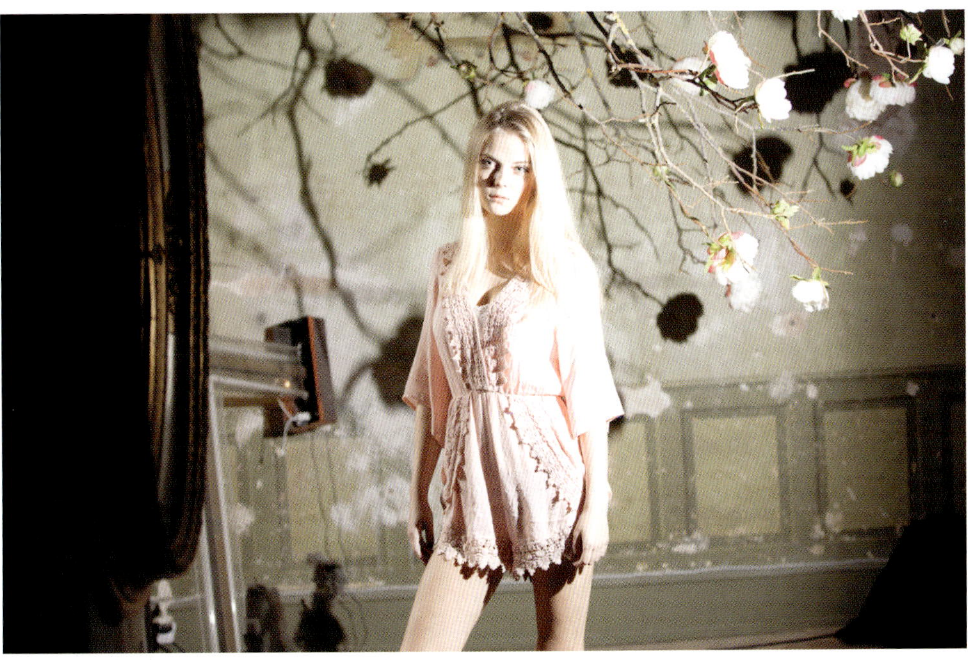

FIGURE 2.41

Solution to the Clashing Moods Problem

Figure 2.42: The solution is to modify our flashes to match the ambient light's color, intensity, size, and direction as much as possible. If you mix the two types of light correctly, it should be difficult for the viewer to discern the ambient light from the photographer's artificial light.

In this case, my first step was to modify the bare bulb flash and use a large diffuser to shoot the flash through. This made the light from the flash bigger, mimicking the window light. Next, I positioned my off-camera flash so that the light came from a logical place in the room. Then I used a ½ CTO (Color Temperature Orange) gel on the flash to give the light a little warmth. Lastly, I dialed the power of the flash down so that it matched the ambient light in the room.

Looking at this photo, you can't tell that a flash was used. The photo looks as if the scene was simply lit by window light. That's what you want. You want it to be hard to differentiate between the two different light sources.

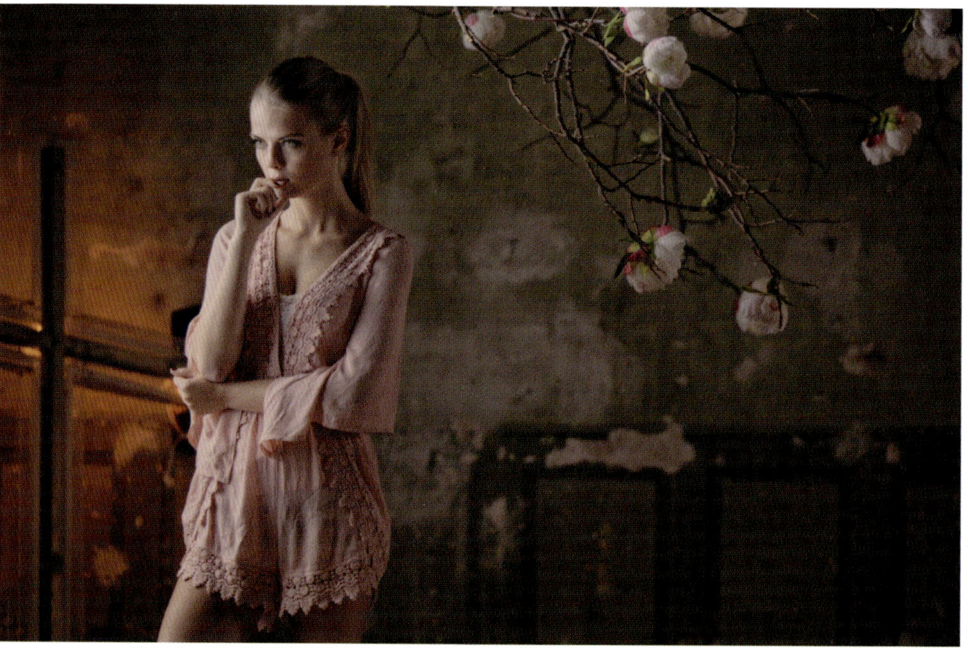

FIGURE 2.42

Final Words on Fixing the Light

Fixing the light means that you are taking a bad lighting situation and turning it into something useful that can satisfy your clients. Fixing the light gives you a proper starting point; it's the first step. Honestly, when I'm in a major rush at a photo shoot, sometimes fixing the light is my only goal. Having the photos is better than trying to be fancy and, as a result, running out of time.

Mastering this chapter will give you a huge advantage at any photo shoot you have. You will no longer be intimidated by harsh sunlight, or cloudy days, or nighttime, or rain. No matter what the challenge is, you will know how to approach the situation to get to a workable photo.

Once you have a good starting point, you can now begin the incredibly fun phase of adding light! By adding light, you begin to function as a truly professional photographer. What I mean by that is this: A photographer who can execute a vision is the real deal! Adding light requires more effort and usually more equipment, but adding light allows you to shoot what you want, not just shoot what you get. Big difference! So let's now move on to the very exciting chapter where we learn to Add Light.

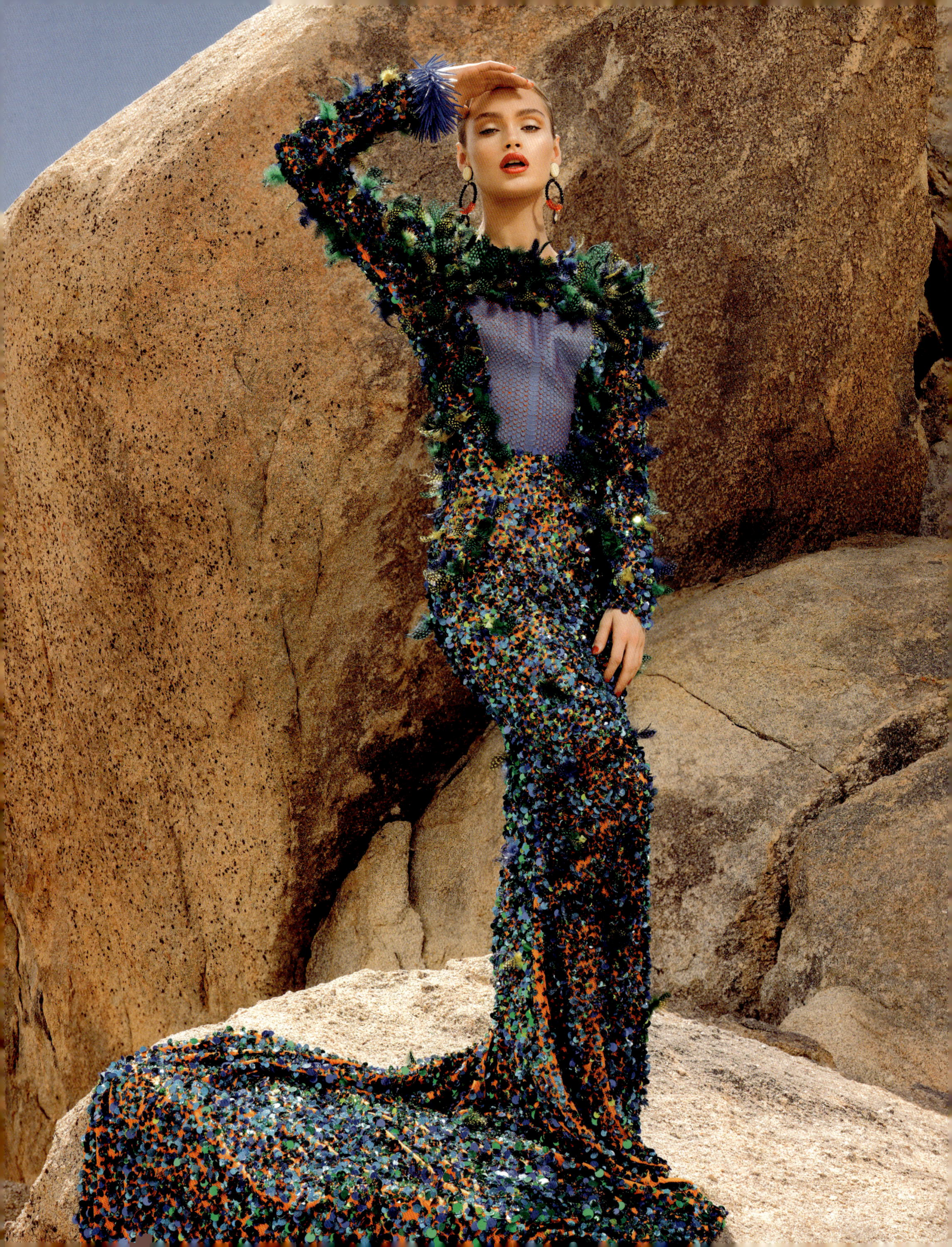

Chapter 3

F
Add Light
C
E
S

Snapshot Versus Photograph Versus Portrait

Adding light to a subject is what transforms a snapshot into a photograph, and a photograph into a portrait. But these three words—snapshot, photograph, and portrait—could all fall under the same umbrella as "photos," right? Well, not all photos are the same. Almost anyone would agree that a quick photo of someone taken using your mobile phone is quite different from the incredible portraits that photographer Annie Leibovitz would take.

It's important to know what it is you are trying to achieve when you point your camera toward a subject. Adding light to a photo of someone is the first step a photographer takes when elevating the act of taking a photograph. Adding light indicates that the photographer has intent, purpose, and a vision for the final outcome.

When I notice that someone is pointing a camera at a person, I always think to myself that the outcome could fall into three categories: a snapshot, a photograph, or a portrait of that person. It's actually quite fun to see which one it will be.

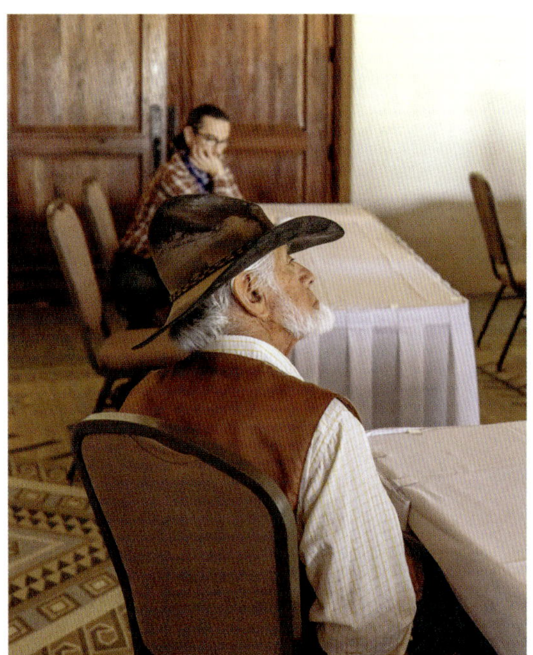

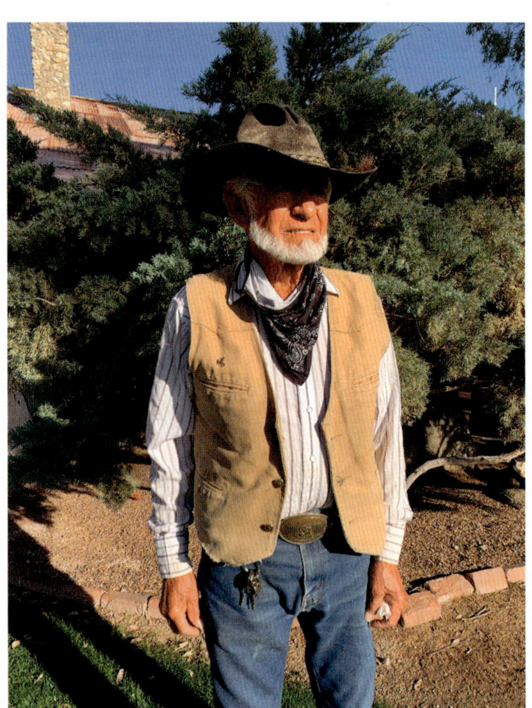

A Snapshot

A snapshot captures a person as they are, at that moment, whether they are aware of the camera or not. It takes little thought to take a snapshot. Therefore, we mainly use our mobile phone cameras to remember the moment. We take snapshots of everything from our food and coffee foam art to quick snaps of friends acting crazy at a party or our kids playing at a park. In short, a snapshot is about capturing a moment. A moment is the reason why you pulled out the camera. During a snapshot, you are not too concerned with posing, lighting, composition, or background.

Figure 3.1: This is a snapshot of Cowboy Joe in Tucson, Arizona, taken by Mandy Krause. Cowboy Joe was sitting down during a class he was modeling for with photographer and instructor Joe McNally. It's clear that there was no thought to lighting, posing, or anything else. This snapshot was just meant to be a candid moment.

A Photograph

A photograph of a person is quite different because it designates that the person being photographed is the main subject. A photograph tells the viewer a little more about who the subject is and gives them a general idea of what that person looks like. Unlike a snapshot, where the intent is more about the moment, a photograph is more about the person's general appearance. A passport photo is a type of photograph. A professional headshot would also be considered a photograph. A photograph of a person could be lit with great lighting or normal everyday lighting. In short, a photograph is when a person is the main subject, and the viewer can see what that person looks like.

Figure 3.2: This is a photograph of Cowboy Joe. The way the photo was taken makes it clear to the viewer that he is the main subject. This allows the viewer to have an idea of what he looks like and what he does based on his clothing. It allows you to see that he could possibly be someone who works outside a lot at a ranch. The lighting in this photograph is not flattering by any stretch of the imagination, but it shows you what he looks like and that he is the main subject. That's it. It's a photograph of Joe.

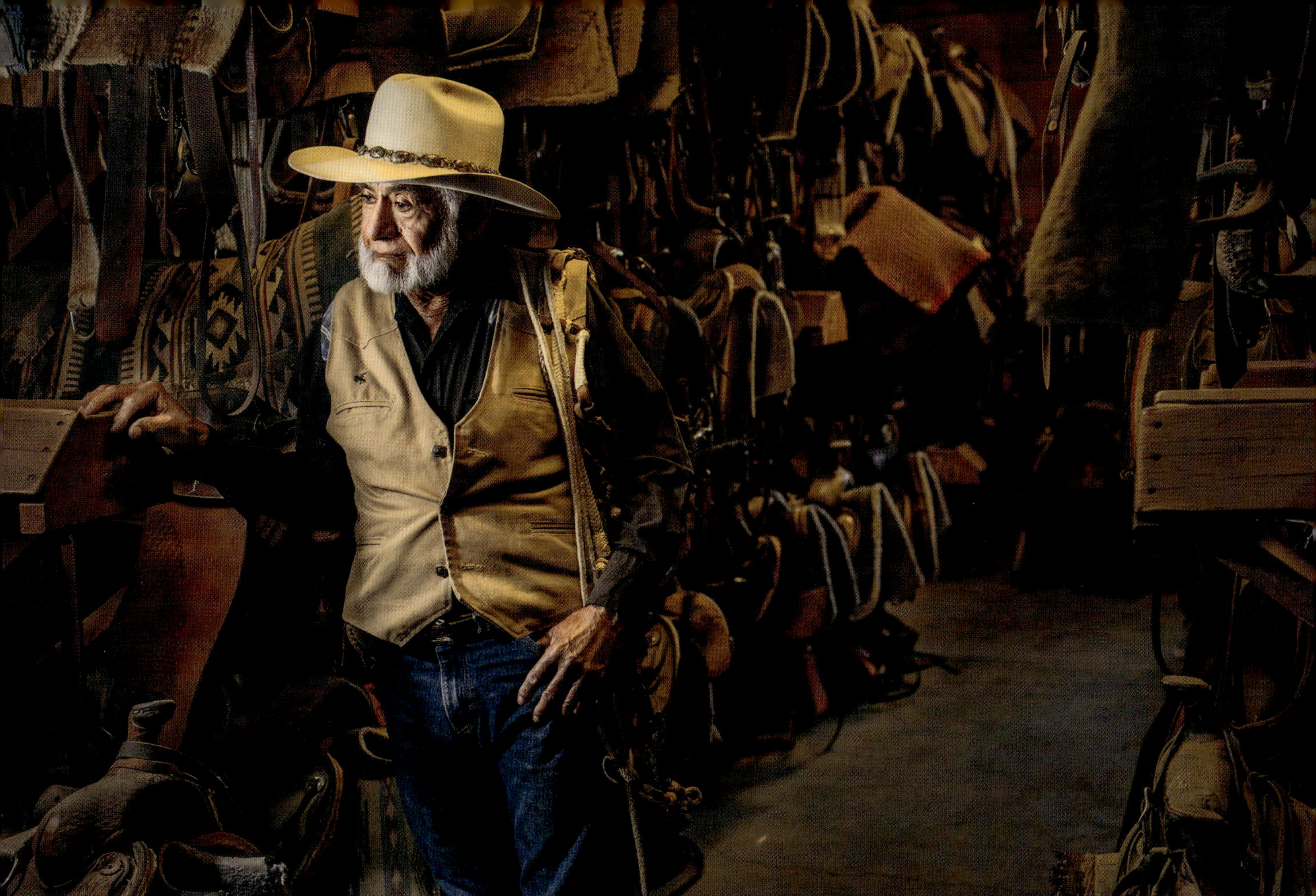

A Portrait

A portrait's essence is more about storytelling. Portraits tell stories about people—where they come from, what they do, what their scars represent, what they have witnessed, and the good, the bad, the pain, and the joy they have experienced. A portrait is the story of an individual told with a camera. How that story is told varies greatly from photographer to photographer by their choices of lighting, composition, posing, camera settings, mood, and location. Ultimately, a portrait is about creatively capturing a person's soul.

Figure 3.3: This is a portrait of Cowboy Joe. You could stare at this portrait for quite a while because this portrait tells a story about Joe. This portrait captures not only what he looks like, but it goes much deeper than that. This portrait reveals his love for horses. His face and hands are a testament to his decades of working outside as a wrangler.

But most important, for the sake of this chapter, is the addition of light. In the previous photograph, Joe's hat completely covered his eyes from the sun. But in this portrait, light was intentionally added to deal with the cowboy hat blocking the light from above.

As a result, you see his face clearly, and you can look deeply into his eyes. A lot can be communicated by considering someone's eyes. Being able to clearly see into someone's eyes is one of the strongest differences between a snapshot, a photograph, and a portrait.

Also, in a portrait, the background or scene around the main subject is not just any random background; it is part of the subject's story. Therefore, adding light to the background also matters! This is a major difference between a photograph and a portrait.

As a side note, photography's ability to turn a snapshot of someone into a portrait, which can be a true work of art, is one of my favorite aspects of being a photographer. With every book I read and every practice session I hold, I am aiming to refine my skills and to improve my abilities, skills, vision, and creativity to turn a snapshot into a portrait anytime I want. It's awesome!

Now that we have fixed the light (in the previous chapter), this chapter is more about quality control of the light and refinement of the light. This book is written in such a way that adding light is the step you take when your lighting situation doesn't need fixing, but it does need improvement and shaping. There must be a very clear distinction between the two. The step of adding light does not come from a place of darkness. It comes from a desire to use average existing light and turn it into gorgeous light!

Adding light is the step you take to create drama, dimensionality, and contrast in a photograph. Adding light is what a skilled photographer must do to take control of the light, rather than being forced to work with whatever light is available. As you become a better, higher skilled photographer, you begin to automatically want to take control of the light. You stop accepting your lighting fate and begin to make your own light exactly how you want it to be.

A great photographer uses light to communicate something about the subject. In the hands of a master photographer, light is a tool that they shape, craft, and chisel, that they use to bring attention to or hide something, that they employ to create a mood according to their vision. This deliberate use of light is what differentiates a true photo creator from a basic picture taker.

THE SIX REASONS TO ADD LIGHT
- Add Light to Achieve the Lighting Benchmark
- Add Light to Create Shape, Contrast, and Drama in a Portrait
- Add Light to Lift Shadows
- Add Light to Create Separation Between Subject and Background
- Add Light to Control Contrast Throughout the Entire Frame
- Add Light to Bring Attention to a Specific Area in the Photograph

Add Light to Achieve the Lighting Benchmark

We talked a little about the Lighting Benchmark in the previous chapter as a means to recognize when you are dealing with a Poor Quality of Light problem. This chapter is about the next step. First you must be able to recognize the problem, then you must do something about it. In this case, we are going to add light so that we can achieve the Lighting Benchmark first written about in my lighting book *Picture Perfect Lighting*. As you are reading this, you might be thinking to yourself "Why do I need to bother with this so-called Lighting Benchmark? What is that again?" Let's take another quick look.

The Lighting Benchmark is a tool you can use to determine the quality of light in any given place, and also determine how much light you need to add to create a lighting quality on your subjects that makes them glow. The Lighting Benchmark helps photographers recognize, create, and manipulate what I consider hands-down to be the most flattering light on location. Here it is again.

OUTDOOR CLEAR SUNNY DAY LIGHTING BENCHMARK

The ultimate Lighting Benchmark on a clear sunny day outdoors is:

- ISO 100, f/4, 1/500 or 1/250

The Lighting Benchmark can be achieved completely on its own by strong sunlight bouncing around objects, walls, buildings, etc., or it can be achieved by including a diffuser, reflector, flash, or LED light to boost the existing light until you achieve the Lighting Benchmark level.

If you haven't read *Picture Perfect Lighting*, you may be wondering how to use these settings and how they represent a benchmark. These are the settings you dial in on your camera. Then, as you walk around outside on a clear sunny day and you find a spot that allows you to achieve a proper exposure on your subject's face at these settings, you have achieved the Lighting Benchmark. That's how it works. It's like treasure hunting, but with light, so I guess we can call it light hunting. It's a fun game, actually.

The Lighting Benchmark is flexible by one stop. Therefore, assuming you keep the ISO and aperture at the prescribed settings above, if you are not able to achieve a proper exposure at a shutter speed of 1/500, but you have a perfect exposure one stop slower at 1/250, you are still good to go!

However, if you need to slow down the shutter speed by anything slower than 1/250—for example 1/125—that will mean that you are two stops below the benchmark;

therefore, this light will need a boost. At this point, you would add enough light with any tool you have available, such as a flash, diffuser, or reflector, to bring the light back up to the Lighting Benchmark.

Use this Lighting Benchmark to test the quality of light on your subject. The benchmark will give you a quantifiable idea regarding how good or bad the light is. This is invaluable information. Remember, the Lighting Benchmark is for testing purposes. By no means am I saying that you can't shoot a single photo with a client until you achieve the ideal Lighting Benchmark. But this benchmark is so engraved in my head at this point that, without even thinking, I can't help but to set my camera to these settings and take a quick test photo of my subject at the location where I'm planning to shoot. If I see that I'm three or more stops below my benchmark, I make the decision to either move to a better spot with better quality of light or add a diffused flash to give the lighting on my subject a needed boost. It's up to you what you do with the information.

Figure 3.4: I included this photo of my friend R'Bonney because I wanted to show you how the Lighting Benchmark looks when you have some depth behind the subject. The quality of light where R'Bonney is standing is around two stops lower than my Lighting Benchmark. Notice how she blends in with the environment. The photo is what most people would call "fine," but we are not aiming for just "fine," correct? We want great!

Well, the lighting on R'Bonney doesn't have to be fixed. It's already clean light that looks relatively flattering. But it's flat, boring, lifeless, and just average. Because I'm two stops lower than my benchmark, I just need to use the help of a flash to boost the light one or two stops.

Figure 3.5: Suddenly, this photo has a pop to it! To create this pop of light, I had someone hold a Profoto collapsible diffuser with handles and shoot a flash through it on Manual mode. The diffuser is camera left just outside of the frame at her shoulder level. To add just a little bit of warmth to the light, I added a ½ CTO gel to the flash head. I always carry a ¼ CTO, ½ CTO, full CTO, and a couple of blue gels in my pocket. If I decide the light would benefit from a little boost of warm color or a cool color, I can quickly reach into my pocket and have it ready to go in seconds. There is no need to go to my bag and hunt for these gels at a crucial time. Otherwise, by the time you find the gel, the flare of the moment is gone.

To me, the most important element here to notice is how three-dimensional the entire photo feels. R'Bonney seems to burst out of the scene. It's remarkable how a little extra light can add so much to a photograph!

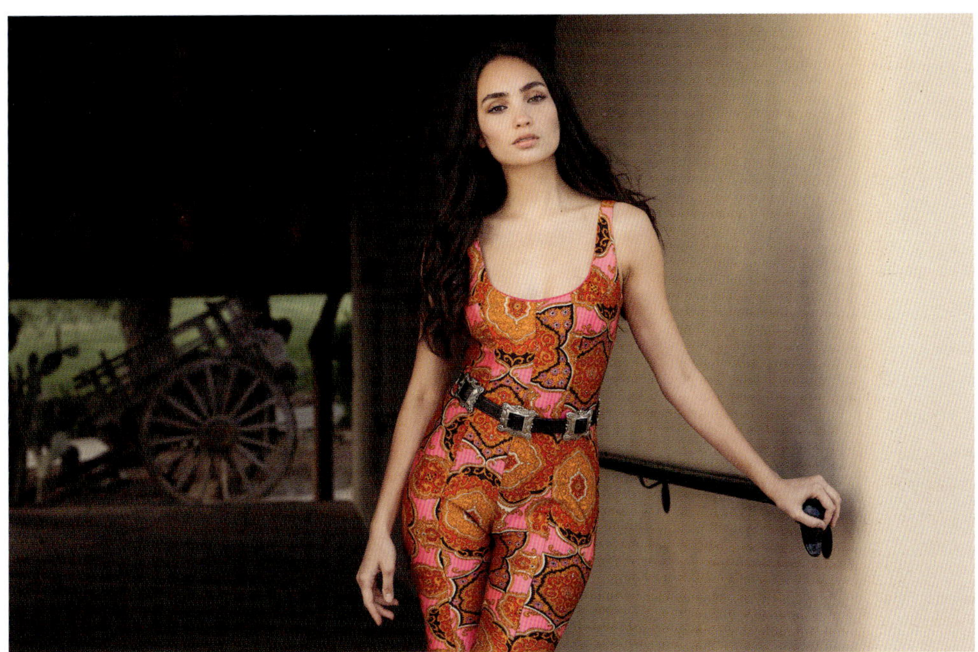

FIGURE 3.4

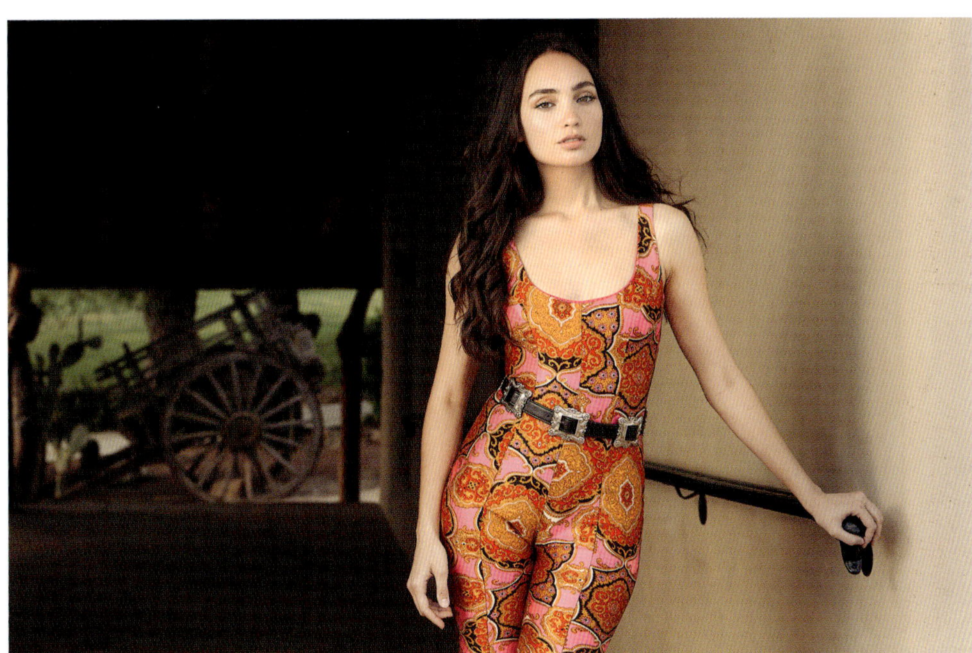

FIGURE 3.5

Figure 3.6: For this photo, both R'Bonney and the wall are lit by the same intensity of light. When both the subject and the background are lit by the same intensity of light, the result is flatness. There is no pop. Furthermore, the light quality here is also between one and two stops below my Lighting Benchmark. Therefore, I need to boost the light to take an exceptional portrait.

Figure 3.7: The effects of adding a little boost of light with a flash shot through a diffuser are even more evident when there is a wall directly behind the subject. Not only does the wall behind her seem to glow now, but R'Bonney really has a three-dimensional quality. R'Bonney pops right out of the wall. It's beautiful, isn't it? In case you were wondering, this photo is taken at precisely my Lighting Benchmark.

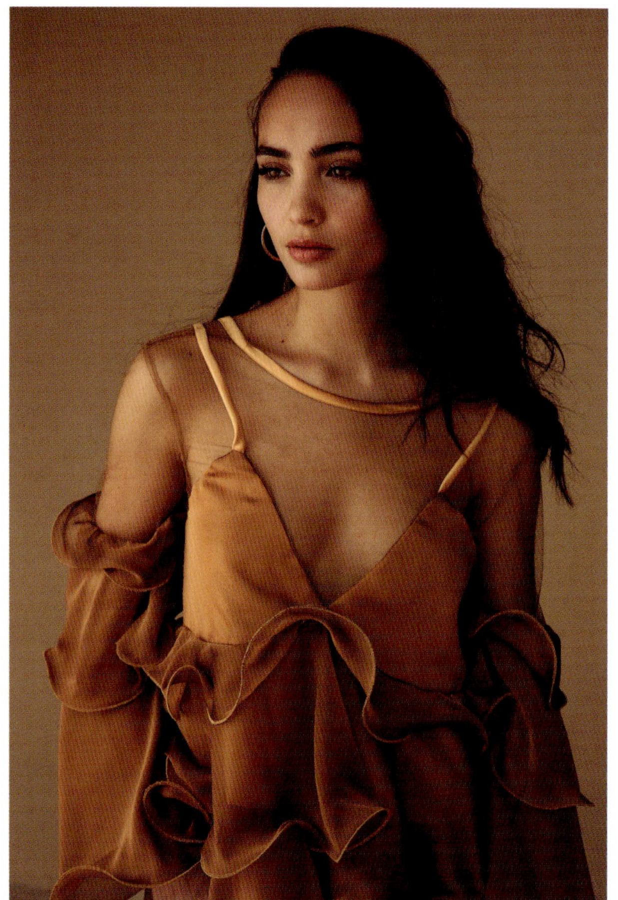

FIGURE 3.6

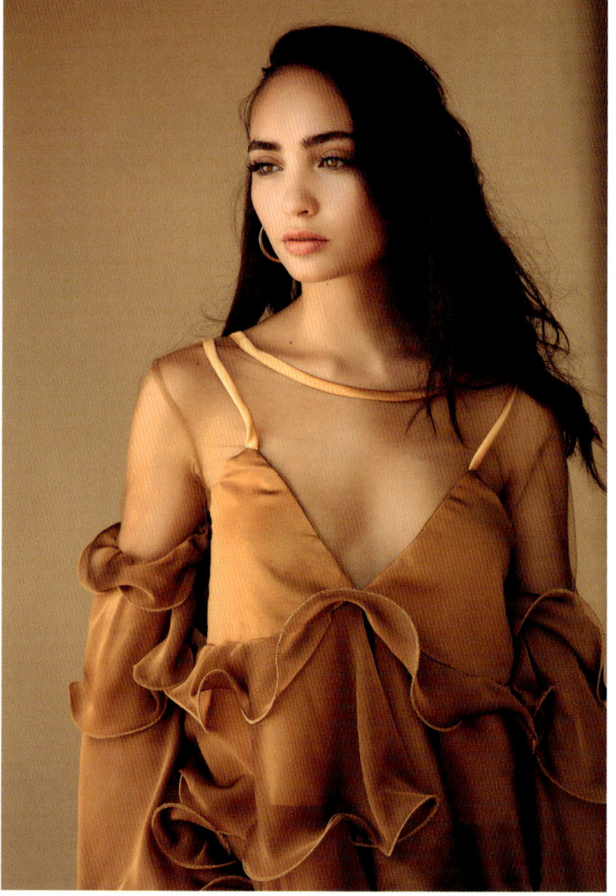

FIGURE 3.7

Add Light to Create Shape, Contrast, and Drama in a Portrait

These are arguably the most exciting benefits of adding our own light to a photograph. A portrait that is lit with flat light looks two-dimensional and uninspiring. However, a portrait that is lit with intention to add shape, contrast, and drama—and thus becomes three-dimensional—appears to jump out at the viewer.

Let's start with the basics. If you situate a person in front of and facing a window, that person will have an equal amount of light on the left and right side of their face. That's flat lighting. It's as simple as that! But, equipped with a flash, you can add more light to one side of the subject's face than the other. Now you'll be adding contrast, shape, and dimensionality to that portrait, which is much better. Adding light to create shape, contrast, drama, and dimensionality in any photograph you take is the primary reason why people buy flashes in the first place. I can say with complete confidence that, for nine out of ten photos, adding any type of modified flash to a photograph will improve it.

Figure 3.8: To demonstrate this claim, let's take a close look at this photograph of R'Bonney at a ranch in Tucson. Since my lighting class was photographing in the desert, there was strong sunlight coming in from camera right. So, you could say, "There is nice lighting on her face with one side lit more than the other. Perfect!" Well, yes, it's a nice photograph and it does have some shape and dimensionality just using the natural light. But let's see what happens if we add flash to an already beautiful photograph.

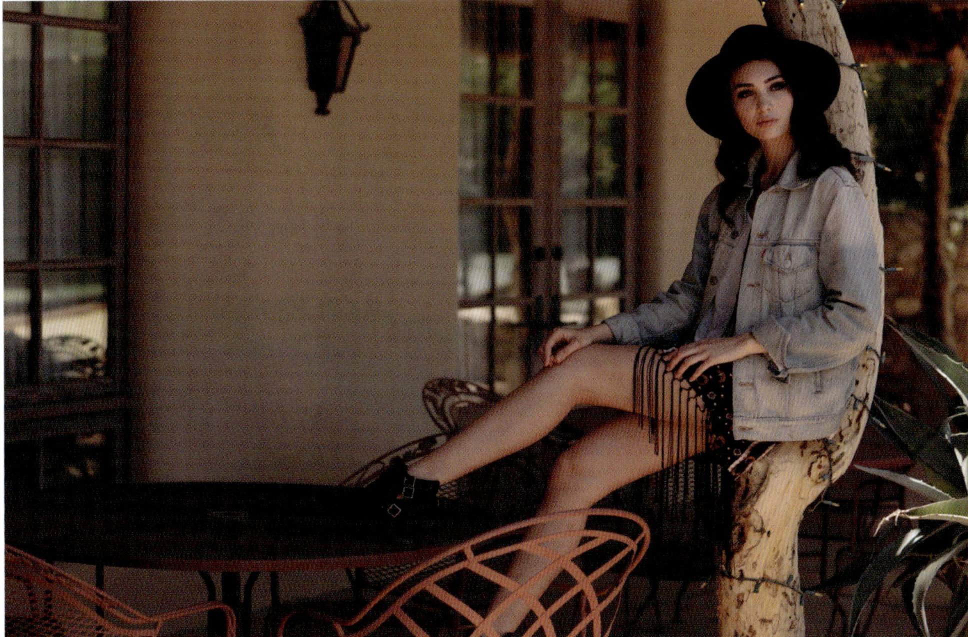

FIGURE 3.8

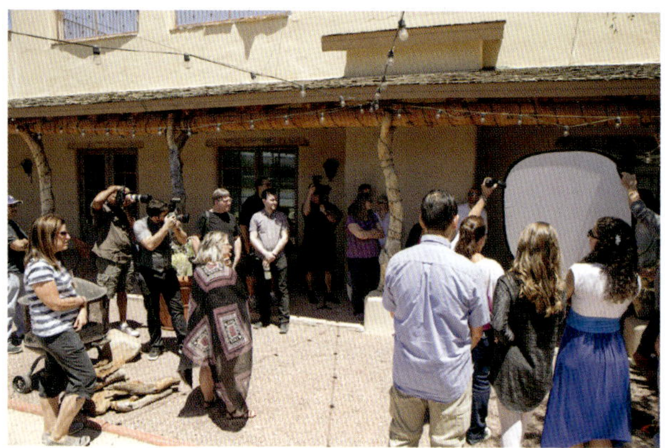

Figure 3.9: With a flash and an easily available diffuser, I was able to give that beautiful natural light a little boost, with the added advantage of choosing exactly where that boost of light would go. You see, with the sun, the light comes from the sky and then it bounces onto the ground back up. Therefore, not much light directly reaches R'Bonney's eyes. But I can position a flash and diffuser to aim the light right at her left eye. The diffuser will soften the light from the flash so much that the viewer will have no idea a flash was even used.

Figure 3.10: What a difference it makes! It's such a gentle addition of light that it does not disturb the beautiful desert light; it just enhances it. The key takeaway here is that by adding a flash with a diffuser, the photographer can choose the exact direction of the added light. This simple act of adding direction to the light is the step most photographers unfortunately miss.

Figure 3.11: I think it would be helpful to see a close-up comparing the two photos. When adding flash through a diffuser, the biggest difference between the two photos is how much R'Bonney's eyes come alive in the photo where flash was added. The second greatest difference is the gentle increase of soft light on the left side of her face. The

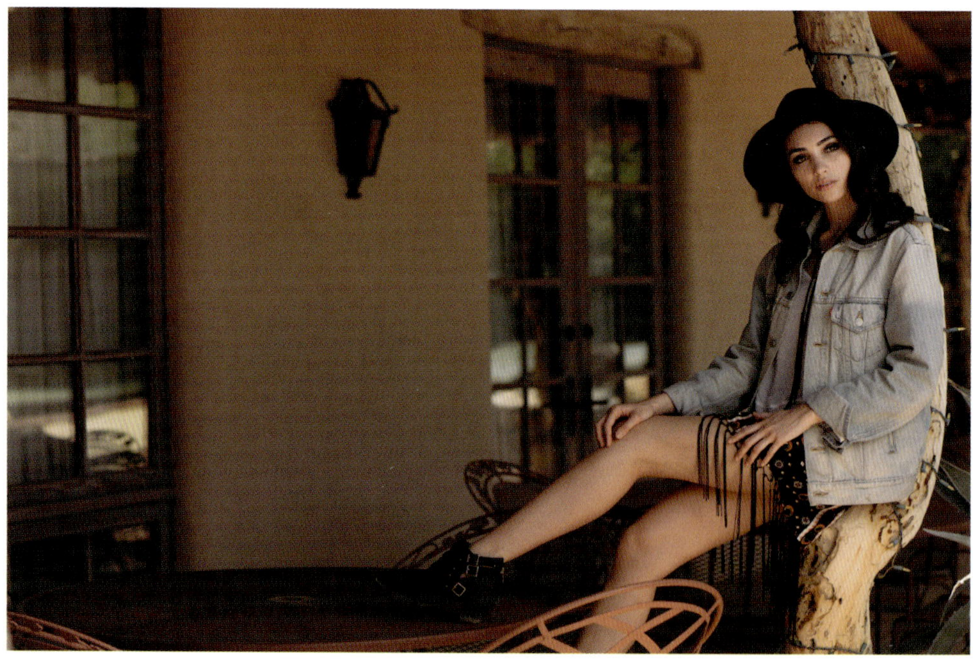

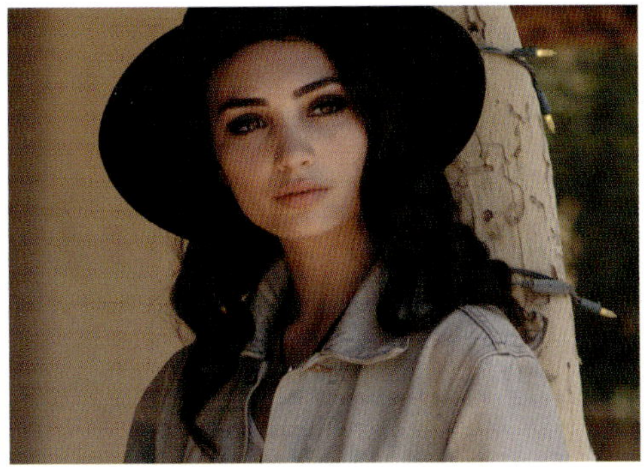

No helper light

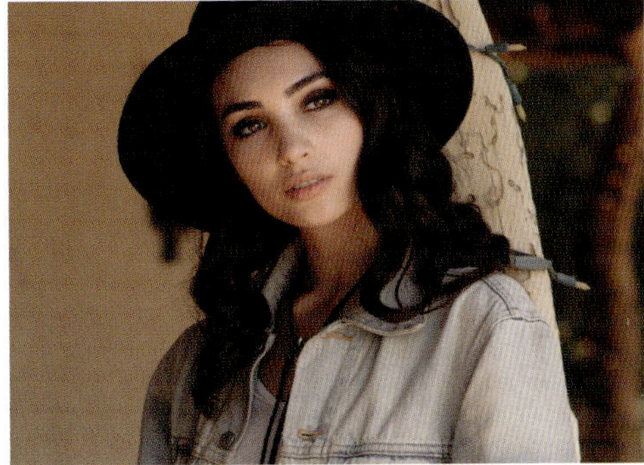

With flash helper light

FIGURE 3.11

third difference is seen in her dark hair. The photo with a flash allows for more detail on her hair to come through. These three differences are significant, wouldn't you say?

Figure 3.12: For this photo, I wanted to bring special attention to the degree of sharpness of the shadow edges on the wall. This photo was taken outside in Joshua Tree, California. I positioned the models against the wall because I was attracted by the wall's color and texture. The problem with this situation was that now the light intensity illuminating the models was exactly the same intensity illuminating the wall. The result was a flat, lifeless image.

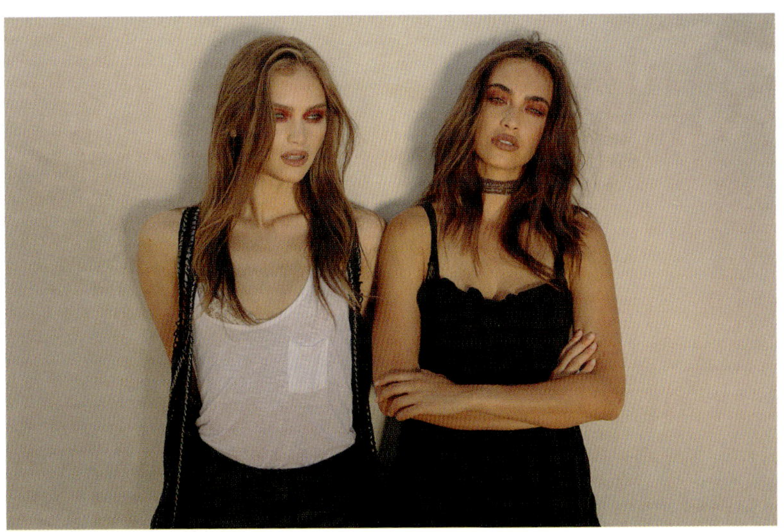

FIGURE 3.12

In order to give this photo a much-needed pop, I added a flash with a medium-sized octabox modifier. Why a medium-sized modifier? Because the models are so close to the wall, a medium-sized modifier would hit them first and then the wall. Had I used a large, six-foot umbrella or any other large modifier, the light would have hit the models and a large part of the wall behind them with almost the same intensity. My goal was to have the models pop, not the wall. Therefore, I went with the smaller, medium-sized modifier to achieve this goal, despite the shadows it produced. But those shadows reveal that the light on the models was soft, but still strong enough to give them a pop to create those shadows.

Add Light to Lift Shadows

Lifting shadows is the most common reason why I decide to pull out a flash during a shoot. No matter how decent the available light may be, adding a well-diffused flash to your subject will lift unwanted shadows from your subject's face and clothes.

At this point you are probably thinking, "Why not just shoot with decent ambient light, and then lift the shadows in post-production?" Well, you can do that. However, lifting shadows in post is never going to look as crisp in print as doing it with light when you take the photo. Manipulating a photo in post always causes damage to the file. Not to mention, it's more work. Having a flash with a modifier always ready to go at all times when shooting on location makes it much easier to use than if you have to pull it out of your bag and set it up in front of your client. The key is to be ready before you need the flash.

Figures 3.13–3.15: A flash doesn't have to be directly pointed at your subject's face; it can also be bounced off existing walls. By bouncing it off a wall, the wall itself will become the modifier, resulting in soft and beautiful light when it reaches your subject. Bouncing the light off existing architecture or anything you bring to the shoot (such as a reflector) is a fantastic way to modify the light without having to bring several modifiers to a shoot.

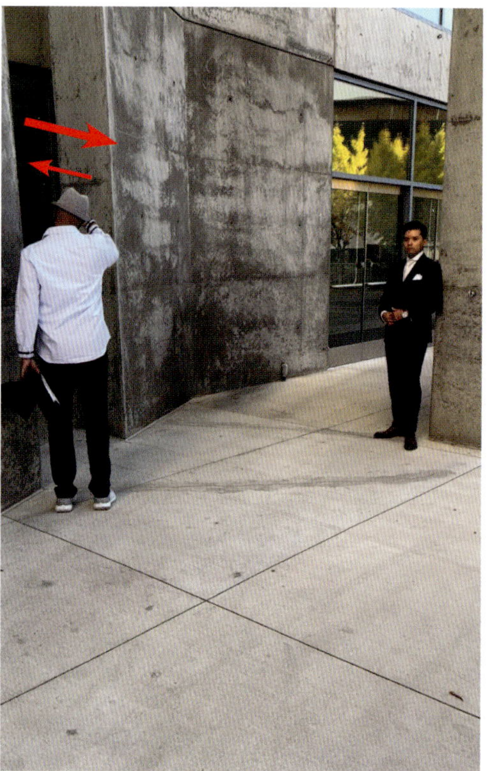

FIGURE 3.13

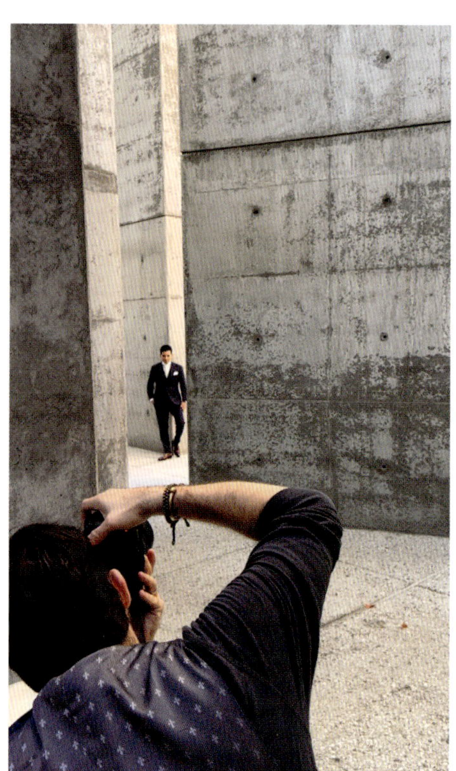

FIGURE 3.14

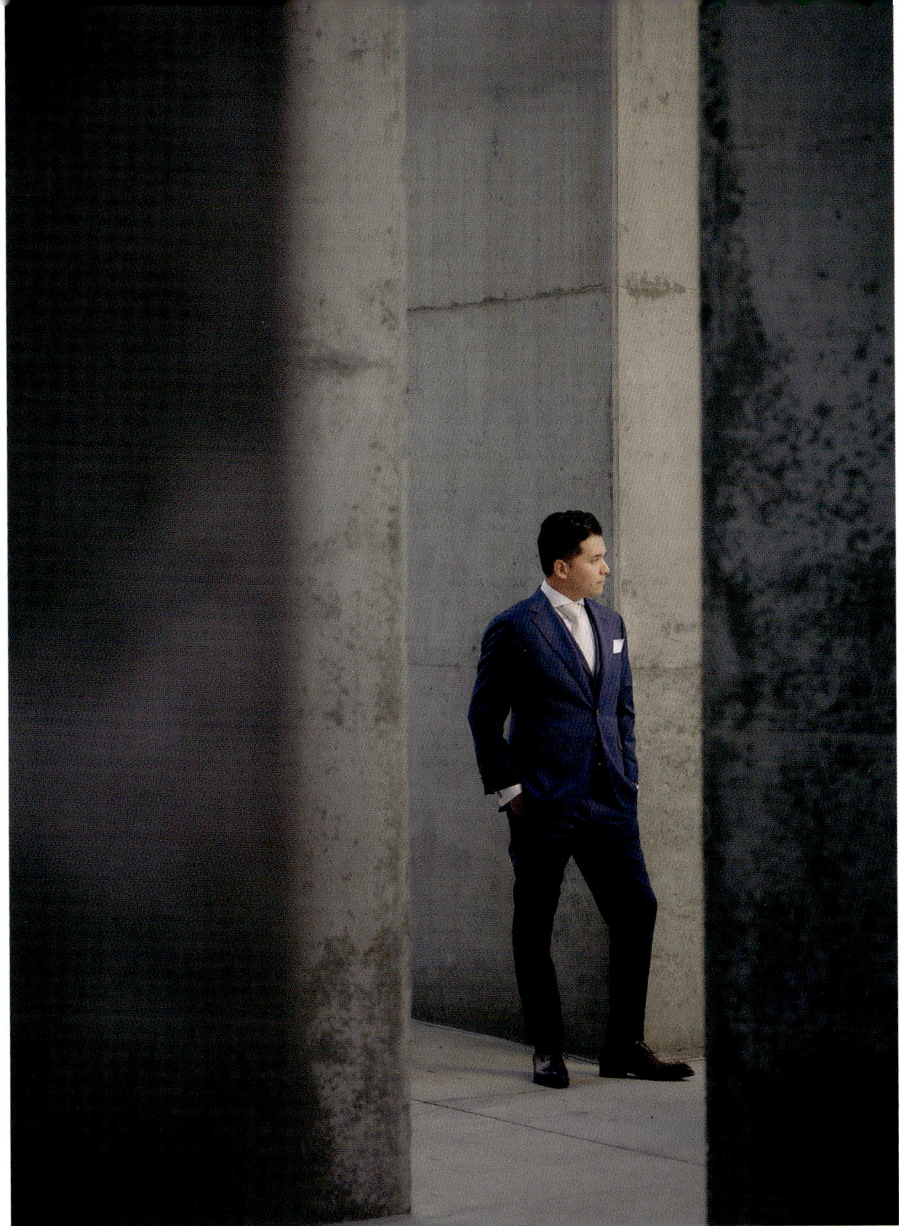

For these photos, I was inspired by the layers of gray wall columns surrounding us on the shoot. These layers of cement beams made for a very interesting composition. However, I wanted to make sure that I featured the groom, Ivan, and not the columns. To do this, I had my friend Andre hold the flash at the height of Ivan's head and point it at the wall in front of Ivan. I then darkened the exposure by using my camera settings. Finally, I dialed the flash output up or down until I could see Ivan turning brighter than the columns surrounding him, but the light had to be soft enough to not give away any telltale signs that a flash was used.

You can clearly see how the beautiful lighting on Ivan would have been impossible to achieve without the use of a flash. Also, notice how the shadows on his face and blue suit have been very gently lifted, resulting in a very flattering portrait.

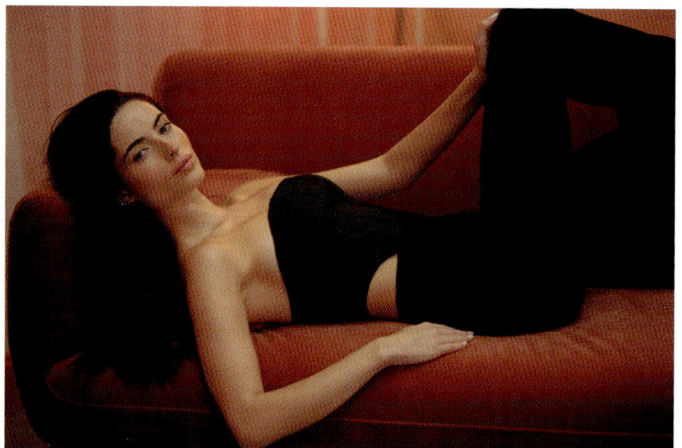

Figure 3.16: This photo was taken with just the ambient light in the room. Almost everything in this photo is top notch! The model is gorgeous, the room is themed, and her styling looks on point. But unfortunately, the lighting is flat, boring, and lifeless. To make matters worse, model Renee's hair is black, and her outfit is also black. If you don't use a flash to lift the shadow detail on her hair and black outfit, it will look like black mush when you try to print it. Also, you can't see any details in her hair. In my opinion, we can do much better than this. Relying on post-production to bring shadow detail back will work to some extent, but it will never have the same level of depth, detail, and volume as we achieve when adding light during the shoot.

Figure 3.17: What an incredible difference light makes in revealing shadow detail! Naturally, when you add light to dark hair, take care that the hair is well placed, neat, and has a good flow, because all that light will bring every detail to the surface whether you like it or not. However, with lighting on the hair and attention to the hair styling, the photo will benefit greatly in post-production to create a masterpiece.

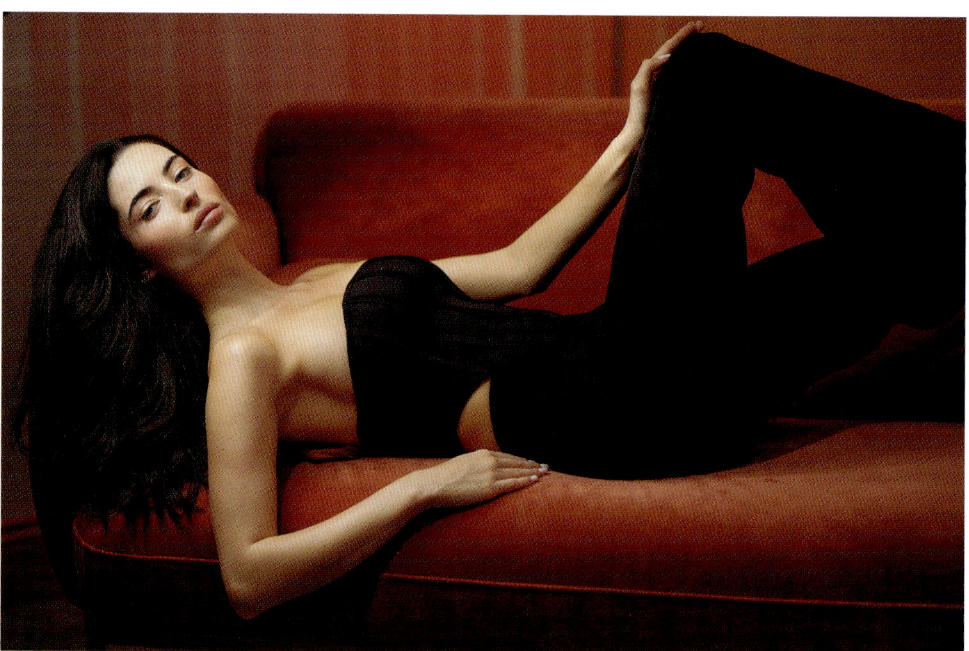

Add Light to Create Separation Between Subject and Background

There are times where the background should be lit separately from the subject. For many years, I never considered lighting the background with my flashes. I always thought that the flashes and modifiers were meant for the subject, and the background would just stay how it was. But I was wrong! I finally discovered the benefits of lighting the subject and the background separately.

One benefit is that the photo will take on a more painterly feel. Another benefit is simply that most photographers never use this technique, so if you do, your photographs will automatically stand out. The third—and my favorite—benefit is the unique look that results from the combination of dramatic lighting on a subject with a separately lit background. The reason why this is so compelling is that when the background is well lit, the shadows that make up the dramatic lighting on your subject's face become more accentuated.

Figure 3.18: That is precisely what I did on this photograph of model Angeline in Zurich, Switzerland. The background was just the right distance away from her to make it a perfect opportunity to squeeze in a light from above, pointing down at the painted canvas. It's quite clear how the lighting on the background gives the illusion of darker shadows on Angeline's face. This is a very effective technique for creating dramatic and impactful photographs. If you have never tried it, you should give it a shot. You can also try this technique on headshots to give them more dimension than your standard headshot taken in the studio.

Figure 3.19: Just for a bit of fun, I decided to try this technique on a white background. I added a light magenta gel to the flash illuminating the otherwise plain white background. I thoroughly enjoyed it when some of that magenta-colored light bounced back from the white background and hit my camera's sensor. It gave Renee a look that is hard to explain in words. This photo would have been an ordinary three-quarter profile of a beautiful person, but now it looks more like a piece of art you would hang on the wall. This background lighting technique is very versatile.

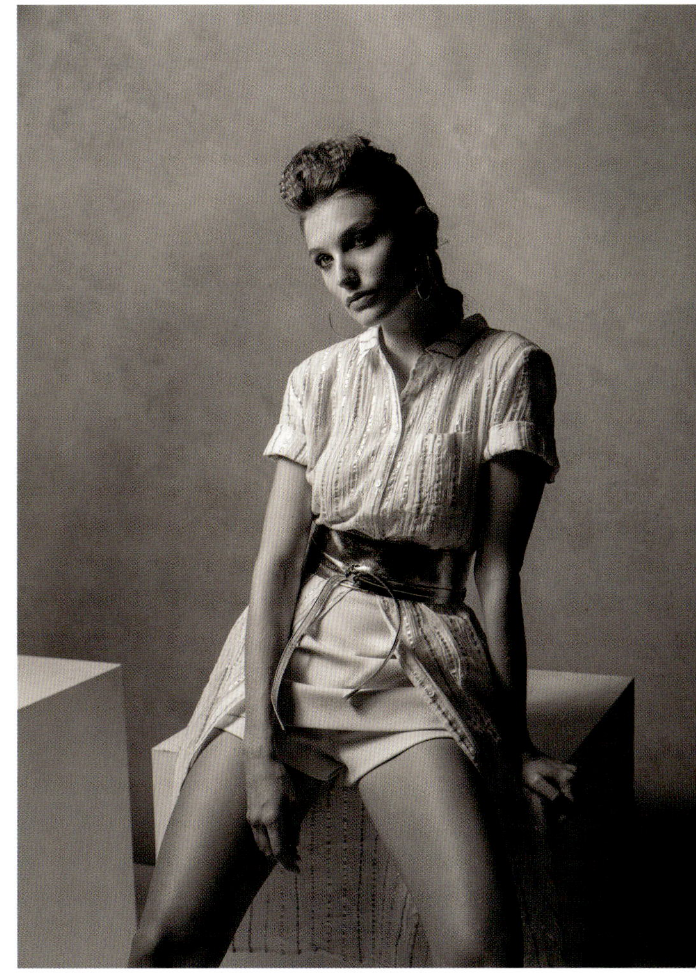

FIGURE 3.18

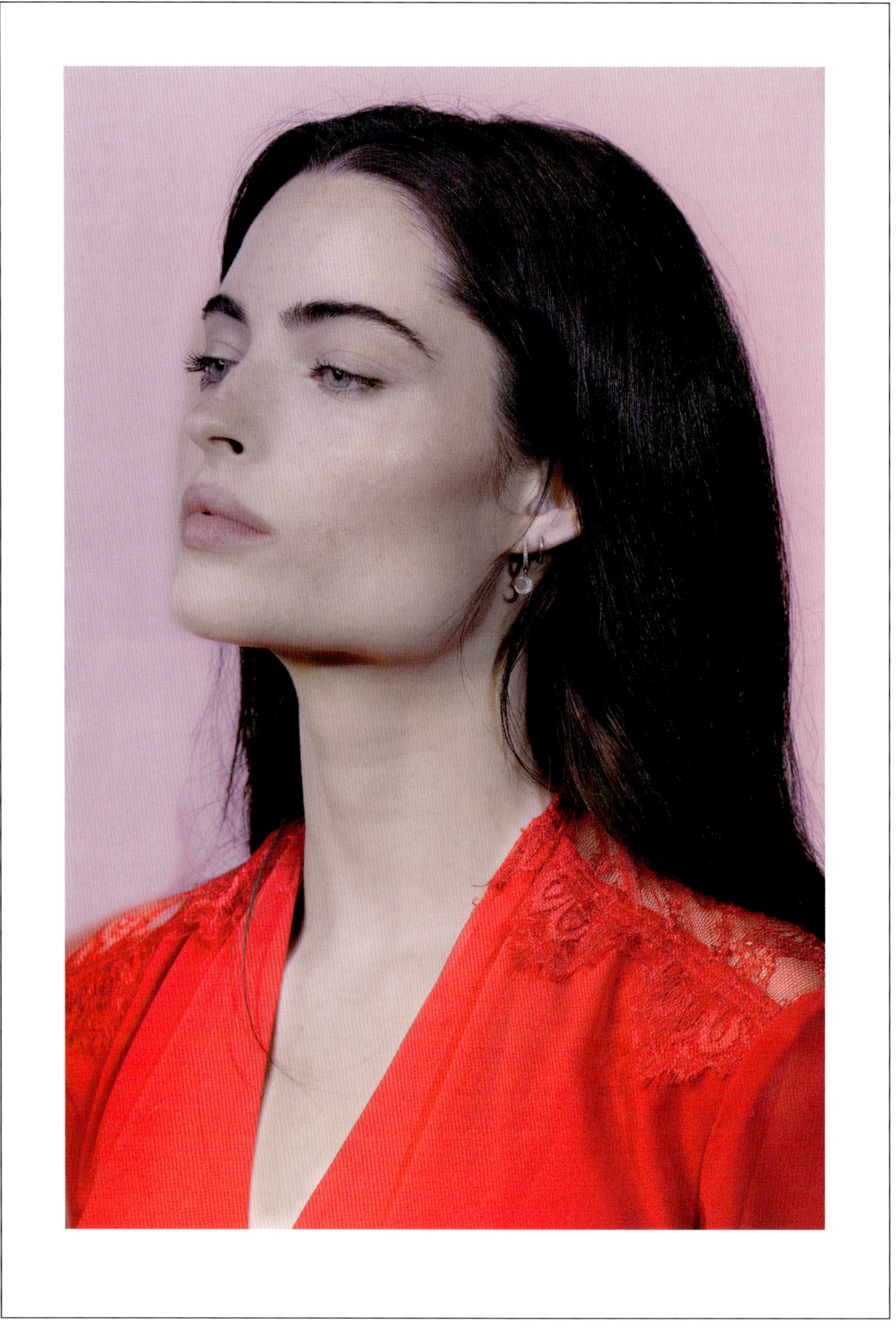

FIGURE 3.19

Add Light to Control Contrast Throughout the Entire Frame

How many times do you go outside for a shoot, find a nice spot to start shooting, then notice that although your subject is standing in clean light, the background is cluttered with hot spots from the sun's hard light illuminating bright buildings, grass at a park, sidewalks, etc.? This fluctuation of dark areas and bright areas throughout your frame is extremely distracting to the eye. Not to mention, your eyes are drawn to hot spots in a photo, so we need to be able to deal with these situations.

The way to work with high contrast scenes like the one I just described is to lower the contrast throughout the photograph. If the sky is too hot (bright), use your camera settings to bring it back down. If your subject is now too dark because you were trying to fix the overblown sky, then use a modified flash to bring the light on your subject's face/body back up near the same level as the sky. By bringing the light on your subject up and the light from the sky down, you have in fact reduced the overall contrast in the scene. The size of the modifier determines how well the light from the flash will blend with the natural light.

Figure 3.20: Look at this typical contrasty scene. It's such a bummer to have a beautiful sunny day such as this. You go outside to do an on-location shoot with an attractive person wearing a beautiful red dress, but then the sun ruins it by striking the grass in the background, causing a major distraction. The three callouts highlight what I saw when analyzing this scenario. First, the face is a bit dark, and it's too close to the grass, which causes a subtle green color cast on her face. The grass that's directly hit by the sun in the background is the second issue that must be addressed; otherwise, it will be an eyesore. Third, all that intricate texture and design on her dress is completely lost due to the flat and low quality of light illuminating the dress.

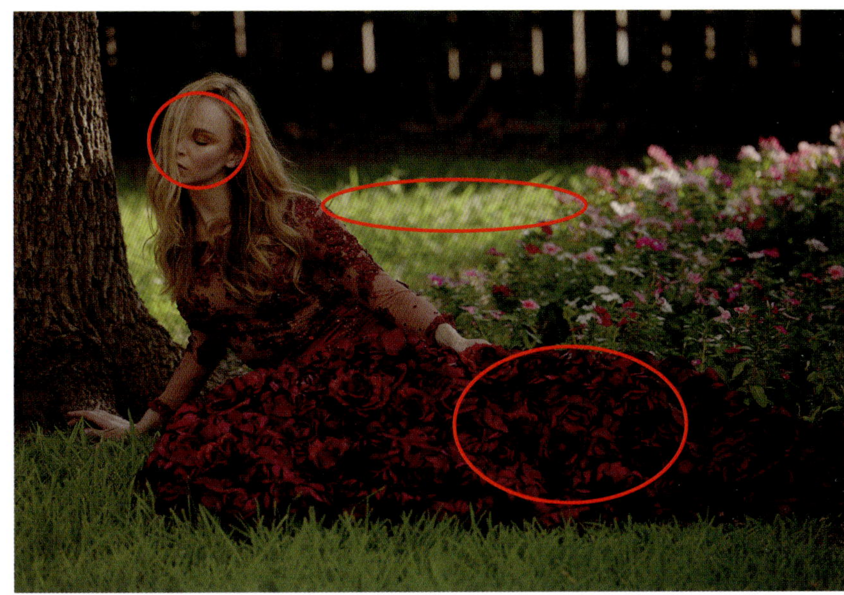

FIGURE 3.20

Figure 3.21: To fix all three problems and obtain this fantastic result, all that was needed was two modified flashes. The green grass distraction was controlled by just using my camera settings to bring down the brightness of the grass behind her. Once I saw that the grass was under control, I had to bring the light back up everywhere else. For Alisha's face, I could have just used a typical softbox and fired the light toward her face. That would have certainly taken care of the low quality of light on her face and fixed the green color cast. But instead, I decided to use a hard light modifier called a beauty dish to not only illuminate her face, but to add shape, drama, and sculpting with shadows to enhance her beautiful facial features.

Finally, to fix the flat and boring lighting on her dress, I used a large softbox pointed at her dress from an angle. The angle is very important in this situation because you don't want to illuminate the intricate texture straight on. That would reduce detail. What you want to do is to hit the dress from an angle. That way, the light hits the fabric differently, creating texture. Just two lights were needed to turn a flat photo into something that looks as if it could be on the cover of a fashion magazine.

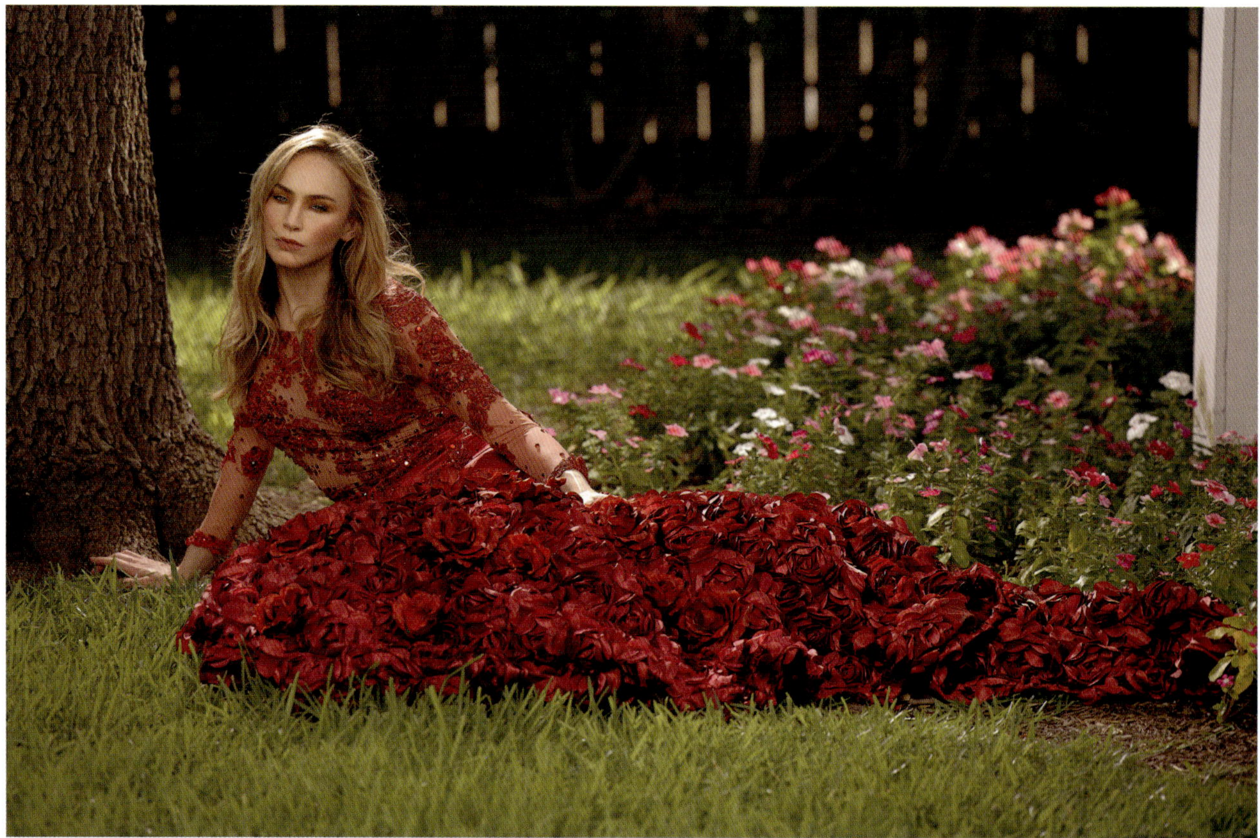

FIGURE 3.21

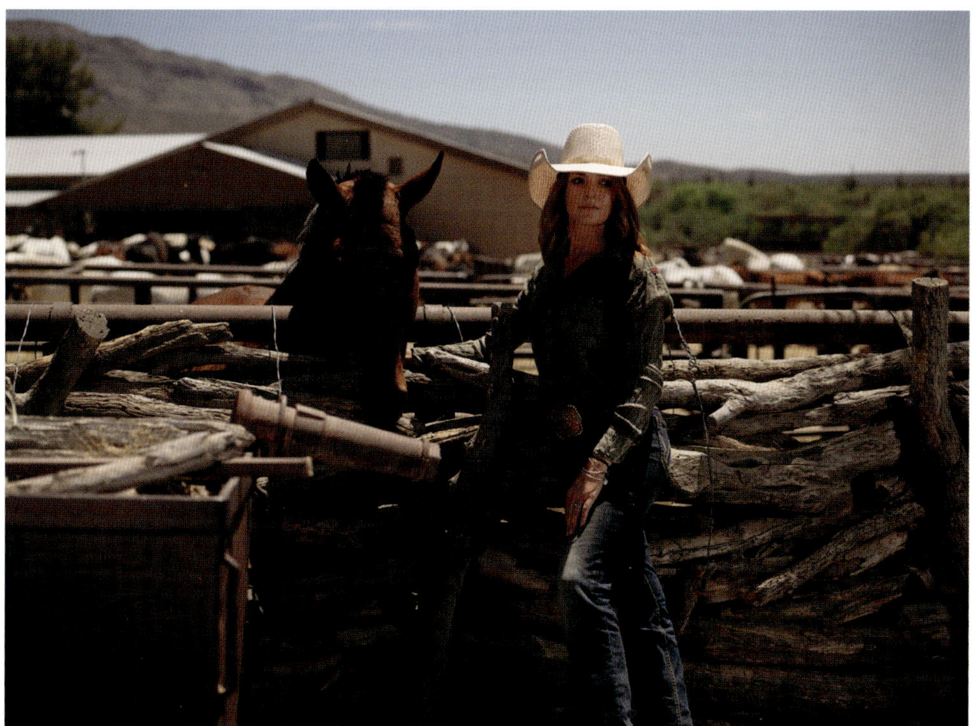

Figure 3.22: Consider this scene at a ranch in Tucson. It is just a typical day outdoors in the desert. Wood, metal, sky, horses, and trees are all lit by the sun, creating a high contrast lighting mess. The reason you can see blue in the sky is because I took this photo to expose for the sky, which made everything else rather dark. But all of this, including the shadow under Hope's hat, was fixed with just one flash and a medium-sized modifier.

Figure 3.23: To give this portrait context, I wanted to shoot at this precise location since Hope, at that time, was the head wrangler at the ranch. Remember, a portrait tells you a story about who you are photographing. Therefore, I had to tell the story of what she loves to do!

Here are my thoughts to tackle this situation. Clearly, we were outside in the middle of the day. Therefore, it was completely natural to have some hot sun spots here and there throughout the scene. I wasn't going to worry too much about that. I just wanted to control the big ones, which in this case were the big bright sky and the exposure on the wooden fence. I darkened my exposure until it looked just under control, not too much. I only had one flash with me, so I used it in combination with a medium-sized modifier

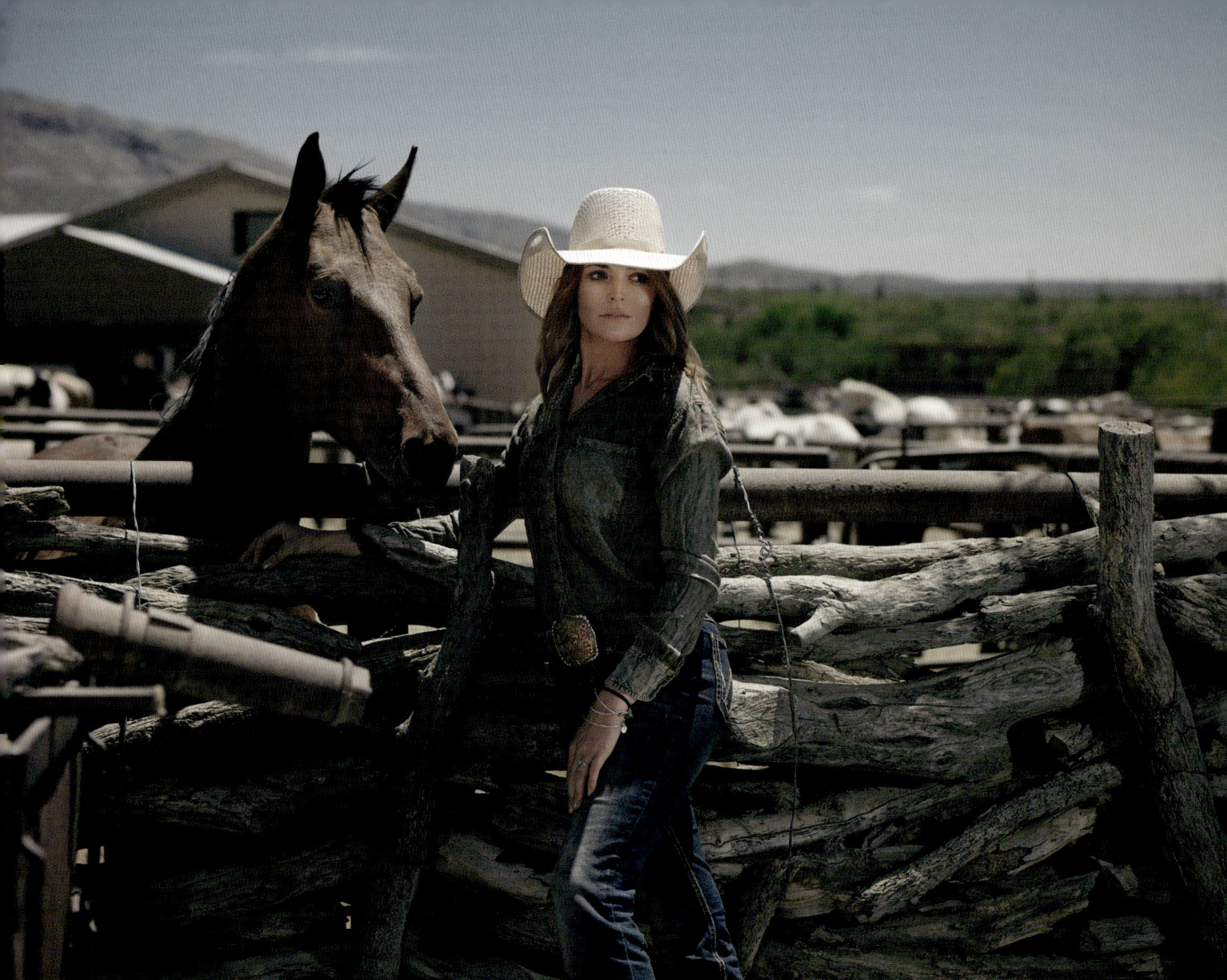

to focus the light mainly on Hope's face and shirt. I didn't want the modifier to be too big and spill light all over the wooden fence by her knees. That wouldn't look natural. Therefore, a medium-sized modifier was perfect.

On Manual mode, I simply turned the power of the flash up or down until the blend between the natural and the artificial light was seamless. I asked Hope to raise her chin, just enough to make sure the light from my flash would fill all the shadows created under her cowgirl hat. Making sure her eyes were well illuminated but still natural looking was the key to making this portrait one of my favorites. The lesson is, you don't need three, four, or five flashes to create something special. As you can see, one flash might be all you need to do the trick.

Figure 3.24: This example is a very important and desired look from magazines and publications, at least in the United States. It's a very low contrast look. This means that almost everywhere you look, the tones are nearly all at the same luminosity levels. To achieve this look, you will need a very large modifier—the bigger the better. Because it's not easy to carry around a huge modifier, there is usually a surprising solution: bounce the flash from big walls or low ceilings!

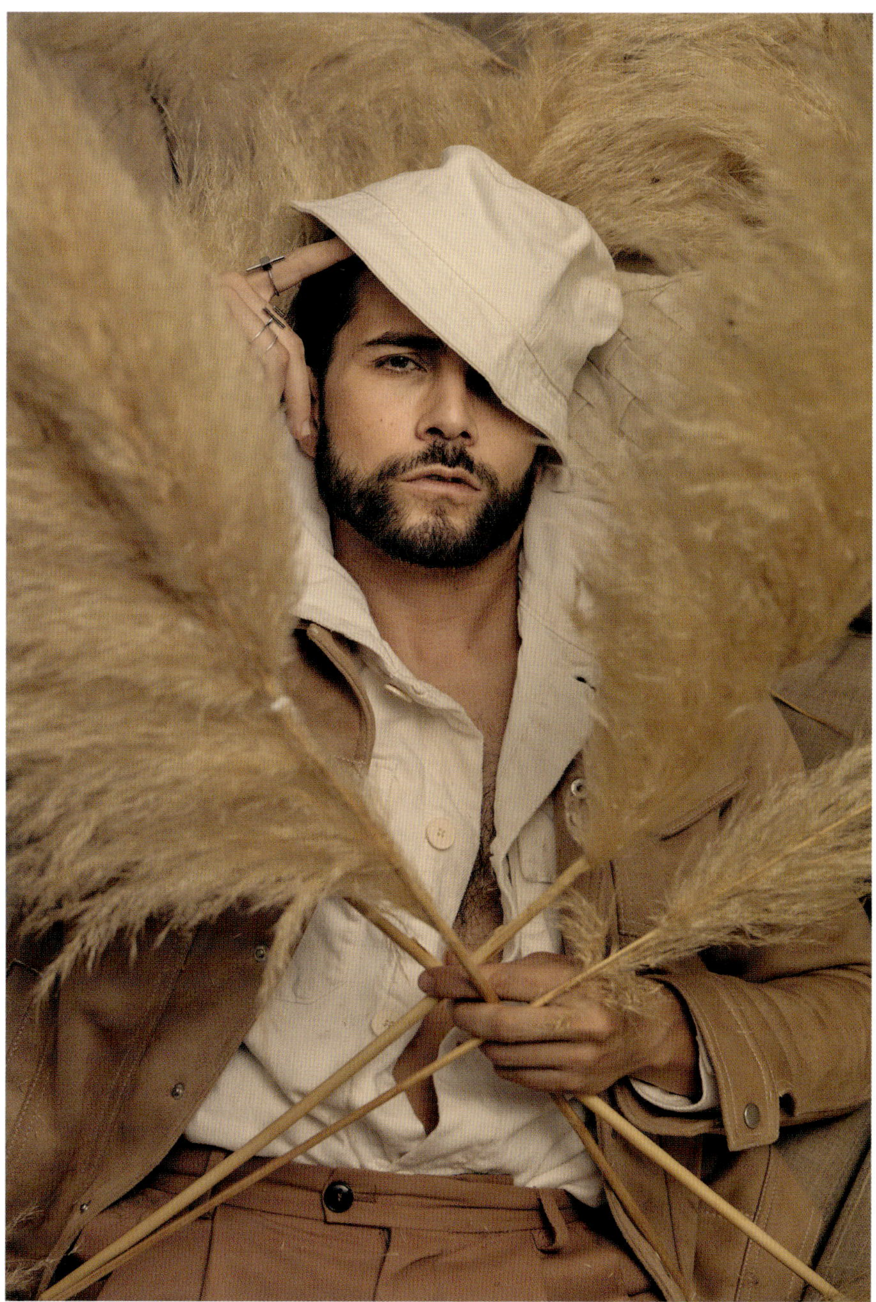

In this case, I went with the ceiling option, because it was low enough to achieve the desired effect. When the light hits the ceiling, the ceiling becomes a huge light modifier. When the light bounces back and strikes the subject, it will do so at nearly the same intensity throughout the frame. As a result, you have a very low contrast look. It's perfect for magazine covers or editorial articles featuring a celebrity. This photo shoot was indeed of actor Fernando Noriega for an article about him in a magazine.

If you don't have a large wall or a low ceiling nearby, you can always buy a cheap six-foot umbrella from Westcott (or the largest umbrella from any company). These large umbrellas work very well for this look on location. But just remember, the umbrella (modifier) has to be almost as large as the person you are photographing.

Add Light to Bring Attention to a Specific Area in the Photograph

Welcome to the world of highly specific lighting. This is where most fashion and commercial photography lives. This type of pinpoint-accurate lighting is actually a lot of fun! Usually, you need at least two lights for this. One is to be used as the main light that illuminates the general area, and the other light with an extremely narrow beam of light is used to point directly at the product or piece of fashion you are trying to feature, such as a purse.

Figure 3.25: The results of this type of lighting are stunning and eye-catching, because the light directs the viewer's eyes straight to where you want them to look. This wasn't a fashion shoot, but I was trying to create a compelling portrait of this beautiful woman in Italy. When I entered the room, which had a Victorian-era vintage mirror, I thought this was the perfect time to put this lighting into action. You can accomplish this with a 5-degree grid or a spotlight adapter on any of your flashes.

In this case, I didn't have that equipment, so I used a paper towel roll to focus the light through the tube. To avoid light from spilling all over the room, I used the paper towels themselves to wrap around the flash and the cardboard tube to make sure that no light could escape traveling through the tube. In photography, light can be modified with everyday objects more than you can imagine. Sure, it's fun to keep buying gear, but honestly, it's not always necessary.

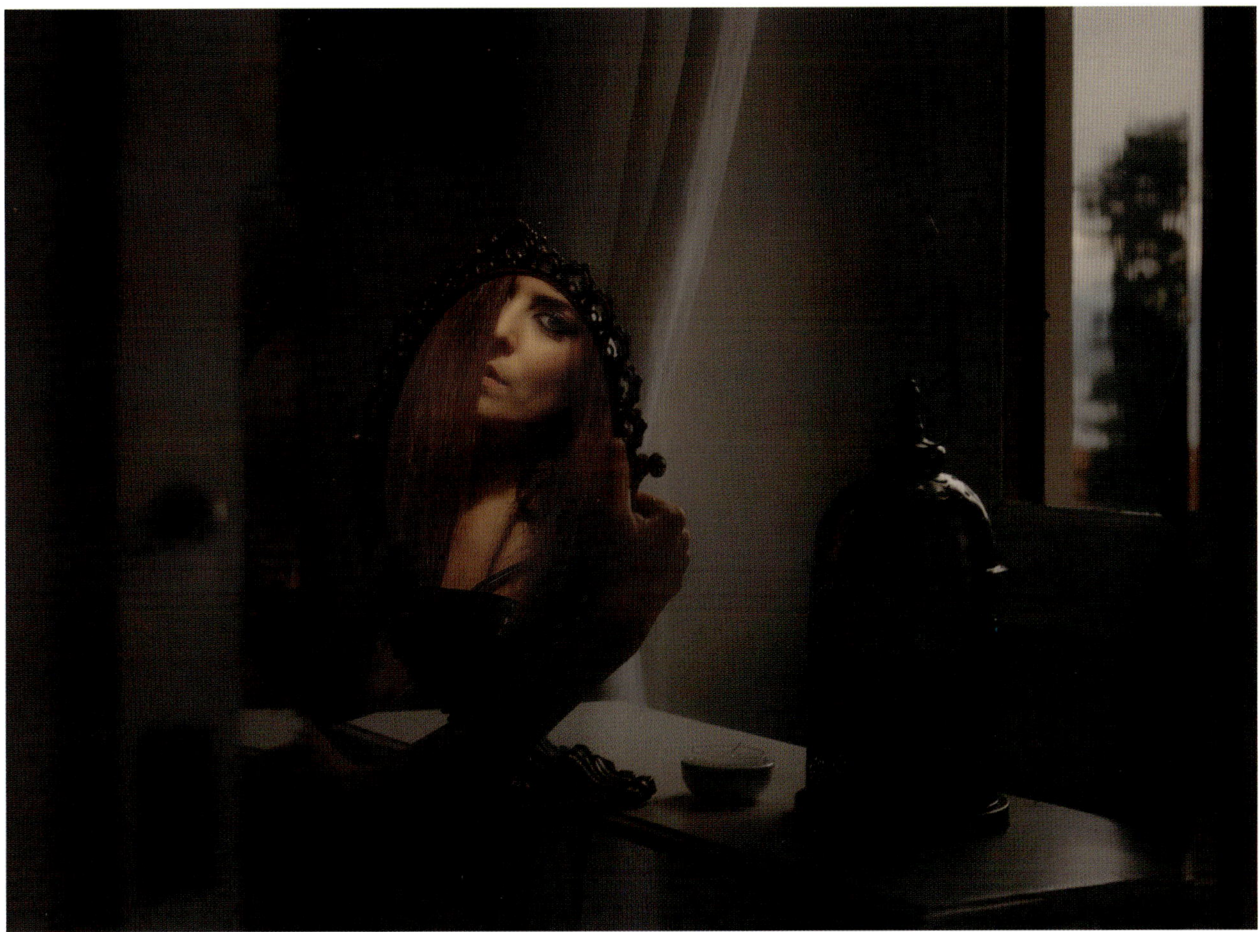

Figure 3.26: For this photo, I was indeed trying to feature the pearls for a commercial shoot. The amusing part is that I once again used paper towels and the tube to create this image, very similar to the last example. The only change was that I kept adding paper towels to the light to achieve the perfect exposure on the pearls and on the model's back. I know it sounds crazy, but sometimes paper towels work better than any other professional modifier for specific jobs. Therefore, I carry a roll with me every-where I go, no matter how big the job is.

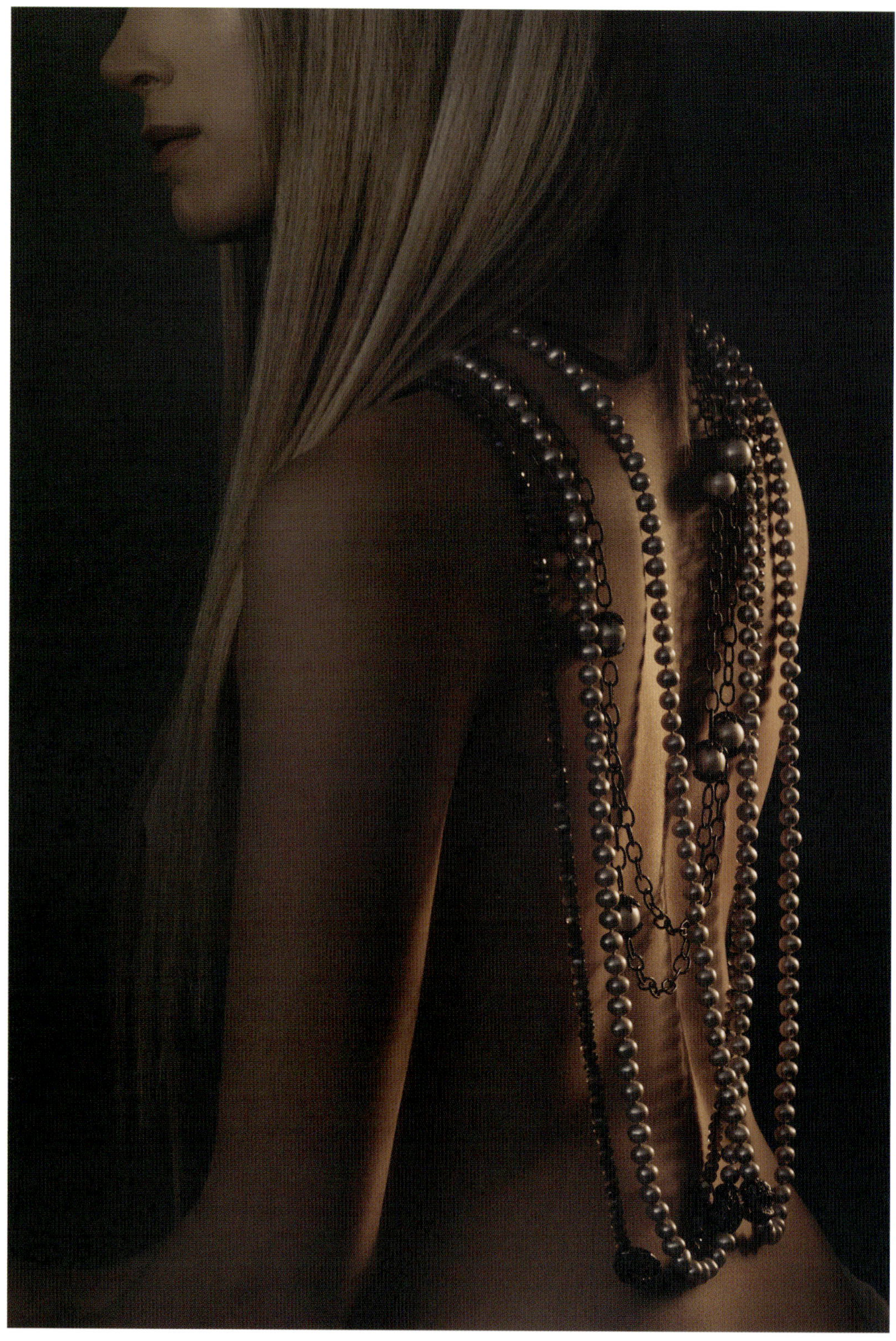

FIGURE 3.26

Figure 3.27: I call this a highlight feature. You add light that has a specific recognizable geometric shape, such as a rectangle or circle, to add drama to a portrait or editorial shoot. This technique probably wouldn't work for fashion photography, but it is great for editorial work.

If, before you read this chapter, I said to you, "Add light to a portrait," you probably would have just added light in the direction of the person you were photographing. But it is my hope that by reading this book, you know that you now have six options to choose from when adding light. This is how you grow as a photographer.

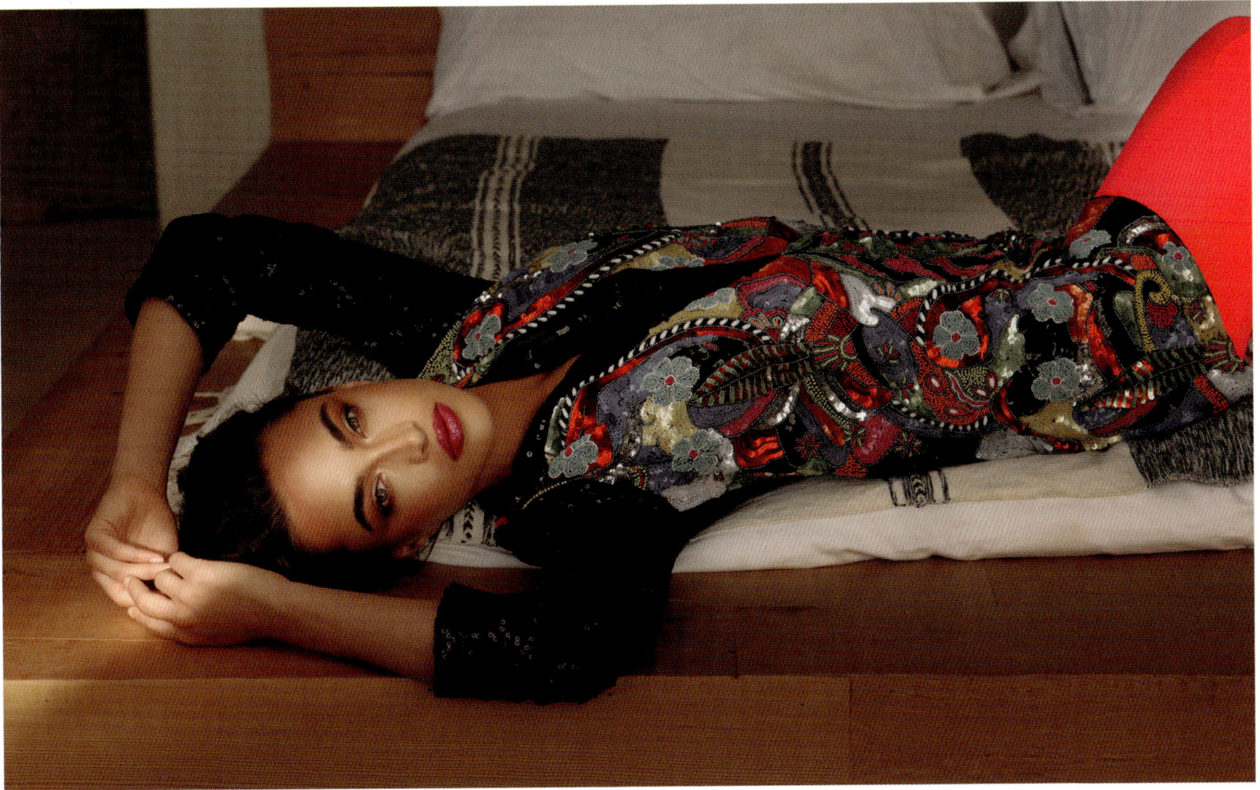

FIGURE 3.27

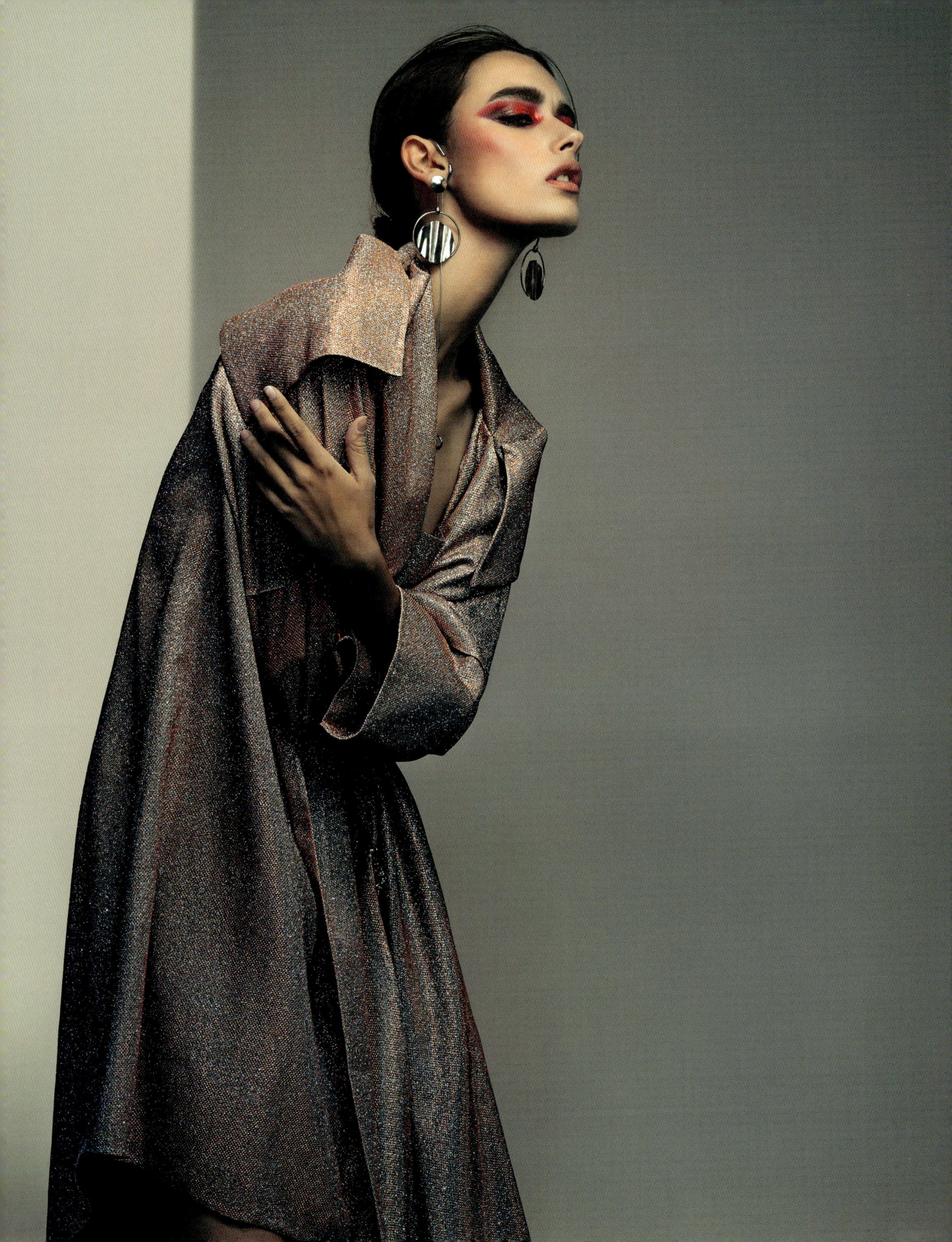

Chapter 4

F
A
Create a Mood
E
S

The next major option you have when working with flashes is to create or change the existing mood of a location, usually indoors. Why should we be saddled with a standard mood that doesn't inspire anyone? Isn't the point of lighting to bring life to a photograph? Locations are, for the most part, very neutral and boring. Without doing something about the mood at a location, the result is often very predictable photos. They might be nice photos, but they won't have that "Wow!" factor. In my opinion, changing the existing mood of a place is the most effective way to impress your clients with your skills as a photographer.

Creating mood means shooting with purpose; it means changing or altering the current ambient light and transforming the scene into something different, more interesting, more flattering, and more cinematic. Creating a mood means that the photographer has an idea, a message he or she wants to communicate to the viewer during a specific portrait session. The question to ask yourself is, "Am I accepting the mood that is already there because—let's be honest—it's just easier, or am I inspired by the subject or location so that it propels me to create something special that will resonate with the viewer?"

Changing the existing mood of a place does not have to be complicated. It can be achieved with just a few lights. The easiest way to change the mood quickly is by changing the color of the location by using colored lights or colored gels on your lights. Another way to create a mood is to make graphic elements by casting light and shadow on a wall or a room. Shoot what you want, not what you get. Before putting your finger on that shutter button, question the mood of a place and decide if you want to change it or improve upon it. You are clearly interested in improving your skillset as a photographer; that's why you bought this book. No one buys a book like this because they are lazy. Let's look at an example of how you can make drastic changes in mood in a single photo shoot.

Figure 4.1: This is a standard photograph of Lindsay. It is lit with two Profoto 1x4 strip boxes on either side of her, thus creating soft light. The light looks complimentary, and it clearly shows you what she looks like. Lindsay is an actress, so clean photos like this are very important for her. The problem with these types of ultra clean photos is that they don't give you much information about what she would look like with more creative lighting. When selecting an actress, a director or casting agent does want to see what she looks like in a straightforward way, but they also want to see what she is capable of looking like with a different, more creative lighting setup.

Figure 4.2: The mood in this photo is completely different from the previous, standard photo. The difference is that for this photo she was lit by a single Profoto reflector placed above her and slightly to the right. The hard light creates much stronger shadows, and although you can still see what she looks like, this photo takes on more of a character portrait rather than a straightforward "here is what she looks like" photo.

Figure 4.3: It is always incredible to me how much impact the mood has on a portrait. Mood cannot be underestimated, because it really defines the overall look of any photograph you take. In this photo, the model Lindsay appears almost unrecognizable. The mood takes over her physical appearance. The mood in this portrait can give a casting director an idea about the versatility of her expressions under different lighting conditions.

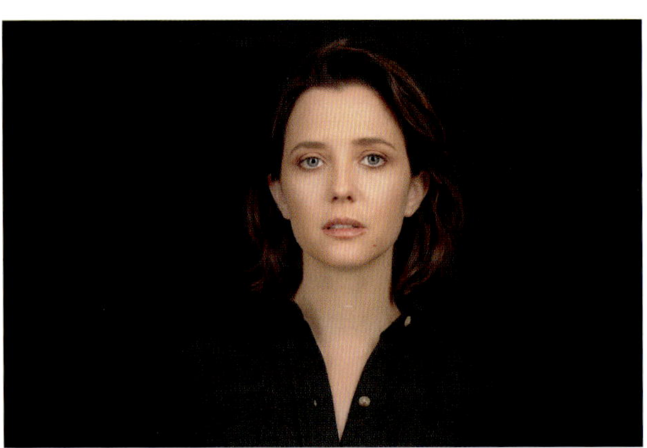

FIGURE 4.1

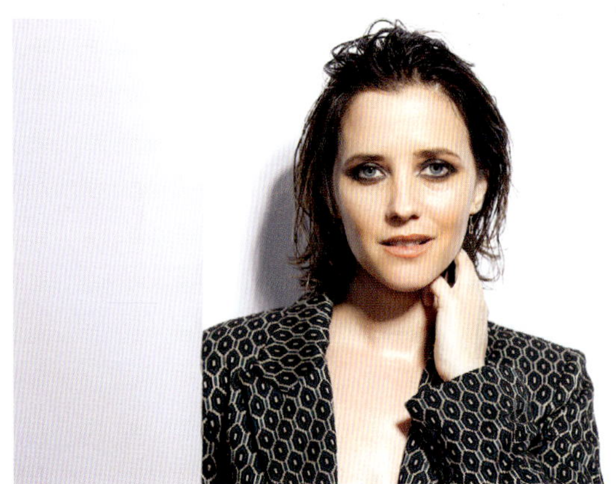

FIGURE 4.2

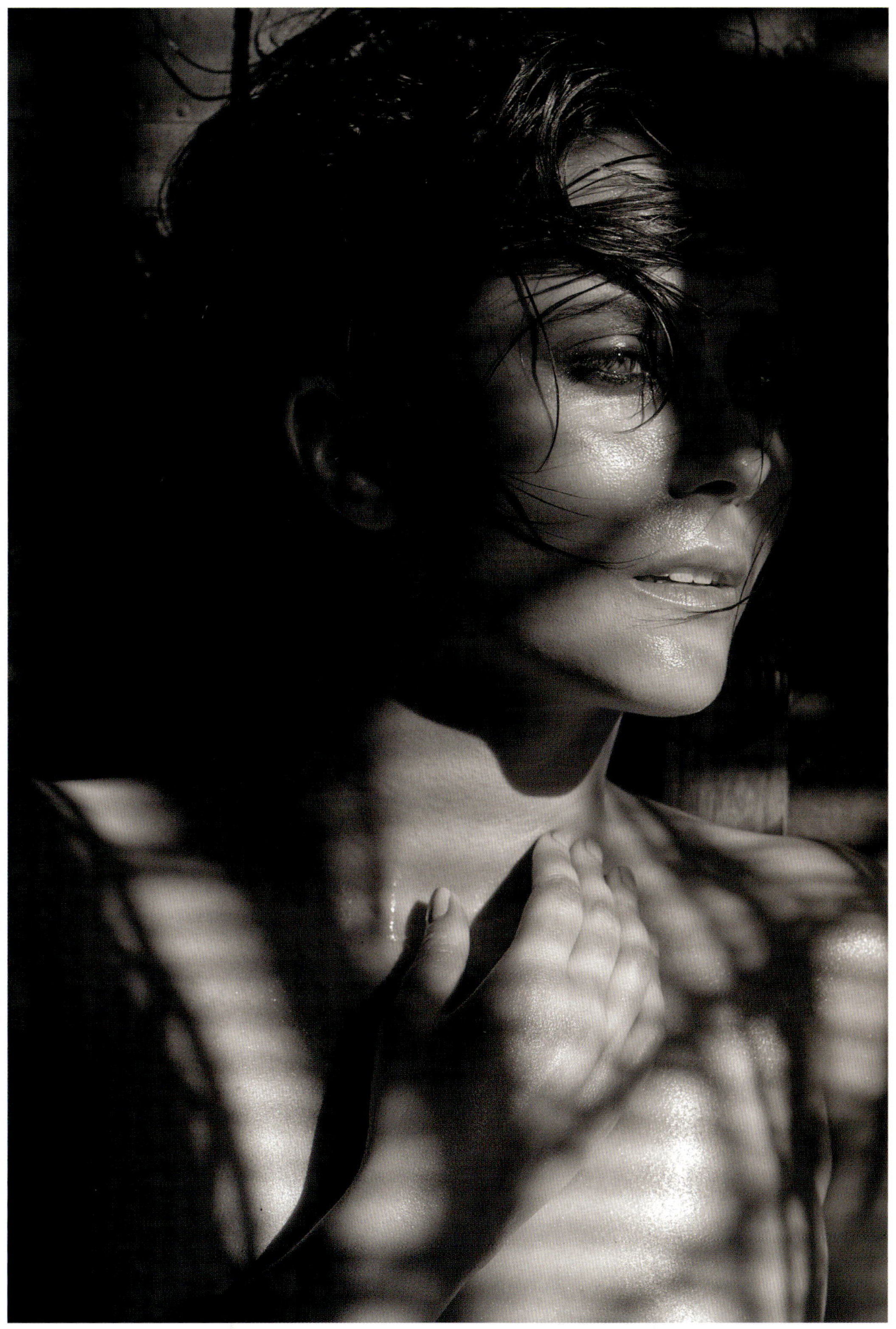

FIGURE 4.3

This portrait was created by allowing the direct sunlight to pass through a window and then through a metal shelving device that I have in my studio. The metal shelves are responsible for creating those shadow patterns that you see on her face and body. It's hard to believe that these three photos are of the same person, taken just minutes apart from each other.

The key is to remember that each of these three photos was created with an intentional mood. In this situation, the sun was used to create this lighting. But it would be very easy to replicate this look with a strobe fitted with a zoom reflector to concentrate the light on a small area. That light could be shot through the same metal shelving, and there you have it!

When I walk into a room now, I don't take the current mood in that location for granted. I realize that with my lights, I can change the mood completely. This is important, because it gives you a great deal of possibilities for the same room. Experimentation is key.

FOUR TECHNIQUES TO CREATE MOOD WITH LIGHT

- Hard Light Mood Versus Soft Light Mood
- High-Key Mood Versus Low-Key Mood
- Create Mood with Colored Gels
- Create Mood by Shooting Light Through Objects

Hard Light Mood Versus Soft Light Mood

The decision to use hard light versus soft light is usually the very first lighting decision that a photographer has to make as they are thinking about adding a strobe to improve the scene. Both qualities of light are equally valuable; they just communicate different things.

Soft light is synonymous with beauty and flattering light. Soft light does a good job hiding wrinkles and texture. A soft light portrait doesn't produce many shadows, and the shadows that it does create have a very soft edge to them. Soft light creates a low-contrast portrait that looks great, but it also flattens a face making it look more two-dimensional. Naturally, this is all affected by the position of the soft light in relation to the subject's face.

Hard light, on the other hand, produces a dynamic and high-contrast portrait. The shadows produced by a hard light source are strong, and the shadow edges are highly defined. A hard light portrait can be much more interesting and exciting. If I were to shoot a character study for an assignment, I would immediately choose my hard light modifiers to create the portrait. However, if I were shooting a bridal portrait or someone's headshot for their business, I would choose soft light.

Figure 4.4: One thing that I have noticed about hard light is that it can be very sexy. The hard light from the sun or a strong strobe illuminating a person's face creates strong shadows and adds a sense of mystery to the photo. That makes it sexy or exciting, whichever term you prefer. For this boudoir photo, I wanted to create a hard light look to give this photo a more glamorous feel. Therefore, I simply had a small but strong light source close to my subject's face from the outside window directed into the room. You can see the beautiful shadows that small light source created on Jordan's face. By the time the light reaches her ears, it is already dark.

Figure 4.5: The client has very defined cheekbones and strong edges throughout her face. Just beautiful! Inspired by these strong facial features, I chose a strong light modifier again, this time a hard, standard-sized white beauty dish. The beauty dish itself produces hard light, but the white coating inside it and the size of the beauty dish relative to her face softened the light a bit. If you look closely, her upper body is lit by much softer light, but her face appears to have more punch. That is the hard light doing its job.

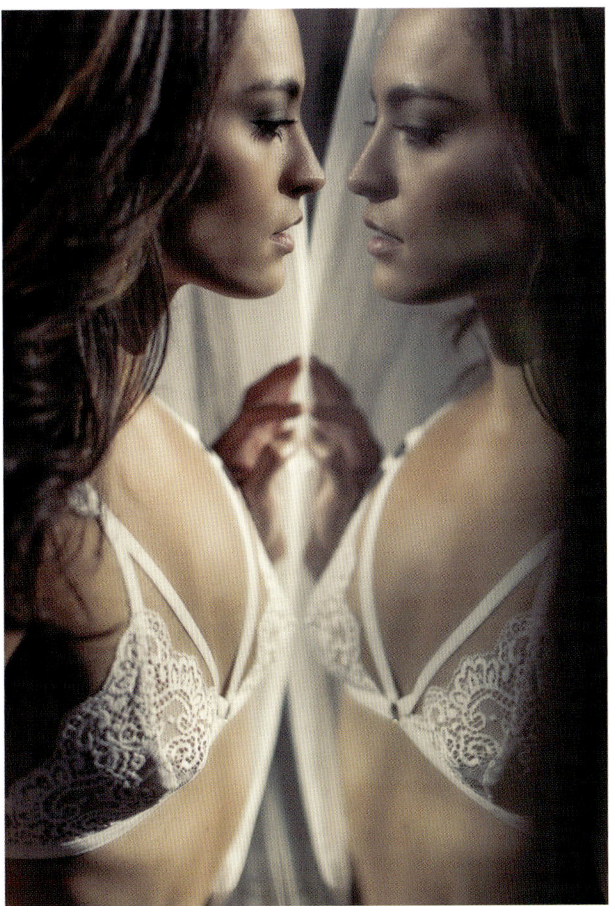

FIGURE 4.4

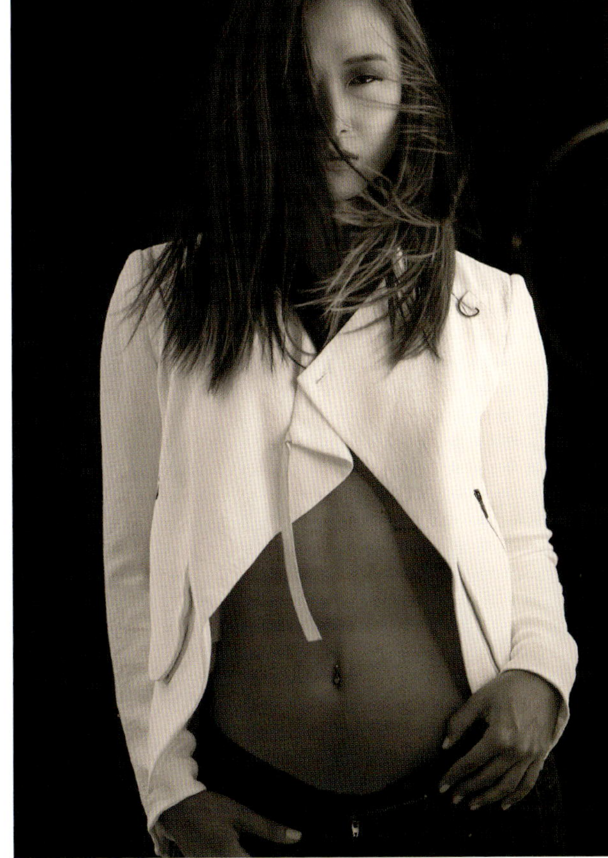

FIGURE 4.5

Figure 4.6: I use this setup regularly. It needs just two lights. One large light illuminates the entire body evenly and softly. The second light is a hard light that gives an edgy mood to the face. For this to work well, you must use a 10-degree or a 5-degree grid on a hard light modifier. If you don't have the grid, too much light will spread to the background. This has been a very successful look for me. My clients love it, and it's easy to create.

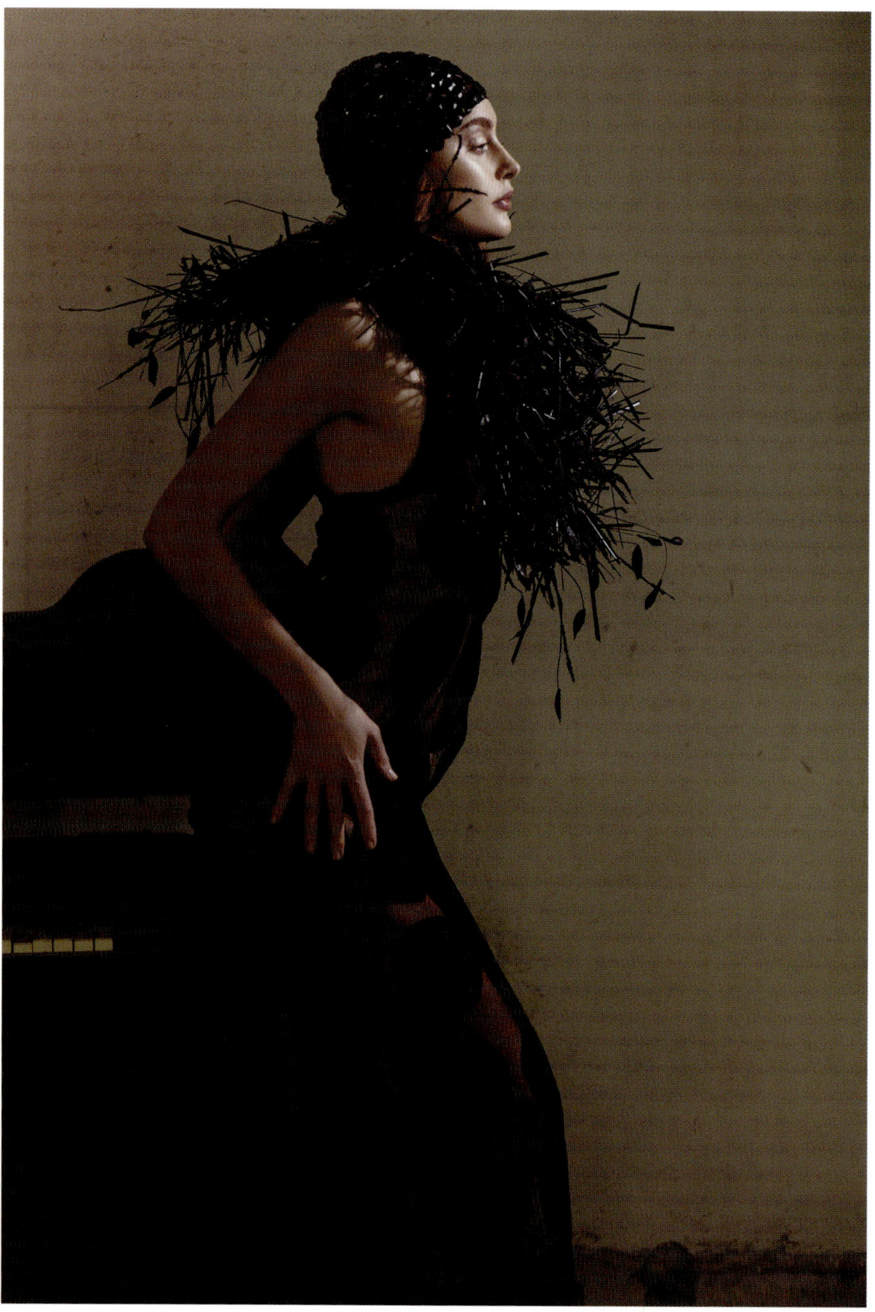

FIGURE 4.6

High-Key Mood Versus Low-Key Mood

High-key portraits are usually bright from edge to edge. A great deal of white and light make up most of the frame, except for the subject. In a studio, you would use white seamless paper, and light it with two lights to make it pure white. On location, you can use a blown-out window to make a white background, or find white walls or a bright building wall, or anything big and white as your background.

Low-key portraits are dark and moody by nature. You start with dark-colored elements that make up most, if not all, of the frame. Then you underexpose the scene using your camera settings to make it even darker. Once you achieve the desired amount of darkness, you then add touches of light to draw the viewer's attention exactly where you want it. When shooting low-key portraits, you will have to use the shadow recovery function in a RAW editor (such as Lightroom or Capture One) to bring back the shadow details so they balance nicely with the rest of the photograph. For this reason, it is important to know that shooting low-key images with the lowest possible ISO is of paramount importance. I often use a tripod, if possible, with an ISO of 400 or lower.

Figures 4.7 & 4.8: Some would argue that these two photos don't really depict the same person. The main difference comes from the approach to creating the mood, using lighting to create high-key and low-key moods. The second biggest difference is that the high-key photo has soft light as the main light source, while the low-key photo has a hard light with a grid illuminating the face.

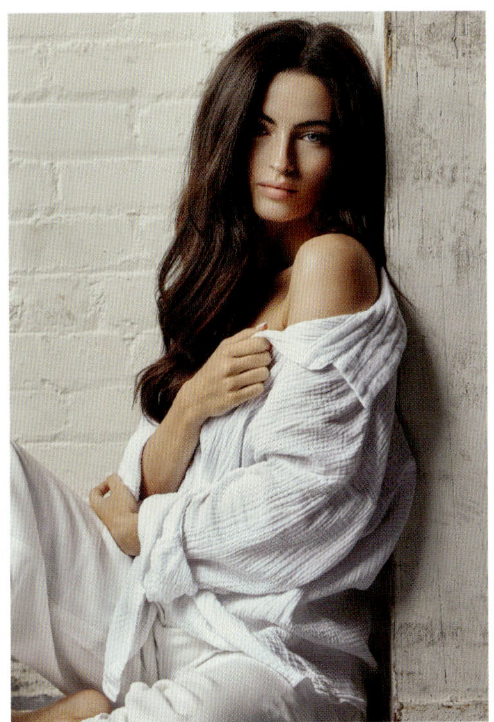

FIGURE 4.7

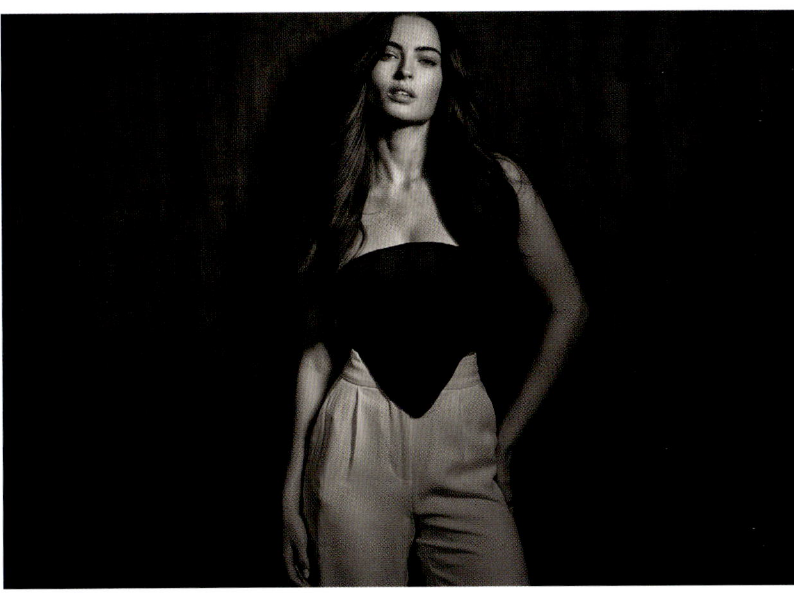

FIGURE 4.8

Figure 4.9: Low-key lighting can add a beautiful sense of mystery to a photo. It's a great tool to use when you want to create a mood instead of just an impression. Low-key lighting should be precise in terms of the spread of light; the light should be placed in precise spots to create a more visually compelling portrait. Everyone is different, but I find low-key photos much more compelling to look at than high-key photos. With high-key, everything in the frame is brightly illuminated, and there is no mystery.

Low-key photos like this one require heavy use of grids to control the light spread as much as possible. You just want the light to strike the subject exactly where you want it and nowhere else. It depends upon the modifiers being used, but I use Profoto 5-degree, 10-degree, and 20-degree grids. By using these grids, you will discover that controlling the light spread is actually quite easy to achieve. Without grids, you will find yourself frustrated when the strobe goes off. There is just too much light everywhere, and it's hard to achieve the mood you want. When appropriate, I feel compelled to try a low-key mood during my sessions. Low-key feels quieter, calmer, relaxing, and romantic.

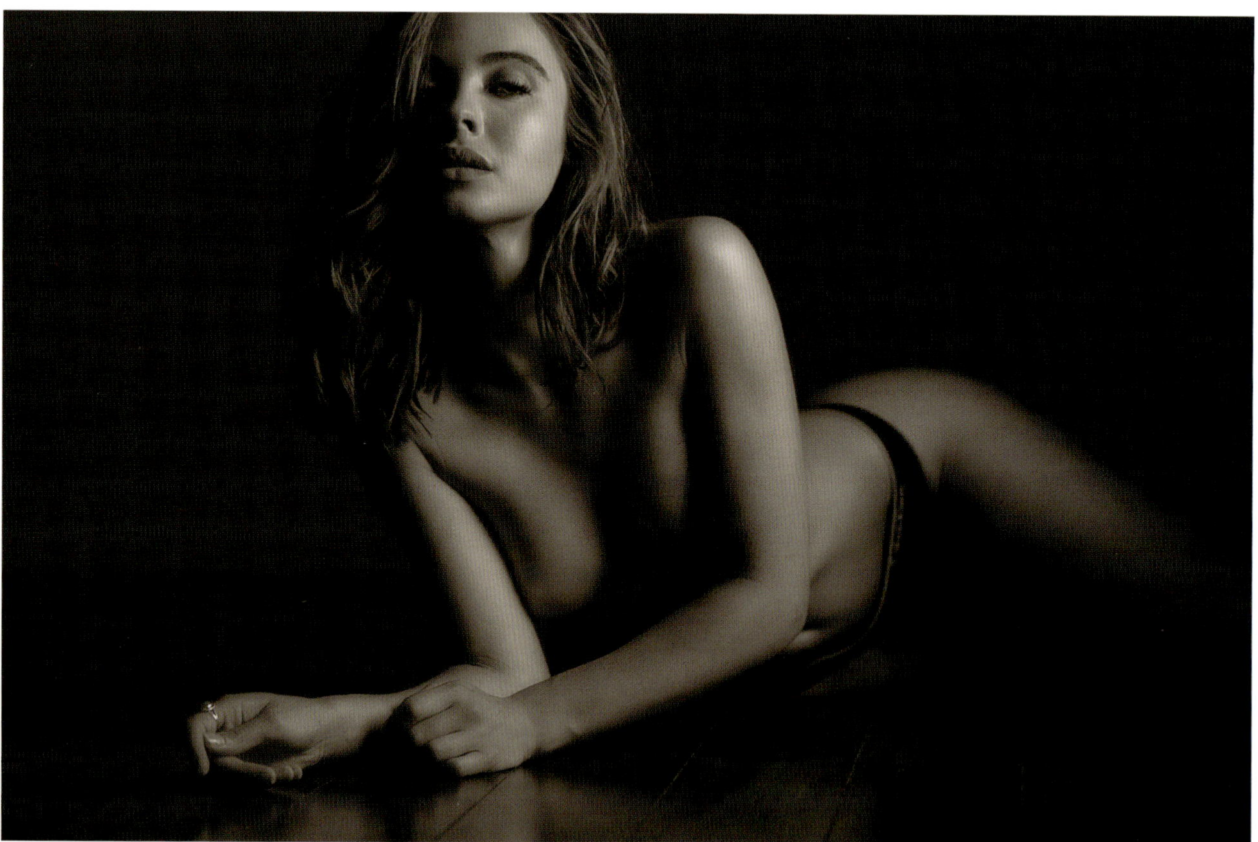

FIGURE 4.9

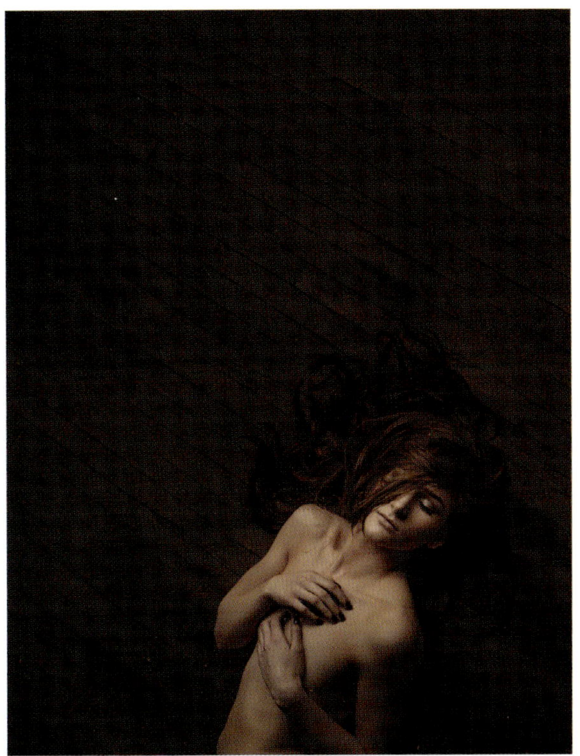

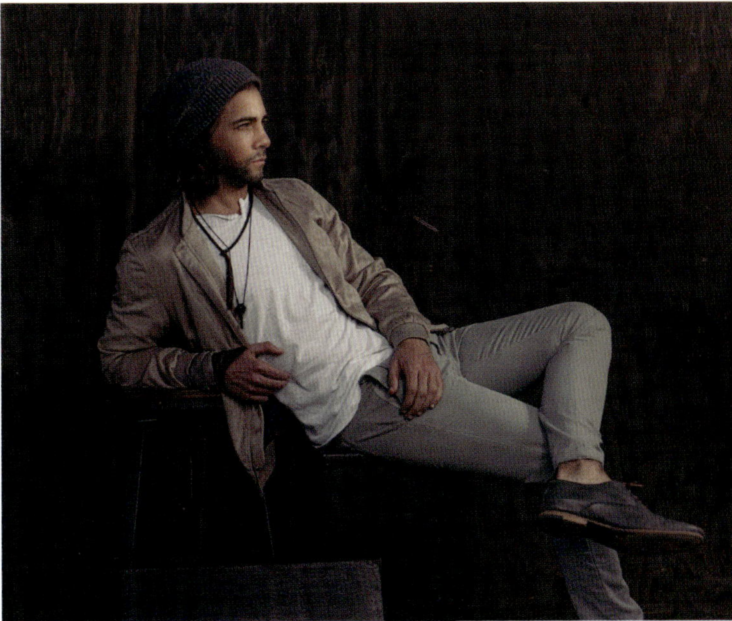

Figure 4.10: Notice in this fine art portrait that the floor has perfectly even lighting all the way through the frame, and the subject has her own light source illuminating just her and nothing else. This is the result of a highly controlled spread of light. The original photo was about a stop and a half underexposed. Using Capture One, I could bring back clean shadow detail because I set my ISO to 100 for this photo.

Figure 4.11: This low-key portrait of an actor was shot with three lights. One light was for the body and one light was just for the face. The third light was a large light source behind me, a six-foot umbrella, that evenly illuminated the wood background to the desired amount. Once again, I set my ISO to 100 and used my lights to provide me with enough power to keep my ISO at 100. When possible, I set and keep my ISO at 100, and everything else from my other camera settings to my light's output depends upon that ISO being fixed at 100.

Figure 4.12: Let's move on to some high-key examples. High-key is quite simple and much easier to do than low-key photos. That said, you can't just throw a lot of light toward your subject and call it a day. To take a quality, high-key photo, there must still be intentional separation between the subject and the background. This particular photo was taken with just one really large umbrella behind me. To create that important separation with just one light, I kept putting more and more distance between the background and the subject until I was happy with the balance. The light will illuminate the subject first, and as it travels to the background, it becomes much weaker, creating the desired luminosity separation.

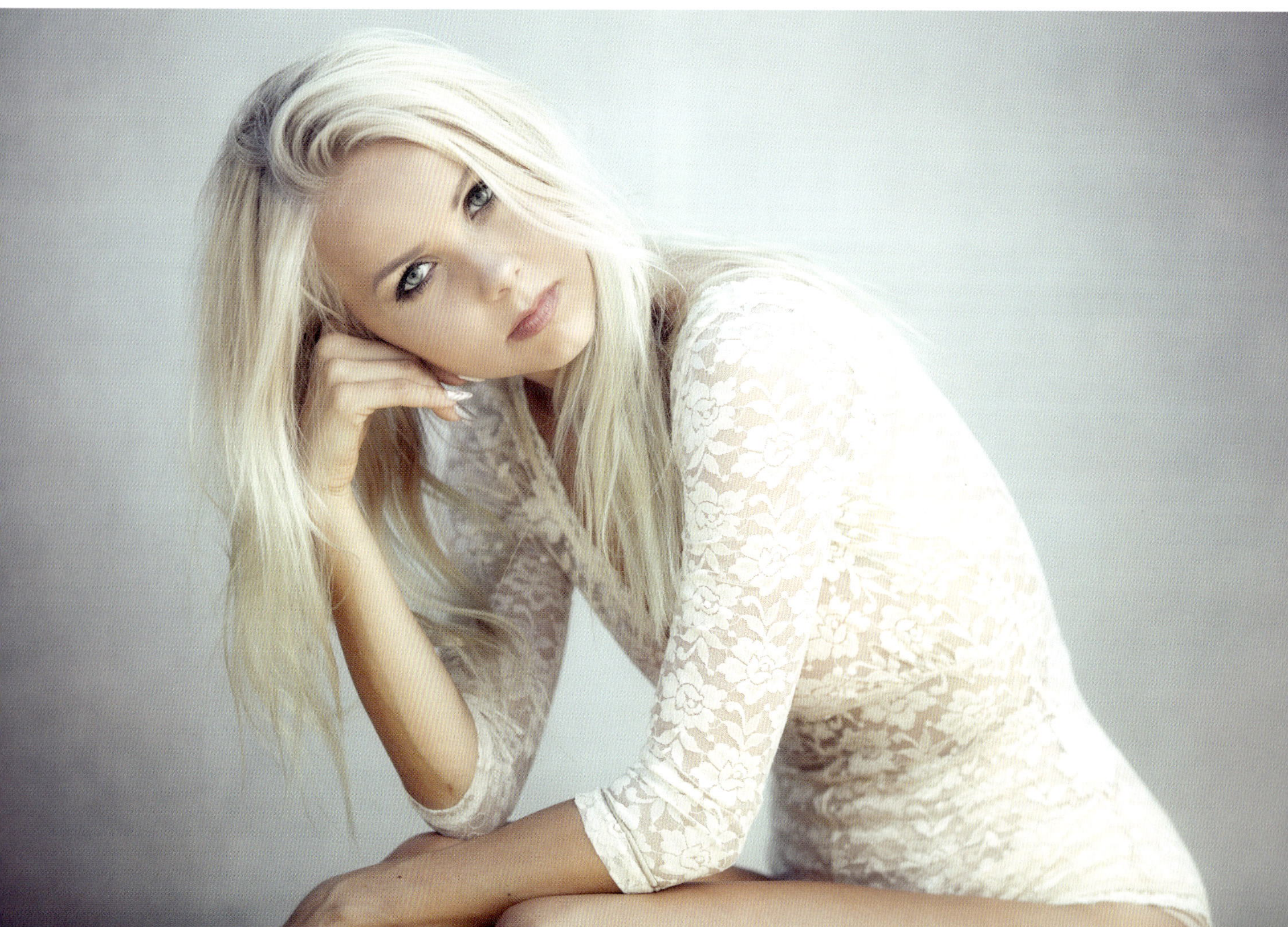

FIGURE 4.12

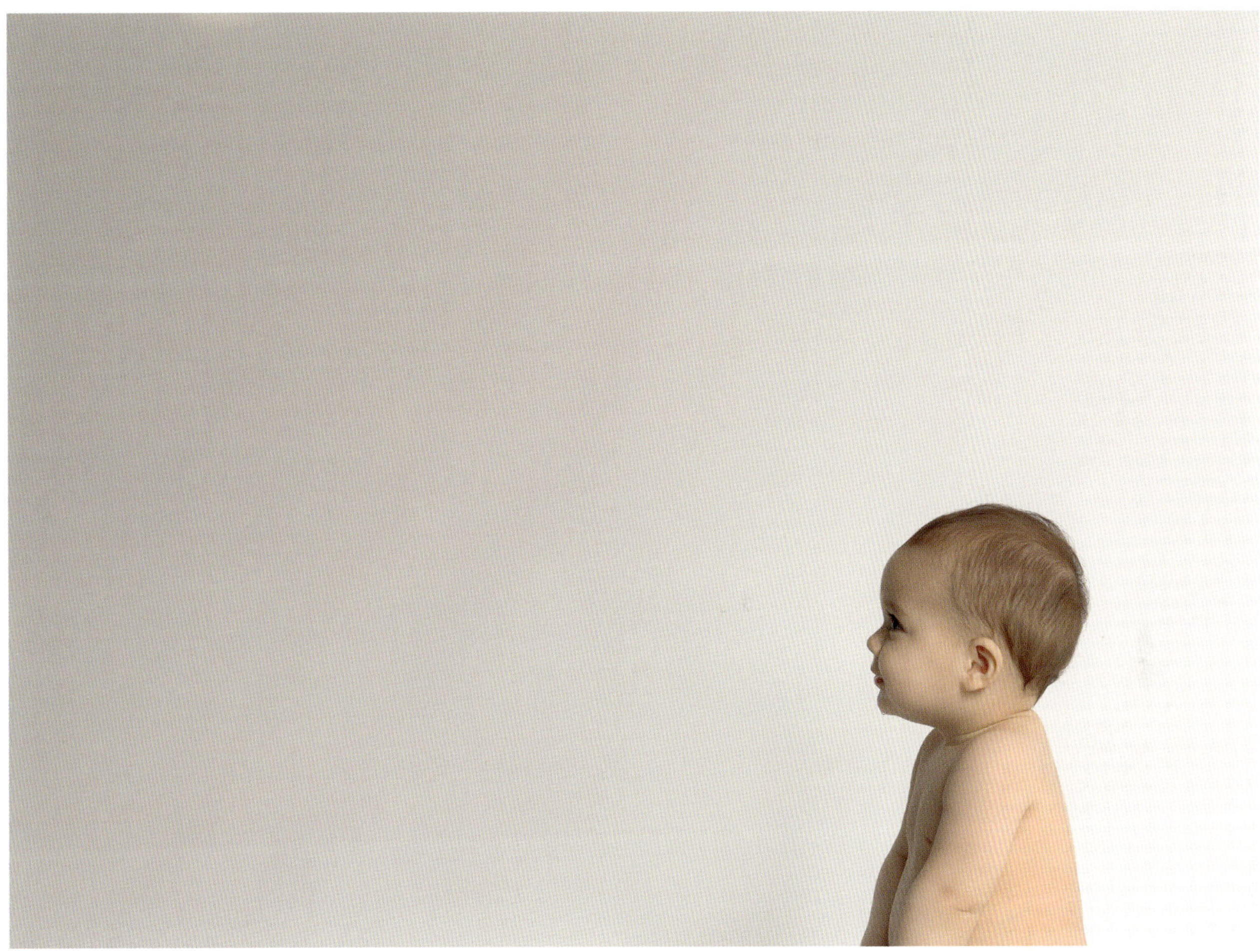

Figure 4.13: This is a portrait of my baby, Lucas, when he was less than a year old. I think high-key images look absolutely stunning with cute little babies or children. High-key gives the photo a fresh, serene, and elegant mood. The technique I used for this photo goes against common practice. Instead of putting the main light in front of Lucas's face, I did the opposite, and put the main light at his back. To still maintain detail on the front of Lucas's face, I propped up a reflector in front of him. The idea is that the light pointed toward his back bounces off the reflector in front of him, lifting the shadows in a subtle but effective manner. When done correctly, this lighting technique can add more three-dimensionality to a person's face.

Figure 4.14: When working with a model who has dark hair, I don't worry as much about having that important luminosity separation between the background and the subject, because the hair itself creates the needed contrast. However, it is imperative that you softly illuminate dark hair. If you don't, the hair will lose too much of its detail and look like a cluster of dark ink when printed.

For this photo, I used just one six-foot umbrella. The light came from the left side to clearly illuminate that side of the model's hair. The other side of her face, closest to the supporting beam, is contoured by the shadow created by her hair. Therefore, although there is no real luminosity separation in this high-key photo, the dark long hair framing her face creates all the contrast I need to separate her from the rest of the white throughout the image.

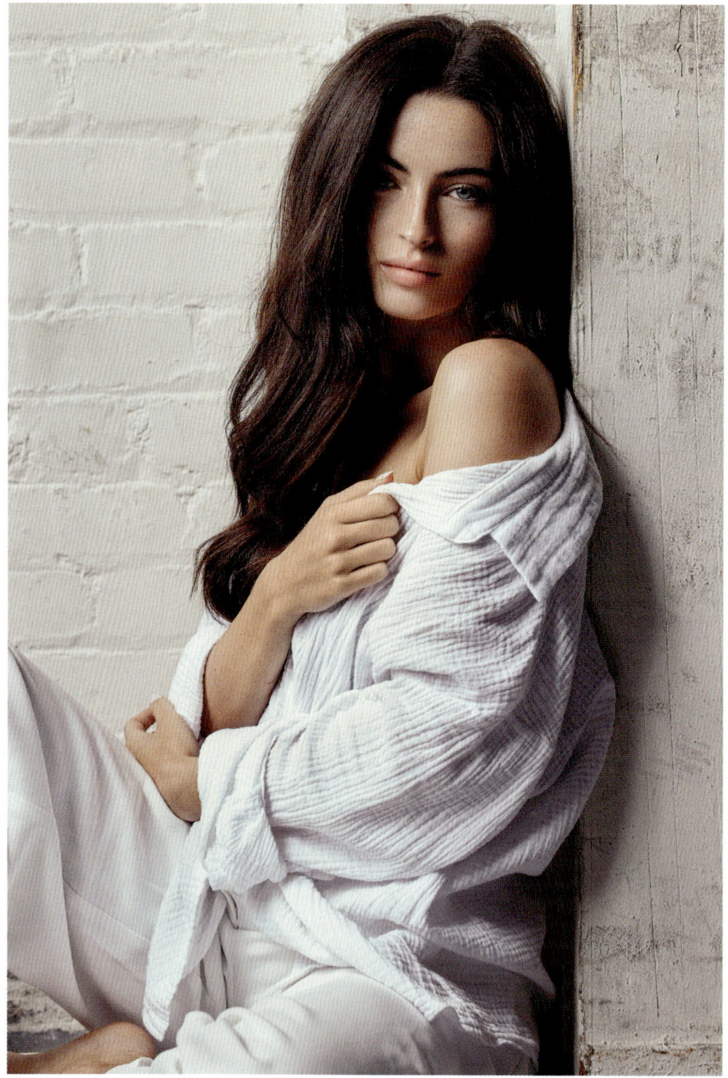

FIGURE 4.14

Create Mood with Colored Gels

The topic of colored gels could be a book on its own. It is a vast subject that has many applications and can yield impressive results. One problem I often see is the sloppy use of gels: not using them intentionally and/or overdoing it. To do a good job with gels and not make it look tacky, you have to be intentional with your vision and precise with your lighting. That's the key.

Figure 4.15: This portrait of Hope is one of my favorite examples of using gels in a way that makes sense. What I mean by that is the gels I used here were very intentional, so they blend with the environment instead of throwing a set of scattered colors all over the place without reason. When the gels blend nicely with the environment, the results are refined, elegant, and show much more skill than when they do not blend.

Study this photo carefully. Look around and try to see what I did to create this portrait. You should know that this bar was closed when we entered. There were no lights on and the room was quite dark. We used portable strobes and gels to bring a dark and boring looking room back to life. Now that you've looked at the photo, let's break it down little by little, so that you can follow along.

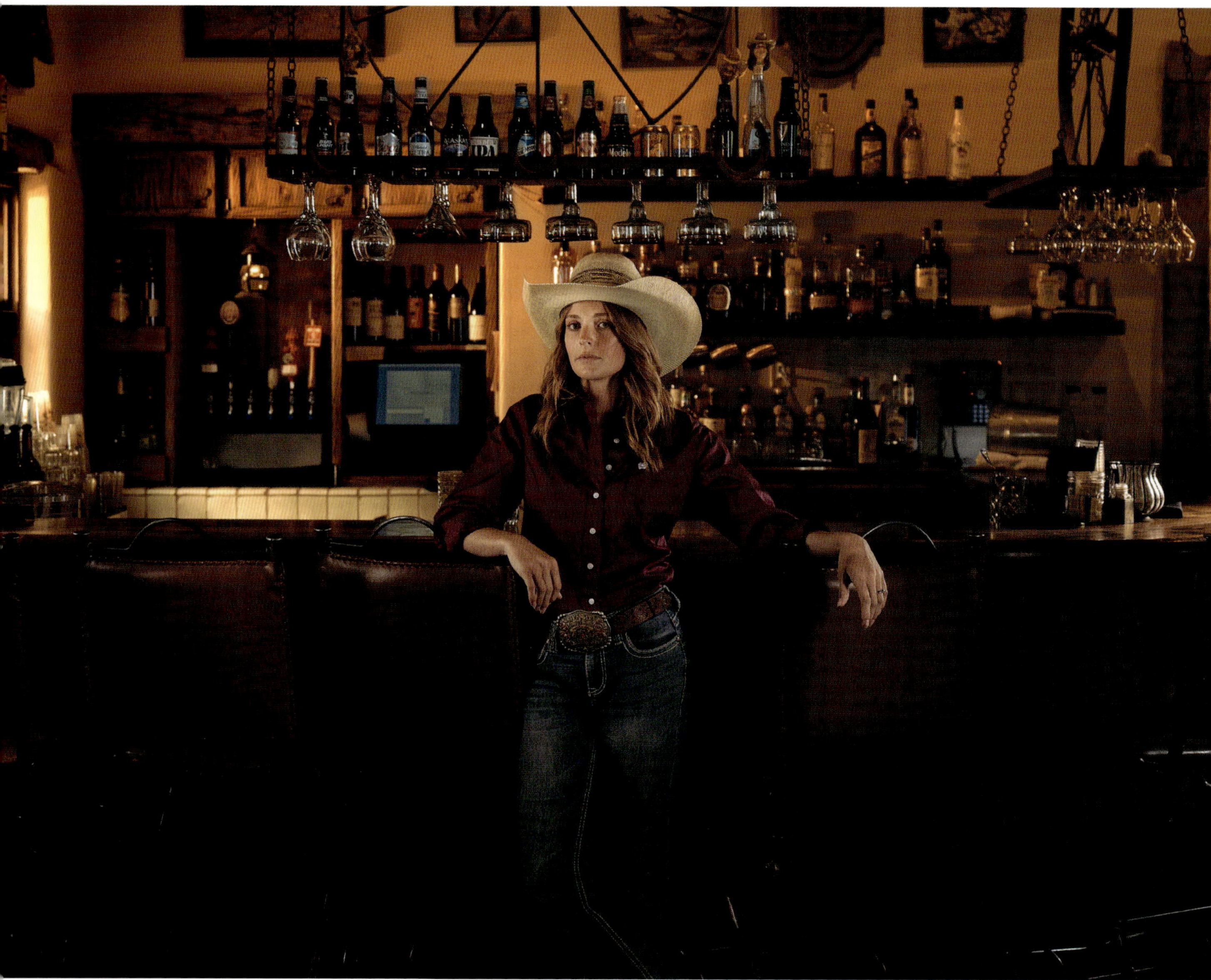

Figure 4.16: Here is where it all began. You can see how dark it was inside the bar. We turned on the bathroom light (top right corner) and we turned on the modeling lights (right side) to begin.

Figure 4.17: The next step was to begin lighting some of the objects at the bar. We needed to light the glasses hanging over the subject's head and the alcohol bottles on the shelves behind her. But first, we used a Profoto 1x4 strip box with a grid to bring light to her face but not to the rest of the bar. Everything had to be lit separately. The grid on the modifier kept the light from spreading everywhere.

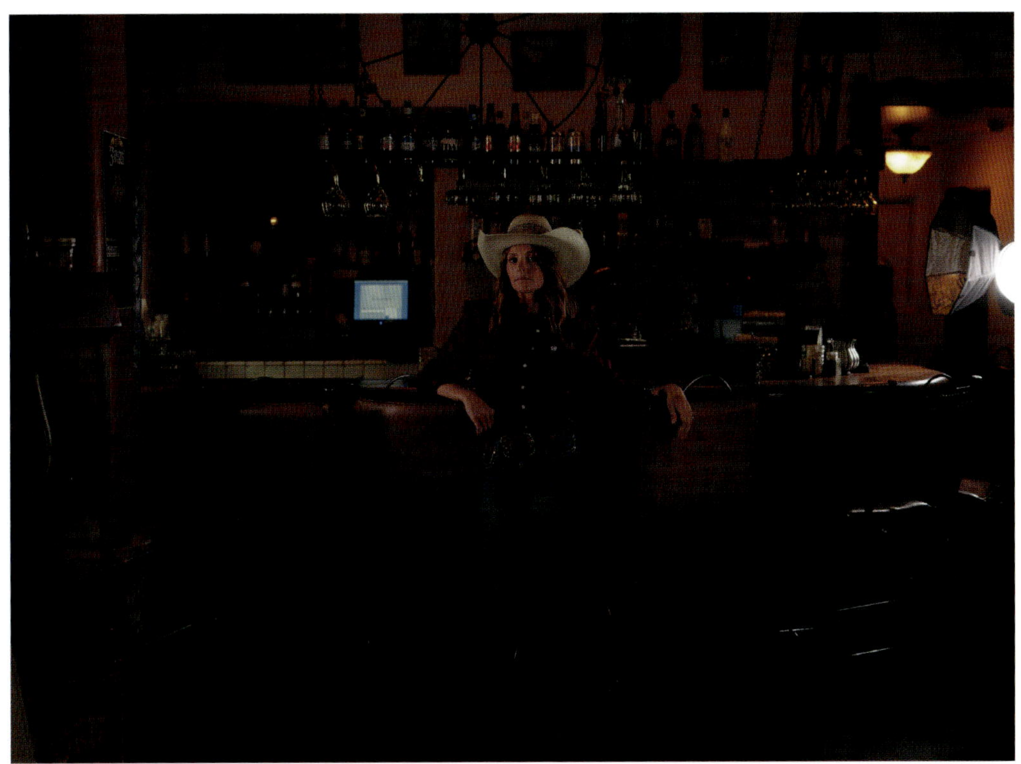

FIGURE 4.16

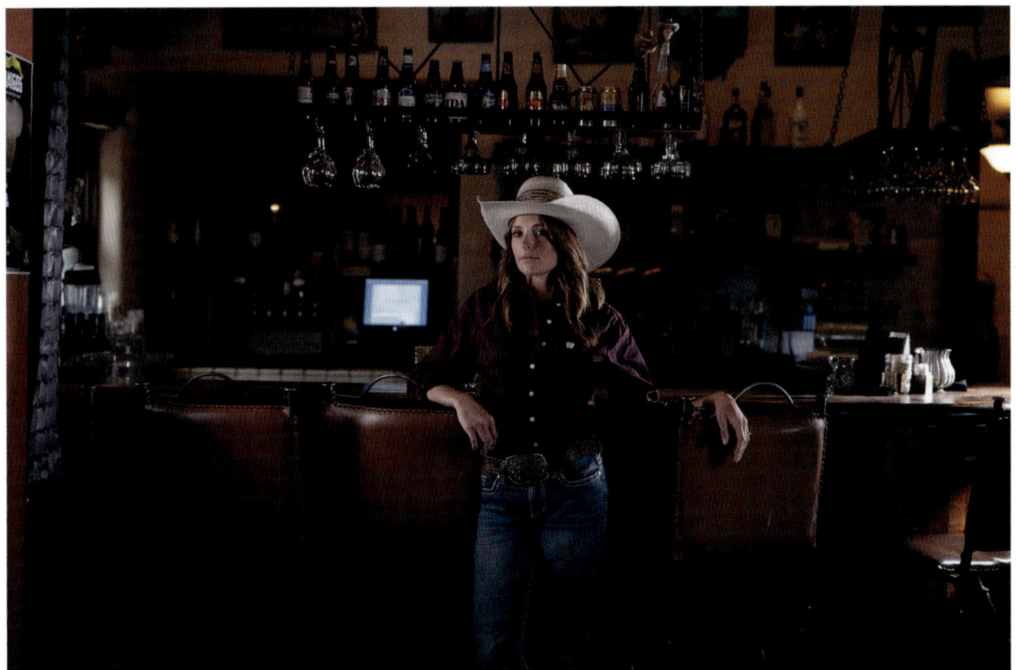

FIGURE 4.17

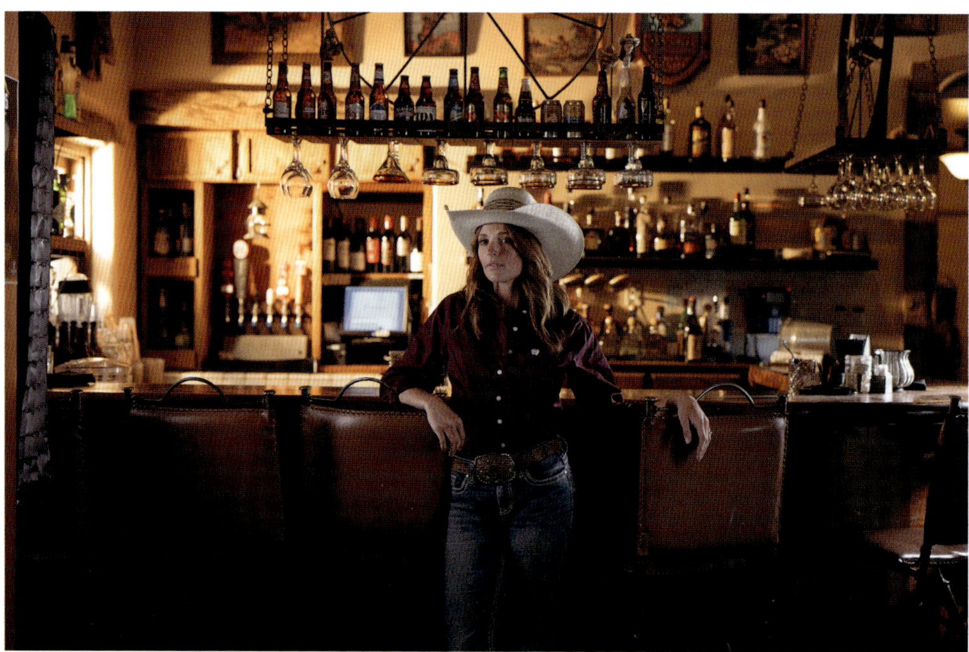

Figure 4.18: To give the bar the mood of afternoon light, we placed a Profoto strobe outside the window, directed it inside, and added an orange gel, or CTO. This is the most important light because it gives the portrait its late afternoon mood and character. But as you can see, the light is too strong. This can be easily fixed by turning down the light or placing a paper towel over the light to further diffuse it.

The last lighting setup was to place a couple of Canon flashes behind the subject, also with grids and blue gels, to lighten up the margarita glasses hanging above her. I chose blue for this light to allow for some contrast and in-camera color grading from the rest of the warm amber light color that dominates the mood. You don't see the blue light influence on its own because I don't have a photo of that, but you can see the results from the hint of blue in the final photo.

One thing to notice is how subtly the use of gels is applied. The gels here add to the overall mood of the bar. My final visual test is to see if I blended the gels with the overall mood properly. I look at the image and ask myself if it is difficult for someone to tell that colored gels were used. It should all look like one cohesive mood. In my book *Picture Perfect Lighting*, I wrote about Circumstantial Light Elements. One of those elements, the last one actually, is called Lighting Reference Point. This refers to a photographer's ability to use gels or any other means to seamlessly blend the light from the environment with the artificial light the photographer added. In this case, the reference I used was the amber bathroom light that you see at the top right corner of the final photo.

That was the only "real" light we turned on in the bar. Since that bathroom light was a warm amber color, I decided to use similarly colored gels to keep that color consistent throughout the bar. If you can control the impulse to use every available color gel that comes in that variety pack, you will gain incredible benefits from being more intentional and strategic regarding your use of gels.

Figure 4.19: For this example, I used just one strobe with a ½ CTO gel. The last example with Hope at the bar required many lights, because I was starting from scratch. But this bar in Toronto was open for business. Had I not used my ½ CTO gel for this portrait, the model's face would have been far too white from the flash, and the mood would no longer make sense. However, with the gel, I could quickly and subtly match the lighting on her face with the overall feel of the rest of the bar. I think it looks quite attractive, and it was simple to do.

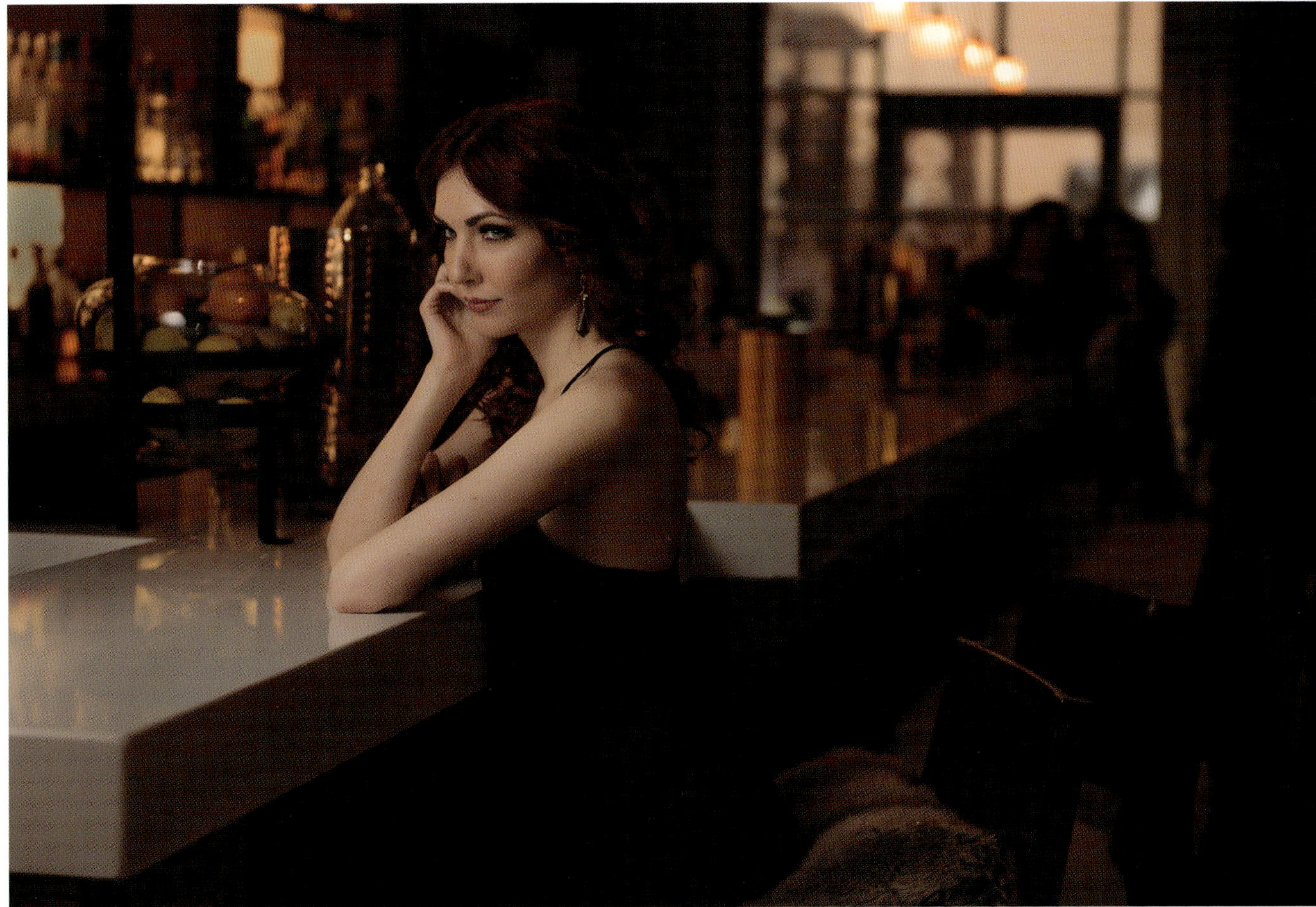

FIGURE 4.19

FLASH FLARING TECHNIQUE

Flash flaring is one of my favorite creative techniques that I use with flashes and gels. You don't need a gel to execute a flash flare, but it could be very smart to use one. Flash flare is created when you point a flash directly and in close proximity to the lens without the lens hood. I usually have the flash pointed straight into my lens within six inches of the front glass element. Depending on the lens being used, the aperture, your ISO, and the power of the flash, you will obtain different results. When implementing this technique, my recommendation is to just start, experiment, and adjust your settings (aperture, ISO, flash power, etc.) until you have the results you like. I discuss this technique more in the next chapter.

Figure 4:20: For this example taken in Ho Chi Minh City, Vietnam, I used a CTO gel to create this vintage effect. It was raining quite hard during the shoot, and we were forced to take cover and wait out the rain. The scene looked depressing and mostly gray. That's what gave me the idea to use the flash flare technique with a CTO gel. I knew that I could turn the scene from what it was into a vintage scene from the past. I didn't have an assistant for this, so I asked for help from my taxi driver. I asked him to hold the Profoto B10 flash with a CTO gel quite close to my lens. He was fascinated, to say the least!

Another Profoto B10 was used to illuminate the model's face under the non la (Vietnamese hat). The flash bulb by

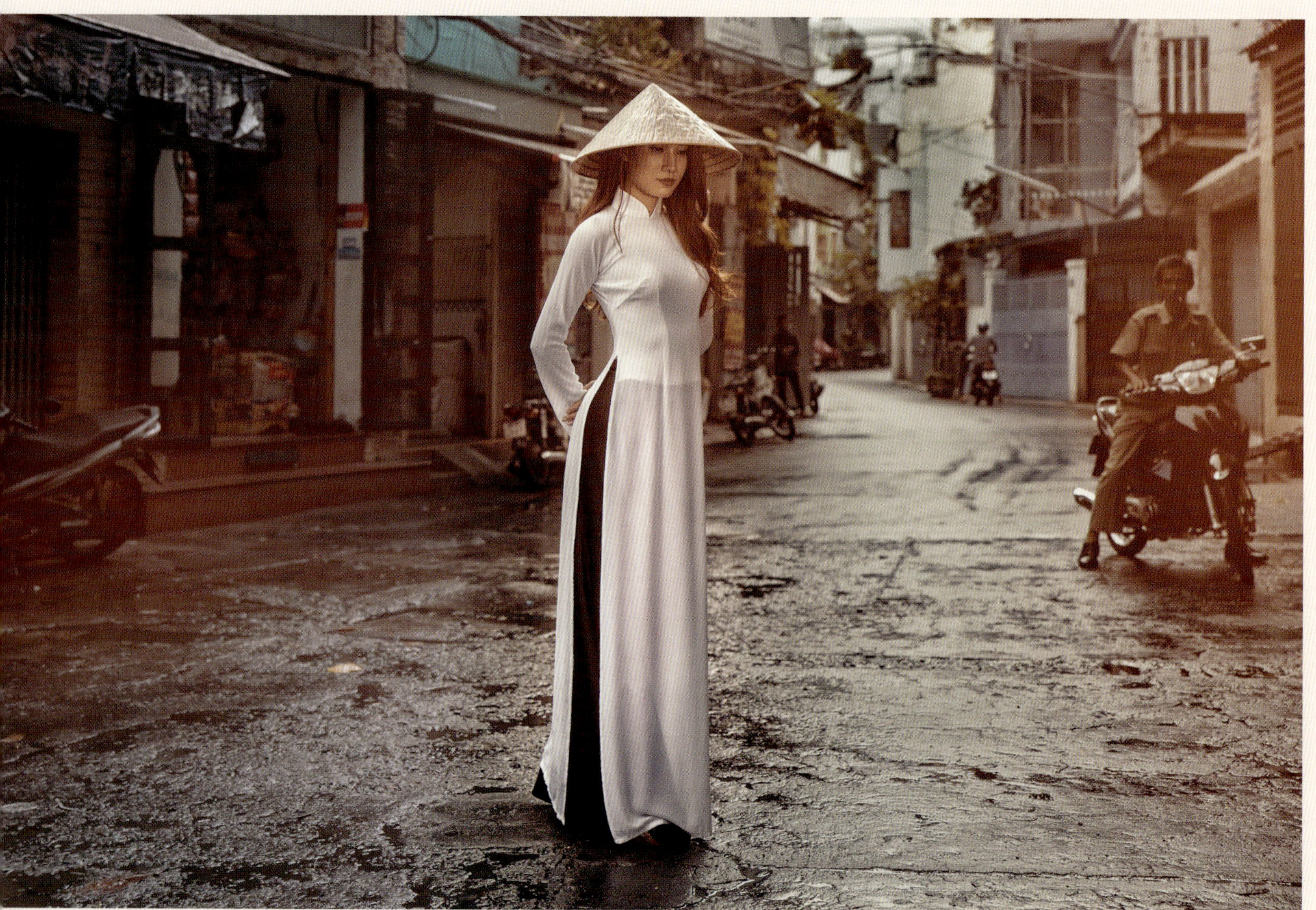

FIGURE 4.20

itself would have been much too harsh, so I asked one of the street vendors selling fruit if she could spare some napkins. The napkins were placed over the flash and held in place by hand to diffuse the light to my heart's desire. Once these two lights were in place, I took the photo, which has become one of my all-time favorite photos that I have ever taken.

To my surprise, when I got back to the hotel, I noticed the man smoking his cigarette sitting on his motorcycle to the right of the frame. What an amazing gift! This all happened naturally, and I laughed, because I couldn't have posed or positioned him better if I had tried.

Notice the subtle orange hue on the edges of the photo. Notice how nicely diffused the light is on her eyes. Without that strobe pointed at her face under the non la, her eyes would have been totally dark. This is why I love using flash so much! You can do things that are otherwise impossible with just natural light. Yes, using flashes is a little more work, but the difference is night and day!

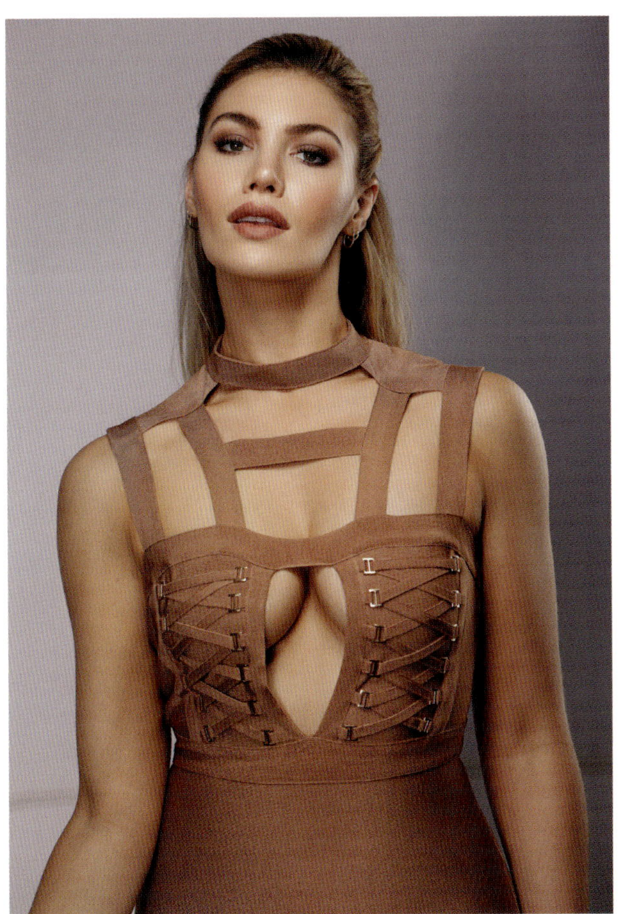

Figure 4.21: Another technique I often use on location or in the studio is to change the color of the background to something a little more interesting. Most of the time, we have white walls or a white seamless paper background in the studio. That's great, and there is nothing wrong with that. However, let's be honest: it can get boring. The solution that I use, and which my clients love, is to add a subtle color to the background. The key word is "subtle." In this case, I used a purple gel on my Profoto strobes pointed only at the background. The model, Meredith, was standing in front of the gelled lights. In order to cover a great deal of the vertical paper as evenly as possible, I used a Profoto 1x4 strip box on both sides. The light on the left had more power than the light on the right. This is by design. Not only did I add a hint of purple to the background, but by having different power settings on each light, I also achieved a nice gradient.

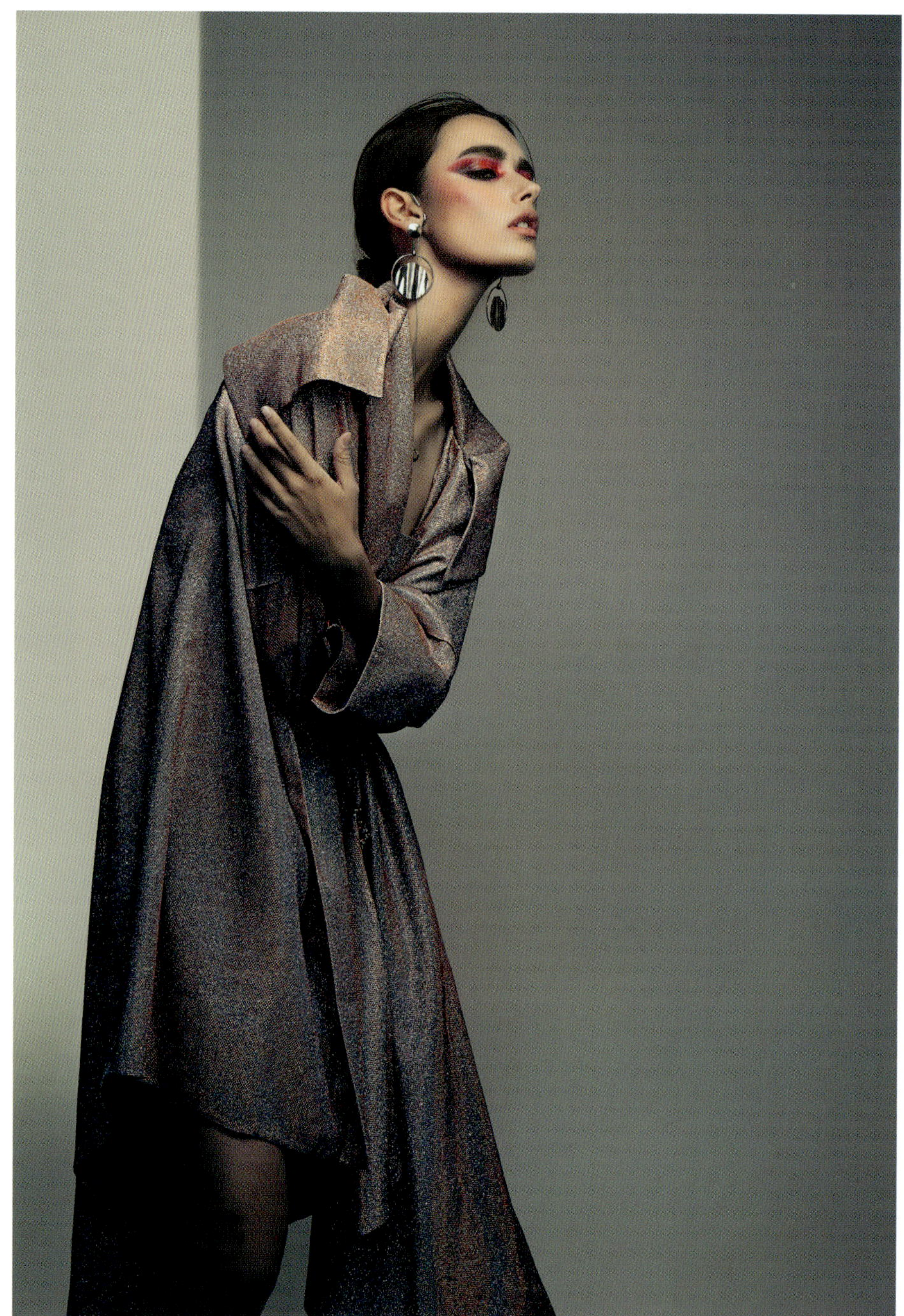

Figure 4.22: I admit this is a bit more advanced, but it's not difficult. I wanted to add this example to inspire you to try it and not be afraid of its technical nature or the multiple lights needed to create this photo. The first thing you should know is that the background is nothing more than a roll of nine-foot seamless white paper. That's it.

Figure 4.23: Here is the behind-the-scenes shot of the setup for this shoot. The model is wearing a different outfit, but the setup didn't change. Since this was shot for a fashion editorial, the background and setup must remain the same to keep the story cohesive. But, as you can see, it's nothing more than ordinary background paper. The final photo looks the way it does due to the beauty of properly used gels.

Okay, back to the final photo (Figure 4.22). Four lights were used to take this photograph, and each light had a very specific purpose.

Light #1: The big light was behind me using a six-foot umbrella. This light's purpose is to illuminate the entire scene, but mostly the dress. No gel was used for this light.

Light #2: I used two colored gels on top of each other to illuminate just the background. Using two gels helped create a deeper color. The light was placed behind the model Sam and to the right. We used a relatively large parabolic modifier for this.

Light #3: The third light was right next to me to create the vertical strip that you see at camera left. We created this strip by mounting an Aputure Spotlight Mount to a Profoto B1. For this light, we used a single gel of the same color as the background. Remember that the background looks darker and more saturated because we doubled up on the same color gel to create a deeper color.

Light #4: The last light was a Profoto B1 with a beauty dish over Sam's head. That light has a ½ CTO gel to create a warm look on her skin. This also creates a complementary color in the photograph.

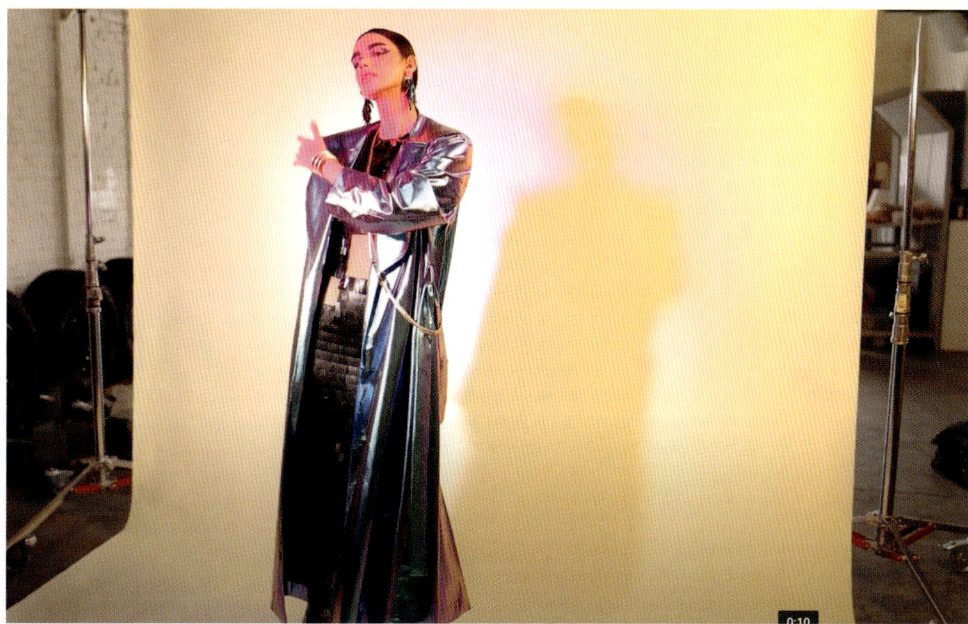

FIGURE 4.23

Finally, color grading was applied in post-production to clean up the edges and refine the light colors. It sounds complicated, but it isn't. Every light had a very clear job. We did not add any more lights than we needed. The key to creating a photo like this is very simple: practice. I became bored with all the white seamless paper backgrounds that I had to use for fashion editorials. To entertain myself, I began to explore different ways to bring visual interest to that white paper. I didn't need a model or anyone else to practice with, since I was just trying to make the background more interesting. After a bit of practice, suddenly I knew that I could turn any white wall on location or any white seamless paper in the studio into something very interesting! I love it!

These next two photos show the power of experimenting with complementary colors for a stronger look or analogous colors for a subtler look. See **Figure 4.24.**

Figure 4.25: The gel technique used here is a very subtle one. Gels are usually overdone and used in such a way that they take over the image completely. But gels can do more than alert the viewer that gels were used. How about adding gels to create a subtle mood in a simple portrait? If done correctly, the results can be understated but stunning.

To turn a simple portrait into something a little spicier, I positioned the model Renee's hair with both sides down. On one side of her hair, I used a small Profoto softbox with a blue gel, and on the other side the setup was repeated but with a red gel. Now that her hair had subtle color on each side, I needed to put clean white light on her face. I placed

COLOR RELATIONSHIPS

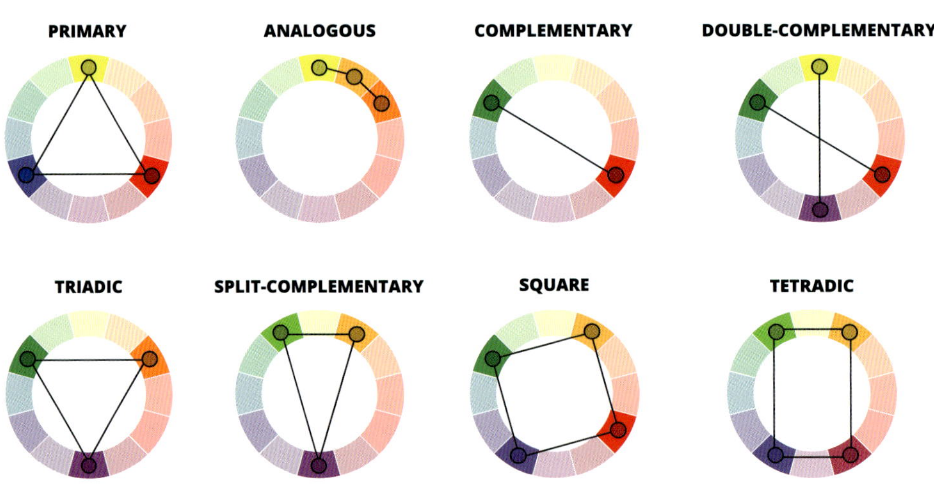

FIGURE 4.24

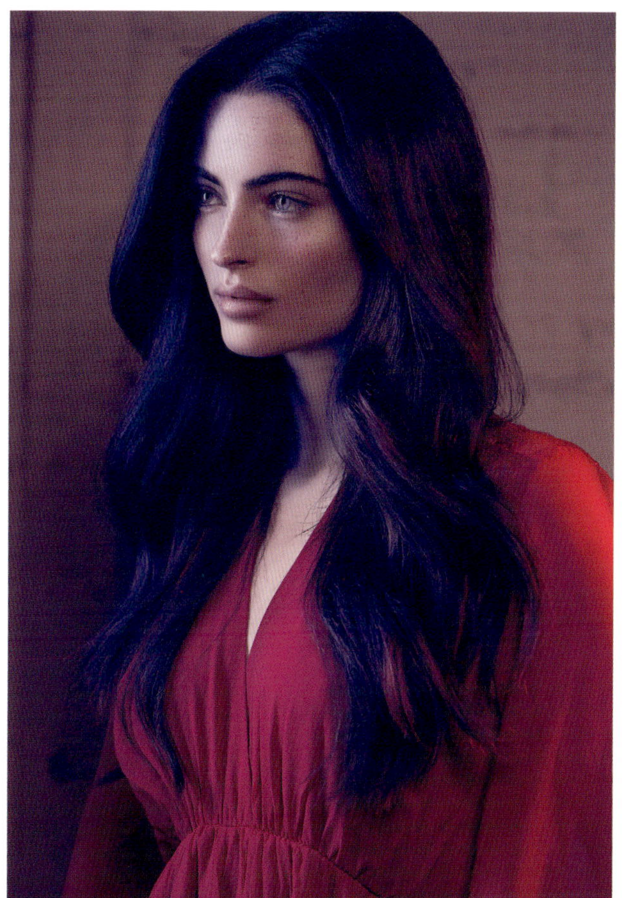

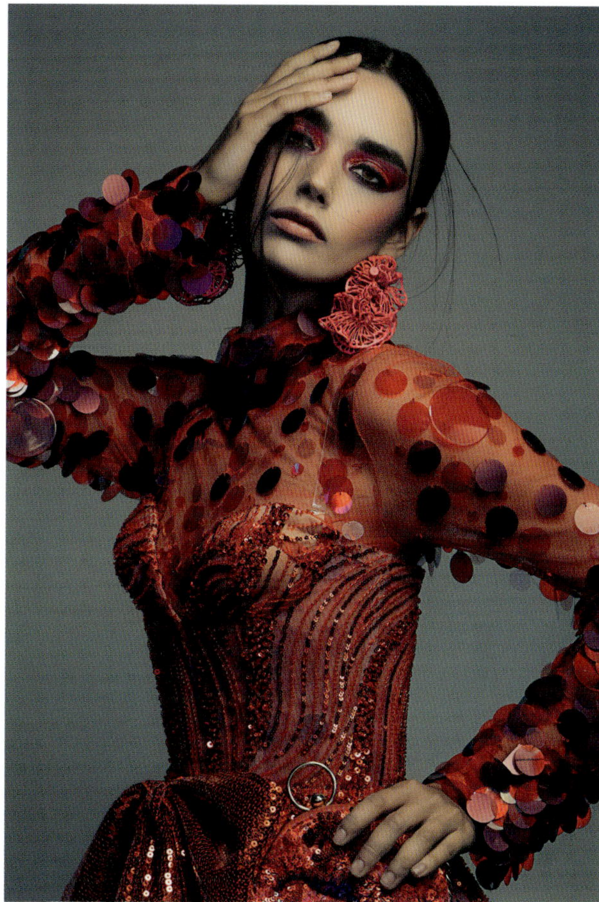

a Profoto 1x4 strip box with a grid on it and gently turned her head into that light. This three-light setup is easy to do, and the results are surprisingly beautiful!

Figure 4.26: This is an example of a very similar setup as the last image, but this time I used analogous colors to make the gel effect subtle but still effective. Just as last time, both sides of the model Sam have a strobe with a dark turquoise color. You can see it if you look closely at her cheeks by her ears. Even though it's very gently done, the effects of the color are all about the mood of this portrait. Without the subtle use of these gels, the photo would be nothing more than a simple portrait with daylight balanced light and a white seamless paper background. The main difference between this example and the last one (Figure 4.25) is the modifier used to illuminate the face. For this example, I used a Profoto white beauty dish in front of and over Sam's head to contour her beautiful face.

Figure 4.27: Another technique that you can add to your gel arsenal to create mood is to do selective gel placement. This is simply when you add a gel to just a part of the body or face to create a different mood altogether. For this photo, there was a bare strobe bulb with a red gel sitting on the floor pointed toward the background to make it red. Remember to keep the studio as dark as possible when doing these techniques, or it won't work. The second strobe was a Profoto B10 with a blue gel. This light was flagged with a black flag to block the blue light from spilling over her face. We adjusted the black flag to block the light until only her forehead was illuminated by the blue light.

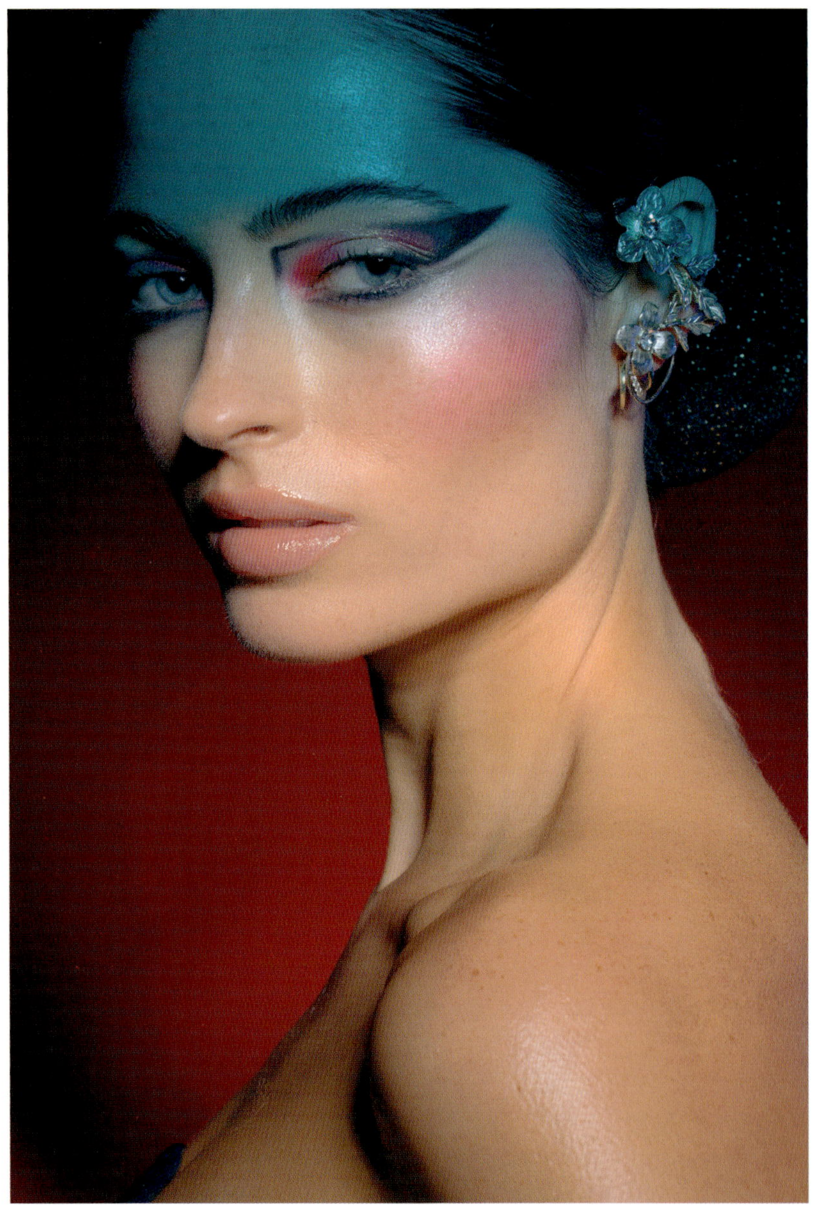

FIGURE 4.27

Figure 4.28: Speaking of flags to block the light, this is an incredible technique that causes people to think that you are some sort of magician with light. When you block the light from strobes, you need to do it as closely to the subject as possible to make the shadow edges crisper. If you hold the object to block the light too close to the strobe, you will not have clean results.

For this photo of actress Meredith, we blocked the light from the left side of her face, but we went the opposite way with her body to give the photo a balanced feel. So we added light to the right side of her face and only her left shoulder. Flagging lights will go a long way toward impressing your clients with a final look that seems very hard to achieve. It's very simple to block the light and create shapes with the objects you are using to block it. This technique works best with headshots. The more of the person's body you show, the more difficult it is to achieve a good result.

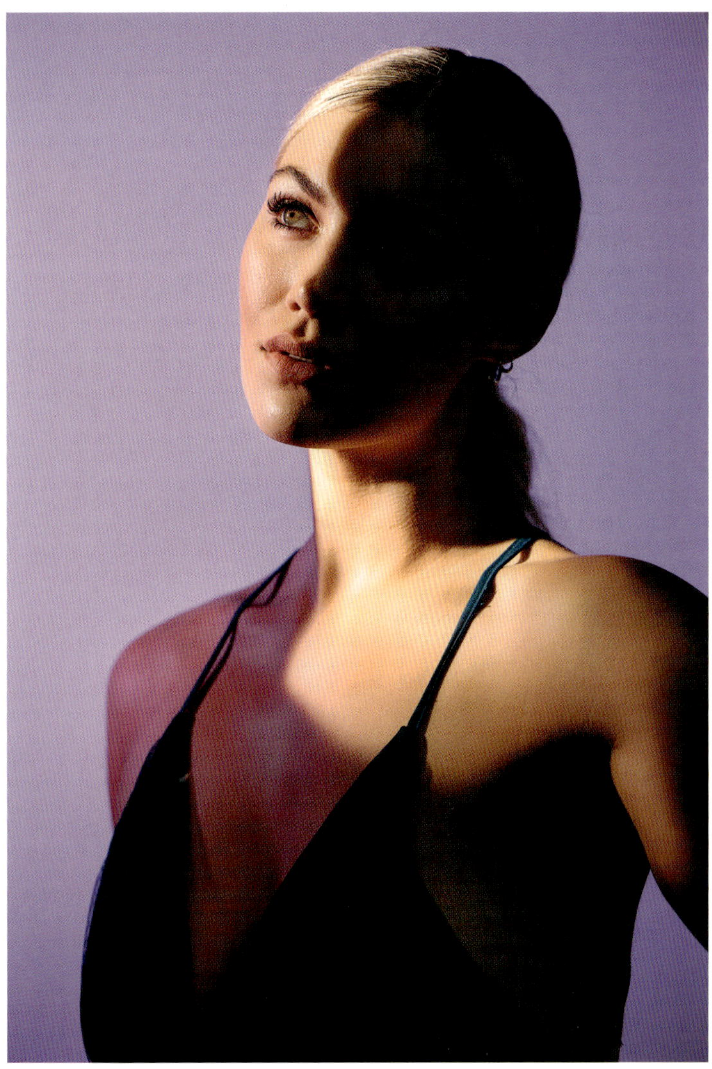

FIGURE 4.28

Create Mood by Shooting Light Through Objects

Shooting light through objects to create a mood with a light/shadow graphic is nothing new, but it is underused. Why? Because implementing this technique adds complexity to the shot. Now, you must contend with correct shadow placement being in the right place on the face or part of the body. The biggest challenge for photographers first attempting this technique is to understand the relationship between light placement and the object you are shooting that light through, relative to the subject.

SHADOW DEFINITION CHEAT SHEET

Defined shadow edges: To create highly defined shadow edges when shooting through an object, the strobe must be modified with a hard reflector to make the light as hard as possible. Next, the object that creates the design or graphic must be as close to the subject as possible.

Figure 4.29: You can see here that the light beam is focused. You can achieve this by placing a grid or egg crate over your modifier to narrow the spread of light. You want as many direct rays of light hitting your object as possible in order to obtain the most out of its design. Lastly, the object itself must be as close as possible to your subject to achieve shadows with highly defined edges.

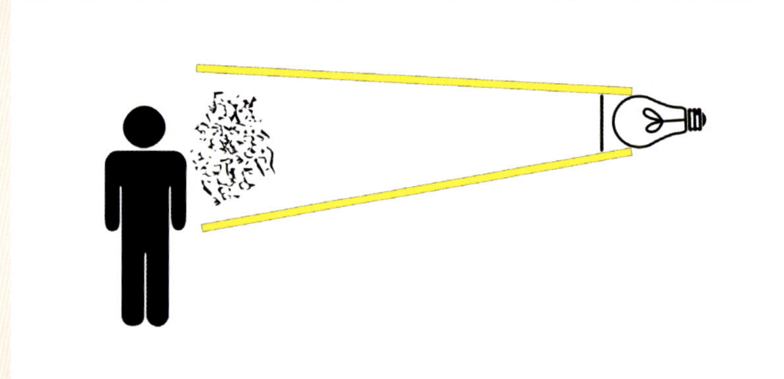

FIGURE 4.29

Soft shadow edges: To create soft shadow edges, the object you are going to fire the light through must be closer to the light source and further away from your subject. You must experiment with the distance back and forth until you obtain the desired shadow edge softness. See **Figure 4.30**. You can also see that the light spread is not as narrow or focused as the light in Figure 4.29.

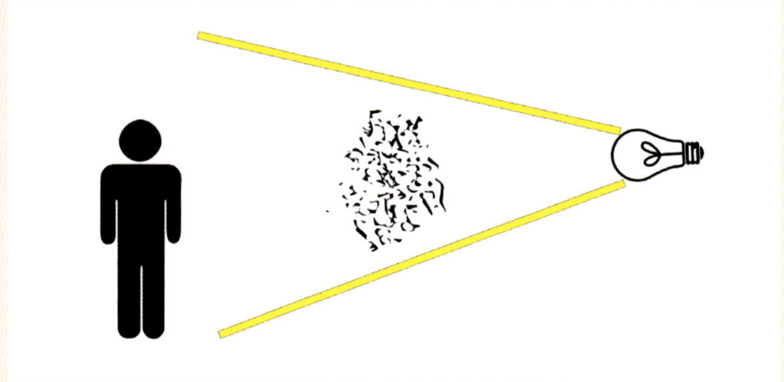

FIGURE 4.30

Figure 4.31: Let's begin with a photo of my beautiful friend and Miss Universe 2022, R'Bonney Nola Gabriel. I drew inspiration from her jacket's fringe design. This was a very simple setup. I asked R'Bonney to lift up her arm to allow the fringe to cover only part of her face. Next, I set up a couple of Stella Pro Reflex S lights eight feet away with a spot attachment to control the spread of light. That's it! This photo has so much more mood than without the fringe shadows on her face. This is a simple technique with very effective results.

Figure 4.32: This photo was mostly created by the sun's rays passing through an ordinary metal bookshelf near a window. In this case, the sun was providing enough light to create the strength in the shadows that I was looking for. The key to making this type of light work is to add a strobe that provides big and soft light to lift the shadows throughout the scene. Without the strobe, the photo would still look good, but it wouldn't have that extra wow factor. This photo has the strobe bouncing against a wall opposite Meredith. However, in the next example, you will see that the results from the strobe lifting the shadows are much better.

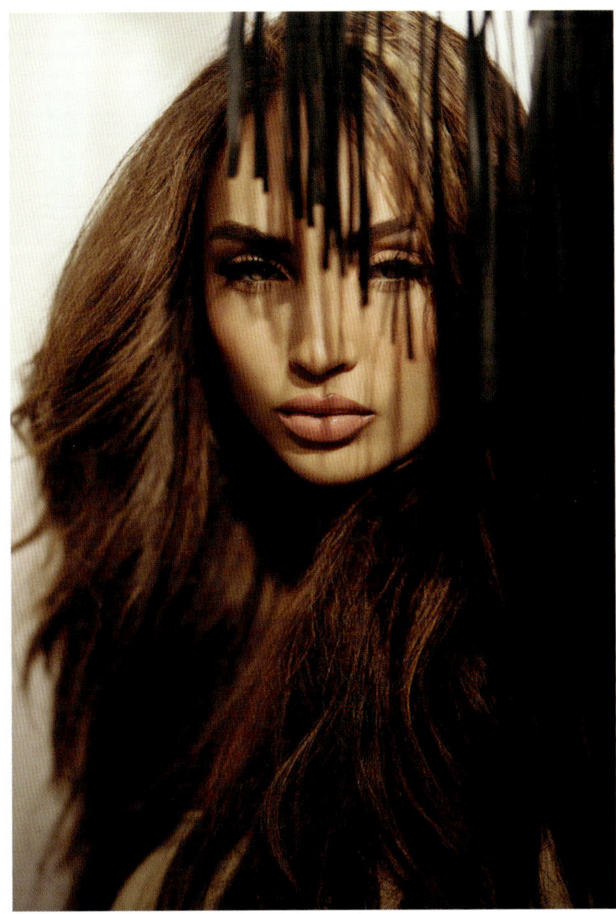

FIGURE 4.31

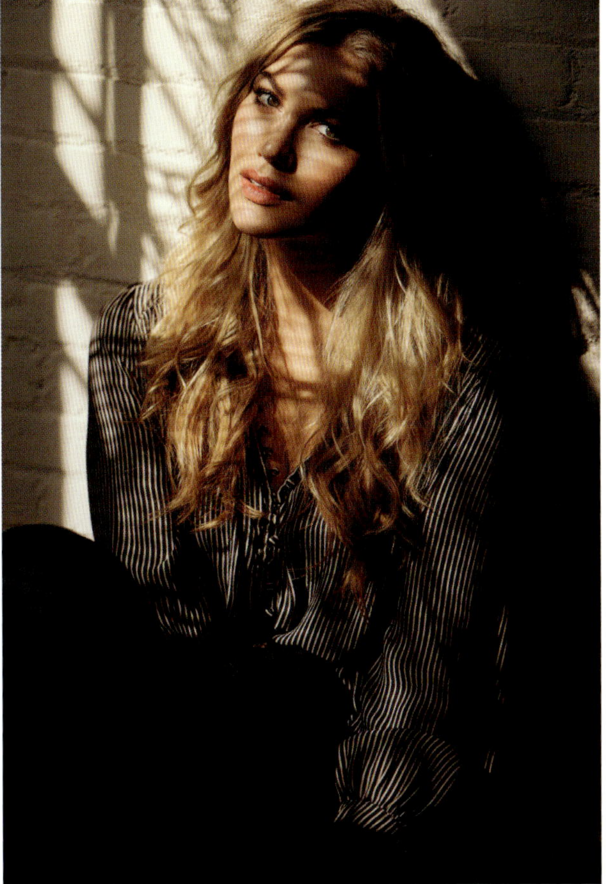

FIGURE 4.32

Figure 4.33: This is a book about flash and portable strobes. Therefore, it is important to me to relay the information to you that will make your photographs reach much higher standards. This photo was part of a fashion shoot that I photographed in Australia. The sun provided the wonderful graphic lighting on the wall from the window, but the rest of the scene was lit by my flash. What does the strobe actually do? Notice that the models are wearing black outfits. Without the strobe, no visible details would be able to be seen in their clothes. That's bad for business in fashion photography. The strobe softened the shadow side of the walls to allow for some detail to show through.

In this case, the strobe was shot through a large umbrella with a diffuser. This technique is simple. Put the flash on Manual mode, and crank it up or down until you achieve the desired results. You don't want to overpower the shadows with the fill light. You just want a gentle lift so that the photo doesn't lose its mood.

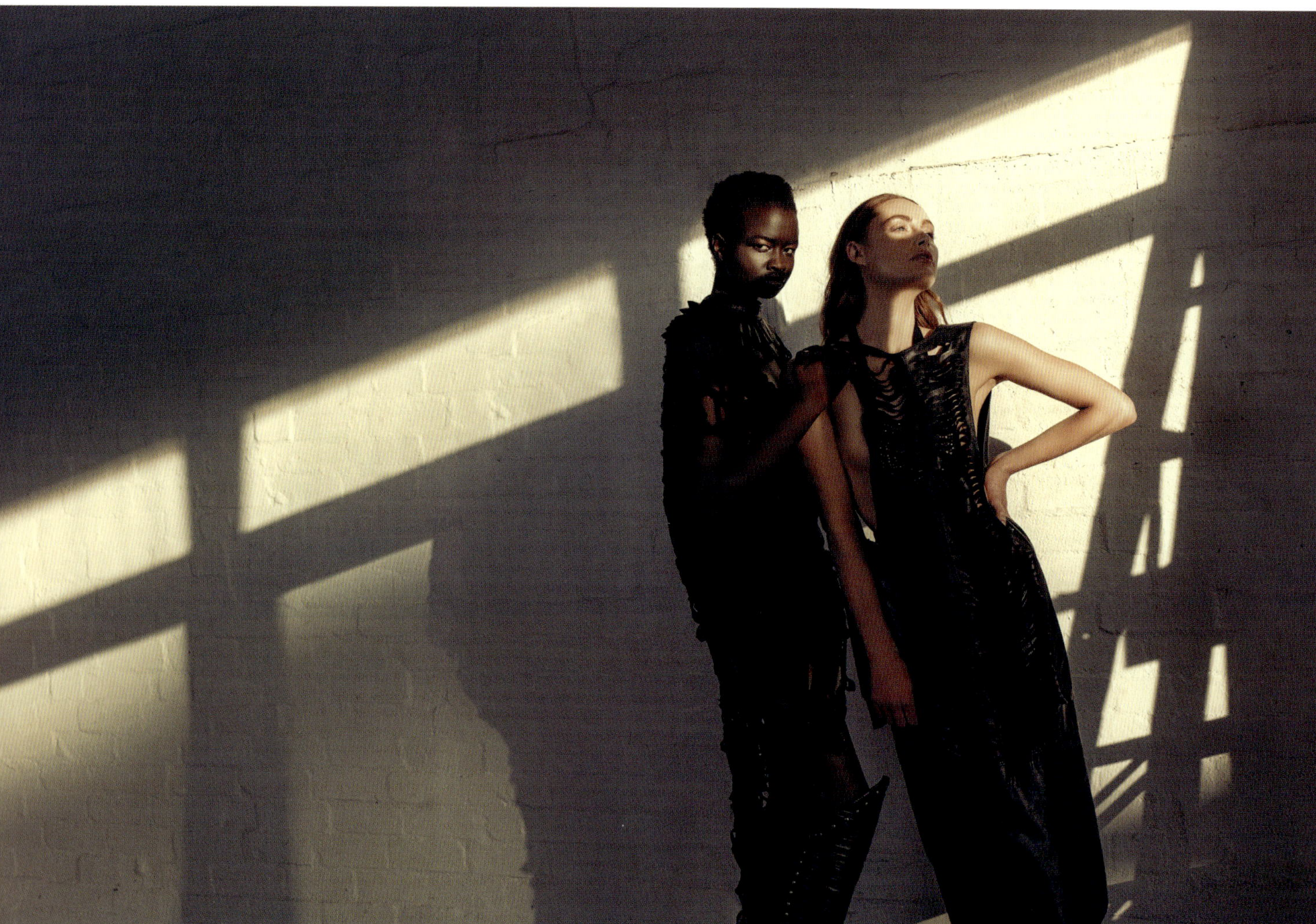

Figure 4.34: For the final technique in this chapter, I want to show you how to add mood to a simple white wall or seamless paper background by shooting light through a GOBO (which is short for **Go B**etween **O**ptics). A GOBO is a small disc with a cutout that creates a pattern when you shine a strong light through it. You have probably seen one before. There are GOBOs that are patterns of trees/leaves, windowpanes, stripes, and many other designs.

For this photo, I used an Aputure Spotlight Mount with a drop-in to insert the GOBO. When you turn on the light, you use the focusing ring on the device to project the pattern on any surface (like the wall here) with any degree of clarity or sharpness you wish to have. Once the pattern was projected on the background, I used another Profoto light with a 1x4 strip box with a grid to illuminate the clothing separately. The point of the strip box was to lift the shadows to show a bit of detail.

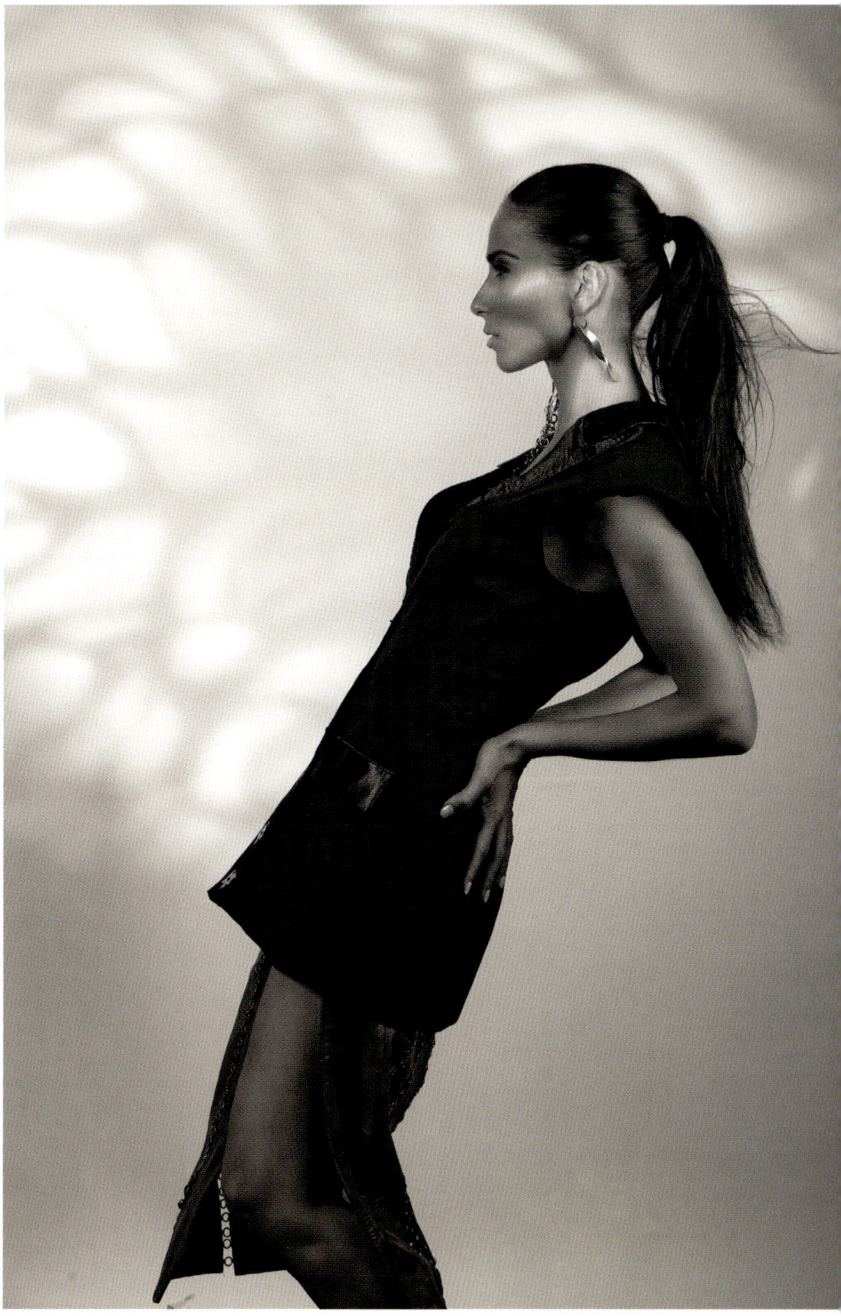

FIGURE 4.34

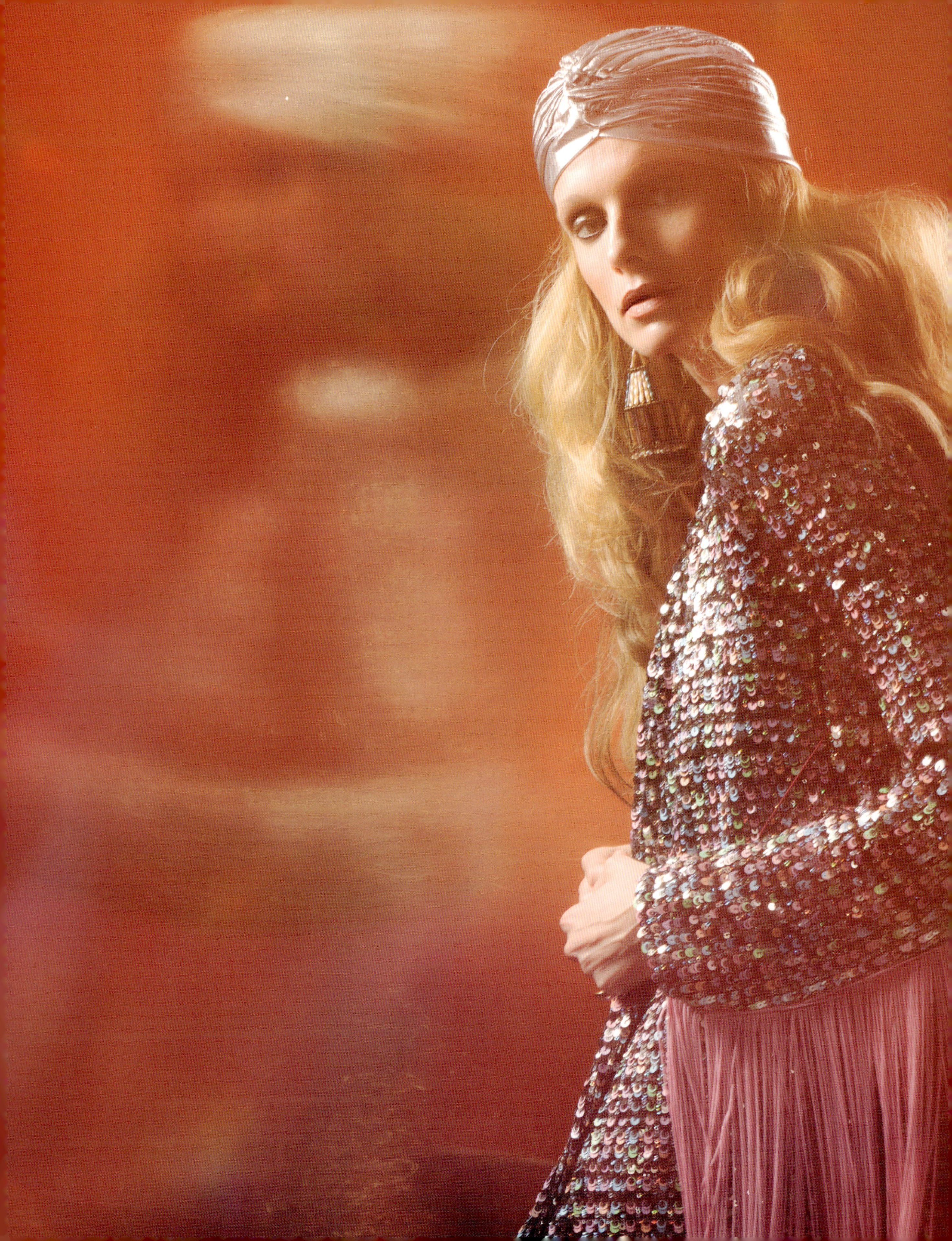

Chapter 5

Effects with Flash

Special effects are similar to a dessert after your meal. They are fun to create, and people are enamored of them. However, you don't want to overdo the effects, either. The reason is simple: Effects with strobes are different, and most people are not used to seeing them in photographs. Most photos that people see are clean, simple, and well lit. The two main characteristics that make a "normal" photo special are likely the location and the styling of the model.

With strobes, though, the results are not what people expect to see. That is why it's so shocking to people when they see the photo straight out of the camera. With special effects, what you see is definitely not what you get! I realize that flash can be perceived as complicated, and adding special effects to your work using flash seems out of most people's comfort zone. However, as with everything in life, a little practice goes a long way.

The effects I'll cover in this chapter are truly not difficult, but they do require a little knowledge about how these techniques work. Once you understand it, it's all downhill from there. But a word of warning: What you don't want to do is to think that you understand the principles these techniques require and then attempt them during an actual shoot without a lot of practice beforehand. Understanding a technique in theory is very different from really experiencing and knowing that technique firsthand. Understanding how a piano is played is not the same as your own fingers playing a piece by Chopin.

These techniques and effects are fun, but they can also be crucial tools you can use when you need to turn things around during a bland shoot.

FIVE TECHNIQUES TO CREATE SPECIAL EFFECTS WITH FLASH

- Freezing Motion Via Flash Duration Speed
- Multiple (Multi) / Stroboscopic Mode
- Dragged Shutter
- Multiple Exposures
- Flash Flaring

Freezing Motion Via Flash Duration Speed

Understanding all the math behind flash duration speed is not only too technical for this book, but it is also unnecessary. What you do need to understand is the basics of how it works without going down a rabbit hole of math, charts, fractions, and inverse relationships. My goal is to make you comfortable with the concepts so that you can use and apply them right away.

There are two types of measurements that companies use to describe their lights' flash duration speed. They are "t0.5" and "t0.1"—let's look at each one individually.

If you are asking yourself, "Why do I need to know these measurements?," the reason is because they tell you how much freezing power the lights have at a particular power setting.

Let's say you are trying to completely freeze a moving person or object in the air with your camera, but the object always appears to have motion blur. Well, that can be very frustrating, and you might think you are doing something wrong. But you are not. The reason behind the motion blur could be a lack of freezing power based on the type of lights you are using and at what power setting you are using them. That's why you need to know what the t0.5 and t0.1 measurements are for your lights. It will help you avoid a headache.

t0.5 Flash Duration Speed Measurement

t0.5 is a measurement used by flash manufacturers to let the photographer know how fast their lights go from zero output to peak output, and back down to 50% of peak output. So, the flash spec might say something like this: "Flash duration speed t0.5 = 1/32,000." What does that mean? It means that it takes 1/32,000 of a second for the strobe to go from off to full power to 50% down from full power. That entire sequence takes 1/32,000 of a second. That's quite impressive.

The problem is that t0.5 is measured at 50% down from its peak power. That means 50% of the light is left trailing until the flash is completely off again. That's a lot! If you try to freeze movement, that 50% trail of light can really give you a headache, because that 50% of light from its peak power is still being picked up by your camera's sensor, thus creating a blur. That is not ideal! Your goal is to completely freeze something moving fast and not have it become a blur. So, why do companies use this type of measurement? While it is a legitimate measurement, the main reason manufacturers tout this specification is because it sounds better (than the t0.1 measurement, which we'll discuss next). Think about it: What could you possibly not freeze completely when the light's flash duration speed is an incredible 1/32,000 of a second?! You can think of a flash duration speed as the light's version of the shutter speed.

t0.1 Flash Duration Speed Measurement

t0.1 is a measurement that tells the photographer how fast the light can travel from zero output to full power, and back down to just 10% of the peak output. Dealing with 10% of light trailing at the tail end is much better than dealing with 50% of light trailing at the end. With 90% of the light completely gone, there is almost nothing left for your camera's sensor to record.

If a strobe's t0.5 flash duration speed is measured at 1/32,000 of a second, this means that its t0.1 measurement will usually be quite a bit less than half of that—in this case, approximately 1/10,000 of a second. Another example: if the light's t0.5 measurement is 1/18,000 of a second, the t0.1 measurement would be 1/6,000 of a second. Instead of trying to calculate this perfectly, the easy way to do it is simple: just remember that the t0.1 is usually less than half of the t0.5. Therefore, if you really want to know how long the strobe takes to go from off to full power and back down to almost zero output, consider the t 0.1 number and *not* the t0.5 number.

Flash Duration Speed Depends on Your Power Setting

The freezing power from your flashes depends on how much power they are putting out. If you put your flash at full power, it is naturally going to take longer for the energy to dissipate. A flash at full power will decrease the flash duration speed significantly. But if you lower the flash output to a weaker setting, the flash will be able to fire and dissipate much faster, giving you a significant increase in freezing power. Flash power and its corresponding flash duration speed have an inverse relationship. The higher the power, the slower the flash duration speed. The lower the power, the faster the flash duration speed.

If you would like to see the exact flash duration speed for each power setting of your flash, the documentation provided online from the manufacturer should tell you exactly that. However, for the purposes of this book, just know that if you are trying to freeze something and it's not freezing, your flash could be too far from the object or your power setting could be too high. If you need more power from your flashes for exposure purposes, simply gang up two or three flashes together and lower the output of each to increase the flash duration speed. Ganging up your flashes will help with the exposure, and it will keep the faster duration speed at lower flash output settings.

Figure 5.1: This photo would be impossible to create with only natural light. This image required the help of a very fast duration speed from my strobes to completely freeze each string on the model Kiara's dress. Kiara had to move very quickly to cause the strings to move in this way. I had to play with the flash's power output by lowering it until I could see every string completely frozen in the air. Even if my camera's shutter speed was not incredibly fast, I knew that I could count on the flash's fast duration speed to do the freezing for me.

That's important because, when shooting with strobes, you are still limited by the camera's flash sync speed. On most mirrorless cameras, the flash sync speed is either 1/250 or 1/200, and that's not very fast. Therefore, you must rely on the flash duration speed for freezing motion, not your camera's shutter speed. Trying to bypass this shutter speed limitation to freeze a fast-moving object would force you to try to use your camera's and flash's High Speed Sync setting. In most cases, this would fail because when using High Speed Sync, you weaken the power of the flash significantly, resulting in a dark exposure.

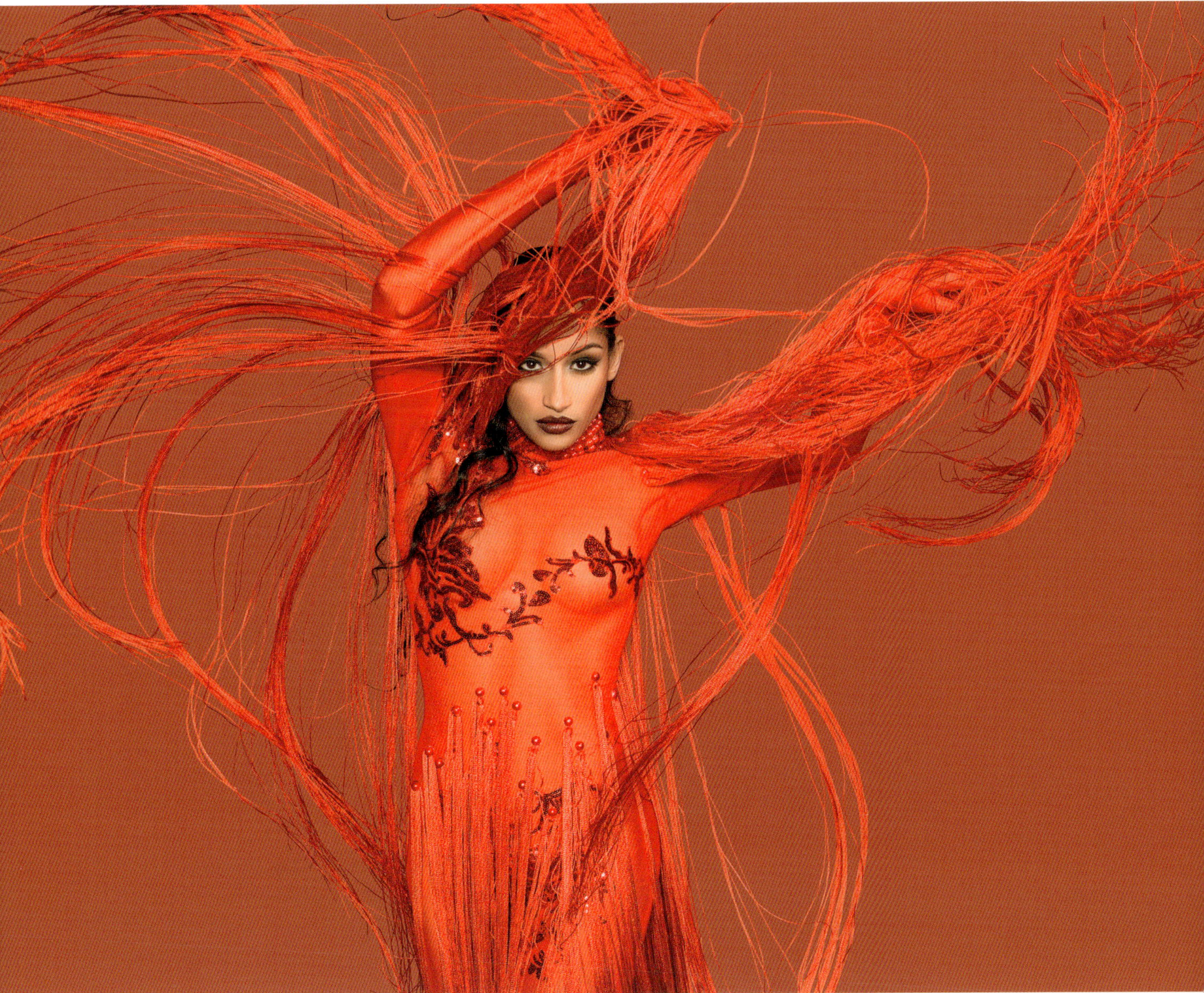

FIGURE 5.1

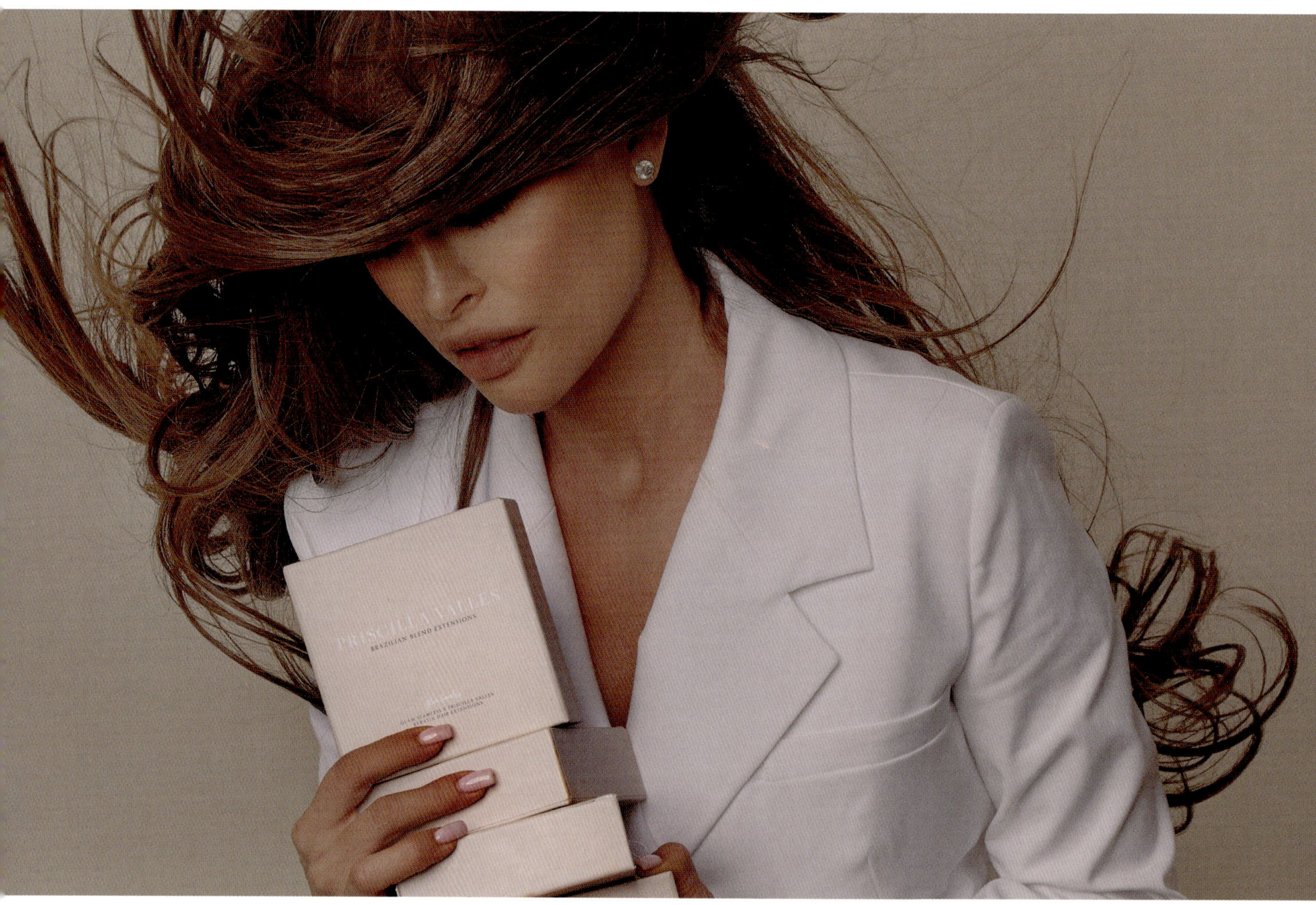

Figure 5.2: This image comes from a sequence of photographs that I shot for a product campaign (hair extensions) that took advantage of flash duration speed as the core photographic technique. We wanted to create a dynamic photo with hair movement, and we wanted high energy and action to make the photo much more powerful.

The model had to move her head as quickly as she could while standing above a powerful fan, so that the fan's wind directly hit her hair and lifted it up into the air. There were a lot of fast-moving parts, but it was not a problem for the flash duration speed. I put the flash as close to her hair as possible and started to experiment with the flash power until I found the freezing ability that I was looking for. Look closely and you can see every strand of hair perfectly frozen, though it was all moving very quickly. That's really cool if you ask me! Arm yourself with all of these tools, and you will not be limited by anything.

Multiple (Multi) / Stroboscopic Mode

Multiple/Multi, or Stroboscopic, mode is usually found on modern hot shoe flashes and less so on portable strobes. Stroboscopic is a setting that most people don't even know about, or if they do, most people have never used it. However, it is a flash setting that can provide you with the most impressive results. Stroboscopic is basically multiple bursts of light that are all recorded in a single exposure. By the way, different brands have different names for this mode/function. Some call it Multi, some call it Stroboscopic. But rest assured that if you have a relatively modern hot shoe flash, it will have this ability.

When done correctly, you can create an exciting image that shows a dynamic sequence of movements all in one image—for example, the motions of a dancer, a drummer, a sword fighter, a fencer, etc. This technique is simple to explain, but since the concept may be new or unusual to you, it will take a few practice runs to understand it and apply it seamlessly.

Four Settings You Need to Know for Multi/Stroboscopic Mode

Hertz (Hz): The first decision to make is how many flash bursts per second that you want. This is measured in Hertz, or Hz. So, if you choose 5 Hz, this means 5 flash pulses per second. If you have 12 Hz, this would be 12 pulses per second. As you can imagine, the higher the number of flash pulses per second, the harder the flash must work. To accomplish this, the flash limits how powerful each pulse will be so it can satisfy your decision about the number of flash pulses per second. Even though this sounds very mathematical, it's actually quite simple. It's just about how many pulses per second you want. That's all.

Number of Flashes: This is the second decision you must make. This is simply asking you how many total flashes you want. The key word here is "total." If you want 10 total flash pulses, the flash will fire a total of 10 times throughout your exposure. Of course, you will need to have a long enough shutter speed to accommodate the number of total flashes you want. More on this in a moment.

Power: This setting is asking you how powerful you want each flash pulse to be. This number is measured in a fraction, such as 1/16 or 1/32. The highest flash power you can reach is 1/1, and the lowest can be around 1/256 or lower, depending on your flash model. As mentioned above, when using Multi or Stroboscopic flash mode, most likely you won't be able to set the flash to full power per pulse, because flashes simply cannot repeatedly put out that kind of power, quickly recycle, and do it again and again, multiple times per second. It is just not possible.

Exposure Time (Shutter Speed): For this setting, you have to use the most basic math from elementary school. Your shutter speed setting is important because the shutter must stay open for the entire duration you picked for the total number of flashes divided by their frequency per second (Hz). Let's say you selected 10 total flashes at a frequency of 5 pulses per second (5 Hz). What is 10 divided by 5? The answer is 2. Therefore, your shutter speed should be a minimum of 2 seconds in order to execute your stroboscopic flash settings properly. Here is the formula:

$$\frac{\#\ of\ Flashes}{Frequency\ (Hz)} = Minimum\ Exposure\ Time\ (Seconds)$$

To apply the formula again with another example:

$$\frac{30}{10\ (Hz)} = 3\ seconds$$

In this case, we selected 30 total flashes at 10 pulses per second. So, 30 divided by 10 equals 3 seconds. Set your shutter speed to 3 seconds and fire! That's not so difficult, agree?

HOW TO BEST EXECUTE STROBOSCOPIC FLASH

Setup: Much like using colored gels (discussed in the previous chapter), the stroboscopic flash technique also works best with a black background in a dark environment. You want to eliminate as much ambient light as possible, because it will contaminate the final result. When I am shooting these kinds of images, I will go as far as wearing a black shirt to eliminate any unwanted light reflections. The only light you want your sensor to record is the light from the pulses of your flash. That's all.

Settings: How do you know what settings to choose? This will require some experimentation. Remember that if you choose a high frequency of pulses per second (Hz), this will prevent you from firing your flashes at more powerful outputs. To fix this, simply gang two or three flashes to work together. The more flashes that you have firing at the same time, the more power you can achieve. The frequency per second and the number of total flashes will depend on what you are trying to capture. There is no better way to figure this out than to run some trials, then make adjustments as you go to obtain the perfect photo. Even with a significant amount of experience using this technique, I still experiment and make adjustments by trial and error until I'm happy with the result.

Communication: This technique requires quite a lot of communication between you and your subject. You want to make it clear how to move, how fast to make the movement, and to make sure that your client stays within your focal plane so that they stay in focus during the entire movement. In my experience, this kind of clear communication will go a long way toward nailing the shot.

Figure 5.3: This photo embodies the reason why we should learn these obscure techniques. It is a very powerful image. However, it is powerful only because you can see and almost feel the incredible and precise movements of a trained ballerina's footwork. The only way to show this sequence of highly choreographed movements is through the use of the Multi or Stroboscopic flash function.

For this image, since both of the dancer's legs are equally important, it was clear that two flashes were needed: one for each leg. I didn't want her legs lit directly from the front. Therefore, I positioned the flashes behind her—one on each side of her, directed at her legs at 45-degree angles.

Figure 5.4: This is a screen grab from a video to show you exactly what the setup looked like. It is very simple actually! The camera settings were ISO 160, f/7.1, 1.25 seconds. The total number of flashes was set to 5, and the frequency (Hz) was 4 pulses per second, or 4 Hz.

Had those two flashes been used in a more "normal" way, the resulting photo would have been standard and expected, with no wow factor. Turn on this Multi mode, though, and the results from the same flashes are now incredible!

Figure 5.5: This photo had the exact same setup as the previous example. The main difference was in the movement. For this photo, I had the dancer, Ellie, take a step back as she repeatedly tapped her tutu to lift and distribute the baby talc that we had laid on top of it to create another layer of visual interest.

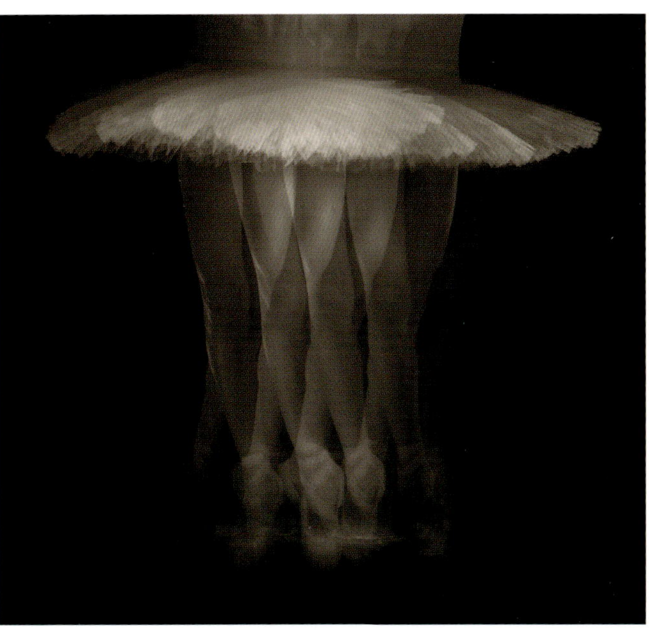

FIGURE 5.3

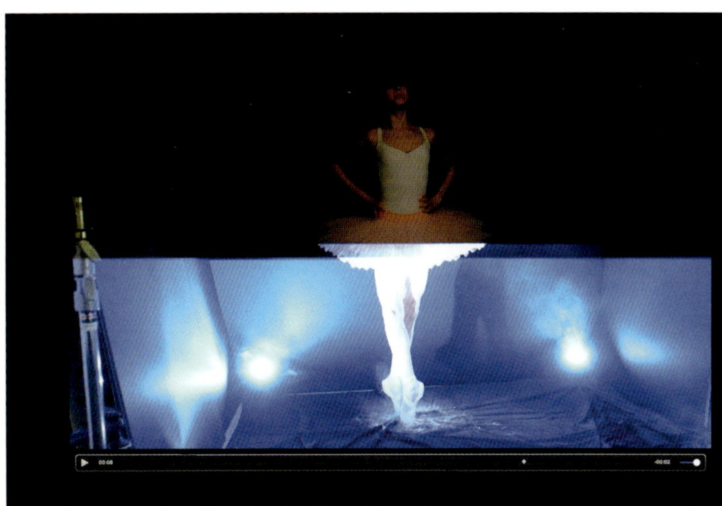

FIGURE 5.4

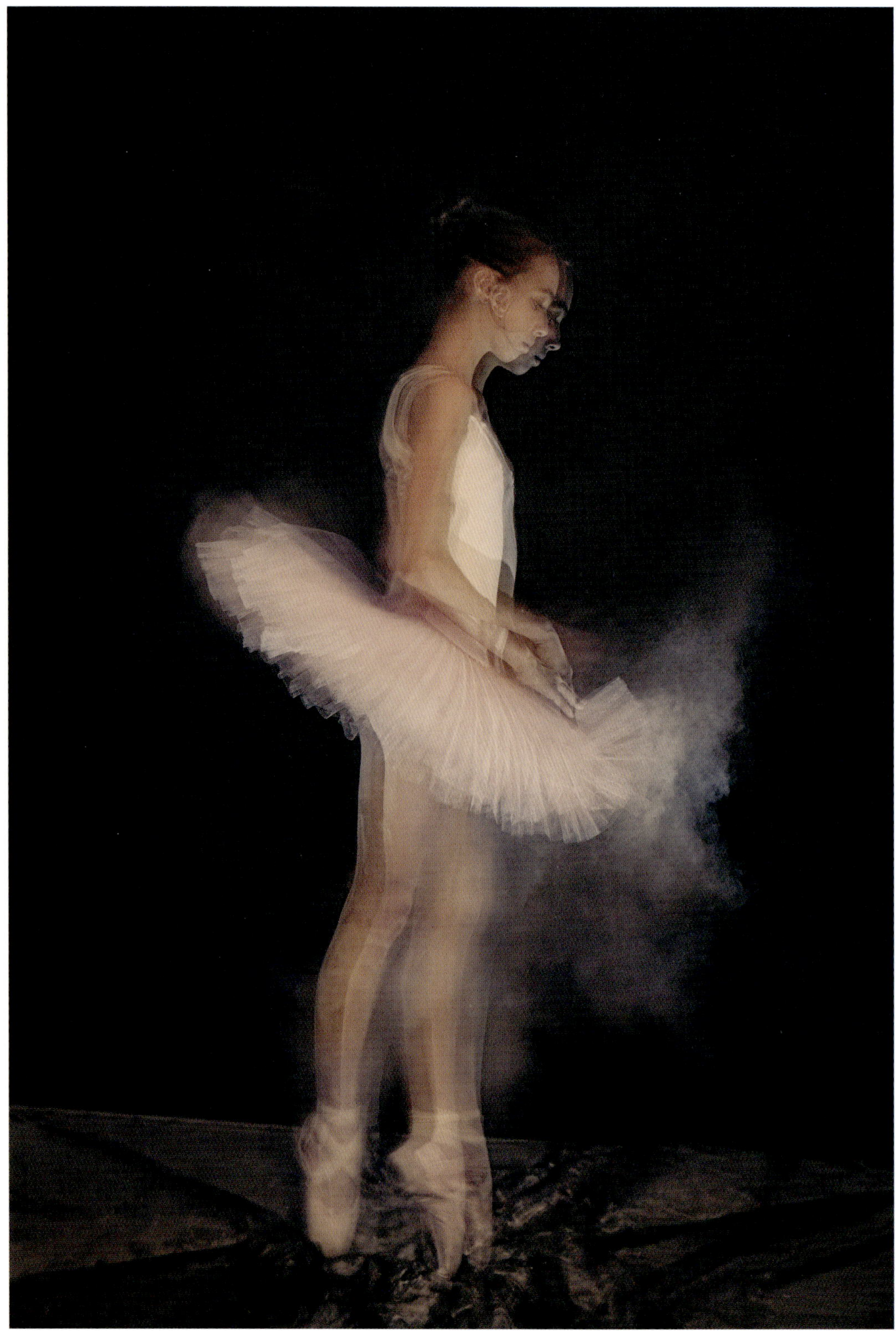

FIGURE 5.5

Dragged Shutter

Next is the very popular effect called "dragged shutter." Most photographers have tried it at least once or twice. Dragged shutter means that the shutter stays open for a longer than "normal" time. This usually means a half second or longer.

The most common, non-flash version of dragged shutter is panning, when a photographer carefully and very steadily tracks a moving object and everything else appears to be a blur from the combination of the object's speed and the intentional camera movement. This technique is very popular when the photographer wants to show a sense of speed and action. This technique is so popular that some modern cameras have a built-in aid system to help you track objects more steadily. My current flagship Canon camera has this feature in the Shooting menu, and it's called Panning Assist. Currently, this feature only works when shooting with a full electronic shutter. Panning Assist will activate image stabilization as well as subject blur stabilization; they work together to give you a much higher chance of success.

If you would like to try this technique outside during the daytime, I recommend that you get a three- to six-stop neutral density (ND) filter. That would do the trick. An ND filter is like sunglasses for your camera lens. You need an ND filter because, when shooting with a longer shutter speed outdoors during daytime, without the ND filter there would be so much light hitting your sensor that the entire image would often be completely blown out. The ND filter reduces the overall exposure based on how strong it is.

I use Kolari Magnetic Clip-In Filters, which are placed directly in front of the camera's sensor inside the mount. Since the ND filter fits behind the lens and not in front of it (as ND filters typically are), this means that you can use these filters with any lens you own, instead of having to buy a filter specifically for each of your lenses. That's a great advantage! I carry a three-stop and a six-stop ND clip-in filter in my camera bag at all times. I mostly use these filters when shooting portraits outside in broad daylight and I want to use my strobes within the camera's flash sync speed limit while at shallow apertures such as f/2.8 or even f/1.2.

Dragged Shutter with Flash (1st and 2nd Curtain Sync)

I will go into more technical details explaining the mechanics of 1st and 2nd Curtain Sync in a later chapter dedicated to this topic. Here I want to show you the artistic applications of these techniques in action.

Figure 5.6: During a lighting workshop, I wanted to demonstrate to the attendees how great this technique can be. To set this up, I set my camera to ISO 100, f/8, 0.4 seconds. That's a shutter speed of almost half a second. Next, I set my Profoto strobe with a hard modifier at camera left. Lastly, I asked the model to take a leaping step forward toward

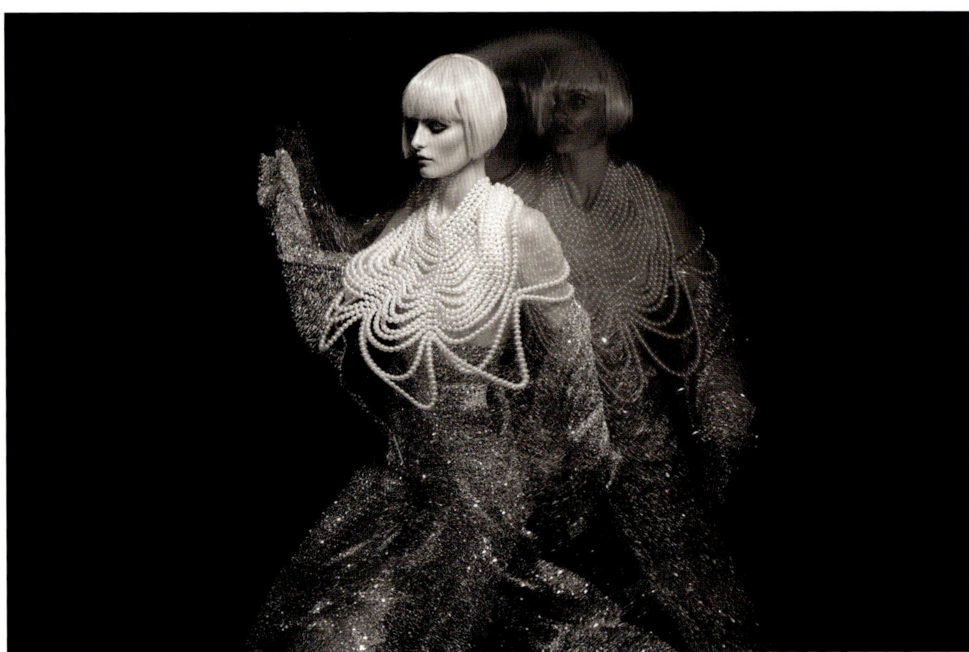

the flash on the count of three. As soon as I said "three" and spotted the slightest hint of movement, I pushed the shutter button to begin the half second exposure. I set my flash to 2nd Curtain Sync for this shot. This means that the flash fires at the last moment before the shutter closes and the exposure ends.

As the model leaps forward during the opening of the shutter, you can see the ghostly trail it leaves behind. However, the moment the flash fires, the instantaneous burst of light at a high duration speed close to her face completely freezes the motion at the end of the exposure.

The results of this technique can be stunning, fun, and definitely eye-catching. Not only does this technique force the photographer to shoot with movement (which is usually recommended for better posing), but it also creates an unexpected, perfectly sharp photograph.

Figure 5.7: This next photo of model Jayden had a very similar setup as the previous example. The main difference here is the creative movement that was rehearsed by both Jayden and me to create this two-face effect. When shooting with dragged shutter, you don't have to just shoot and see what comes out of it, aimlessly. You should take a minute to think about your final composition, and try for that. What do you want to create?

In this case, we both wanted to create a relatively sharp yet ghostly image to the right of the frame at the start of the exposure, and then end with a powerful and completely sharp image to the left of the frame, facing toward the ghostly impression. We had a plan, and we executed that plan. Most people shooting dragged shutter don't have a plan at all, just the technique. Try combining both—the technique and a plan for your final image. That's what will make you talented, instead of just average.

Figure 5.8: For this photo, we had a simpler outcome in mind. We decided on a 2nd Curtain Sync dragged shutter technique with a simple rotation of the model Meg's head from one side to the other. We started with her chin down. As the shutter dragged on during the exposure, I asked her to rotate her head and bring her chin up during the rotation. At the end of the exposure, the flash fired and froze her movement perfectly, despite the slow shutter.

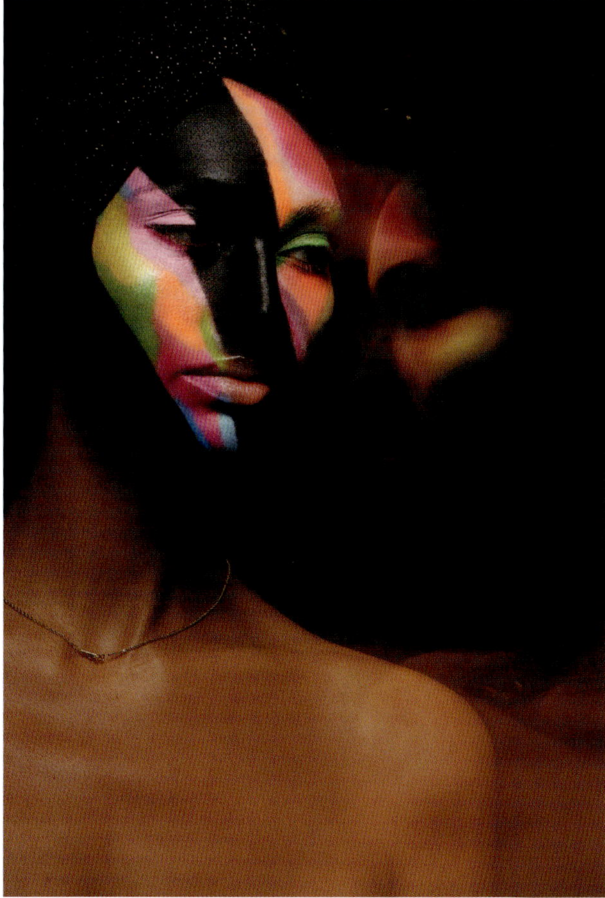

FIGURE 5.7

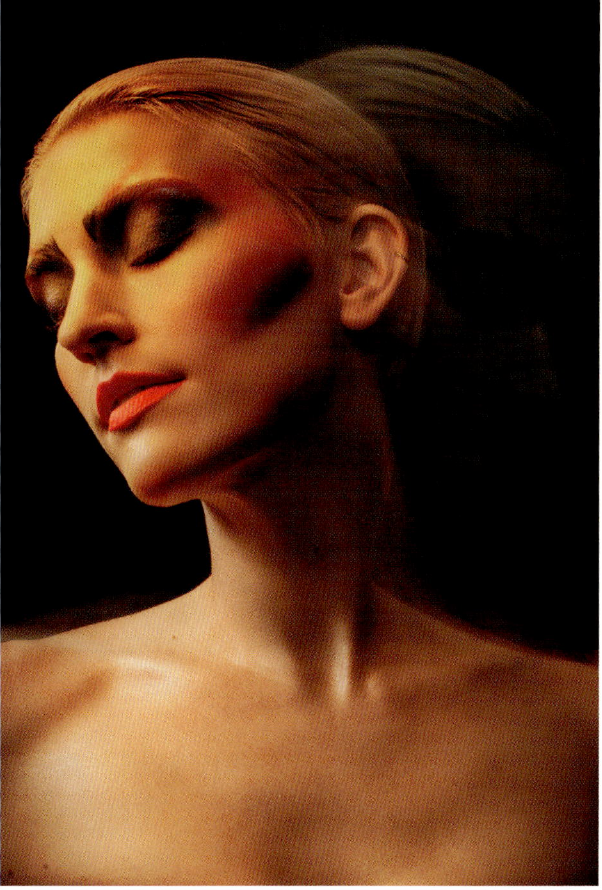

FIGURE 5.8

How cool is it that we can create an image that has both the look of a slow shutter, which yields motion blur, and a tack sharp image, which (seemingly) requires a super-fast shutter speed? It's quite the gift to be able to implement both a slow shutter speed in camera and a very fast flash duration speed from the strobe—combining them together to create remarkable special effects photographs.

Multiple Exposures

The Multiple Exposure setting is a feature that most cameras have these days, and it allows you to merge, add, or otherwise combine multiple exposures into one single photo. The results can be polarizing. People either love them or hate them. There's not much opinion in the middle. So why have this section in a book about flashes and portable strobes? By adding flash to your creations of multiple exposures, it will elevate the results to very high levels of creative imagery. And since this book is about opening your mind to the possibilities and advantages that flash can bring to your work, it is very fitting to add multiple exposures to the list.

THE MULTIPLE EXPOSURE SETTING BLENDS IMAGES IN FOUR WAYS

Additive: This method stacks images on top of each other. If bright areas on two separate images happen to overlap each other, their combined brightness will increase in the area where the overlapping occurs. A bit of underexposure per image is recommended with this method.

Average: With this method, the camera automatically underexposes each image. The goal is that the final, combined image will have the same overall exposure level that a single image on its own would have. This is a good choice when you know you will be overlapping images from the same scene. This method helps you avoid overexposure in the overlapping areas and in the overall final photograph.

Bright: This method evaluates each image separately, giving more importance to the bright areas of each image. This means that if you are shooting, for example, at night, the darker areas will not become progressively brighter as the images are combined, but the bright areas will be displayed at full brightness.

Dark: This method does the opposite of Bright, giving more importance to the darker areas of each image. This method can help with unwanted light reflections or bright, distracting objects in your combined multiple exposure.

You can combine up to nine photos together depending upon your camera make and model.

Figure 5.9 & 5.10: For these two photographs, I used two Profoto lights. One light is to light up the background, and the second light is to illuminate the model, Jayden. For both of these photos, I used the Dark blending method, because I wanted to protect the darker areas of her face. I also wanted to eliminate the possibility of unwanted reflections. For Figure 5.9, we had to move the Profoto light for each photo we created—from the left side in one photo to the right side for the other. Two exposures were taken and then blended together. For Figure 5.10, again, two lights were used, but this time we didn't have to move them left or right, since the main photo was of Jayden looking straight at the camera. For this multiple exposure, three photos were blended together for the final image.

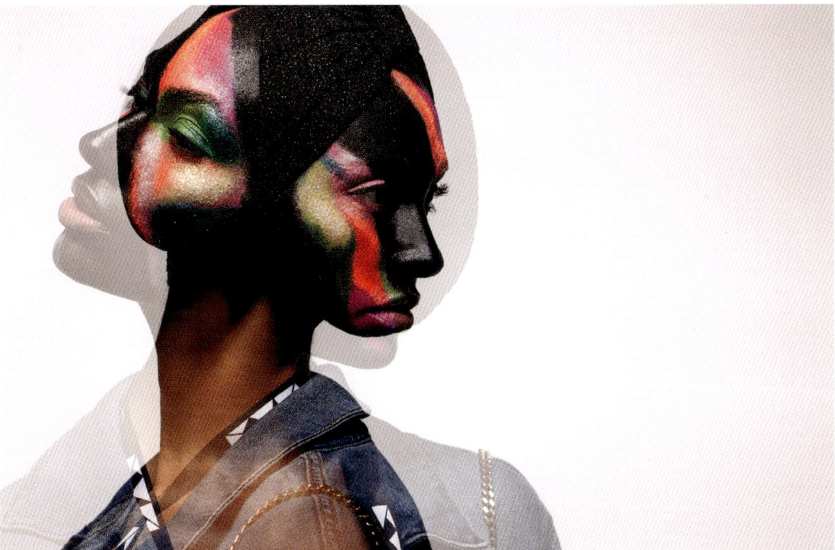

FIGURE 5.9

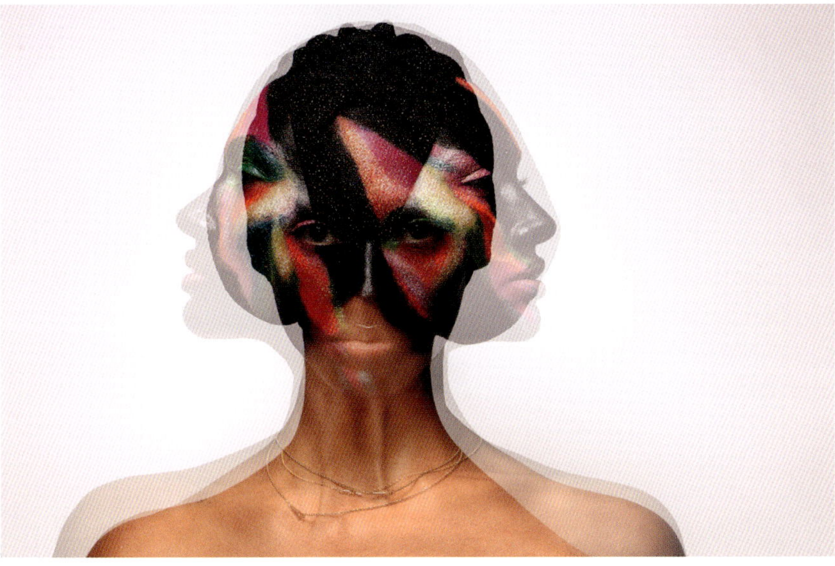

FIGURE 5.10

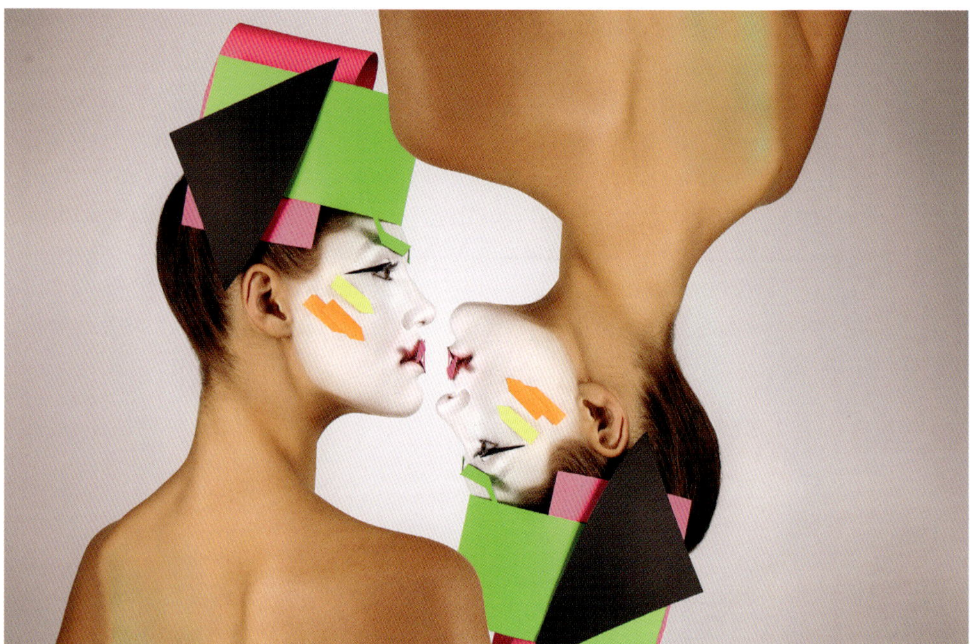

Figure 5.11: This photo is the result of two exposures being blended together using the Additive method. I used this blending method because I simply wanted to stack the two images together. I created the photo of Meredith upside down by simply turning my camera upside down for the second exposure. Only two Profoto flashes were used for this photograph: one for the background and one for Meredith. Note that without the flashes, these multiple exposure images would not have the wow factor that they possess. The use of flash is what makes these photos so unique.

Figures 5.12–5.14: The first two images are the two source files used to create the final optical illusion photograph. This shoot took place live during my Canon demo talk on the Canon Main Stage at the Imaging USA conference. I used two Profoto lights with blue and purple gels on either side of the camera. To create this optical illusion, in which the couple seems to be trapped inside the material, I used two multiple exposure photographs and the Average blending method. The Average method blends the two photos together by underexposing each image and then combining the luminosity levels throughout the frame from both images to create one final image. This averaging of the luminosity levels created the illusion that the subjects being photographed were trapped inside the background. This works with highly reflective material, such as this Mylar material. But different types of material will yield different results. Experimentation is key.

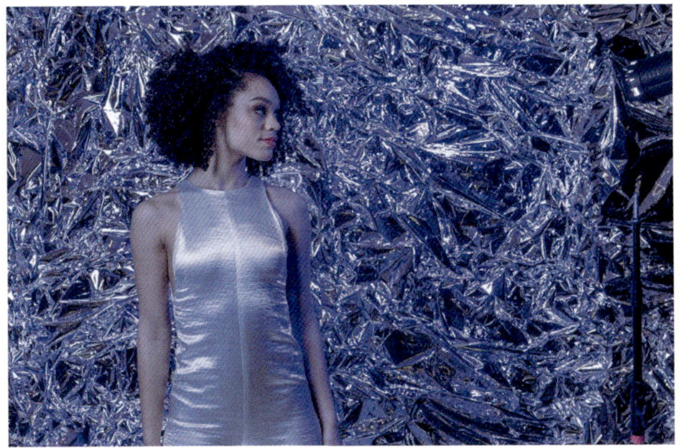

FIGURE 5.12

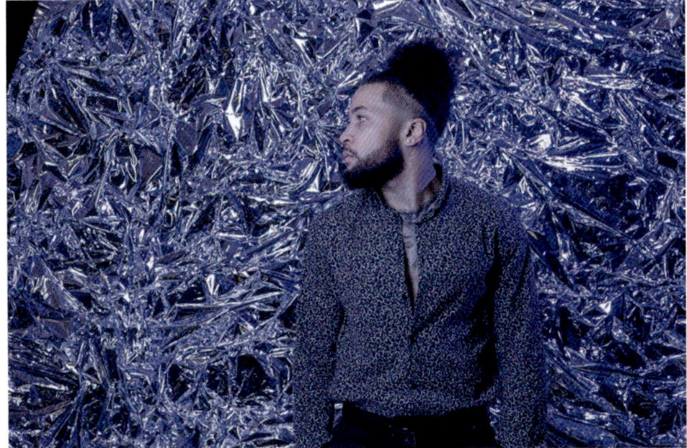

FIGURE 5.13

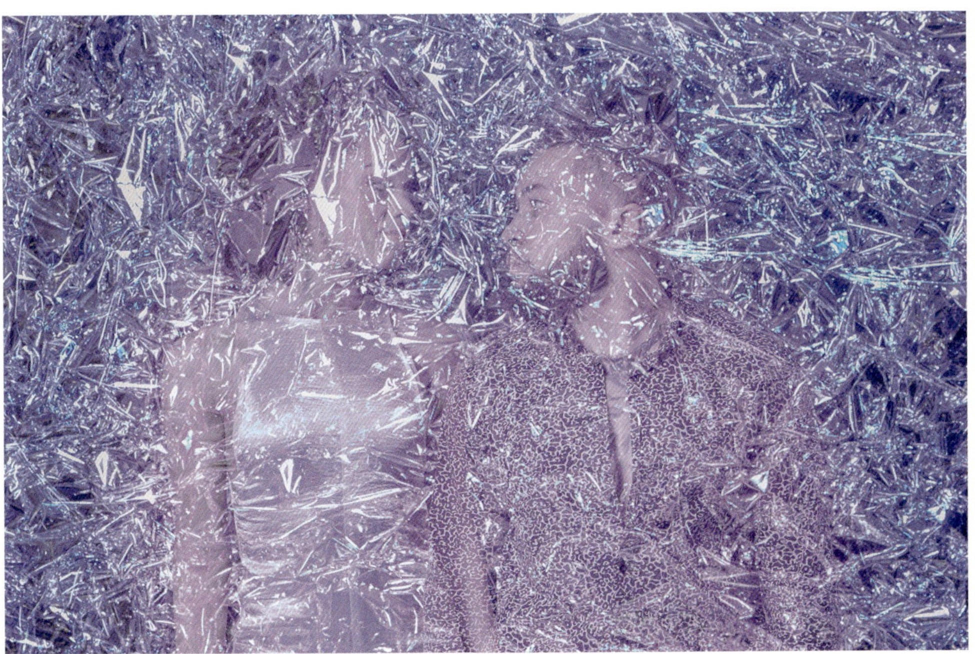

FIGURE 5.14

Figure 5.15: This multiple exposure is simpler than the previous example. The idea was to have a red gel on the woman and a blue gel on the man. I used the Additive blending mode because I just wanted the camera to stack the images without worrying about shadows or highlights. Without creating a multiple exposure, this image would not be possible, because the blue gel would spill on her and the red gel would spill on him. This image could be used for an album cover for a band. As you read this, think about what you would like to try with multiple exposures.

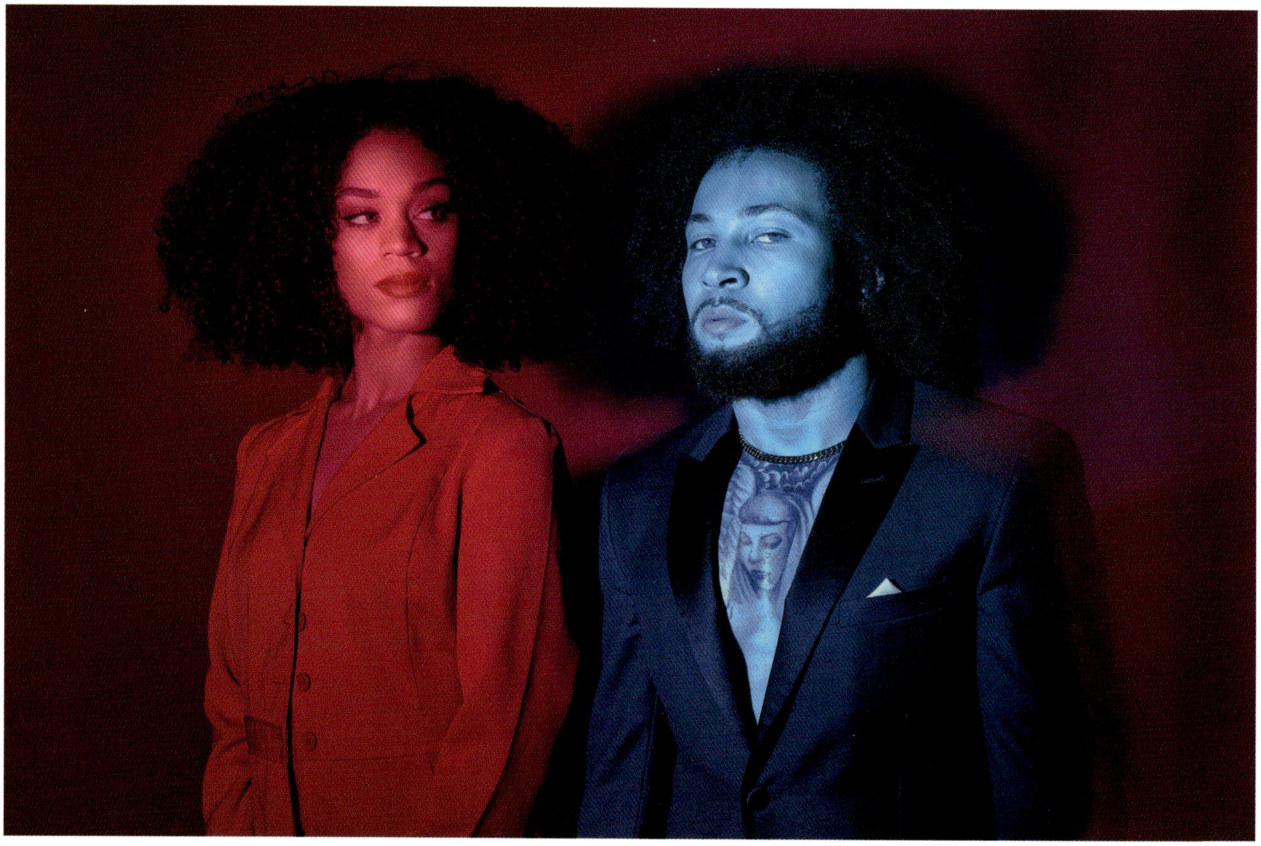

Figure 5.16 & 5.17: I took this photo for the grand finale of an exhibition shoot I was hired to do for Canon during the Adobe MAX Conference in downtown Los Angeles. I'll be the first to admit that this was a complicated setup. However, I want to include it here so you realize how impressive the results can be when you combine flash with the Multiple Exposure setting on your camera. It's truly incredible what you can do right out of camera!

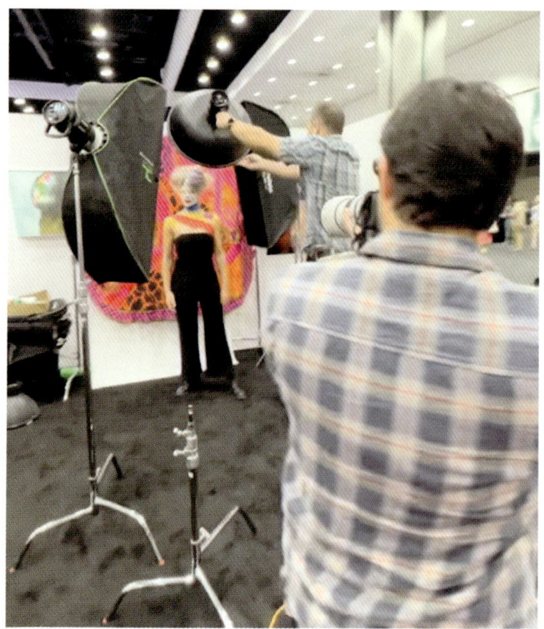

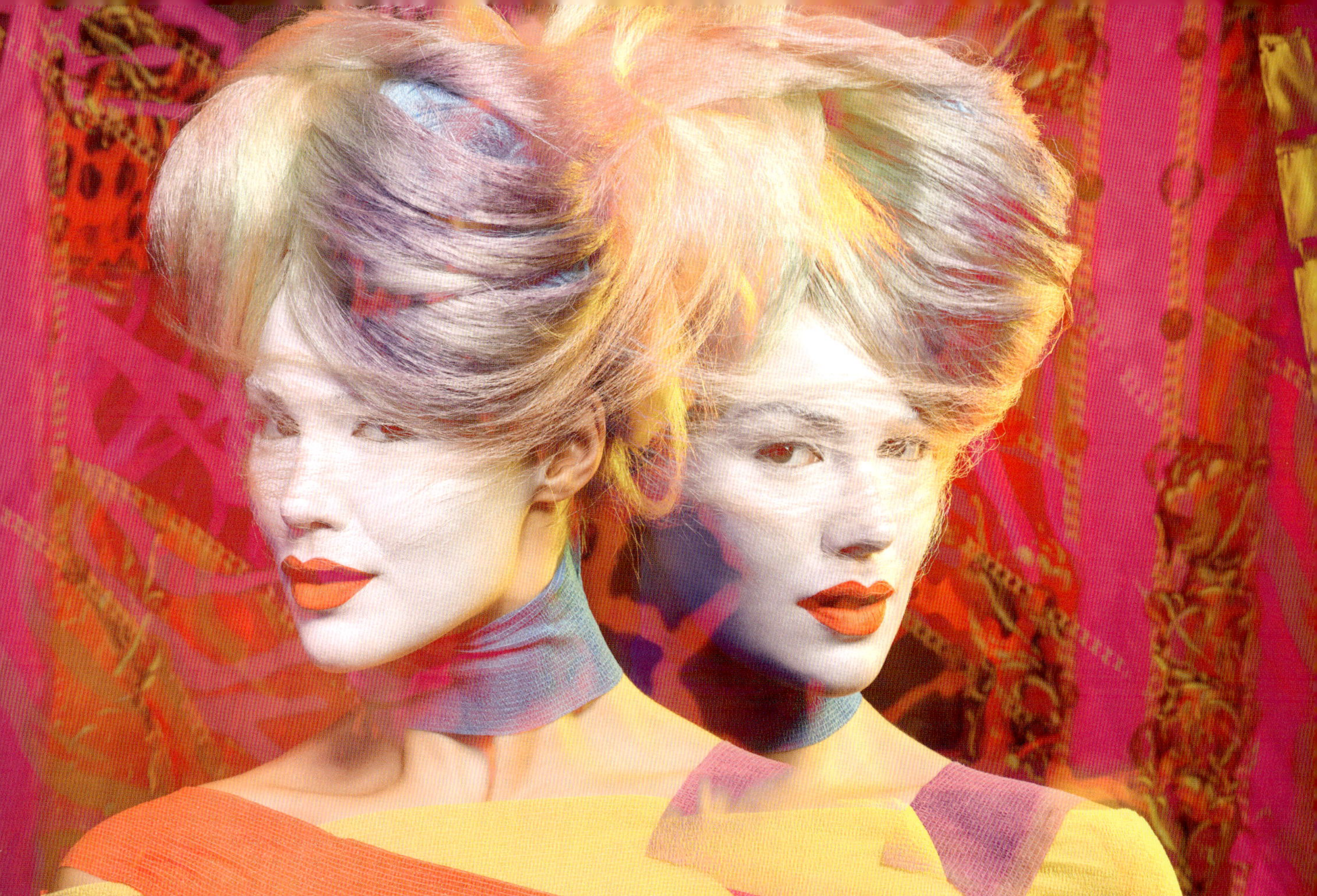

Flash Flaring

I discussed this technique a bit in the previous chapter, but it's worth looking at again here in the Effects chapter. Flash flaring is a flash technique that I use quite often. It produces dream-like lighting, and it is very easy to do. To create this effect, all you have to do is point a strobe directly toward your camera lens without the lens hood on. When the flash fires, the light will directly hit the camera's sensor and create this exciting lighting effect. This is a great technique, especially when you find yourself in a bland environment. You have to experiment to find the result you like: Turn the flash power higher and lower, and then compensate for the change in power by adjusting your aperture and ISO.

Figure 5.18: This photo was taken on stage at the largest photography show in the world called Photokina. Unfortunately, the show doesn't exist anymore. However, at their last show, I was able to shoot on their main stage. Since there was nothing motivating or inspiring about the environment, I thought it would be the perfect time

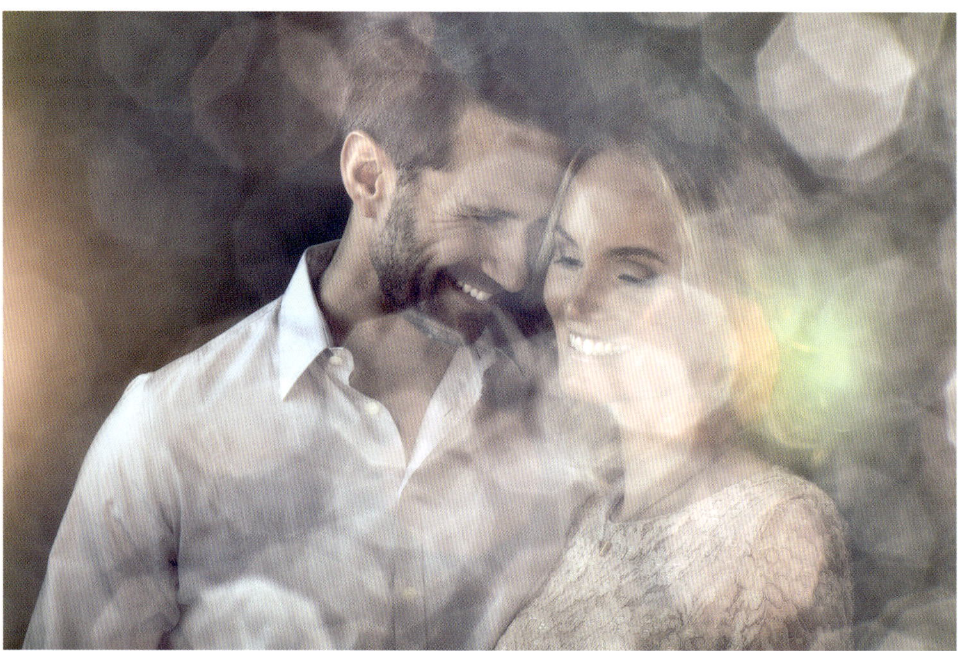

to implement the flash flaring effect. For this photo, I set my camera to ISO 100, f/13, 1/200. I cranked up the power of the strobe almost to full power, and I had an assistant point the strobe head directly into my lens without the hood. It took a couple of adjustments to make the flare look just right. In the end, it worked out beautifully.

Figures 5.19 & 5.20: I discussed this image a bit in the previous chapter, but I think it's worth looking at again to see what an incredible difference flash flaring can make in a photograph. During this shoot on a random street in Vietnam, the rain was coming down hard, so we took cover for a few minutes. Then I realized that I could use the rainy day to my advantage with a flash flaring photo. I wanted to transform this ordinary scene into something vintage from the past.

To do this, I placed a full CTO gel on the Profoto B10 that you see here aimed directly at my camera. The flash was at a relatively high power to emphasize the effects of the flare throughout the scene. The man wearing the white shirt and holding the other Profoto flash was pointing the flash toward the woman's face to illuminate her eyes under the non la (traditional Vietnamese hat). Now, turn your attention to the final image. Doesn't the image have a vintage look from the 1960s or thereabout? The effects of the orange gel really come through—but in a subtle manner so that it is not too obvious.

No matter how long I've been doing this work I will always become excited when shooting. My blood will always pump so much faster when I have these tools as part of my skillset, and when the results pay off when I take risks implementing them.

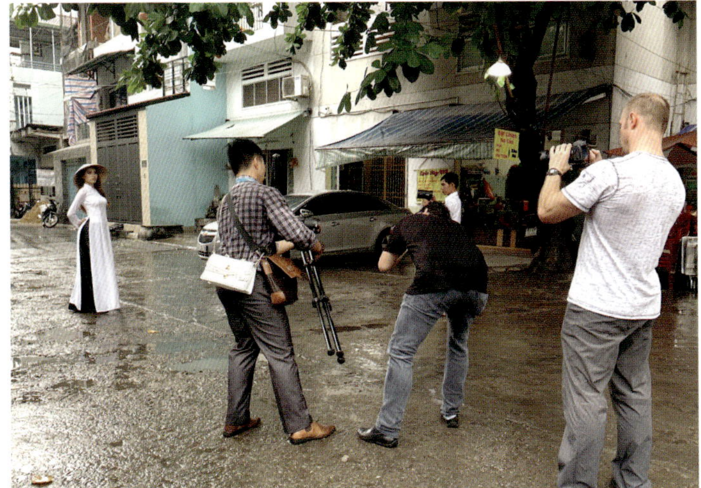

In summary, these effects are incredible, but remember to use them wisely. You don't want to be at an actual shoot trying these effects for the first time. I highly recommend that you take some time to experiment with them; get a feel for how they work, and how long it takes for you to reach a satisfactory result. Lastly, keep in mind your clients, your audience, or whoever you are shooting for, because as great as these effects can be, they may not be everyone's cup of tea.

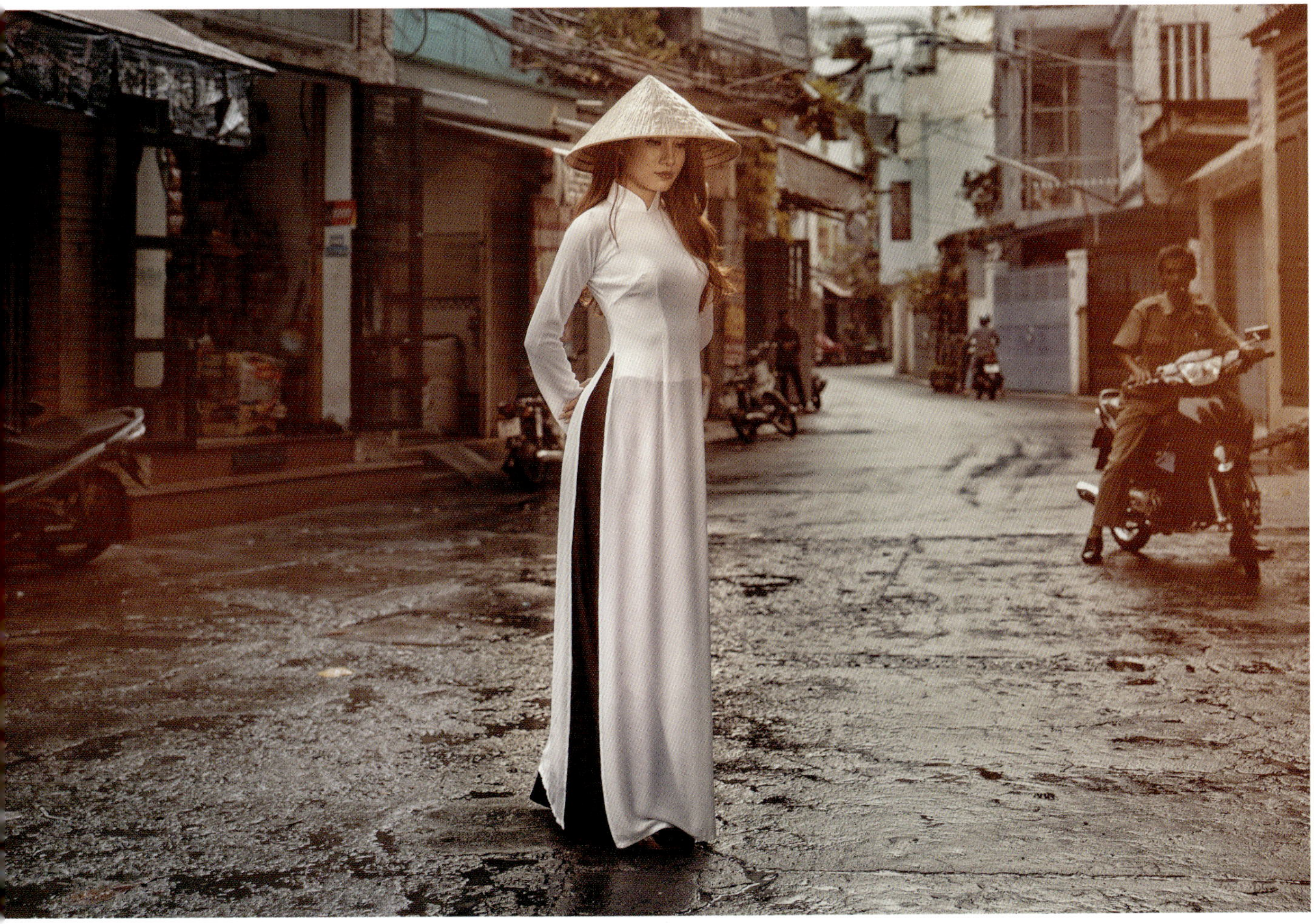

FIGURE 5.20

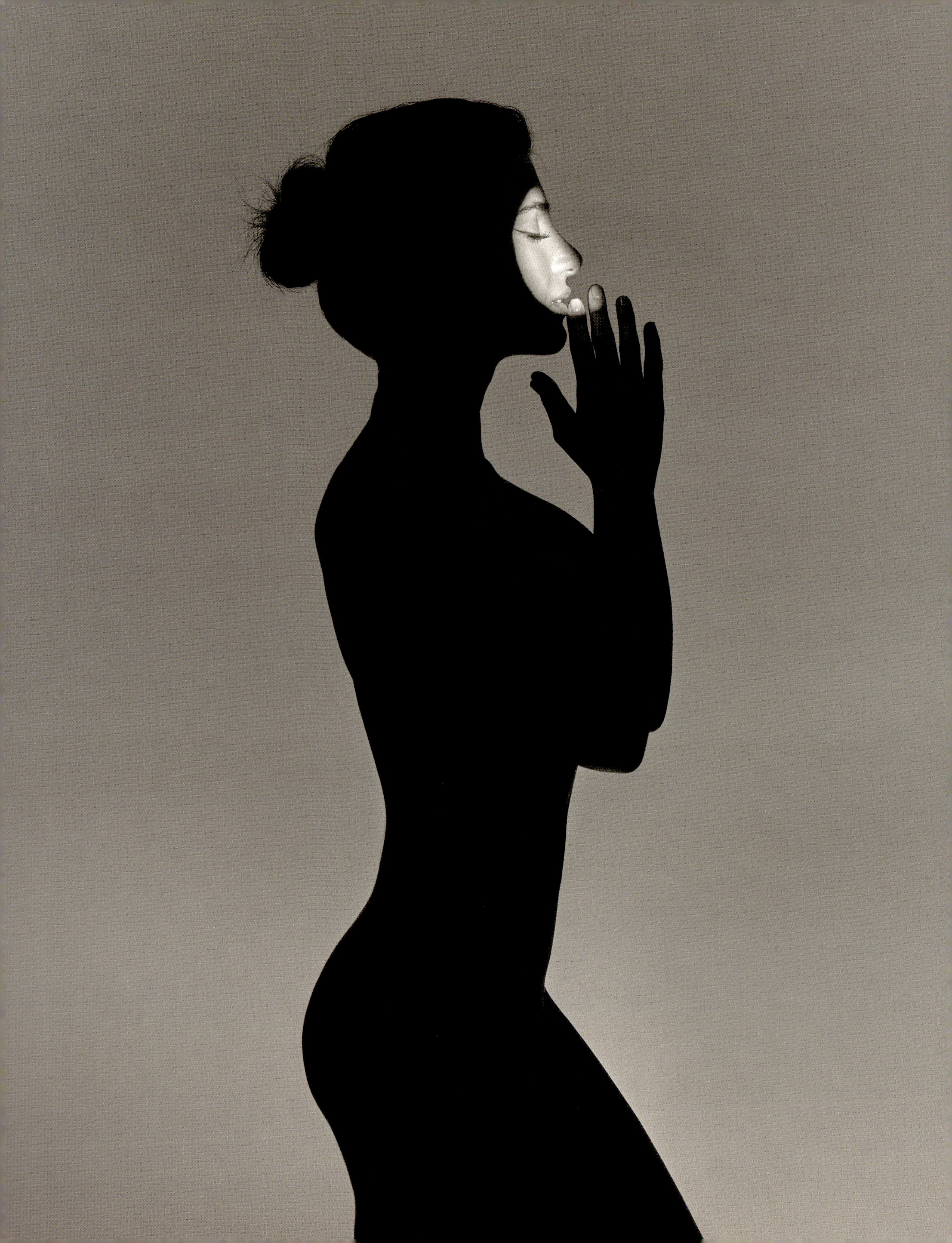

Chapter 6

F
A
C
E

Sculpt the Light

Sculpting light in your photographs is very important. In my opinion, nothing is more boring than a flat photo with no dimensionality or shape. Buying a flash and directing it toward someone without any thought or purpose other than to illuminate that person with the flash is *not* light sculpting. Sculpting light is a technique that requires the right equipment and the manipulation of light sources in order to achieve depth and drama in a precise manner.

People photography benefits greatly from light sculpting, because implementing sculpting creates a visually compelling portrait. Adding drama to a portrait means purposeful placement of both light and shadow to achieve a vision. A portrait without that light and shadow—with just a lot of light covering every inch of the person's face—would result in a two-dimensional, flat portrait. That's not necessarily a bad result, by the way. It's just flat.

But creating a portrait with density and with shadows in all the right places is a portrait with drama and a wow factor. This is a relatively short chapter, but it's a crucial one. Sculpting light is easily a topic for an entire book. However, for the purposes of this book, we will cover the tools, the importance, and the benefits of sculpting with light.

Figure 6.1 & 6.2: To whet your appetite, look at the difference in impact between these two photos of the same person taken just minutes apart. Figure 6.1 is lit more evenly throughout the frame, and it's a flatter image. The subject's chin is lit by the same light intensity as his nose, eyes, forehead, and cheeks. The image looks nice, and it's a well-lit photo.

But by no means does it have the wow factor of Figure 6.2. It's no contest! The bright but well-exposed front of the subject's face has much more intensity of light than the rest of his face. Look at his cheeks and neck. There is so much going on with the ups and downs of light and shadow. The result is a photo that appears sculpted. The photo is also more exciting to look at because the light sculpting draws your attention to all the corners of the portrait.

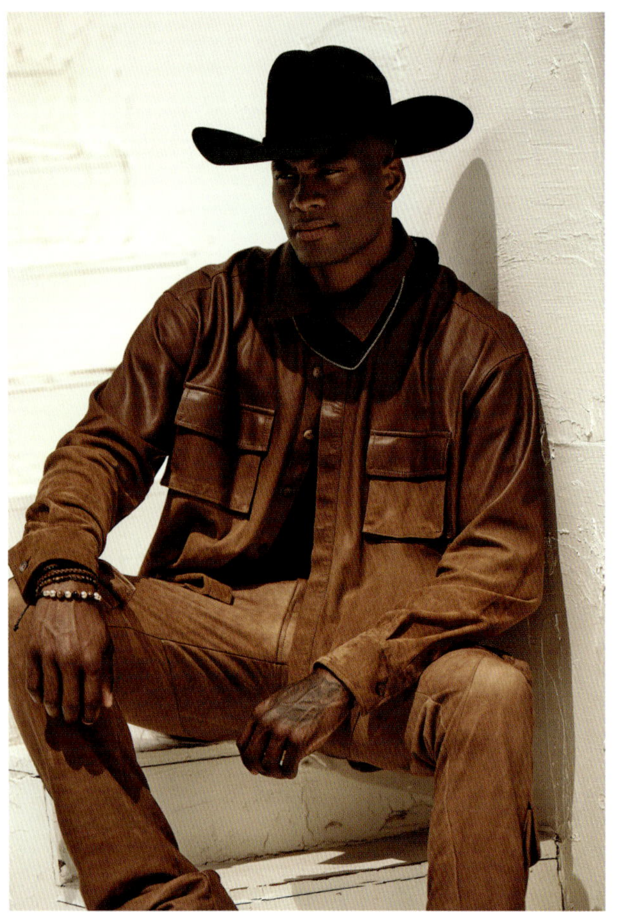

FIGURE 6.1

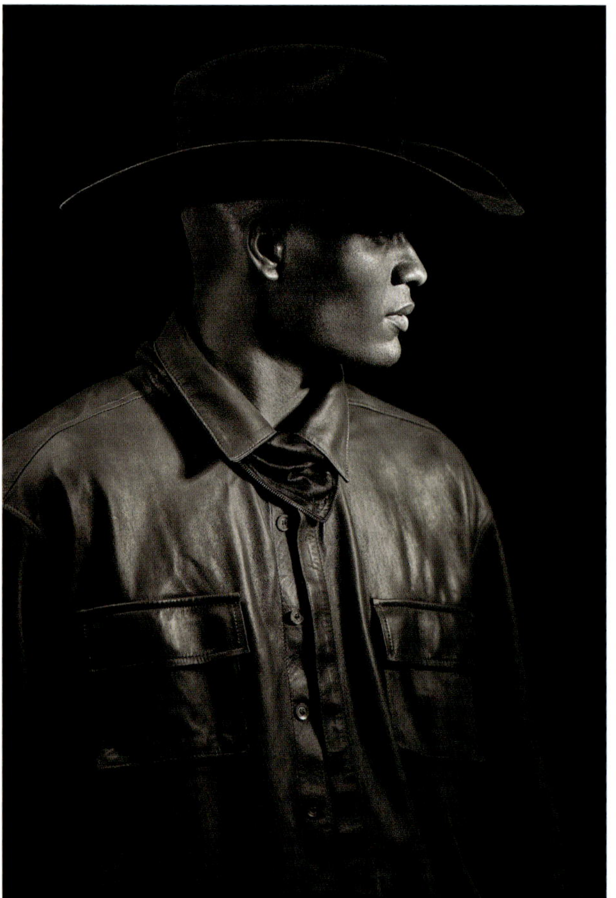

FIGURE 6.2

To make light sculpting easier to implement, you must understand how light behaves, how shadows are created, what makes hard and soft shadows, and the tools you need to sculpt the light, such as light shapers. This might seem like a lot, but the great thing about light is that its behavior is predicable. The laws of physics that control light never change. Therefore, once you understand these concepts, you are always good to go. From then on, you can improve and refine your skills with each of these elements. This is the most exciting part of people photography!

Sculpting Light by Increasing the Intensity of Light

As you read this section, you will begin to visualize what happens as you increase the intensity of light striking your subject. When you expose for the brightest part of the face lit by the strobe, everything else that is not as bright as that will go darker from your exposure.

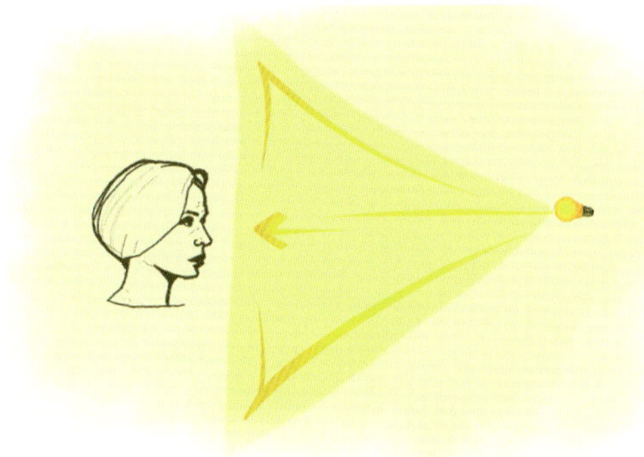

FIGURE 6.3

Intensity of Light Explained

Let's define what "intensity of light" means. Practically speaking, increasing the intensity of light means that more light is striking your subject. Because light radiates outward from its source, some light energy hits your subject, and some light energy is lost through the spread/dispersion of the light. Therefore, if your light source is very close to your subject, then most of the light rays will strike the subject's face. There is not enough distance between the light and your subject for the light to spread outward much and miss the person's face. Let's look at a couple illustrations.

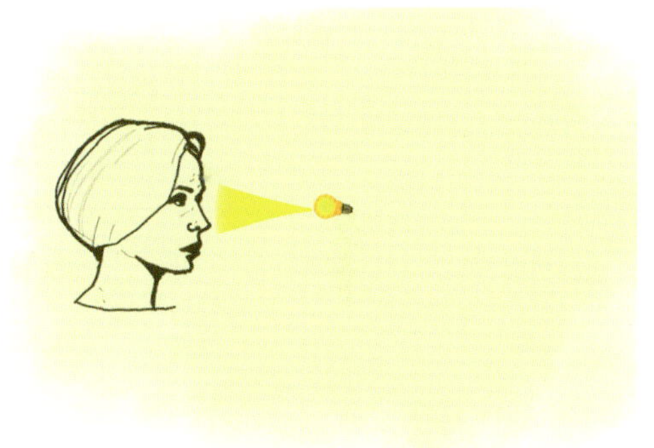

FIGURE 6.4

Figure 6.3: The light source is far enough from the subject such that, as the light radiates out, as it always does, most of the light rays miss the subject. Just a few of the total light rays strike her. Therefore, our eyes perceive the light to be weaker as it strikes the subject from this distance.

Figure 6.4: Now look what happens when the light is close to the subject. As the light spreads, all or most of the light rays strike her face at a higher intensity than the rest of the ambient light, which is represented by the overall yellow throughout the illustration. These illustrations also show why it is so useful to use flash outdoors. By using a strobe, you can add a higher intensity of light just to your subject and not to the rest of the scene. This allows you to create a flattering separation between the subject and the background, thus giving your subject more importance. That's awesome!

Inverse Square Law of Light in Simple Terms

All these mathematical sounding names and graphs can be summed up in a very simple way. In the real world, when light first emerges from its source, it comes out at its strongest intensity. As the light travels away from its source, the perceived brightness quickly dies down because the light radiates out and scatters throughout more space and in all directions. Therefore, the perceived loss of light on your subject happens exponentially, meaning it happens very quickly.

The formula for the Inverse Square Law of Light is:

$$Intensity = \frac{1}{distance^2}$$

If you want to find out how intense the light will be on your subject at a certain distance, perhaps 4 meters away from the light source, simply replace the word "distance" with the number "4" in the formula and square it. 4 x 4 = 16. So, at 4 meters away, you are working with only 1/16, or 0.0625, of the light. If we change that number into a percentage, it makes a bit more sense: 1/16, or 0.0625, is 6.25% of the light you started with. That's not much light at all!

Figure 6.5: This easy-to-follow diagram shows how the intensity of light rapidly changes with distance.

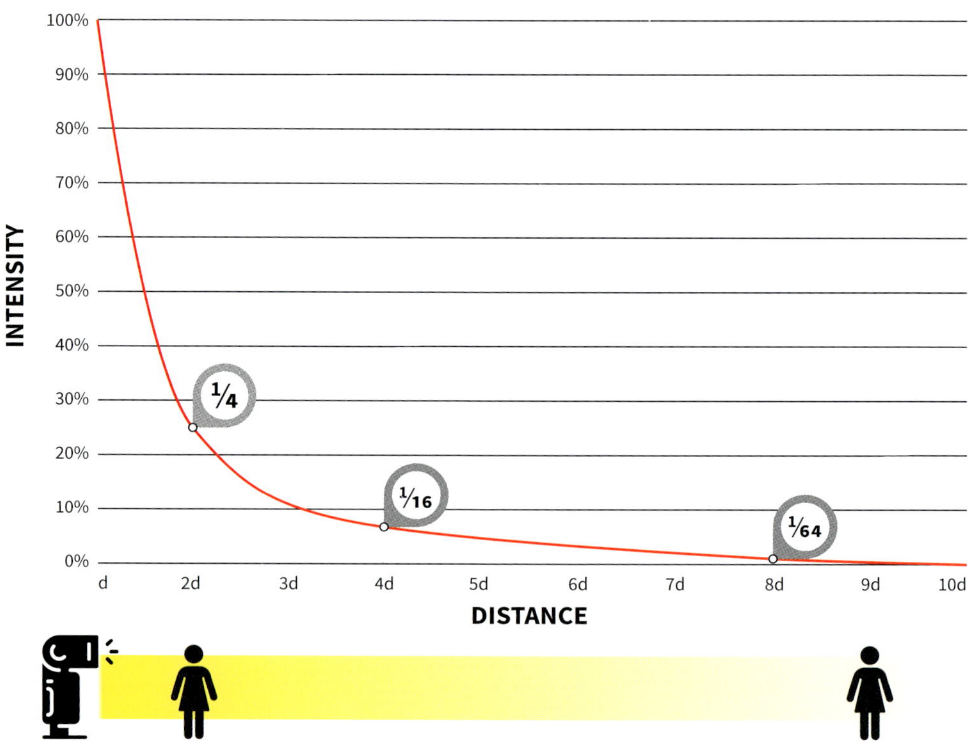

FIGURE 6.5

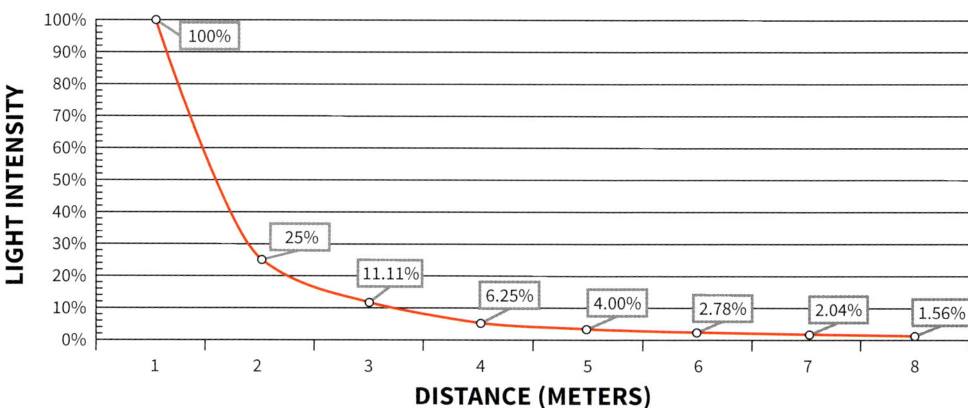

FIGURE 6.6

Figure 6.6: This chart clearly shows how much light is lost through distance. At 1 meter away, you have 100% of the light. When the distance from the light source increases to just 2 meters, you are left with only 1/4 of the light, or 25%. At 3 meters away, you have 1/9 of the light, or 11.11%. Can you believe that? At just 3 meters from the light source, you only have 11% of the light to work with. If you are more of a visual person and don't like math, just look again at Figure 6.5. Notice how the light starts out strong but by the time it reaches the person further away, the light intensity appears to be almost nonexistent.

Controlling the Throw and Spread of Light for Sculpting

As discussed, light radiates out from a source. A flash, a strobe, and even an LED light all radiate out. In certain circumstances, this spread of light can be your friend; however, when you are trying to sculpt light, it is your worst nightmare. The very first thing you need to do is control that spread. To do this, you need light-shaping tools.

Light shapers are to a photographer what a set of knives is to a chef. For any light-shaping need, there is a specific tool that can handle the job better than the rest. To me, controlling light's throw and spread is when photography becomes truly exciting. Anyone can buy a flash, point it at someone, and obtain a good exposure. But imagine looking at a great portrait that draws you in, an image so captivating that you can't stop looking at it. I bet that such a portrait is visually compelling because the light is meticulously sculpted. Sculpting light is creating the desired shape and density of shadows in all the right places.

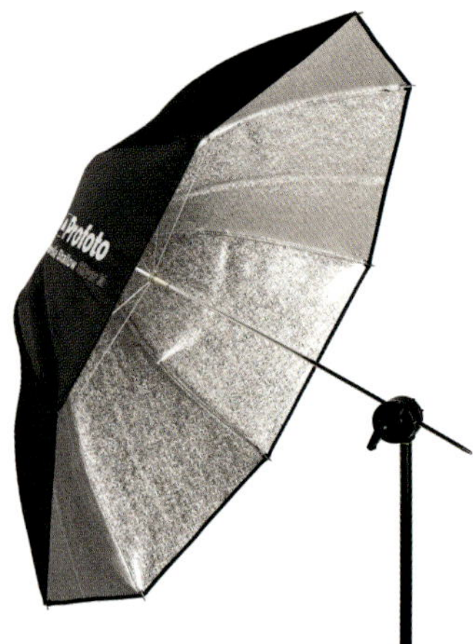

FIGURE 6.7

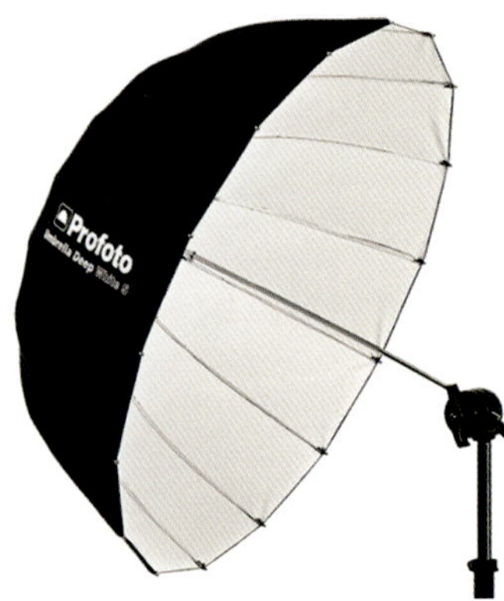

FIGURE 6.8

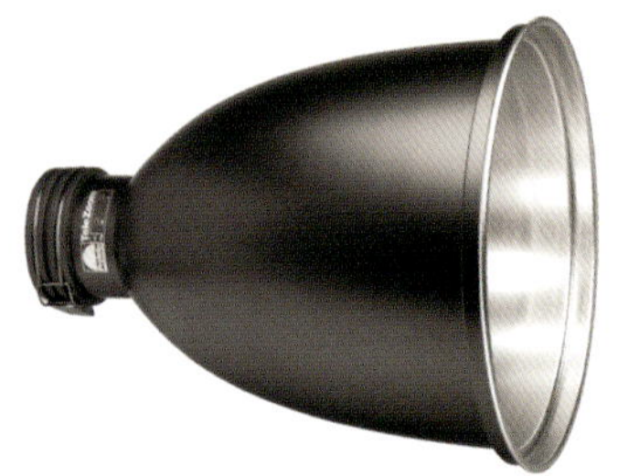

FIGURE 6.9

Shallow Modifiers Versus Deep Modifiers

Here are a few very brief descriptions of the main light-shaping tools that photographers use. This is not meant to be an exhaustive resource for how each of these modifiers exactly behaves. Instead, I want you to have an idea of how the light will act when paired with any of these very popular modifiers. This knowledge will help you decide which is the right light shaper to sculpt the light exactly how you envisioned.

Figure 6.7: This is a basic, shallow umbrella that you can buy at any camera store. Regardless of the brand, they all work the same. A shallow umbrella such as this will definitely help in controlling the spread of light that occurs when the flash is a bare bulb. But since the shape of this umbrella is shallow, and the opening is very wide, the light will still spread out quite a bit. But something is better than nothing. In a jam, these umbrellas can be quite useful because they are cheap and easy to carry. They are also very useful when photographing families or any other group of people because the light spread will reach many people.

Figure 6.8: This is a deep umbrella. Notice that the shape is very different from the shallow umbrella. The umbrella is deep, with an opening that doesn't allow the light to spread as much as the wide opening of a shallow umbrella. With this kind of modifier, you can control the spread of light much more efficiently than with a basic, shallow umbrella.

Figure 6.9: Just looking at the shape of this tele zoom reflector gives you a big hint about how the spread of light will look coming out of such a deep reflector. This type of modifier is a reflector, which you can tell due to the shiny metal surface inside. The purpose of this modifier is to throw a high intensity of light far into the distance. The deep shape and reflective materials on these types of hard modifiers are meant to intensify the light as much as possible with a very narrow spread, so that more light rays strike the subject, even at a further distance.

Figure 6.10: For this portrait of my great friend Andre, I did not use Profoto's tele zoom reflector. Instead, I used something very similar called the Magnum reflector. I used the Magnum reflector because I wanted to illuminate the outline of Andre's face but I did not want any light spill from the modifier to illuminate his hat or sweater. I had a grid attached to the reflector to ensure that the light would not spill anywhere I did not want it to go.

This portrait was created with serious sculpting in mind. It's not your typical photo of a person with light everywhere. The result is a portrait that makes you feel something. The key word there is "feel." Another fill light was used to create soft light on his sweater and on the side of his face, and a third light was used to highlight the outline of his hat against the black background.

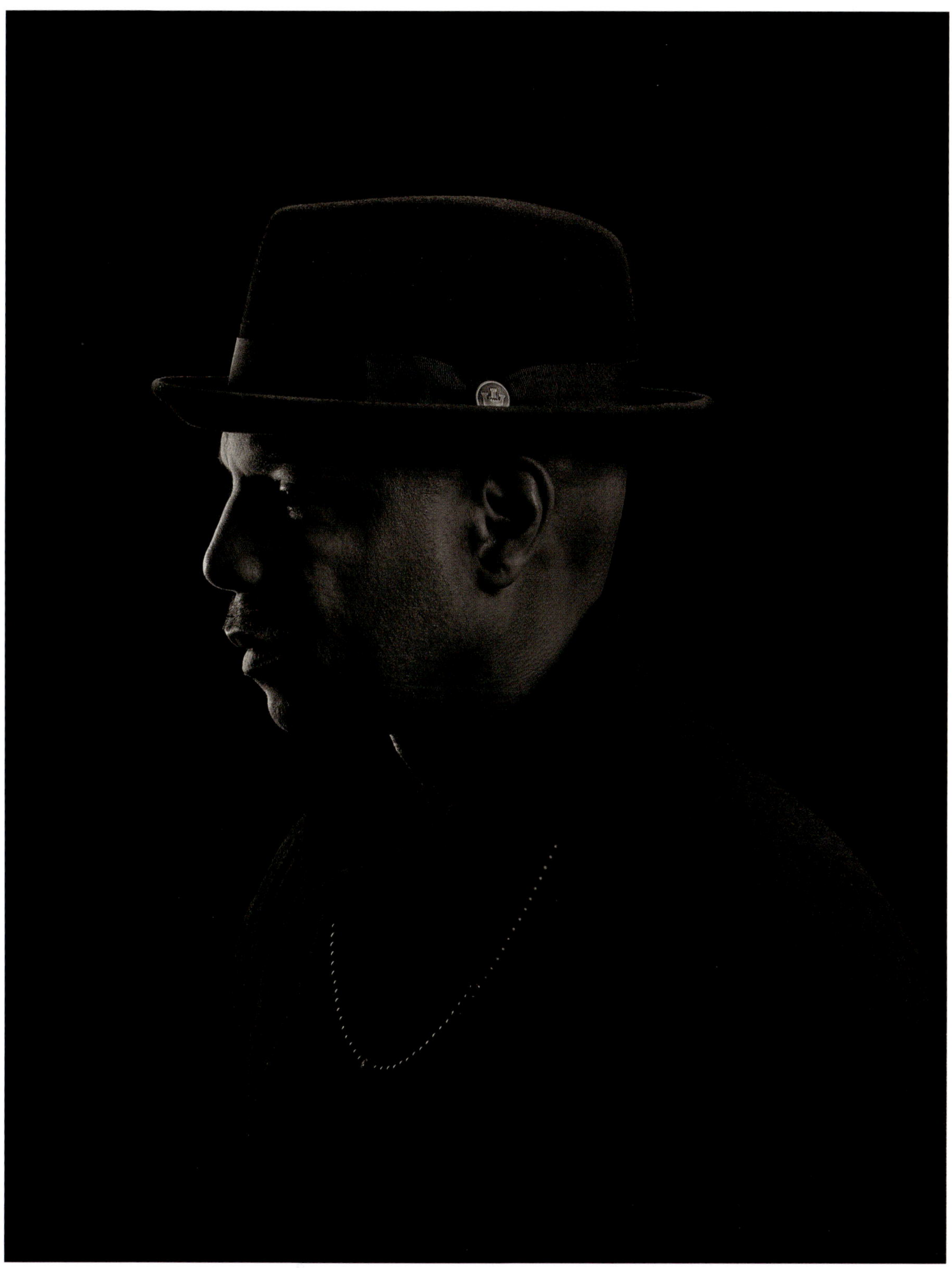

FIGURE 6.10

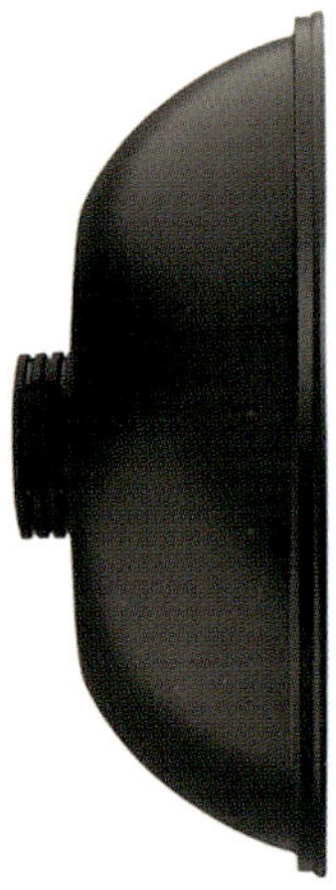

Figure 6.11: This is a beauty dish, arguably a favorite among most fashion/beauty photographers. Its unique shape and size creates a combination of soft light with crisp shadows. It's difficult to beat the flattering look from this modifier. It is best used with a beauty dish grid.

Figure 6.12: The magic of this fashion photograph comes mainly from the use of a beauty dish with a grid positioned over the model's head. The designer of these 3D-printed glasses worked very hard to design and print this work of art accessory. As a fashion photographer, I did not want to disappoint by simply aiming a big softbox toward the model's face and call it a day. I knew some serious light sculpting would make this photo shine!

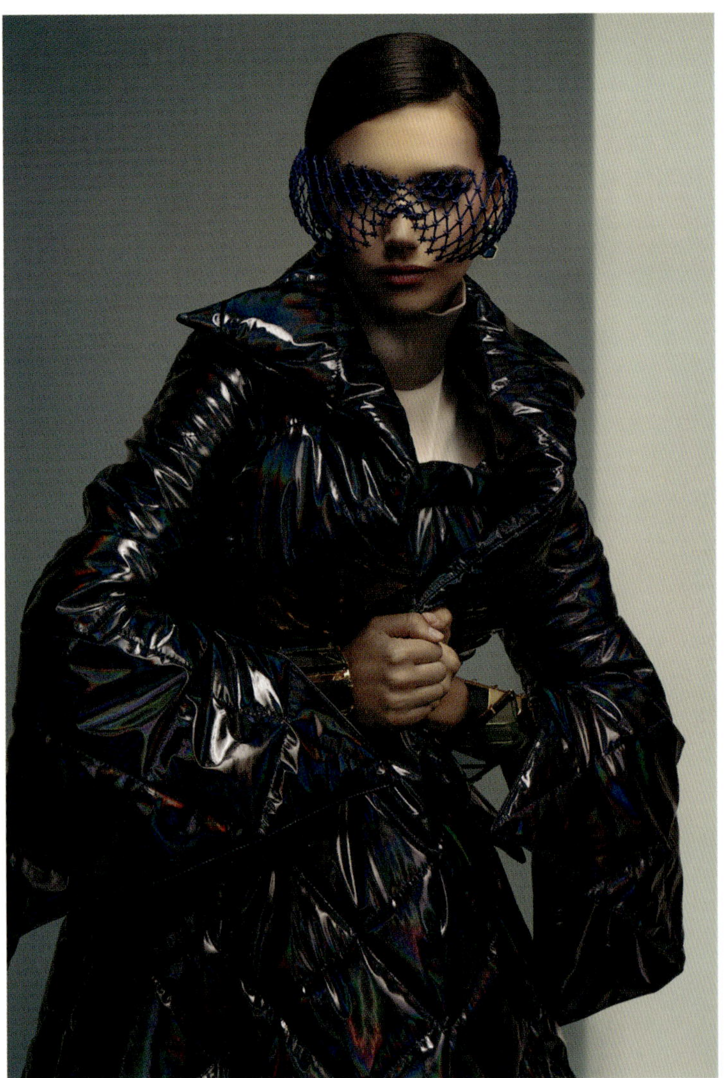

FIGURE 6.12

Quite a few lights were used to create this final image, but let's focus on the behavior of the light on the 3D-printed glasses. The lighting really makes these glasses look three-dimensional. You can feel the curvature of the design. The lighting on the glasses was created with a beauty dish with a grid about two feet above her forehead. By the time the light reaches her lips, the light is much weaker. This meticulous light sculpting allowed for the light to feature the intricate design of the glasses, while providing the necessary shadows on the sides of her face. That's super cool!

Figure 6.13: Grids, or honeycomb grids, are the holy grail of light control. Whenever I buy a modifier, I also buy its corresponding grid. Without grids for your modifiers, it's like playing a guitar with the strings loose and out of tune. In order to gain control of the sound that each string makes, they all must be in perfect tune. It is the same way with modifiers: the grids are the equivalent of well-tuned strings.

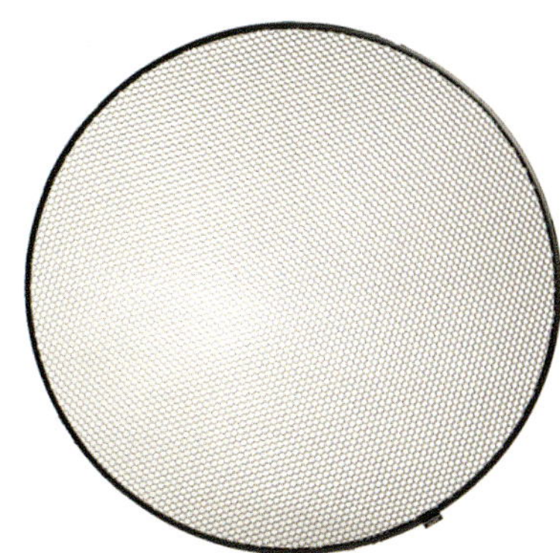

FIGURE 6.13

Grids come in a variety of degrees. The smaller the holes on the grid, the smaller the degree. The degree that is listed on a grid, such as 5-degree, 20-degree, 40-degree, etc., is a measurement of how the light will spread when it emerges from the grid. Grids are made for most modifiers and for most types of lights. Profoto makes them for their entire line of lights, and MagMod makes them for hot shoe flashes. The point is, if you want to sculp light, you will need grids—many of them! When you buy a light modifier, buy it with its corresponding grids. It will save you time, and you'll experience much less frustration.

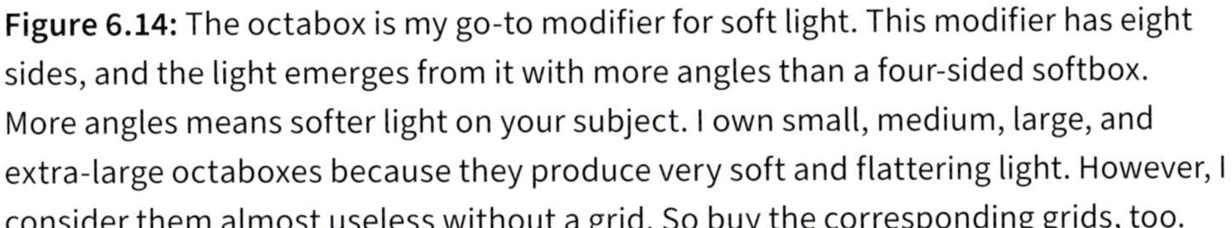

BY USING GRIDS WITH YOUR MODIFIERS, YOU WILL BE ABLE TO:

- Separate your subject from the background by controlling light spill
- Reduce lens flare
- Aim light precisely at a specific area of the photograph

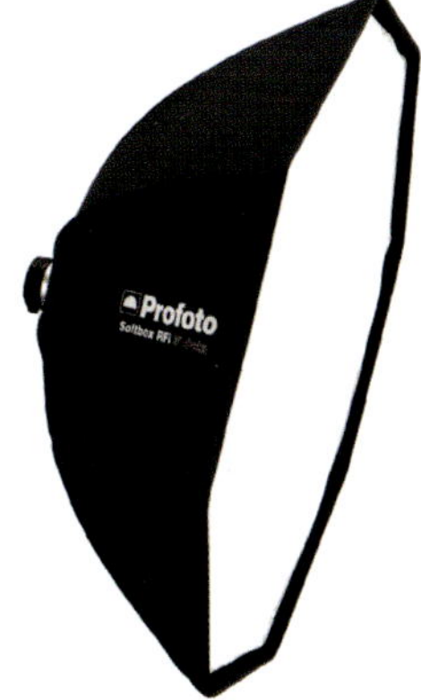

FIGURE 6.14

Figure 6.14: The octabox is my go-to modifier for soft light. This modifier has eight sides, and the light emerges from it with more angles than a four-sided softbox. More angles means softer light on your subject. I own small, medium, large, and extra-large octaboxes because they produce very soft and flattering light. However, I consider them almost useless without a grid. So buy the corresponding grids, too.

Figure 6.15: The four-sided softbox is my least favorite modifier, and I try to avoid using it. The four-sided softbox causes too many light rays to come out from this modifier at nearly the same angle, increasing the possibility of hot spots on people's skin. Four-sided softboxes produce harder light than eight-sided octaboxes.

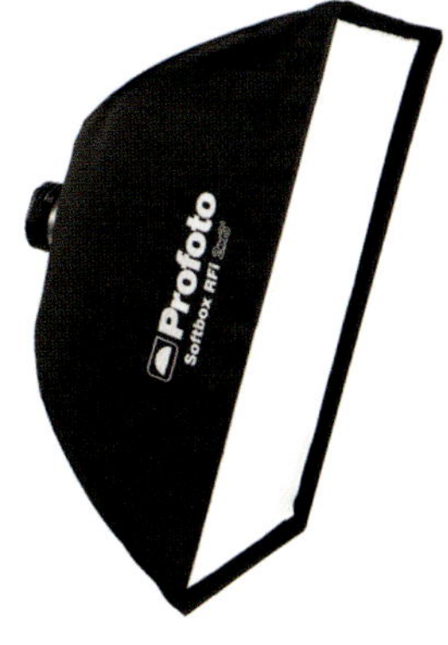

FIGURE 6.15

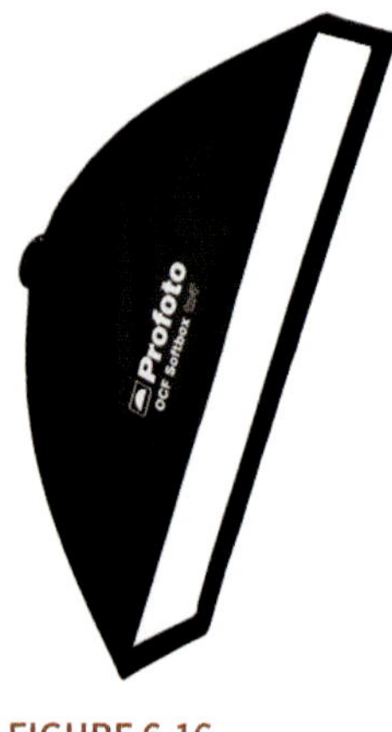

FIGURE 6.16

Figure 6.16: This is a strip box. Strip boxes are very useful, and I own many of them. Their skinny, rectangular shape produces great results for vertical subjects, such as people, articles of clothing, and accessories. Again, buy grids for them or you will have too much light spill.

Figure 6.17: This is my older son, Lucas. I absolutely love the silhouette of his belly and face. Because I wanted to draw the viewer's attention to his face and little belly, I had to sculpt the light. Putting two softboxes to the left and right of him would be the opposite of sculpting. Instead, I used two strip boxes with a grid on each of them. Per the Inverse Square Law of Light, the closer the light is to the subject, the faster the falloff will appear. So I placed a strip box as close as possible in front of him, right out of camera view, at a very high power.

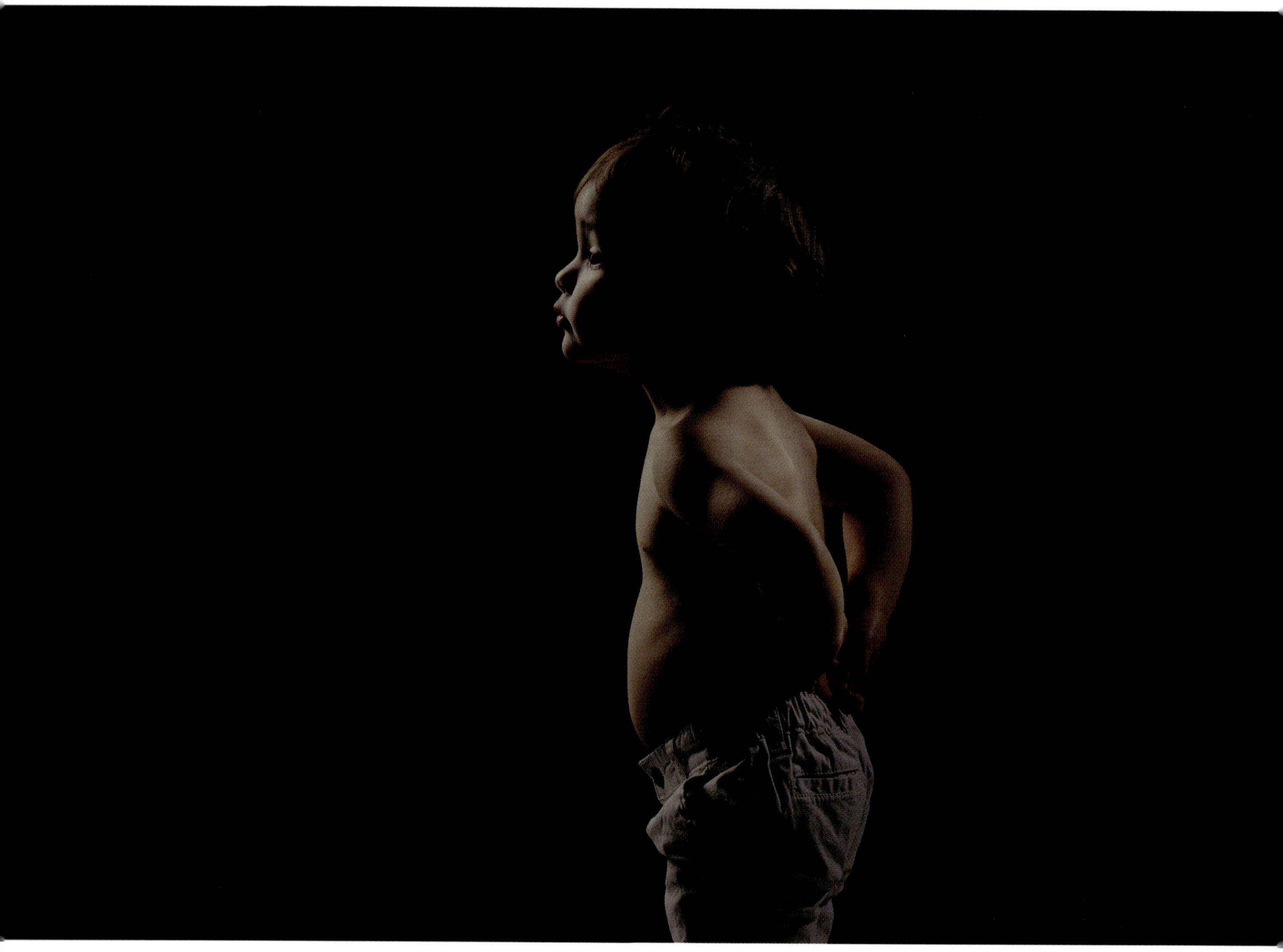

FIGURE 6.17

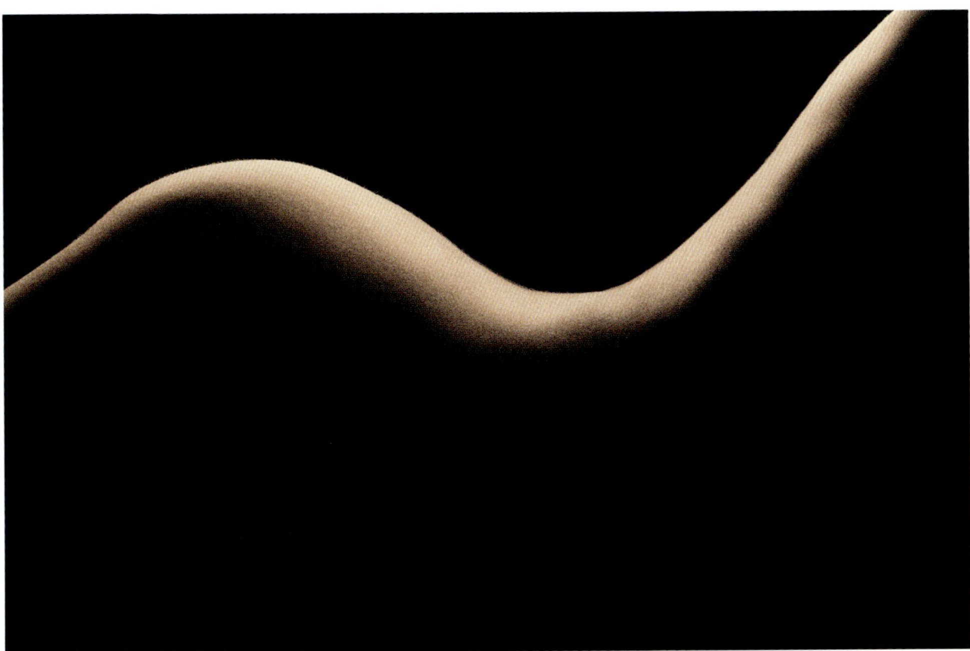

Next, I did not want his dark brown hair to become lost in the black background. To solve this, I used another strip box, with a grid, mounted on a C-stand and pointed down toward him. The top of the strip box illuminated his hair just enough to provide that separation. The middle of the strip box gently illuminated his back, and the bottom illuminated his pants. This is a perfect use for a strip box. Vertical subjects illuminated with a vertical light modifier work nicely together. When you see this photo, you can't help but admire his facial features, chubby cheeks, and cute little belly. This is what sculpting light is all about. Put light and shadows only and exactly where you want them.

Figure 6.18: A client hired me to shoot some abstract nudes of her. Abstract nudes are the perfect subject for light sculpting. To emphasize the beautiful curvature of her body, I again used a strip box held lengthwise to match the length of her body. With a grid attached, no light spill occurred, making the light fall off immediately into complete shadow. The further the strip box was from her body, the more of her body would be illuminated due to light spread.

Figure 6.19: A snoot is considered to be a specialty modifier. It's meant for a very specific purpose: to create a harder, more defined light than a grid can provide. Grids create a narrow beam of light, too, but they do so in a more gradual way. A snoot creates much harder shadow edges for those looking for a clean, well-defined circle of light. In fashion photography, I often use snoots to highlight a small piece of clothing or bring attention to a purse, belt, brand label, etc. If you like the clean lines that a snoot provides but want something a little softer, put a grid over the snoot. That will narrow the spread even further and slightly soften the edges.

Figure 6.20: This example shows the snoot modifier being the sculpting hero of the image. How terrific is it to be able to have the entire person be in silhouette, then add just a perfect little circle of light on her face? You can have so much fun using these modifiers!

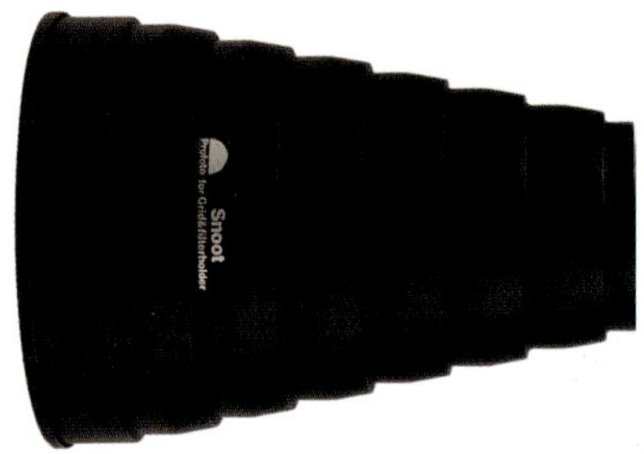

FIGURE 6.19

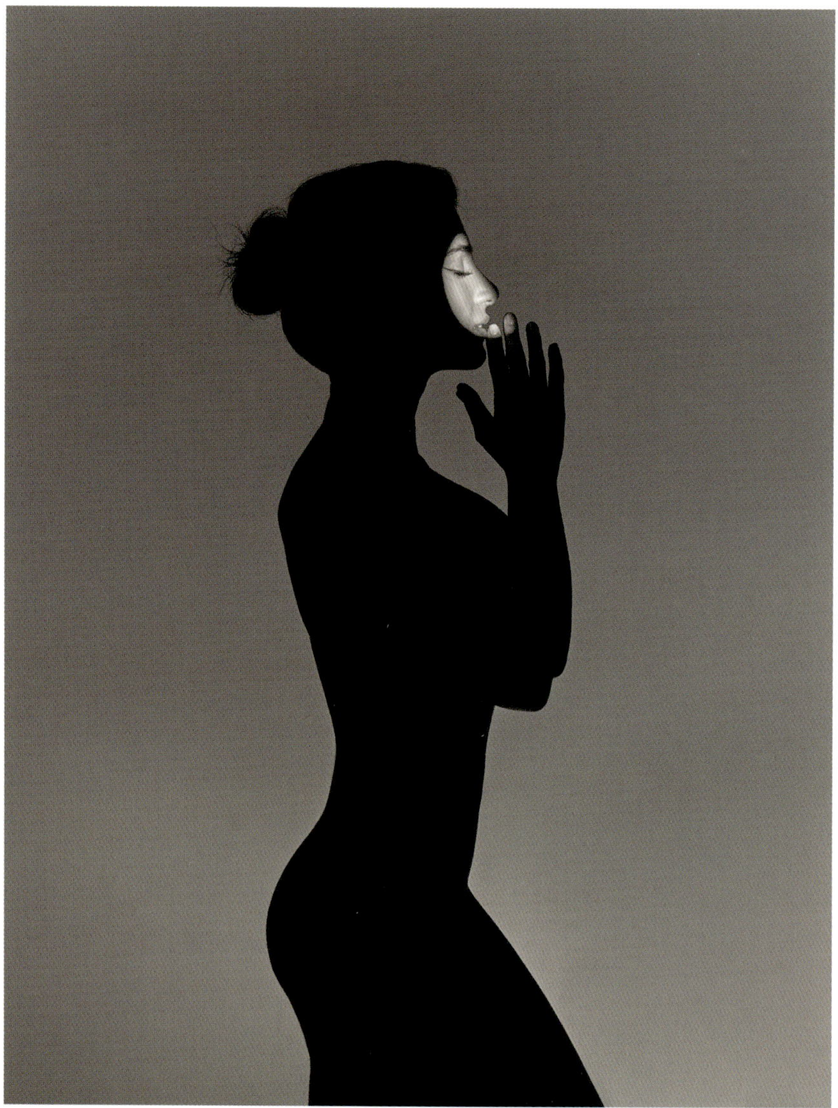

FIGURE 6.20

Light Sculpting Illustrations

For this book to do its job, I feel strongly that you have to feel confident that you have a good understanding of how the math of lighting works visually and how modifiers affect how light is sculpted. In order to help solidify these concepts, I created some lighting diagram examples using a beauty dish with and without a grid at various distances from the subject. These illustrations should help you visualize what happens with distances from light to subject and with or without grids to control light spill.

Figure 6.21: To start, I set up this illustration with a beauty dish without a grid far from the subject. Two lights are being used: one for the background, and the main light is the beauty dish pointed straight at the woman's face. As you can imagine, the beauty dish with no grid spills light all over the room. You can see how much light spill we have by looking at the floor and walls. At this distance and with no grid, you can see that there is no light sculpting at all. Since there is no grid, the light bounces everywhere and illuminates her face as well as her ponytail.

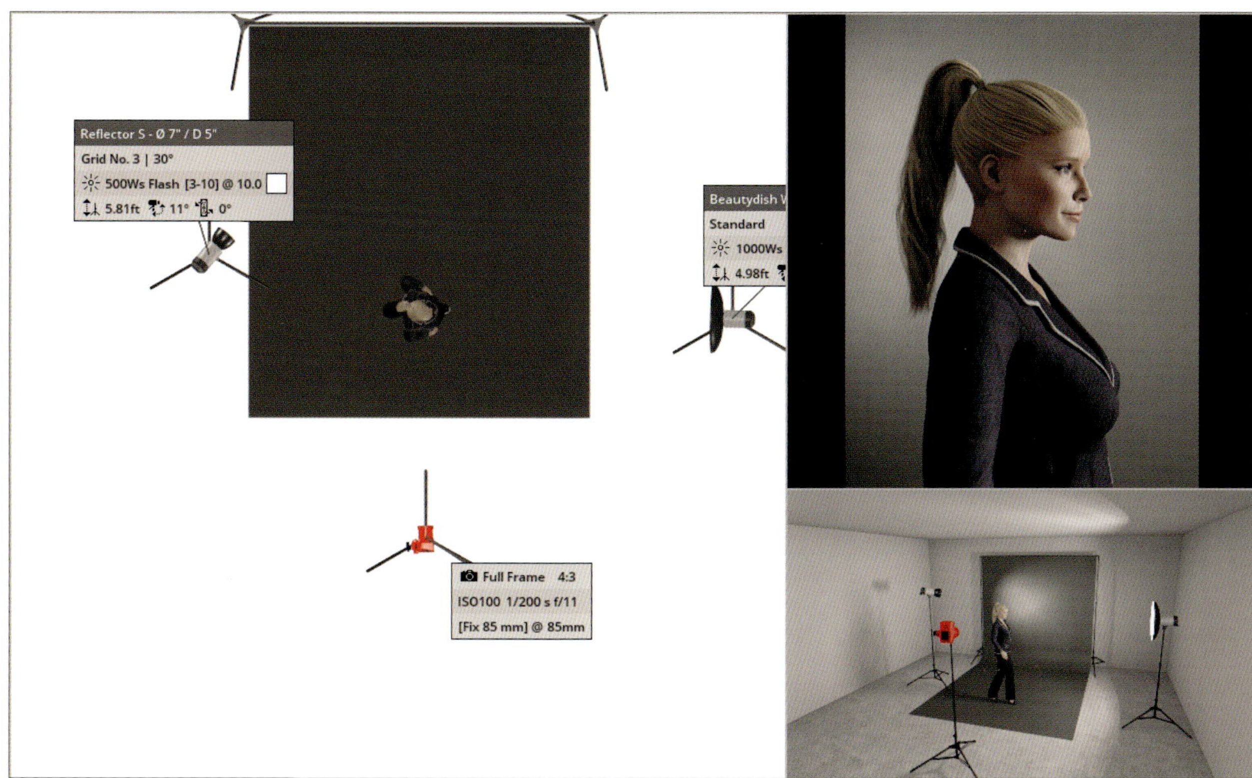

FIGURE 6.21

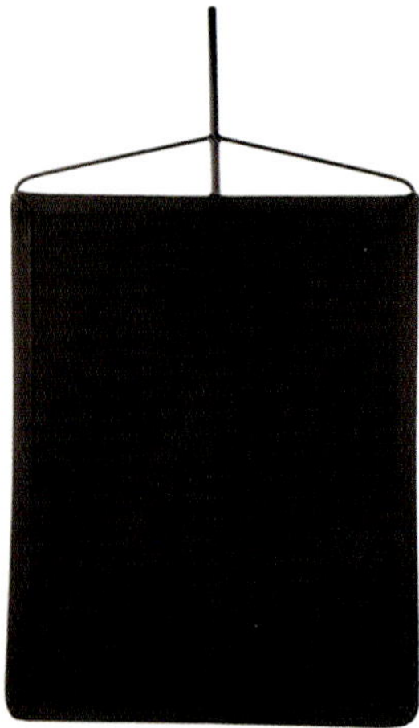

One light spill prevention method would be to use black flags on either side of the subject, as close to the subject as possible but still out of camera frame. Black flags absorb most of the light that strikes them, preventing any light from bouncing back to your subject. For on-location shoots, I bring a couple of portable black flags that have a built-in metal frame (see the next image). Flags do an amazing job of reducing the light on your subject. Regarding their material, in my opinion the only flags that seem to work well are the ones made from a fuzzy-soft material similar to duvetyne.

Figure 6.22: These are the better black flags that you can buy. They don't fold down, so you'll have to check whether you can transport them carefully in your vehicle. The good news is that they come in all sorts of sizes. Companies like Kupo and Matthews make these types of high-quality flags with a 3/8" top pin so you can attach them to a grip head on a C-stand.

Figure 6.23: This is the same setup as in the last example, with no grid over the beauty dish. But there is one key difference: This time, we are using the math behind the Inverse Square Law of Light to see how light falls off quickly when we bring the main light very close to the subject's face. At this close distance, there are two things to

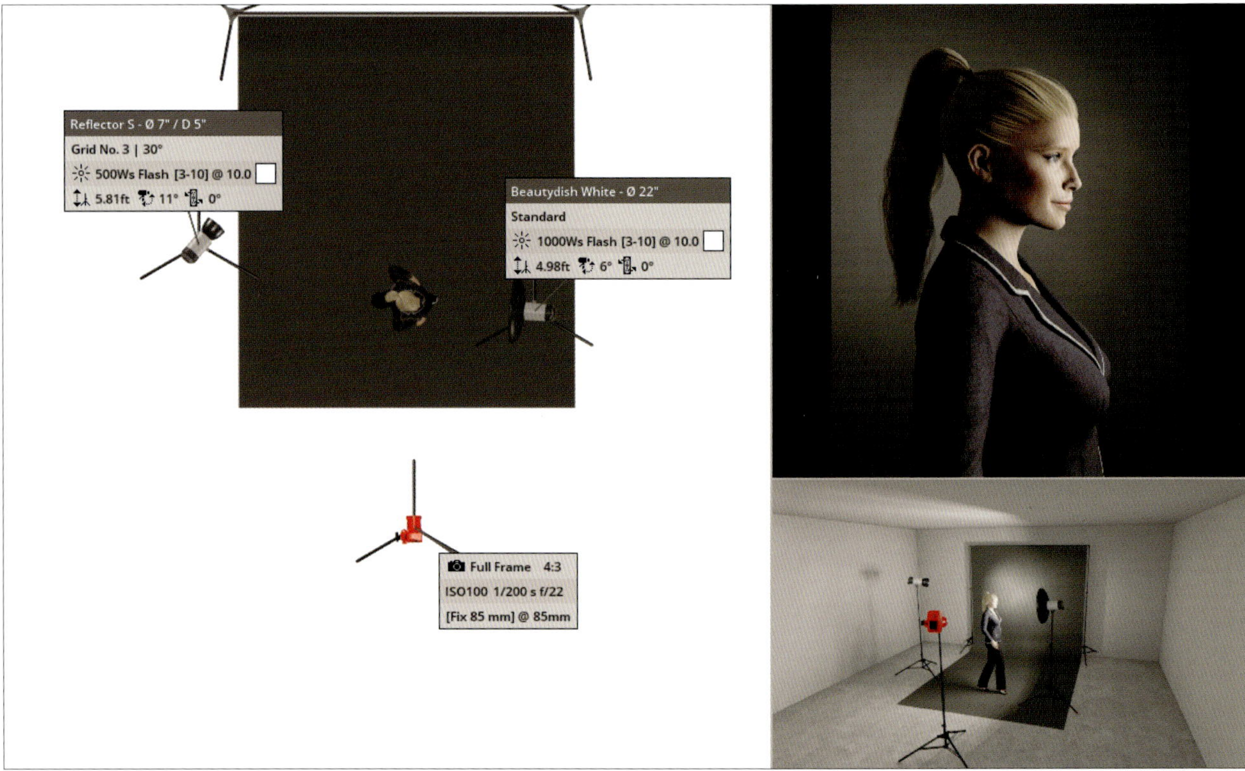

FIGURE 6.23

notice. First, the relative size of the light to the subject is larger, giving us a softer light on the face. Second, notice how much darker the cheeks, back of the neck, and ponytail are in comparison to the previous example. At this close distance, when the light fires from the beauty dish, many more light rays strike the woman's face. Not many light rays escape to illuminate the walls that provided that bounced light in the previous example.

Figure 6.24: Now let's put a grid over the beauty dish. With the grid on, the light can't spread nearly as much as it can without the grid. Pay attention to the floor and walls. You see very little spill this time. The close proximity of the beauty dish to the subject gives you that flattering light with soft shadows, and the grid prevents most of the light from spilling everywhere, which is why her cheeks and ponytail are so dark compared to the other results. This is how you sculpt light.

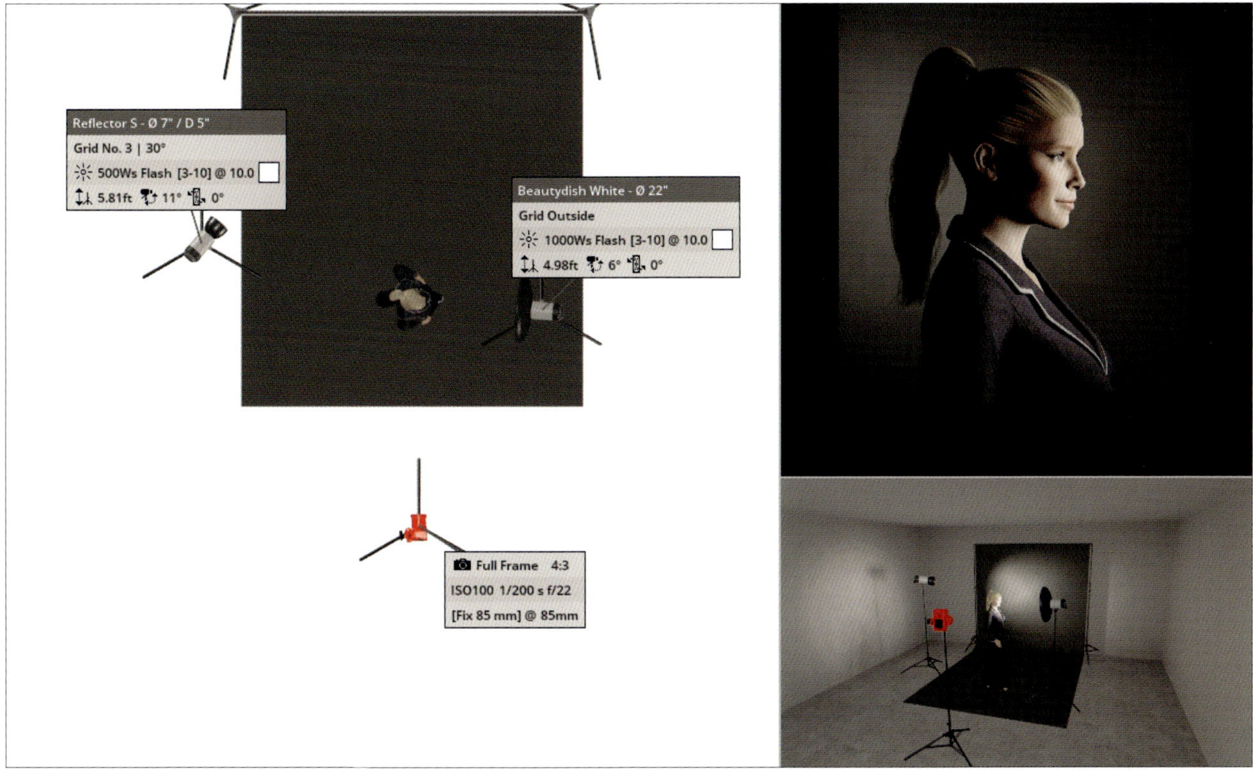

FIGURE 6.24

Final Words about Sculpting Light

I'm very aware that sculpting light is not always easy or even possible, especially if you are photographing outdoors. Trying to sculpt light outdoors and competing with the sun's light requires more powerful lights; 500-watt portable strobes should do the trick outdoors. Furthermore, if you are moving around a lot during a shoot, carrying around light shapers such as hard modifiers and grids can be difficult.

But if you manage to have this type of equipment with you and use it well, you will certainly be creating photographs that very few photographers will be able to match. Most photographers, at most, use a simple light attached to a basic octabox with no grid and simply aim it at their subjects. That's good, but that's not light sculpting. That's just using light to better illuminate the subject or separate the subject from the background.

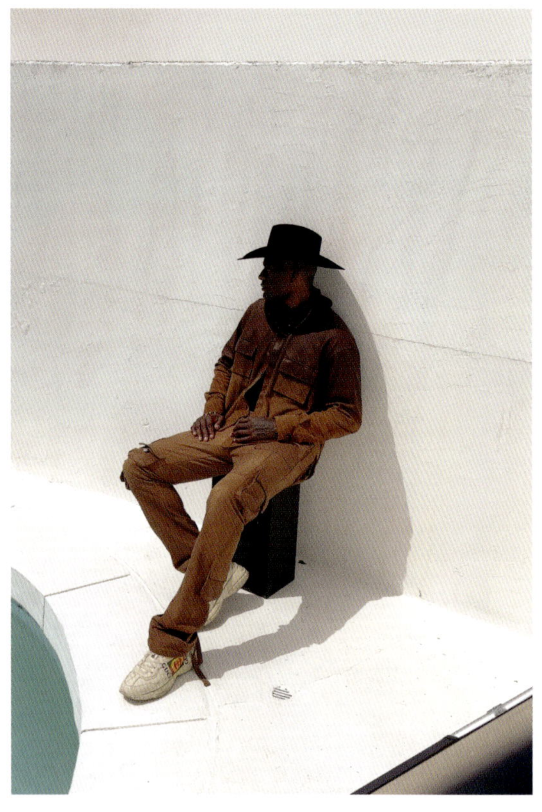

FIGURE 6.25

Figure 6.25 & 6.26: You don't see light sculpting very often in people photography; at least that's been my experience. So, to elevate the photographs I was taking for a Canon campaign for the RF 100–300mm f/2.8 lens, I felt that I had no choice but to sculpt the light on the models, even though I was shooting outside during the middle of the day. I didn't want to deliver "normal" photos for such an exciting lens, so we sculpted away.

In the behind-the-scenes photo, notice how bland the lighting looks as Gary leans against the wall. His cowboy hat was doing its job blocking most of the light from his eyes. Had I taken a photo of this setup as is, it would have been quite embarrassing.

To sculpt the light, I asked my team for a Profoto 500-watt monolight, a Magnum reflector that I could use to intensify the light, and a grid over the reflector to keep all the light rays from spreading much; I wanted the light to strike the front of Gary's face with maximum force. We aimed the light right under his hat so that we didn't accidently cause a shadow from our own light. Precision was key. Another light with a larger octabox was used to illuminate the leather jacket. The results speak for themselves.

This is how you elevate your work to higher levels. What if you had to sculpt the light during your next shoot? What would you do? Sometimes I pretend that the sculpting of light on a shoot is the #1 requirement from the client. This practice forces me not to be lazy. After doing a lot of experimenting during many practice sessions, I figured out a better way to shape the light more accurately than just using a standard softbox directed toward the subject. Sculpting light outdoors is more manageable under the cover of shade, of course, but if you have lights powerful enough, you can sculpt light anywhere.

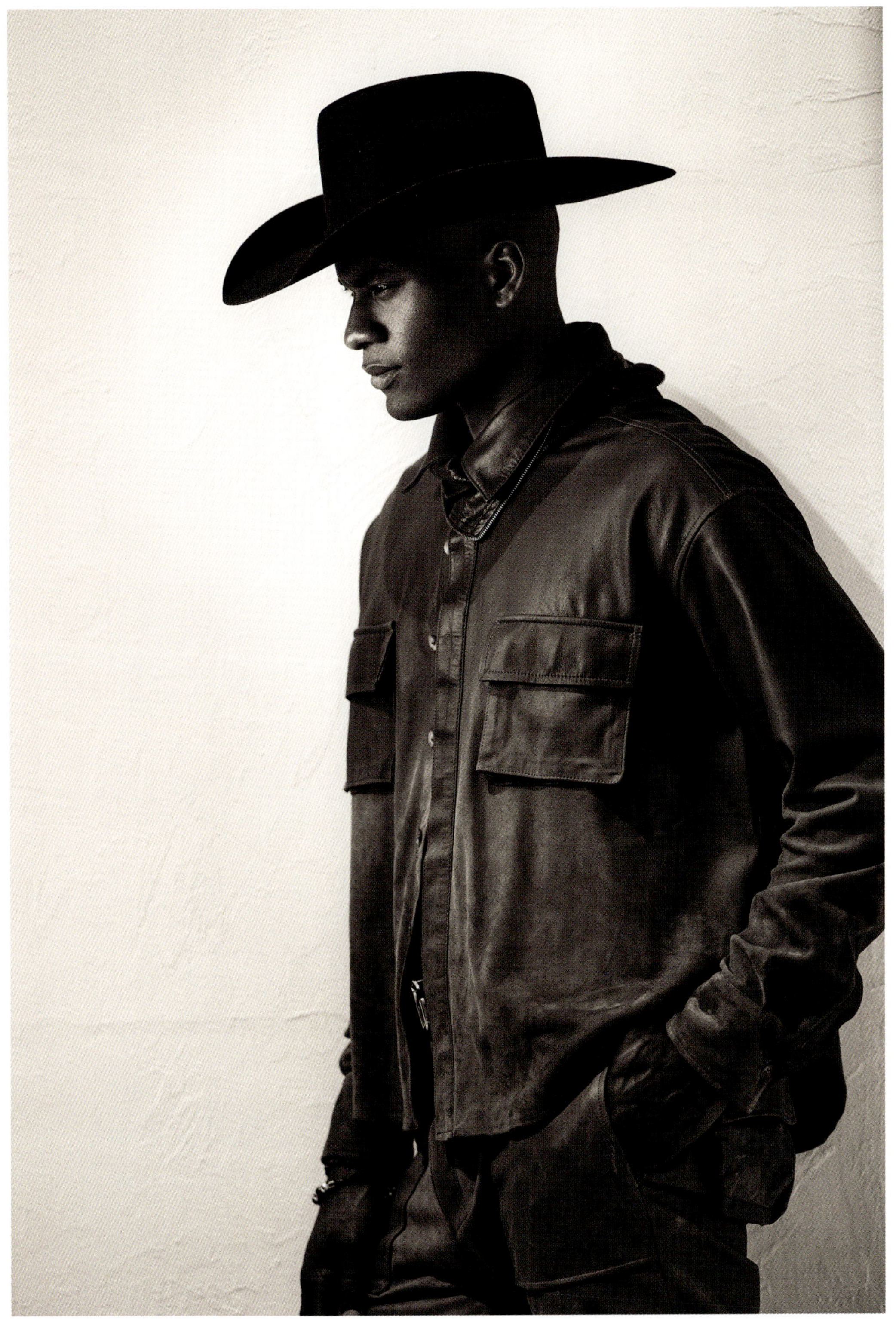
FIGURE 6.26

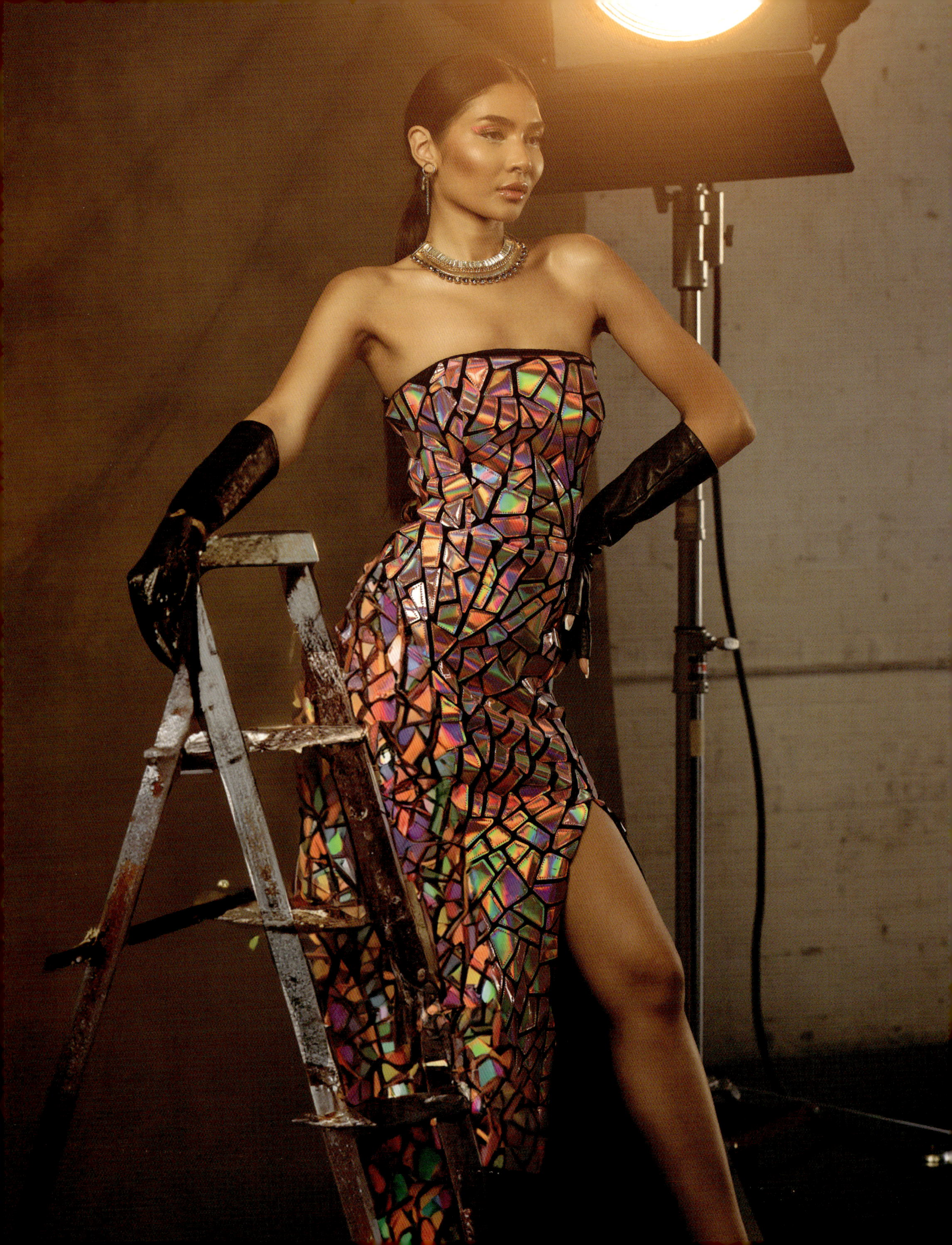

Chapter 7

NAME: Your Game Plan

NAME is an acronym I created to help you remember the steps you must take to bring your vision to life. In Chapters 2–6, we examined FACES and covered all of the choices a photographer can implement to create a vision for their photography using flashes. This chapter is about what is needed to actually execute that vision. FACES is the idea, and NAME is the action! NAME represents the final component of this book's lighting method.

I can't begin to tell you how many times in my career I have had an idea or a vision for what I wanted to do with my lights during a shoot, but when it was time to make it happen, I froze. I didn't know what the first step or the second step should be, or even how many steps I needed for this vision to come to life. After many years of frustration and practice, I devised a step-by-step system to help me through this process. That's what this chapter is all about.

NAME is your game plan. Let's get started.

> **WHAT NAME STANDS FOR**
>
> **N:** Number of flashes, and the grouping required
>
> **A:** Angle of the lights
>
> **M:** Modifiers needed for each light
>
> **E:** Energy output for each light

Number of Flashes and Grouping

Number of Lights

First and foremost, you need to know what you want to add light to. For example, if I'm doing a portrait shoot, I automatically know that I want to add a dedicated light to just the person's face. On a fashion shoot, I need a light just for the clothing and at least one light for the face. If the fashion shoot requires highlighting an accessory, such as a purse, then I need a light just for that purse. If the subject has dark hair, I need a light to illuminate the hair so it doesn't turn into black mush when the photo is printed.

Next is the background. Do I want to add light to the background or not? Do I want to lift the shadows in the room or not? If you refer to Chapter 3: Add Light, you will have a better idea about where you would want to add light to your photograph. In that chapter, I listed six reasons why you would consider adding light to the scene. If you consider sculpting the light on a portrait (Chapter 6), you will probably need more lights and equipment than if you are simply illuminating a subject with light.

Grouping the Lights

Next, you have to figure out how you will group the lights so you can either work with them together or control each light separately. This is how you become organized during a shoot, and how you are able to control each light from your remote on camera. Also, if you are working with less powerful lights, such as a 250-watt portable strobes or even 50-watt hot shoe flashes, you may well need to gang up multiple units together to produce more power working as a single unit.

Angle of the Lights

Direct Angle Versus Indirect Angle (Feathered)

When I first discovered feathered lighting with my light modifiers, I couldn't believe my eyes. I started laughing in frustration that I had not discovered this feature before. You see, one of the reasons why many photographers dislike the "look" of strobes is because it can look harsh and very artificial compared to the softness of natural light. That can be true…until you feather the light!

As light emerges from a softbox, the light from the middle of the modifier will always appear harsher, harder, and more direct than the light from the rest of the softbox. As the light radiates from the softbox (or any modifier really), the light begins to soften, almost like a vignette. The key concept behind direct versus indirect lighting is to illuminate the subject not with the light that emerges from the middle of the light modifier (direct angle) but instead with the softer light from its edges (indirect angle). People are naturally inclined to always point the light modifier directly toward the subject. I rarely do that now. By turning the lights off-axis and using the softer light, you will have a much more natural-looking result.

Feathering the light is not always appropriate or the best look. But it is definitely something to keep in mind the next time you are directing a light modifier toward a person, and the result is too harsh or "flashy" looking. Let's look at some examples.

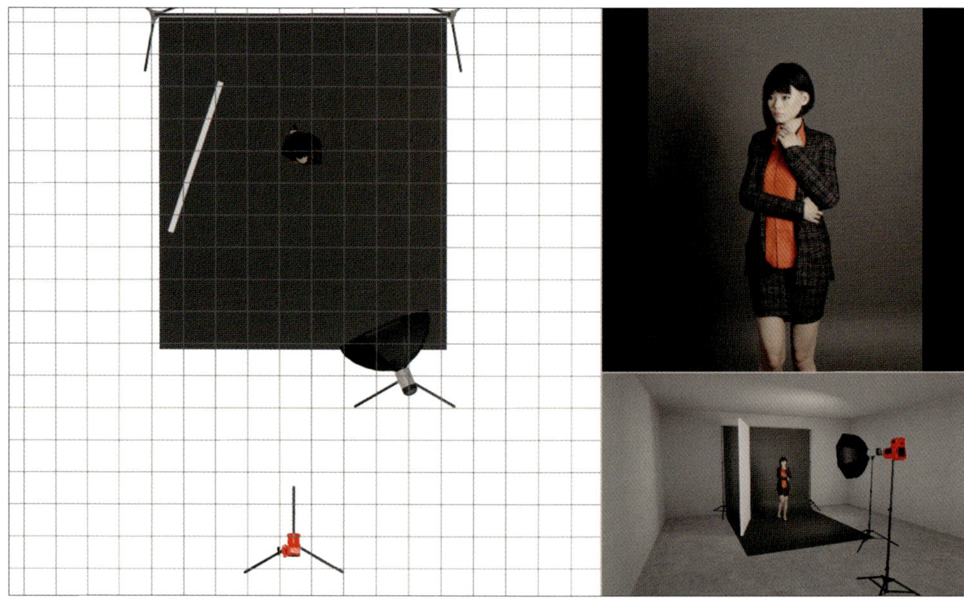

Figures 7.1 & 7.2: In this example, notice that the octabox is directly pointed at the subject. As the light emerges from the octabox, it illuminates the model's face, body, skirt, and legs. The model clearly looks flashed, doesn't she? The problem is that there is too much light everywhere from top to bottom. This method is throwing light at someone, not controlling it. There's a huge difference.

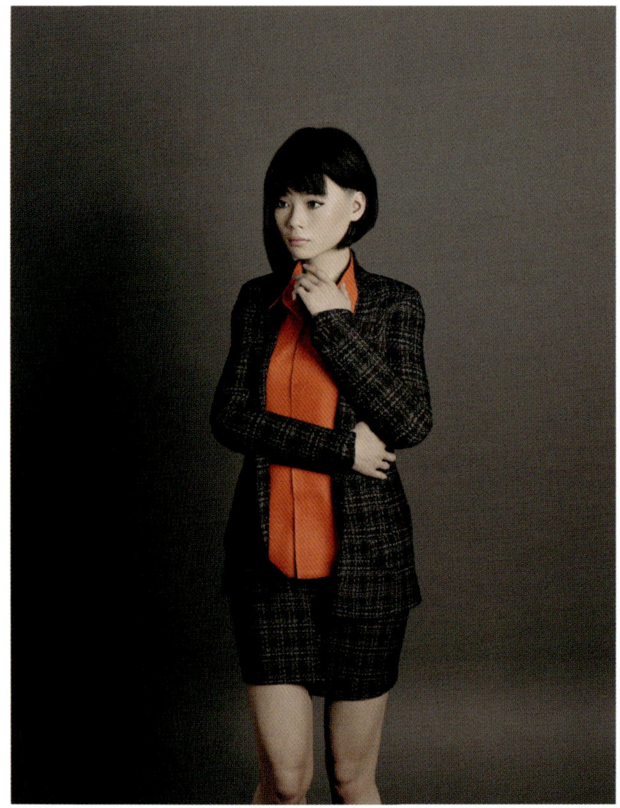

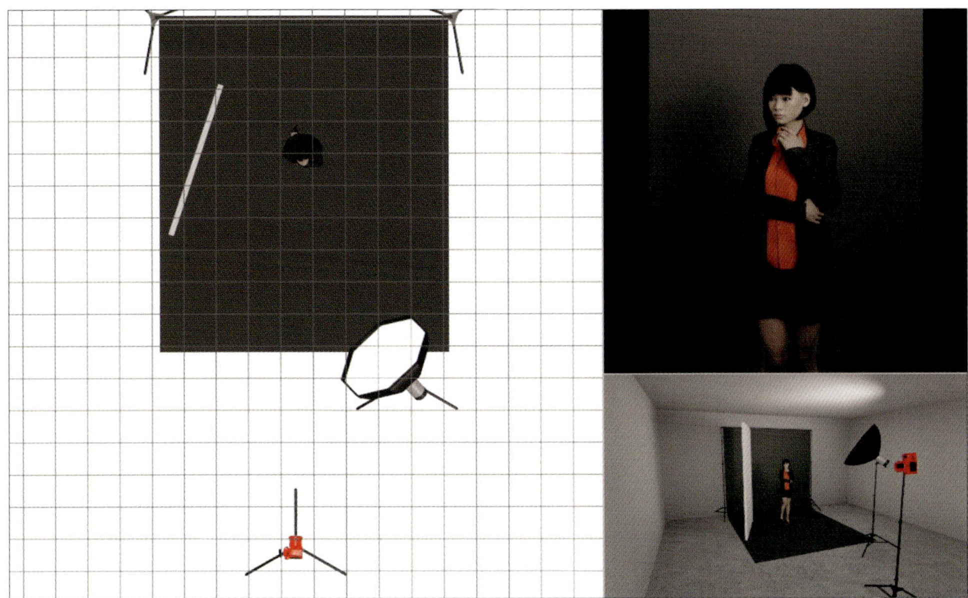

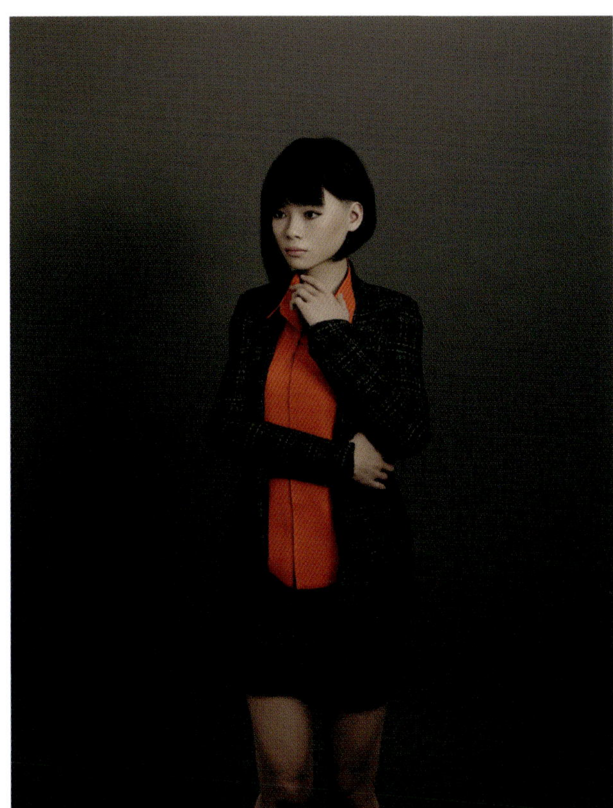

Figures 7.3 & 7.4: In this example, I directed the light far up and to the left. What a difference! Now, most of that harsh direct light travels toward the ceiling out of camera view, and we are left with just the soft light from the octabox on her face. Also, her top and skirt look much more naturally lit, since they are not receiving direct light right on them. In addition to these benefits, you also achieve more emphasis on the face rather than on the rest of the body.

You may have noticed the white foam board used as a fill. In my opinion, when using this technique of feathering the light from a modifier, it's a good idea to have a V-flat or a white bounce card to be used as fill. This fill light will allow you to direct more or less light toward the background. You will be surprised at how different the results can be by simply changing the angle of the V-flat for fill light.

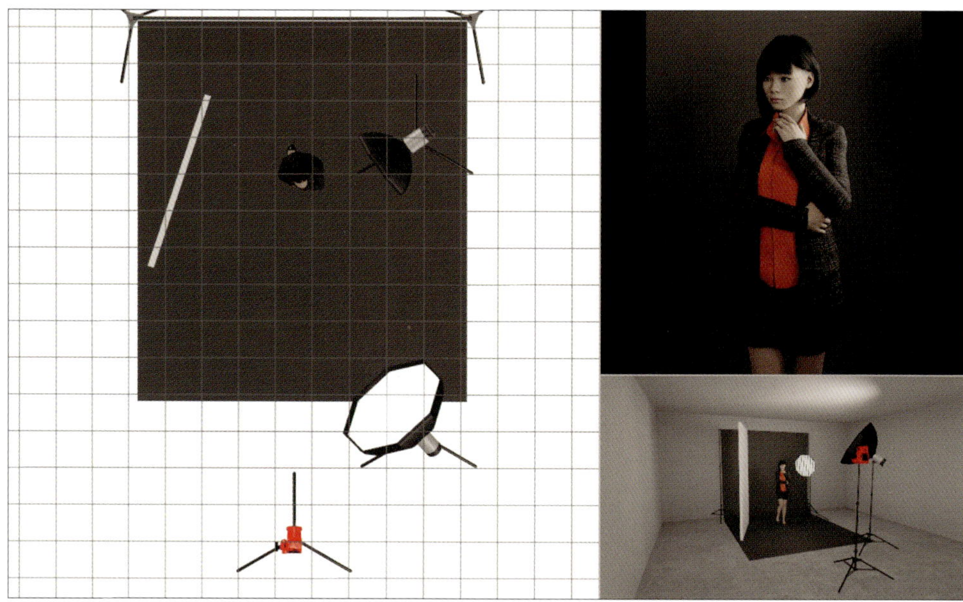

Figures 7.5 & 7.6: This is a bonus technique that I absolutely love! I want to share this with you because I think you will love this technique and use it as much as I do. One of the best ways to shape a person's face is to add a light from the back behind the head and indirectly angle it at the person's face. Feathering this light is very important or it will look like accent light. A light from this angle is very flattering if executed correctly. When printing a photo of a person with this kind of lighting, you will see a very strong three-dimensional quality to the portrait on paper—even more so than on a screen. The back light should be softened with an internal diffuser, gridded, and feathered. From there, you should experiment with the power of this light and make it just a bit brighter than the main light illuminating the front of the subject's face. When done correctly, you will be very happy with the results!

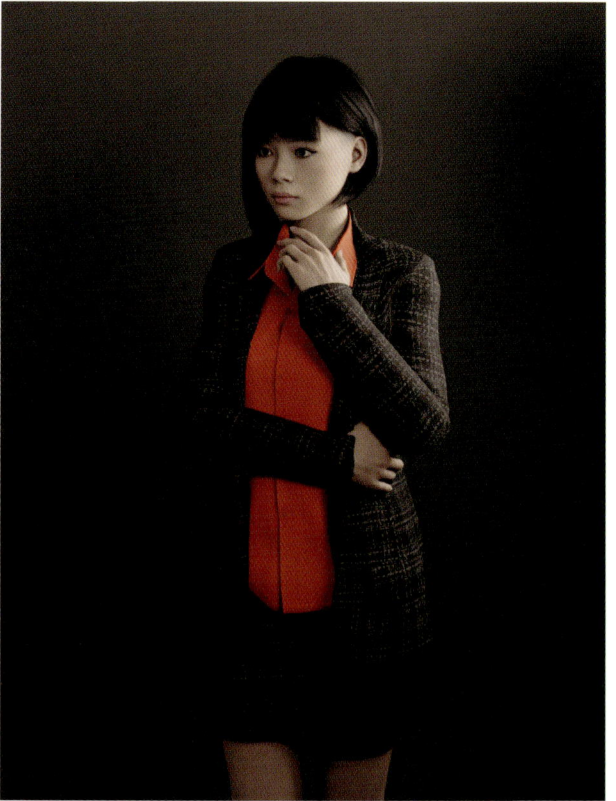

Flash Angle and Color for Mimicking Another Light Source

Imagine a scenario in which you have a person sitting in a moody room, perhaps in a hotel lobby next to a beautiful lamp. The lamp is decorative, and it doesn't provide much light on your subject. In a situation like this, I try to create the illusion that the portrait was lit by that visible lamp in the scene. To achieve that, the angle of my flashes must match the angle of the ambient light source, the lamp. That lamp represents the "Lighting Reference Point" which I explain in my other lighting book, *Picture Perfect Lighting*. Not only should the angle match, but the color should have a similar quality, as well. If the lighting reference is a warm amber light, then the flash you use must also be warm to match the lamp. They don't have to match exactly, but both the angle and color need to be in the same vicinity to make it seem real.

The goal in a scenario like this is for people to admire your photo for the mood that you created. If your use of flashes is obvious, then it will take away from that natural vibe. We have all seen those photographs that people take on the beach, when the sun is about to set completely over the horizon. The scene is lit by hardly any sunlight, and whatever is left of the sunlight is warm and soft. So, what does the photographer do? They grab a flash, position the family with their backs to the sunset, put the flash in front of the family, and take the photo. The result is a photo that has a good exposure on the family, but the lighting doesn't make any sense. The light from the flash is daylight balanced at 5000K, and it's much harsher than the soft look of the last moments before the sun completely sets. This is a setup that should be used only if you must. There is always a way to change the angle of the light and the color of your flashes by using gels, which can help you create a better blend of the two light sources in a situation such as this.

Figure 7.7: This is a portrait of the actress Mithila Palkar in my studio in Beverly Hills. This is a good example of light blending. It appears as if this photo was lit by the window behind her; however, two flashes were responsible for most of the lighting. The angle of each light source is what makes them effective but invisible. The light that appears to be window light is actually my flash, which is positioned camera left and parallel to the window. The parallel angle to the window is what makes the two light sources blend seamlessly. The second light is a big, soft modifier positioned behind me to illuminate the entire scene with soft light. The result is a clean-looking portrait with beautiful light that seems completely natural. The angle at which you place each of your lights plays a major factor in achieving the goal of making the flashes look invisible.

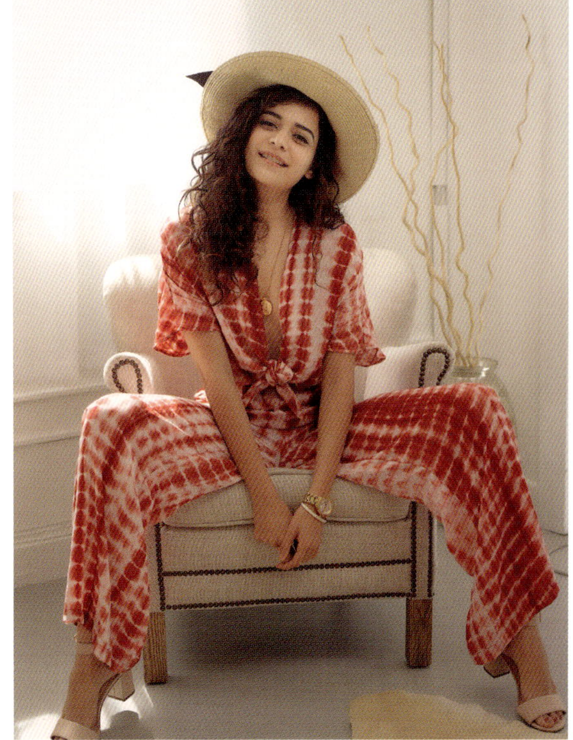

FIGURE 7.7

The Effect of Light Angles on Shadows

The angle at which you choose to put the lights you need for your vision to come alive will always impact the type and size of the shadows you create, particularly shadows in the background, which are usually not wanted. Shadows can be very distracting and unflattering. A quick adjustment to the light angle could be all you need to ensure that the shadows are adding to your photo and not distracting from it.

Figure 7.8: This could have been a beautiful photo of Arianna, but I had to throw it out because of its distracting shadow. The shadow on the right completely takes over the photo, and you can't stop looking at it. How long would it take to seamlessly remove this shadow in Photoshop? Honestly, it doesn't matter. It's much faster to pause the shoot and reconsider the angle of the lights to minimize, soften, or remove the shadow altogether.

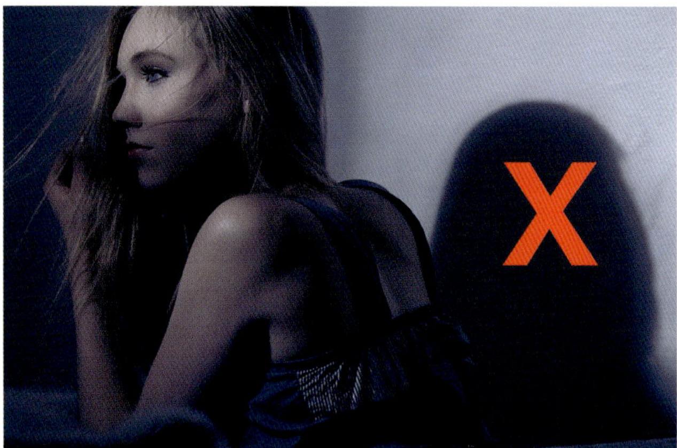

FIGURE 7.8

Figure 7.9: This photo of Saa was taken in a similar manner as Figure 7.8. But notice that there is no distracting shadow this time. There was a key light at camera right pointed towards Saa's face. This key light caused a shadow on both her head and the wall, similar to the last example. I paused the shoot and changed the angle by rotating the key light counterclockwise to feather the light and remove the shadow from the wall. Then we continued with the shoot. All those countless hours I would have had to spend in Photoshop removing shadows from this set was resolved in less than 60 seconds.

Figure 7.10: During a wedding in Los Angeles, I was trying to create a beautiful portrait of the bride in front of a clean, tan wall. However, no matter what I tried with my modified flash, a distracting shadow kept forming behind the bride on her left or right. Finally, I pointed the flash with the octabox behind me toward the intersection of the wall and the ceiling. That light bounced back beautifully and placed the shadow right behind her, completely out of camera view. Angles matter!

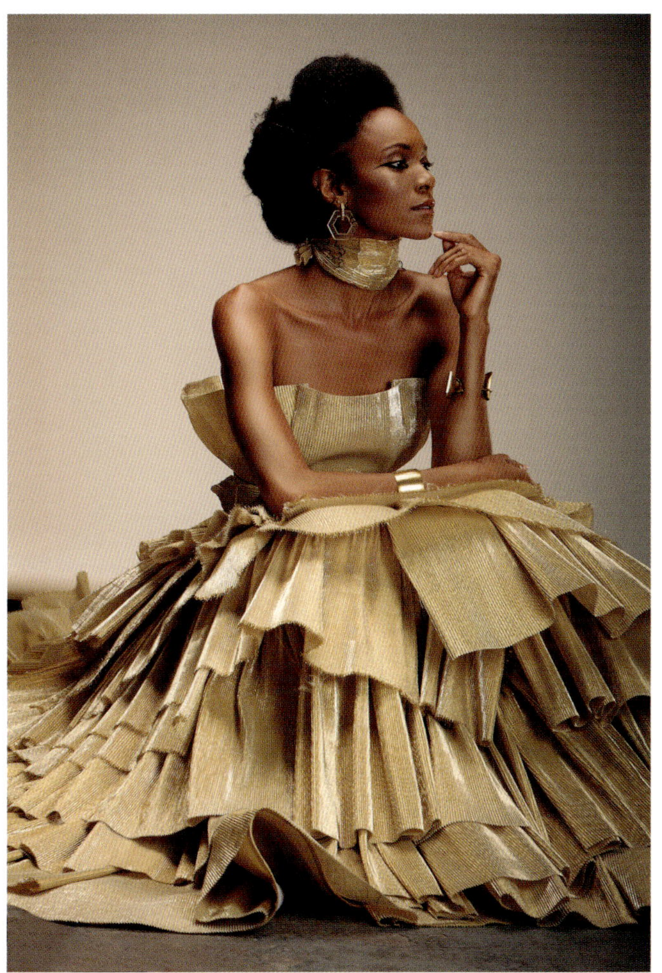

FIGURE 7.9

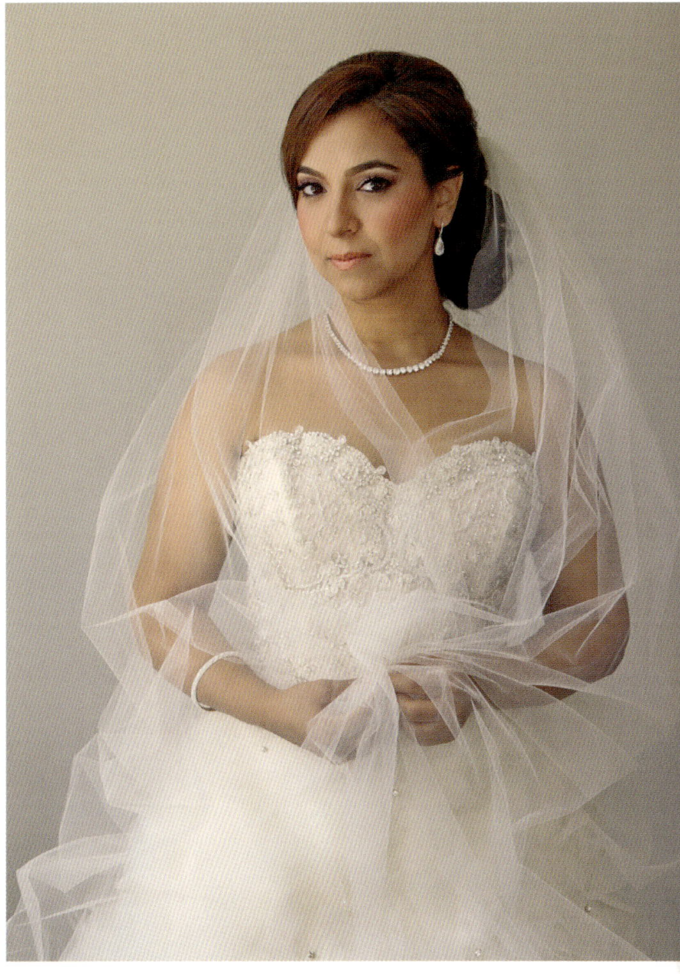

FIGURE 7.10

Modifiers for Each Light

In the previous chapter, "Sculpt the Light," we spent a lot of time discussing modifiers and what they were designed to do. I would like to emphasize "designed to do," because one of the biggest lessons I learned the hard way is to treat each modifier with the respect it deserves. These mods truly are tools of the trade. A chef wouldn't try to fillet a delicate fish with a bread knife, right? But I see many photographers using whatever modifier they can find to do nothing more than shoot light forward. That's bad!

When you pick up a modifier, you should know exactly what that modifier was designed to do. What is the behavior of the light from each of your modifiers? What kind of quality of light can you expect when you use each modifier, either feathered or direct?

How crisp are the shadows from each modifier at various distances? I know what you are probably thinking: "That's nice in theory, but who has time for that?" Well, I'm guessing that since you bought this book because you want to improve, then you do have time!

Honestly, since there are so many resources that explain what each modifier does, it should be easy for you to get started. Once you have an idea how a modifier works, then it's time to try it for yourself.

THE FOUR MOST COMMON TYPES OF LIGHT MODIFIERS

Circumstantial Light Modifiers: These are my favorite modifiers because they don't require equipment. Circumstantial light modifiers are regular, everyday objects in your surroundings that can be used creatively for their light-shaping qualities. For example, the wall of a building can become a very effective reflector, and its large size can produce soft light. A white FedEx truck can also be a great reflector. Tree branches or the overhang of a rooftop can create interesting shadows on a wall when lit directly by the sun. The ground can be dark dirt, which absorbs light. The green grass at a park will create a green colorcast from the ground up. A smooth sidewalk can act as a great light reflector from the ground up.

All the objects around you have a unique way of behaving when lit directly by the sun or any light source, such as your flashes. When you combine circumstantial light modifiers with your flashes, a whole new world of possibilities opens! One of my favorite ways to use circumstantial light modifiers with my flashes on a location shoot is to find a clean white(ish) wall. I fire my flashes directly at the wall to create soft, bounced light onto my subject. Unlike the sun, which you cannot control, you can always dial your flash power up or down, depending on how intense you want your bounced light to be. The best photographers in the world that I have watched work are the ones who have taken this combination of circumstantial light modifiers and flashes to

a whole new level! These people are true masters: they can create the most mesmerizing work anywhere they are and at any time of the day. To them, everything is an opportunity, not an excuse.

Soft Modifiers: Soft modifiers are soft in their construction and are usually made from fabric. Soft modifiers include softboxes, octaboxes, and umbrellas of all sizes. The larger the modifier relative to the subject, the softer the light will be. But practically speaking, soft modifiers usually provide soft light.

Hard Modifiers: Hard modifiers are hard to the touch. They are made from metal or strong plastic. Hard modifiers are great for sculpting light and reflecting light with a higher output. Some hard modifiers can even give you two or more stops of light than the flash can by itself; they do this by harnessing the power of their reflective qualities and shape. The opposite of soft modifiers, hard modifiers usually provide hard light.

Specialty Modifiers (Gels, Grids, GOBOs, Barn Doors, Snoots): These are the modifiers that refine the light and target specific areas that need to be lit. Specialty modifiers are also used to create a different mood from what's right in front of you by using gels and/or a combination of modifiers. GOBOs are used to create interesting graphic shadows on walls or any background. Grids limit the spread of light from any modifier to a specific angle, such as 5-degree, 20-degree, 40-degree, etc.

Your "best friend" for learning how modifiers work is a mannequin torso. They are very patient! If you try to learn with people as your test subjects, you will test their patience very quickly, and it will only lead to frustration. Another great helper is a clean wall or a clean surface on which you can shine a light. This makes it easy to notice the spread and intensity of the light with various modifiers.

I spent a great deal of time learning not only the entire MagMod system of accessories, but I also practiced how quickly I could put various setups together on location. This has become a huge advantage for me, because by having practiced various setups, I can determine if I have time to try something similar during a real shoot. "Knowing" what the MagMod modifiers do is very different from "experiencing" them firsthand. In photography, speed matters. Time is never on your side. If you have to fiddle around with your modifiers because you are not sure how they work or are assembled, or you don't know how long it takes to set them up, you will look quite unprofessional. How well you know and modify your lights can make or break the shoot.

Energy of Each Light

Energy is another word for power, so the final step of the NAME method deals with how much power you set each light to. For this step, think about how lights balance each other out and how the various power settings will result in different brightness levels throughout the image, which will draw the viewer's attention to the desired areas of the photograph.

Energy is also a key decision that informs the mood you are creating in the scene. If there is too much energy throughout the room, you wash everything out. If there is not enough energy, the room or scene will be underexposed. Each light's power setting must be corrected for whatever vision you had during the FACES stage.

During a shoot, regardless of the pressure I may be under, I always tell myself to take good care of the energy output for whatever number of lights I am using. I might be using just one light, or I might be using six lights; either way, I need to ensure that while I'm shooting, I set the power of each light exactly where it needs to be. Trying to fix exposure in Photoshop after the fact is not fun. I would rather get it right during the shoot and be done with it.

The decision you make regarding the energy of each flash is going to result in how well-balanced your photo feels. Energy of lights is about balancing the light so that the result looks seamless, with each light contributing to the scene the exact amount of light it needs to.

NAME Case Studies

Adda

Figure 7.11: When I first envisioned what to do in this space, I was immediately drawn to the abundance of white throughout the room. Pairing all of that white with Adda's black outfit just seemed a perfect way to gain instant separation between her and the room. The outside light was cloudy, so the white room was rather dark. The weak light had to be fixed.

Since this was a campaign photo for Canon, the quality of the final image file mattered. So there was to be no shooting at ISO 1600 to compensate for the lack of light. Instead, I used my flashes to provide all the light I needed. I set my camera to ISO 100 for maximum quality. I wanted this photo to look as if it was lit by only natural light. It seemed to be a good choice considering how clean and soft everything in the room was.

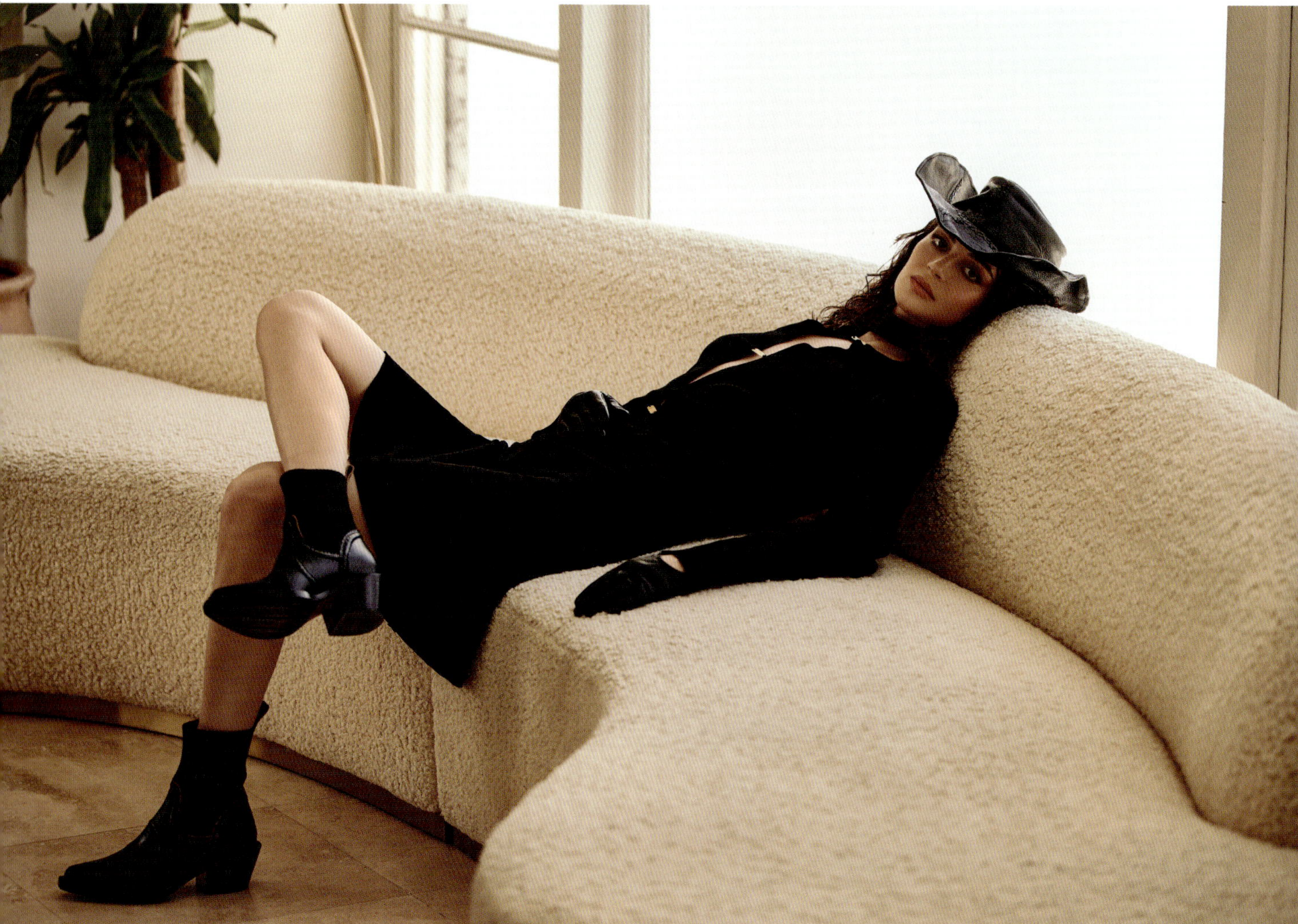

The photo looks completely lit by natural light, and being able to shoot indoors at ISO 100 by using flashes is by far one of the biggest advantages of learning how to use flash properly. Without the use of flash, I would have had to take this photo at ISO 1600 or even 3200, since the ambient light was so weak.

Number of Lights: There were three light sources for this Canon campaign photo. Two of them were Profoto flashes, and the third light was the sun, though it was weak.

Angle of Lights: One light was pointed up toward the ceiling to create clean light throughout the room. The second light was positioned near the plant, camera left, to gracefully illuminate the side of Adda's face. This second light also added some directionality to the light and helped remove the flat feeling from the main light pointed toward the ceiling.

Modifiers: The light pointed toward the ceiling had to seem as if the sun was illuminating the room, not my light. Therefore, we double diffused the large octabox and pointed the entire setup toward the ceiling for further softening. The second Profoto flash was modified with a standard zoom reflector to throw the light completely across the room to illuminate her face ever so gently. To achieve a soft effect, we used a standard kitchen paper towel in front of the zoom reflector. You can see how that side of the couch is lit just a bit brighter than the other side of the couch closer to the camera.

Energy: The main light was raised until I could see a hint of shadow detail on her black dress. It is much easier to catch that detail on black clothing using flash when shooting the photo, rather than trying to fake it in Photoshop. The second light was more of an accent light and was powered half a stop brighter than the main light. That extra bit of power gave her right cheek the lightest boost over the rest of her face.

Fernando

Figures 7.12 & 7.13: This photo of my friend and actor Fernando was taken at his home in California for a magazine feature about him. I wanted to create something with more drama than your average portrait. I found an area near his front door that had a clean backdrop, but the natural light coming in was too weak to give me the drama I was looking for. The solution was to use a strobe and make it look like the sun.

Number of Lights: Only one flash was needed for this portrait. The second light source was the sun.

Angle of Lights: The job of the flash was to provide me with the drama and power that I couldn't get from the natural light coming into the home. Therefore, the angle had to be similar to the angle of the sun. I placed the light up on a C-stand and pointed it down toward Fernando. This angle perfectly mimicked the sun. This is the reason why the angle of your light matters more than you think. Had I put the light at face level, it would have lost that natural light feel.

Modifiers: Again, to mimic the sun, I had to use the correct modifiers. Therefore, I used a Profoto flash with a Magnum reflector and a grid to direct the light rays only to his face and not let them spill onto the wall behind him. Without the grid, light would have been everywhere and would have completely ruined the mood.

Energy: I dialed the power up until the light was strong enough so that the other side of his face had some strong shadows from the light falloff. I didn't want the falloff to be too extreme, so I dialed it back down until the balance felt right.

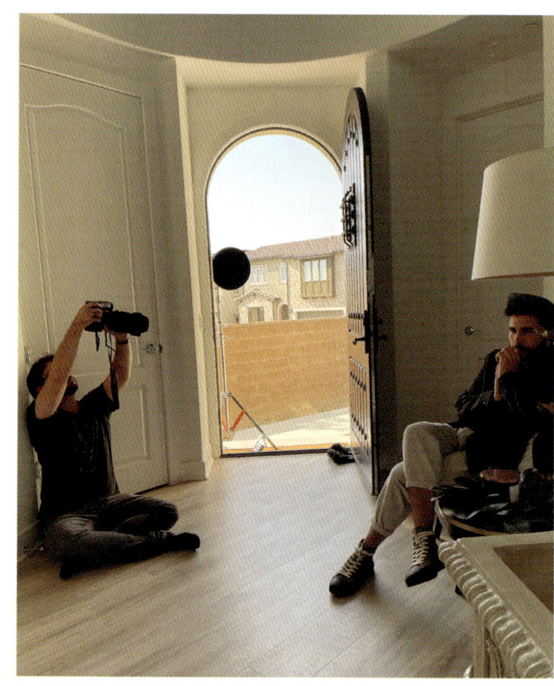

FIGURE 7.12

FIGURE 7.13

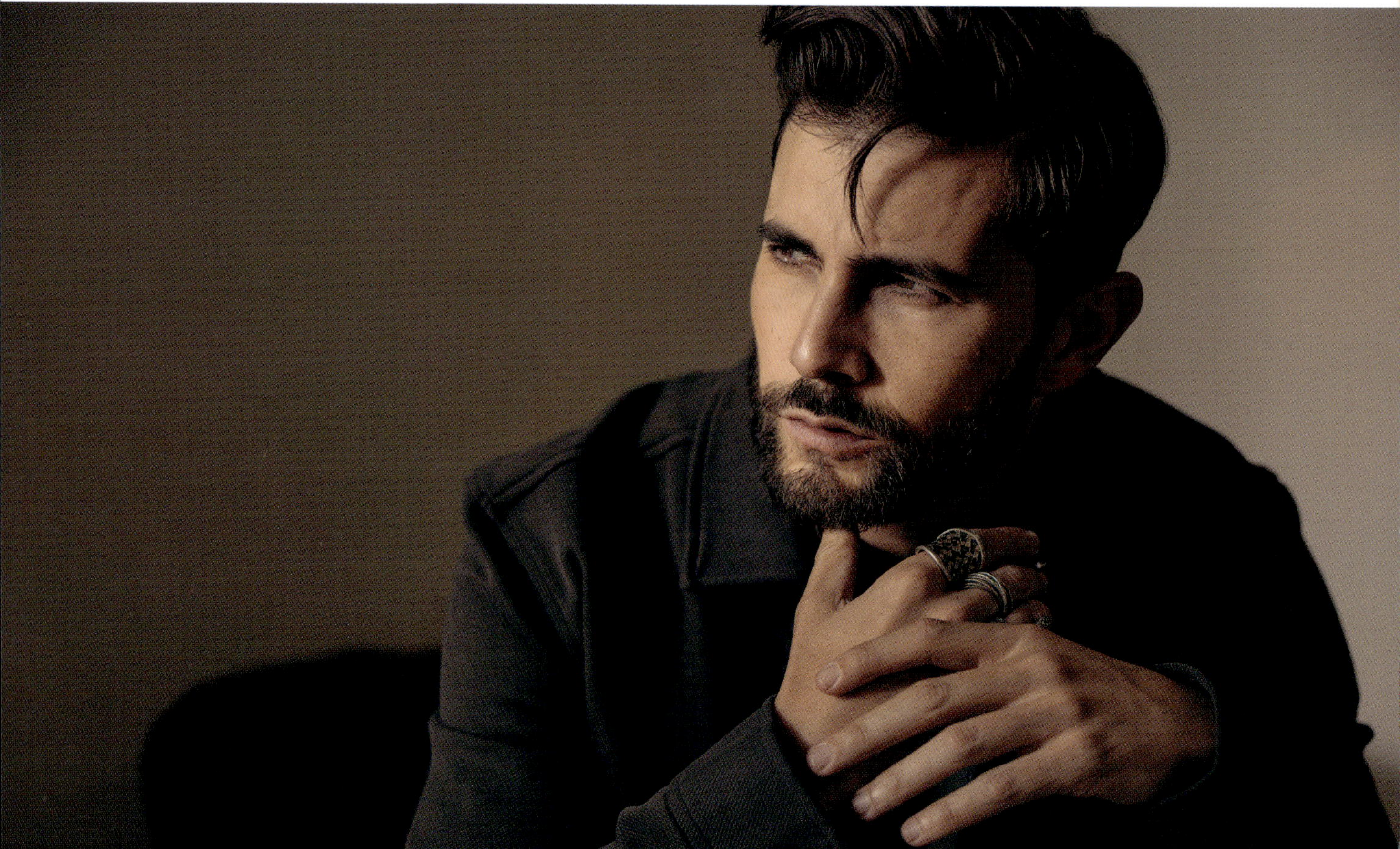

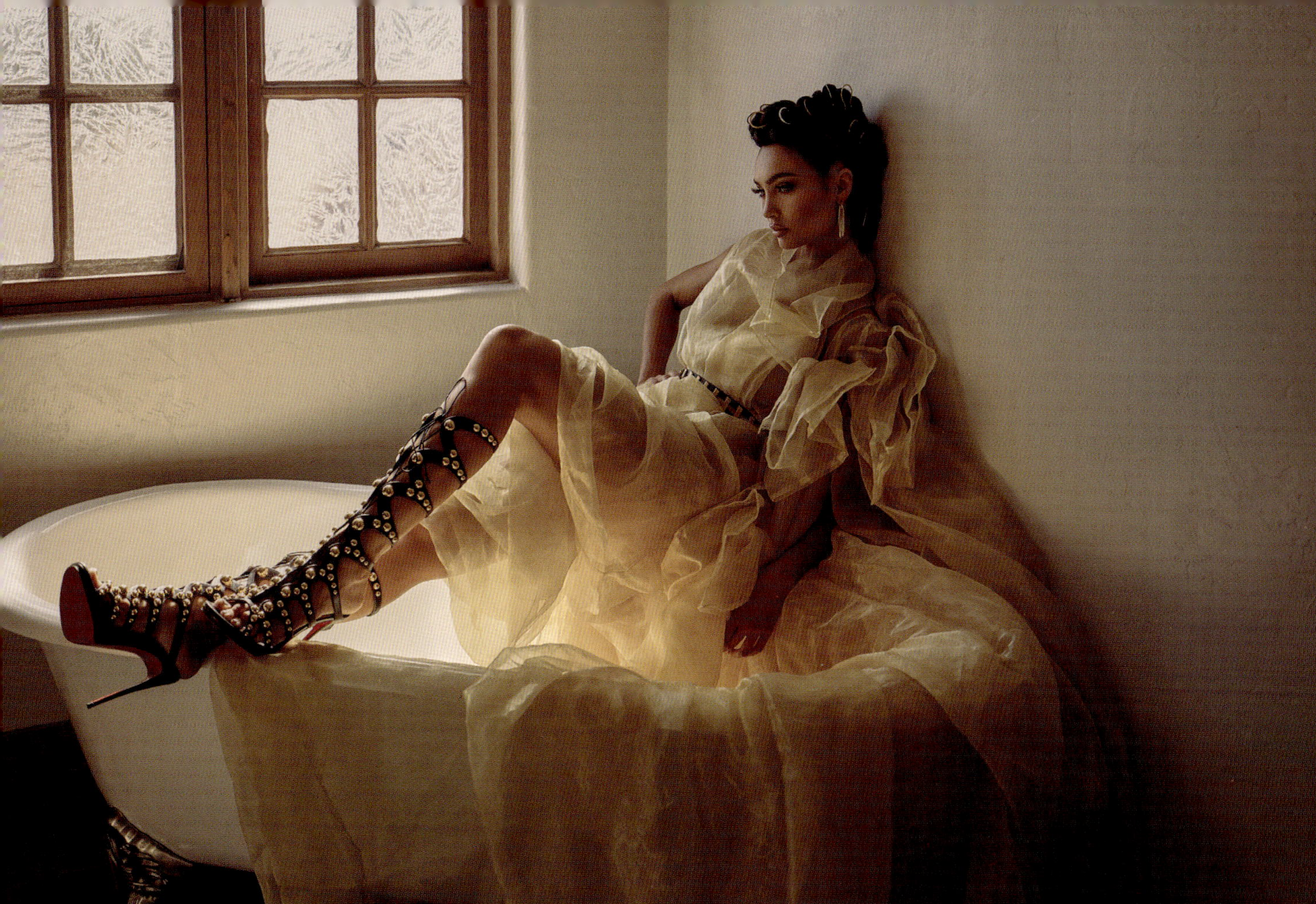

R'Bonney

Figure 7.14: For this photo of my friend and, as of the writing of this book, the reigning Miss Universe, R'Bonney Nola Gabriel, I had to consider two main factors: the mood I wanted, and the texture of the dress, which I wanted to highlight through lighting. I used a yellow and a 1/2 CTO gel to create the warm amber in-camera color grade you see here. Again, this being an environmental portrait, my goal is always that the lights I use need to be "invisible" to the viewer. I want the lighting to create the mood—not distract the viewer with the obvious use of flash.

Number of Lights: Two flashes were used for this portrait. The fill light came from a flash that had a yellow gel attached. The key light had a 1/2 CTO gel attached.

Angle of Lights: The fill light was achieved by pointing one of the Profoto flash heads toward the ceiling corner that was opposite R'Bonney. This allowed the light to hit the ceiling and upper part of the wall and flood the entire room with light, while also giving some directionality to the bounced light. The key light was positioned parallel to the window to mimic the window light.

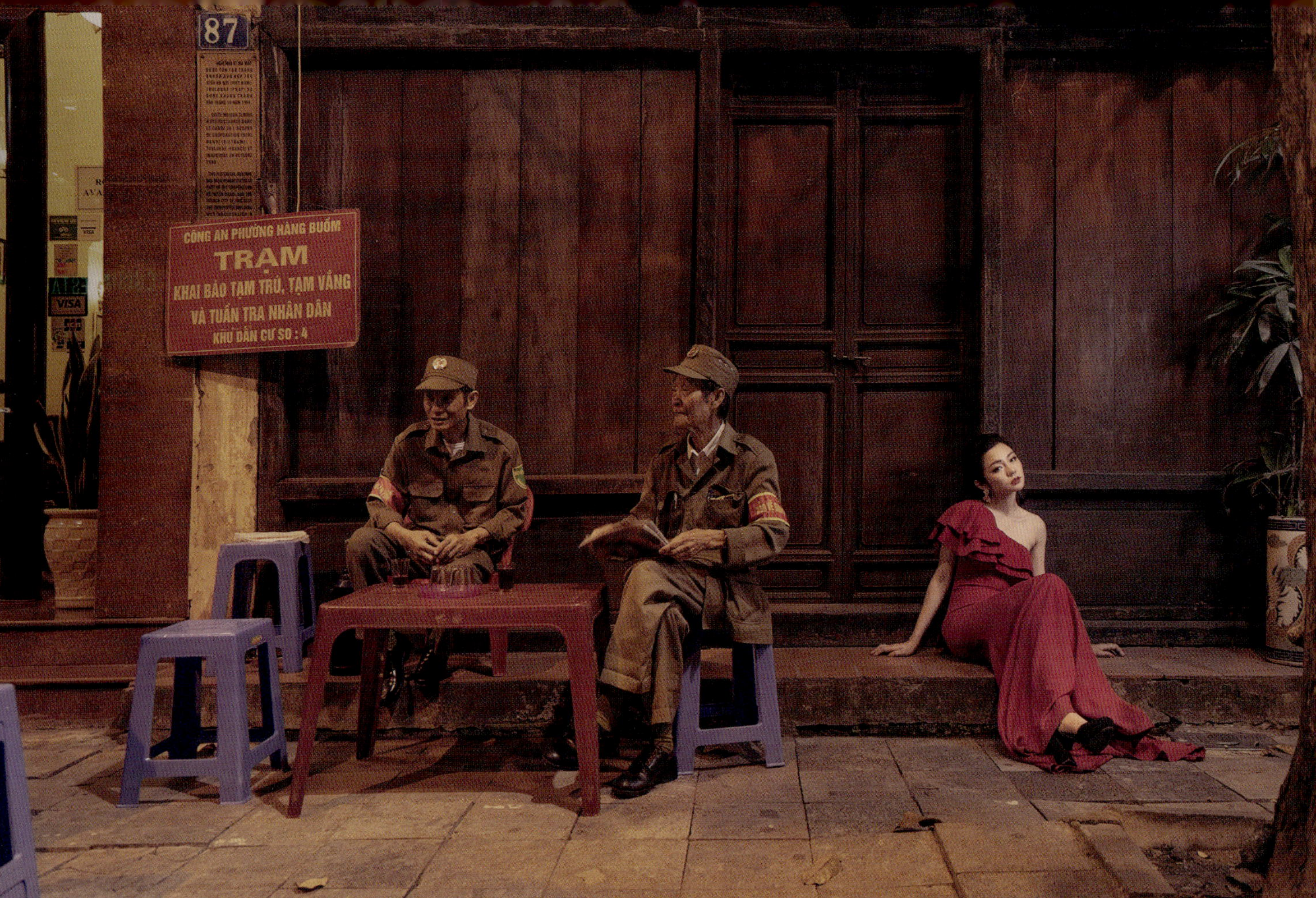

FIGURE 7.15

Modifiers: The fill light did not need any modifier since it was firing toward the ceiling; in essence, the ceiling was the modifier. The key light had a two-foot octabox on it and was pointed from the window toward the dress.

Energy: I began working with the key light first. I wanted to be sure that the light was powerful enough to showcase the texture of the dress by illuminating it with heavily directional light. At the same time, I didn't want the light to be so strong that it would not look natural anymore or blow out the delicate dress fabric. Once that was set, I began to work on the power for the fill light. I wanted my fill to be around a stop darker than the key light.

Hanoi Portrait

Figure 7.15: This street portrait was taken in Hanoi, Vietnam. I loved the look of the soldiers relaxing and reading at a plastic table. I noticed a small space on the sidewalk at camera right that was perfect to position the beautiful model for this portrait. This photo was taken around 9:00 p.m., so all the ambient light is coming from car head-lights, bar lights, and old streetlights.

Number of Lights: This was a narrow corridor on the streets of old town Hanoi. I used two lights angled in such a way to achieve a good blend with the ambient light, but also to highlight my subject.

Angle of Lights: First, I wanted to fix the lighting by adding a large fill light to the entire scene. Since this was a narrow corridor, I pointed my fill light behind me to bounce onto the opposite side of the street and back to where the model was seated. To highlight my subject, I placed the key light at camera right on a stand to elevate the light enough so it mimicked a bar light.

Modifiers: Both lights had a Profoto two-foot OCF octabox. I used an octabox on the fill light because I wanted to have a softer feel to the bounced light.

Energy: The fill light accomplished a lot by providing soft light throughout the street scene. In order to highlight the beautiful model I was working with, I had to raise the power of the key light until it was brighter than the overall light. When you look at this photo, your eyes should be drawn to the girl sitting on the right.

Sarah

Figures 7.16 & 7.17: Remember this photo from Chapter 1? Now you can see how bland the original mood was with only natural light illuminating the space. This is a great example that shows how the use of flash can really make a photo come alive. This photo of my beautiful friend Sarah was taken at The Photo Creators Conference in Tucson, Arizona. As you can see from the first photo taken with only ambient light, the lighting was weak and uninspiring. Basically, it was boring! To brighten the photo and give it some life, I decided to create the look of sunrise using my flashes.

Number of Lights: I used two flashes for the entire transformation of this scene. Just because you have more lights in your bag doesn't mean it's better to use them. Use the correct number of lights and recognize why that's the correct number. You will be more conscious of your decision, and there will be less guesswork.

Angle of Lights: The angle of my light had to mimic the sunrise. Therefore, we placed a light outside and up on a stand to create the angle and shadows that would naturally occur from the rising sun through the window frame. The second flash was a hot shoe flash mounted on my camera and angled up toward the ceiling. The ceiling became the light modifier; the flash itself was bare bulb. The angle of this second light was very important because its job was to fill the shadows with a little light until the scene was balanced to my liking. Without the fill light bouncing off the ceiling, the scene would have been way too contrasty for my taste.

FIGURE 7.16

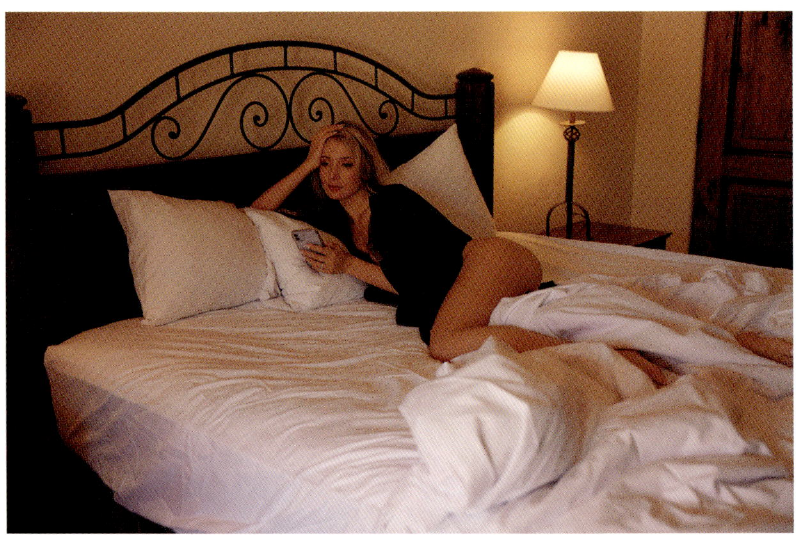

FIGURE 7.17

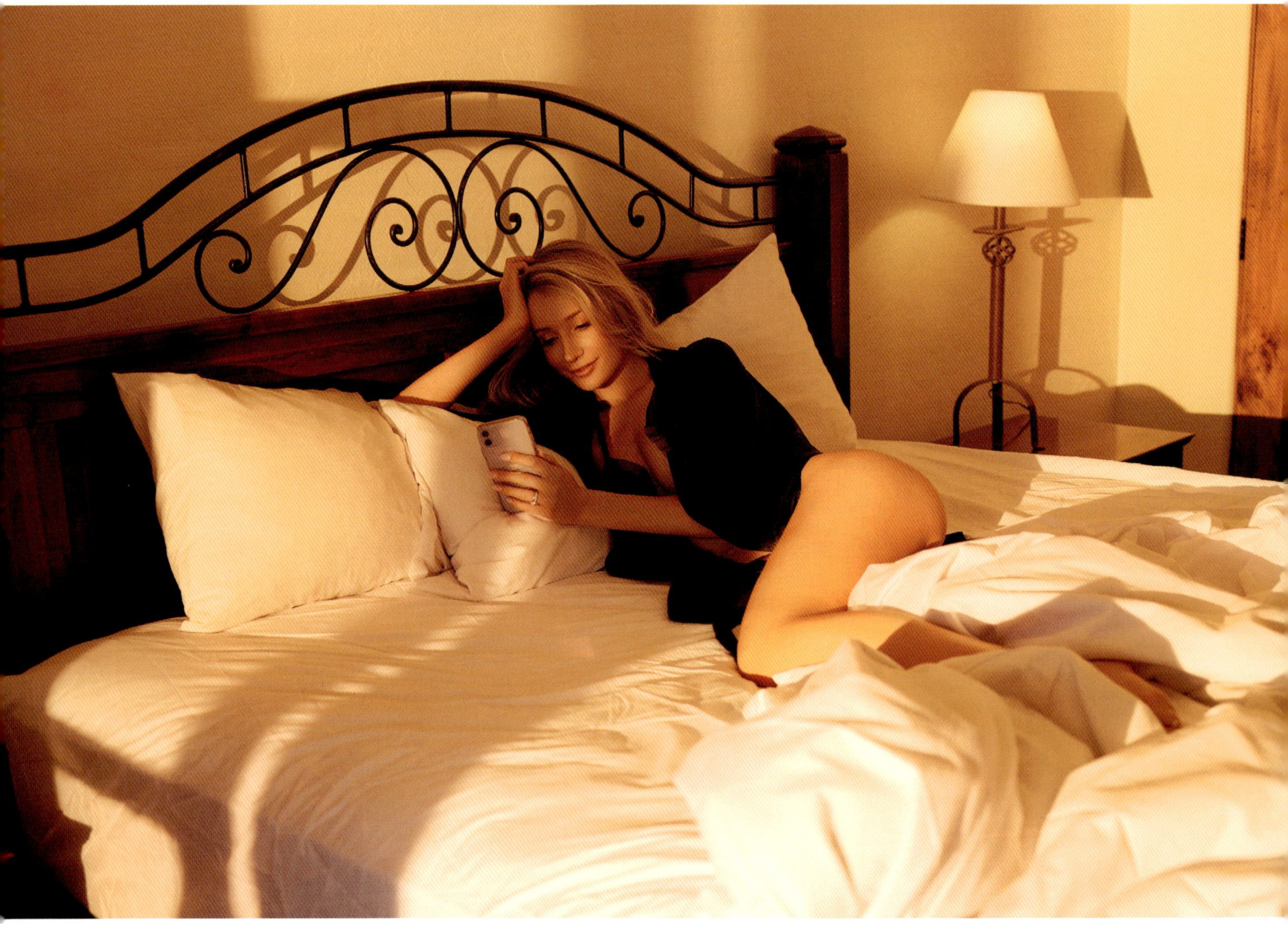

Modifiers: The light outside had no modifier, only an orange gel. The bare bulb best mimics the spread of natural light. As far as the second flash, as noted above, the white ceiling was the perfect fill light modifier. Modifiers for your flashes don't always have to be made for flashes by lighting companies. The secret sauce is to combine professional lighting modifiers with the objects around you working as natural, circumstantial light modifiers (as noted in the sidebar earlier in this chapter). A white ceiling is like a huge softbox placed directly over your subject. Except the ceiling is much cheaper!

Energy: For this image, we had to create realistic light and shadow that mimicked the sun. Therefore, the light had to be placed a good 15 feet from the window outside and pointed toward the room. The power was almost at full power to obtain the morning light vibe that I envisioned. The fill light flash on my camera's hot shoe was raised little by little to achieve the perfect lift of the shadows and reduce the overall contrast in the scene created by the key light outside.

When you are thinking about how much energy you want per flash, remember that it's all about balance. You can balance your flashes with each other, or you can balance your flashes with the ambient or natural light on location. The Picture Perfect Flash System will always be there to challenge you to not always take the obvious photo. Mentally going through the steps of this process (FACES and NAME) will also help ensure you don't forget something important. Remember: You are in control, always.

FLASH BASICS EXPLAINED

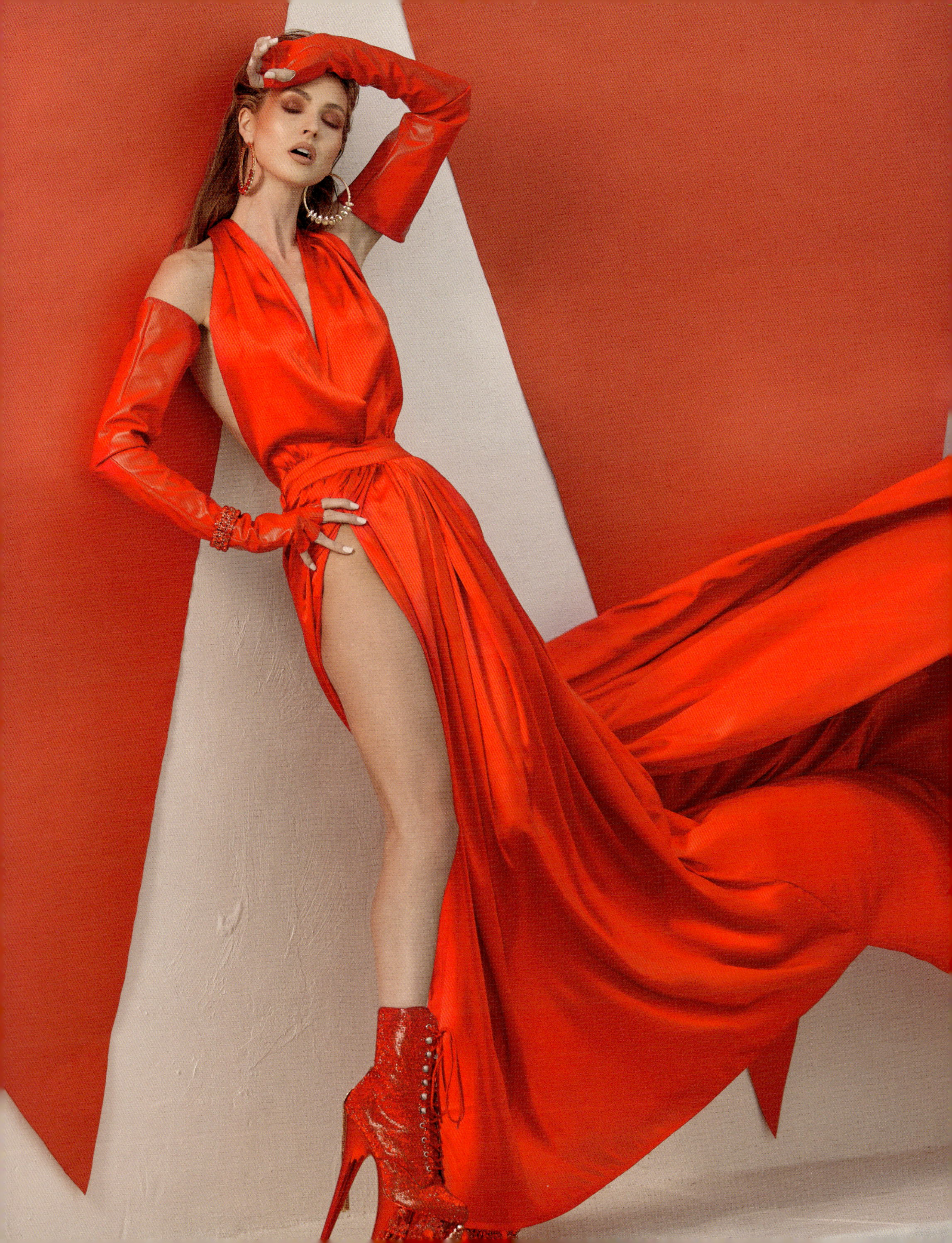

Chapter 8

TTL: Let the Flash Decide

When you first buy a camera flash and turn it on, the flash is pre-programmed to start in TTL mode. TTL is an acronym for "Through the Lens." This technical term means nothing more than that the flash automatically chooses how much power to fire depending on the scene in front of the lens (what it sees "through the lens"). Some camera manufacturers call it E-TTL, or I-TTL. None of these names really matters. Let's just call it TTL.

This technology is a lifesaver, and it works extremely well in most cases. By having the flash mode set to TTL, you can turn on the camera and the flash, then fire the shutter button. The chances that the flash will do a good job illuminating the scene or your subject are very high.

But who is the judge of what a "good exposure" is? In this case, the flash is the judge. The flash only has one goal: to fire off enough flash output to satisfy how it was programmed.

TTL Explained in Simple Terms

Figure 8.1: TTL doesn't care about color. It only cares how bright or dark each object in the frame is. In other words, it only cares about their luminosity levels. Let's try to see the world as TTL sees the world, and it will help you clearly understand why the flash does what it does. Imagine that you take a photo of something—a park, a cityscape, a person, a landscape, it doesn't matter. Mentally, remove the color of everything in the frame so that you are just left with how dark or bright each object is. If you were to put all those shades of black, white, and gray from every object in a blender and mix them up, you would end up with a shade of gray that is like one of those in the rectangle from the chart in Figure 8.1.

Pure Black   TTL   Pure White

FIGURE 8.1

Looking at that chart, the leftmost rectangle represents a photo that is completely underexposed. It's pure black. The rightmost rectangle represents a photo that is totally overexposed. It's pure white. As you can see from the chart, TTL wants to be right in the middle. When you take a photo and your flash is in TTL mode, the flash will fire enough light to bring the photo's overall luminosity to the middle of the chart, or middle gray.

If your exposure of the scene in front of the lens is already to the right of the chart (too bright), the flash will know that flash is not needed. The flash will still fire because it's on, but it will only try to add just enough light to brighten some of the darker shadows in the scene, thereby reducing the overall contrast in the photograph. However, if the camera sees that you're exposing the scene to the left of the chart (too dark), it will tell the flash to output whatever amount of light is necessary to brighten the exposure toward the middle of the chart.

Now that we understand what the flash in TTL mode is programmed to do, we need to understand what the camera uses to determine if a scene is too bright, too dark, or just right. The camera does this using its built-in metering modes.

What Is the Camera Meter For?

Modern cameras give the photographer the ability to have some control over how the camera determines how bright or dark a scene is. The camera has a built-in light meter. The light meter tells the photographer that, with the current camera settings, the photo would be underexposed, overexposed, or just right. The problem is that camera has no idea what your main subject is within the entire frame. How could it?

Figure 8.2: How does the camera know what's in front of the lens to determine the right flash exposure? In simple terms, when your flash is on and is in TTL mode, the instant you press the shutter button, the flash fires something called a "pre-flash." This pre-flash is a tiny bit of light from the flash that travels out to the scene and then returns all the information about the scene's luminosity levels back to the camera via the magic of reflectivity. How remarkable is that? With that information, along with your camera settings, the flash can now calculate how much flash power this particular scene needs to bring the luminosity of the entire photo to middle gray. All of this happens incredibly fast. Note that the pre-flash does not influence the photo at all; it just gathers information like a small spy.

In summary, when you press the shutter button, two flashes go off very quickly. The first flash is the pre-flash, and the second is the real flash that illuminates the scene while the camera shutter is open. Most likely, you will never actually see the pre-flash because it happens so quickly. But trust me, it's there.

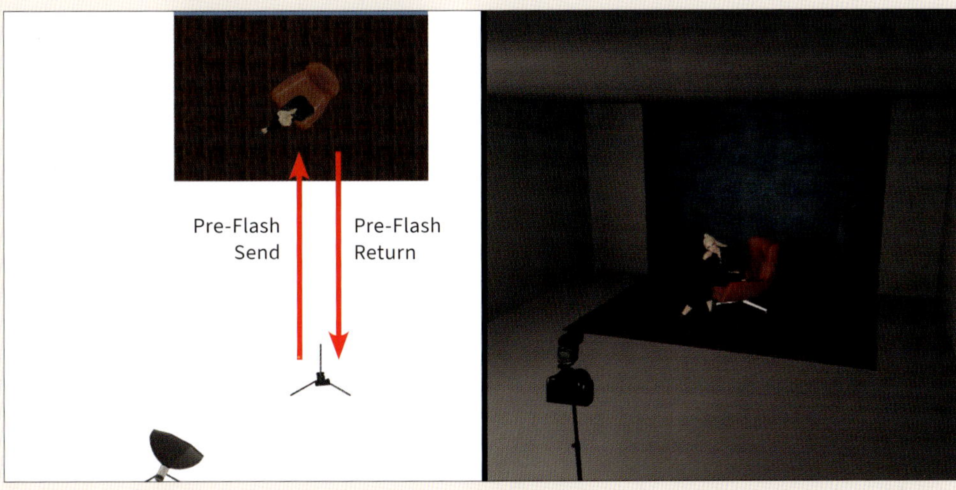

FIGURE 8.2

Suppose that you are photographing a bird flying across a blue sky with clouds. Is your subject the sky, the clouds, or the bird? What if you are photographing a small child in front of a large window? Is the subject the window, the trees outside the window, or the small child? Not to mention, how bright or dark is the background behind your main subject? This is a lot for the exposure meter to handle. By choosing different metering modes, you can help the camera by guiding it to focus on a specific area of the frame.

All cameras have many metering modes to choose from, but we are going to focus on the three most important ones. Every camera manufacturer gives these three modes a different name, but the modes themselves don't change. They are the same. Don't you just wish camera manufacturers would stop making everything so complicated and agree to the same names for the same features?

The Three Main Metering Modes You Should Know

Evaluative Metering Mode

Evaluative metering mode will be your "home base" metering mode. You will use this metering mode well over 90% of the time. **Figure 8.3** shows Canon's icon for this mode. Canon also calls it Evaluative. All you must know about this mode is that it is the "overall" mode. When you buy a camera from any manufacturer, this is the default mode the camera is set to. Regardless of the brand of camera, they all have the same metering modes but with different names. (For example, Nikon calls it Matrix metering mode.)

Don't let the brand-specific name distract you. Let's focus on what this mode does. This mode looks at most of the scene in front of the viewfinder. From corner to corner, almost everything present in the viewfinder is considered for brightness levels. This mode gives a slightly higher priority to the area near the chosen focus point (**Figure 8.4**). This mode does a great job most of the time, but it can be tricked by large areas of bright or dark objects in the viewfinder, which will skew the average toward too bright or too dark.

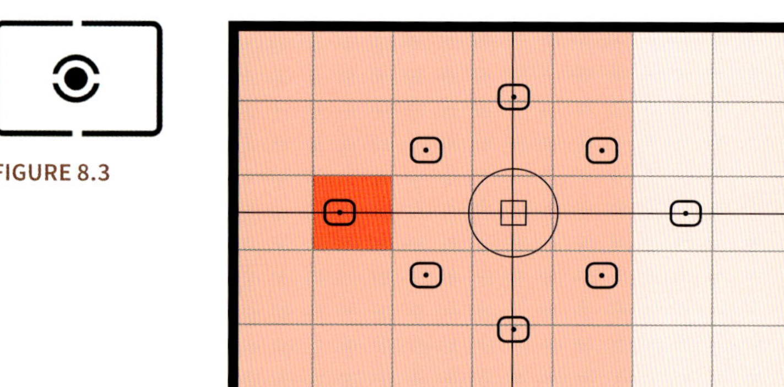

FIGURE 8.3

FIGURE 8.4

Note that if you are shooting in Manual mode, I would just stay with this metering mode, which is the camera's default. With a little experience, you will soon become familiar with how your camera's metering in this mode behaves in most situations. Then you can adjust the exposure accordingly. Only when you are shooting in any of the automatic modes such as Auto, Program, Aperture Priority, or Shutter Priority does the metering mode become more important to know. For this reason, it is worth explaining the other two main metering modes.

Center Weighted Metering Mode

This metering mode (**Figure 8.5**) also measures the light across the entire scene, but it gives higher priority to the center of the frame (**Figure 8.6**). One thing to note with this mode is that it does not consider your chosen focus point. Therefore, it's quite simple to understand because it's always consistent. It measures the whole scene for light, but it gives more priority to the center of the frame.

This is a great metering mode to use for backlit subjects. A person standing in front of the ocean, a bird flying through the sky, or a child standing in front of a large window would be more accurately metered with Center Weighted metering mode.

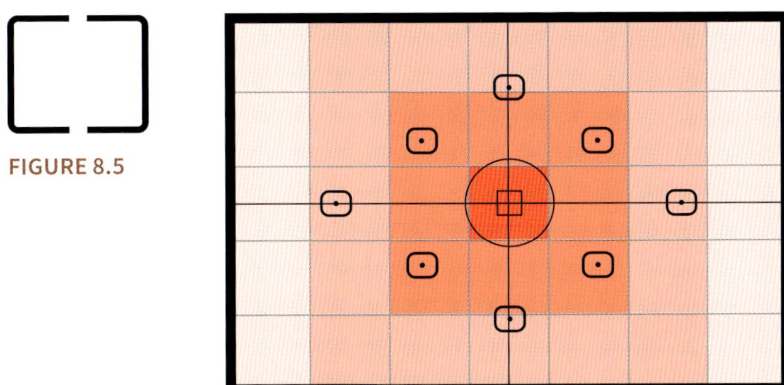

FIGURE 8.5

FIGURE 8.6

Spot Metering Mode

This mode (**Figure 8.7**) is a high-precision metering mode. It only meters around 3% of the entire scene (**Figure 8.8**). This mode determines its exposure calculations based on the tiny area where the photographer placed the focus point. That's really cool! It used to be that Spot metering mode only considered 3% from the middle of the frame and ignored the rest. But, with modern cameras, it is based on the placement of the focus point.

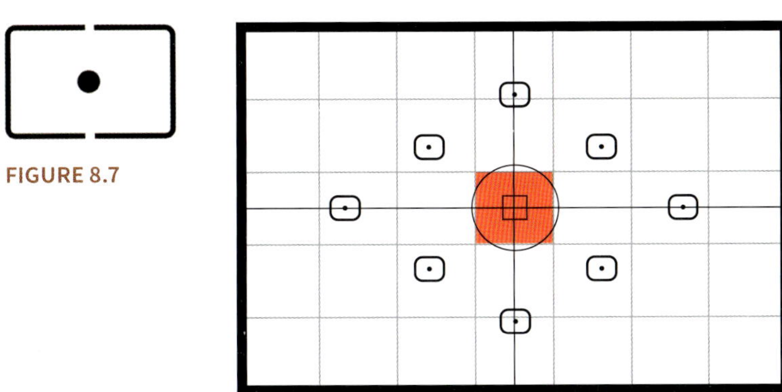

FIGURE 8.7

FIGURE 8.8

Canon has another metering mode called Partial metering mode. This is the same thing as Spot metering except that the area it calculates is approximately 10% of the frame around the focus point. I completely ignore these more obscure metering modes. These modes can be very confusing, for no good reason. You only need to know one or two, particularly the Evaluative metering mode.

Metering modes don't matter very much. They matter even less if you are shooting in Manual mode. However, it is good to know the basics just in case you have some strange exposures.

For example, once I was at a shoot and every photo I was taking was overexposed. I normally shoot in Manual mode, but this time I was shooting in Aperture Priority mode. My exposures were too bright by almost a full stop. With the pressures of the job, I became very frustrated because I couldn't figure out quickly enough how to fix the problem. Later, during a break, I finally looked at my camera settings carefully and noticed that the camera was set to Spot metering mode. I had been experimenting with the metering modes a few days earlier and had forgotten to change it back to Evaluative metering.

Understanding TTL Flash Behavior

You now understand how TTL was programmed to achieve middle gray and how the camera sees the scene through metering modes. Now we can more easily predict how the flash, when set to TTL mode, will behave in every situation. Let's take a look.

Figure 8.9: This is just a software render, but it represents a typical situation that you will often find yourself in, indoors or outdoors. Look closely and try to guess what the flash in TTL mode would do. The background behind the woman is black, and she is wearing a black leather jacket and dark blue jeans. However, she does have light-colored hair and light skin. Would you agree that most of this scene is dark?

When the flash/portable strobe is in TTL mode, the pre-flash will fire to examine the situation, and it will find a very dark scene in front of the lens. TTL is programmed to throw enough light at the scene to turn the entire exposure to middle gray. Well, to turn all that black into middle gray requires quite a bit of light, correct? The result is a highly overexposed person who looks washed out, and the black paper has turned more to gray. This makes sense. TTL is designed to turn everything middle gray. If you wish to keep the black paper and black jacket their true black color, you must underexpose the scene with your camera settings.

Figure 8.10: In this render, we have the opposite problem. Looking at this example, you notice how the scene is overwhelmingly white. The paper background was set to white (though it looks a light gray here), and the woman is wearing a dress with a lot of white in it. When the TTL system sees so much white in front of the lens, it thinks it shouldn't

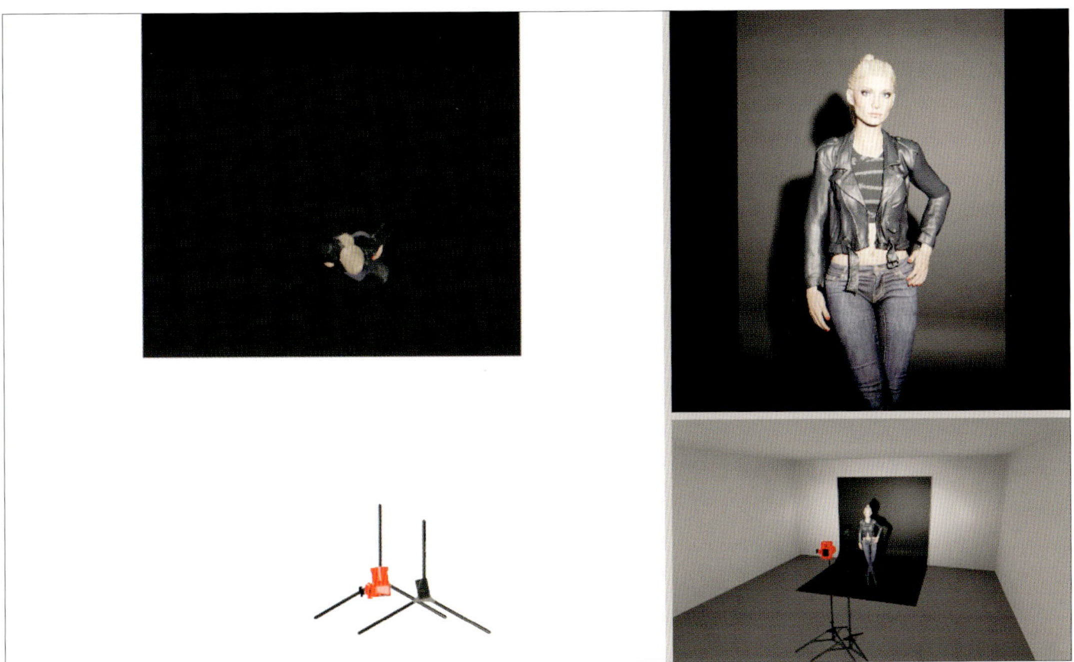

FIGURE 8.9

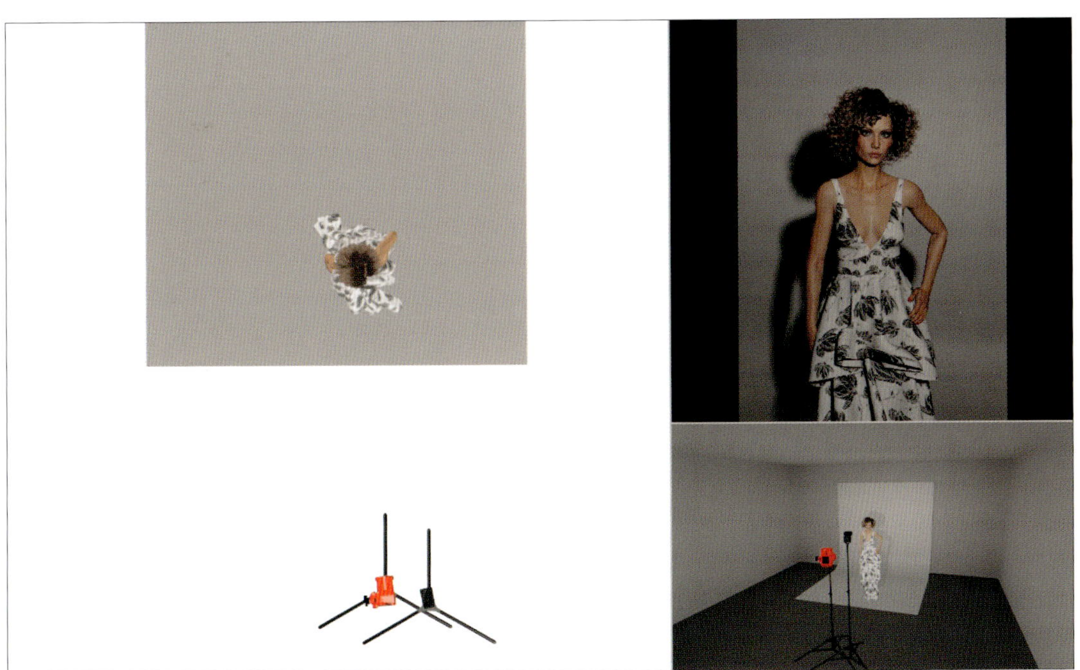

FIGURE 8.10

throw any more light onto the scene, because it is trying to make it gray, not more white. Therefore, the flash barely outputs any light, and the camera's light meter tries to turn all that white into gray by underexposing. The result is an underexposed photograph.

Another problem you'll find on location is when you're photographing someone in front of a white wall. The camera's light meter thinks there is far too much white in the scene, and it will meter to make the exposure middle gray. If the flash is on, the camera will tell the flash to fire just the bare minimum of light to avoid adding even more white to the scene. In these cases, with a lot of white, you must override the camera meter and flash TTL mode and tell it to "overexpose" the scene by whatever amount necessary to keep the integrity of the white. This way, the white will stay white.

Figure 8.11: Isn't this interesting… In this example, the background paper is gray. The woman's clothes cancel each other out because the top is dark and the pants are white, so this gives you middle gray. This is the camera's happy place. In examples like this, the camera's light meter and the TTL flash system will agree that this is middle gray, and it will handle the scene perfectly. When you take a photo, the meter will be spot on, and the flash will emit the perfect amount of light to keep the scene an optimum middle gray.

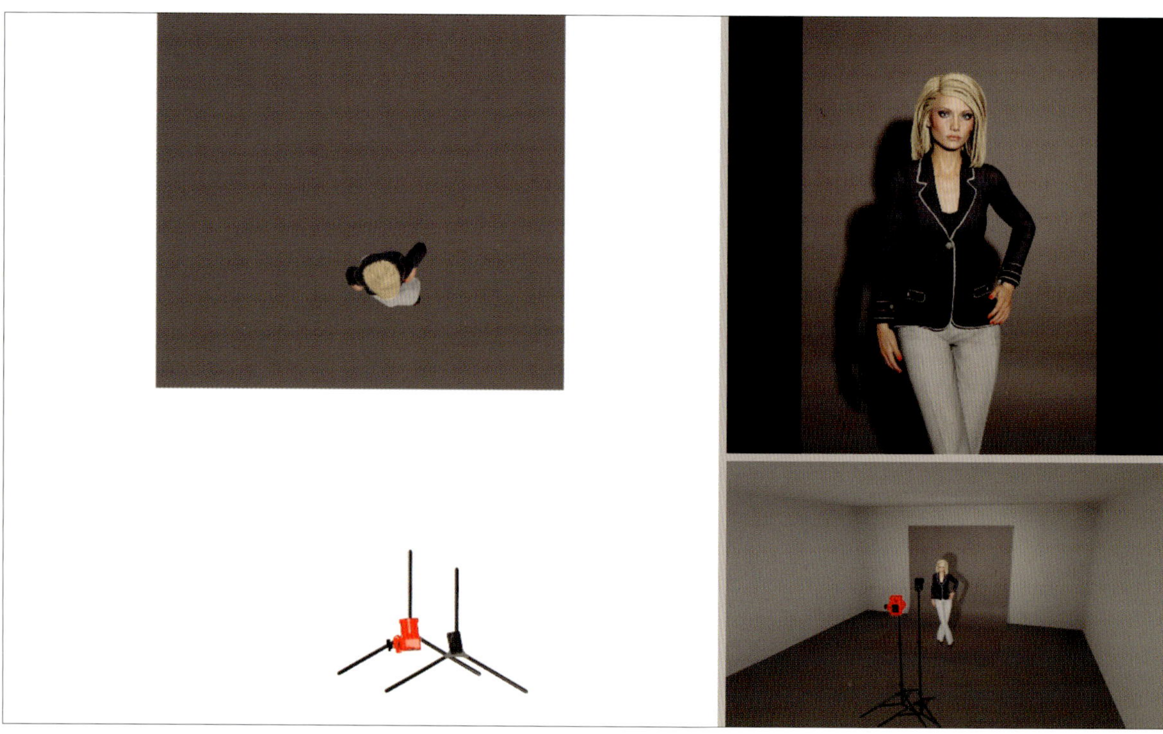

FIGURE 8.11

So Why Bother with TTL Flash?

There are three major reasons why you would want to use TTL flash.

Reason #1: Despite the examples I showed above, in most cases, TTL flash is surprisingly accurate. Technology with TTL is getting better and better. For example, Canon's EL-1 flash uses the camera's eye-detection technology to identify the subject's eye. It uses just that area of the face (face priority) when determining how much flash the subject needs, regardless of how bright or dark the rest of the scene is. How incredible is that?

Reason #2: TTL flash is the best solution when the subject is constantly moving toward or away from the camera. Trying to adjust the flash power manually when the distance between the camera and subject and flash keeps changing by the second would be a nightmare. By using TTL mode, the camera and flash work together to instantly calculate how far the subject is from the lens and the flash at any given moment using the pre-flash. It will choose the perfect (or almost perfect) amount of flash for those given distances.

Reason #3: It is handy when you are in a hurry. Let's assume you have a flash on the camera's hot shoe. Suddenly, you notice something that you want to capture but you are in a low-light situation. You have no idea what your camera settings are. In less than a split second, the camera can focus and determine how much flash it needs for you to capture that perfect moment, even if your settings are not optimized for low light. Your settings could be at ISO 200, f/16, 1/125 in a dark room at night. Your flash will compensate for your camera settings and output enough power to give you at least a decent exposure—which is certainly better than missing the moment altogether. You can't beat the speed of technology.

Many of the top flash experts in the world use TTL mode as a starting point for their flash exposure. Then, they switch over to Manual and adjust from there. Another method is to start with TTL flash and make changes to it by using Flash Exposure Compensation (FEC) to dial the TTL flash output up or down. (This works like Exposure Compensation when you're in Aperture Priority or Shutter Priority mode.) I personally don't work this way, because during most of my shoots, the subject-to-camera distance is not constantly changing. Therefore, I prefer to start with Manual flash. Fortunately, anyone can choose what flash mode works best for their own work.

TTL & Flash Exposure Compensation

Flash Exposure Compensation (FEC) and TTL go hand in hand. As noted, I don't usually work this way, but it's worth experimenting with it and understanding it, so you can always have it available to you in case you want or need to use it.

The second you activate TTL, you should be thinking about having to adjust the flash's power output with Flash Exposure Compensation. Remember, the flash is programmed to output enough power to give you a middle gray exposure. Well, that's very limiting. Not all situations call for a middle gray exposure.

Here's how it works: When the Flash Exposure Compensation is set to "0," TLL mode is going to try to give you middle gray exposure, as previously explained. But what if you're in a moody room—say, a beautiful old library in a historic building—and you wish to stay true to the mood of that room? Regular TTL flash is going to ruin it by blasting too much light to bring the exposure to middle gray.

Figure 8.12: If you try to see a scene like the camera's light meter, you might get something like this. The camera just looks at the different tones throughout the image. It doesn't care what the subject is. Blurring the image allows you to focus on the tones. At first sight, you can see that there is a great majority of gray tones. That's great, right? This should make it easy for TTL flash to give us middle gray.

But look closer. The lady has black hair, and the man has a black suit on. Also, the lady's dress is dark gray with black stripes. Therefore, as soon as you activate TTL flash for a scene like this, your brain should already be considering all the dark or black tones in the scene. What is the flash going to do here in TTL mode? Well, for the most part, the flash sees gray throughout most of the photo, so it's super happy. But when the black tones enter the camera's light meter, the flash will say, "Oh, there is quite a bit of pure black tone here, so I need to output more light to turn those blacks into gray." And there you have it: now you have an overexposed photograph. The couple's skin tone will be completely washed out due to the flash trying to compensate for the black tones in the hair and clothes.

Figure 8.13: This photograph was indeed taken in TTL flash mode. I normally don't use TTL, but I did here. Because I took into account the black tones, and I learned how the camera's light meter sees a scene, it was easy to know what to do to compensate for what would have been an overly bright flash output. As soon as I turned on TTL, I immediately used FEC to dial it down by a whole stop. That decision was correct. This photo is the result of activating TTL and dialing FEC down to –1 stop. You can always take a test photo and check out the results. From there, you can make changes to FEC. But with experience, you'll get better and better at this, and eventually you'll be able to do it without the need for a test photo.

Figure 8.14: This is an illustration of the screen on the back of a typical camera. In this example, there is no Flash Exposure Compensation because it's set to "0" as you can see inside the orange box.

Once you take a photo when using TTL mode, you can use your camera's menu system or your flash itself to dial the Flash Exposure Compensation up or down from a middle gray exposure. Looking at Figure 8.14, you can see how you can dial the compensation up or down by three stops. That's a lot of range! So, this gives you the flexibility to use TTL for speed, and then dial the power down to maintain the mood of a dark room, for example. Once the FEC is set, it will stay that way until you return it back to "0." FEC does not automatically reset to zero. Remember that.

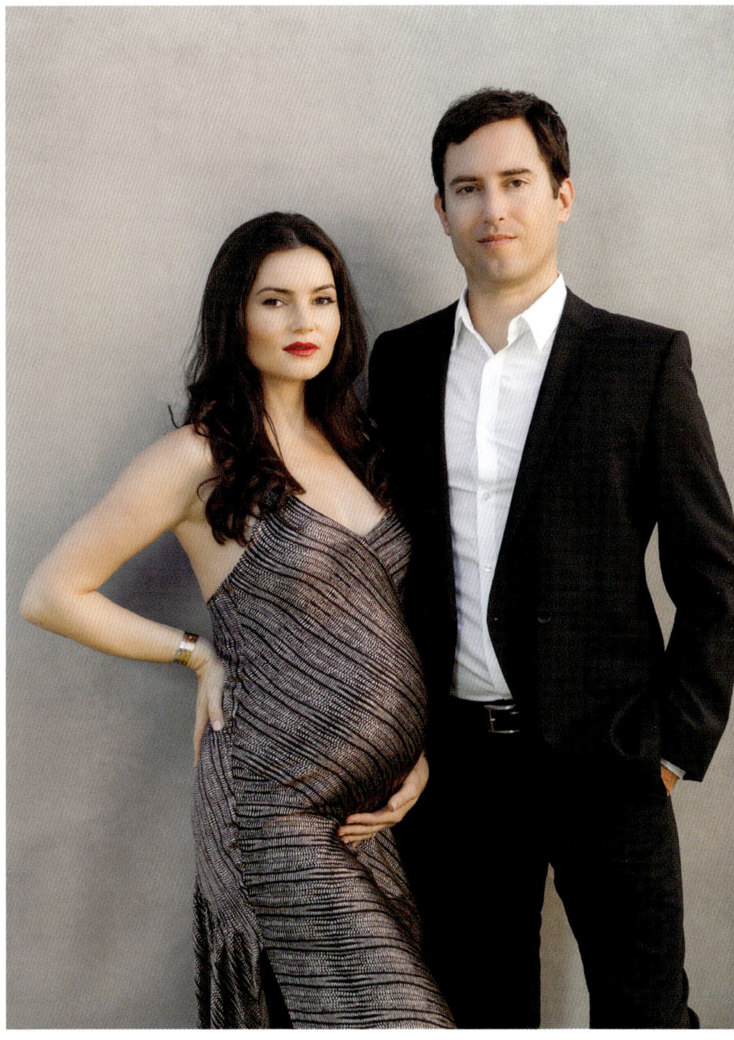

FIGURE 8.13

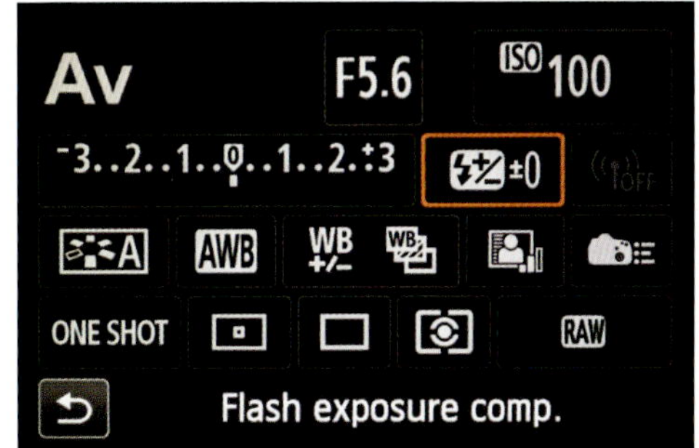

FIGURE 8.14

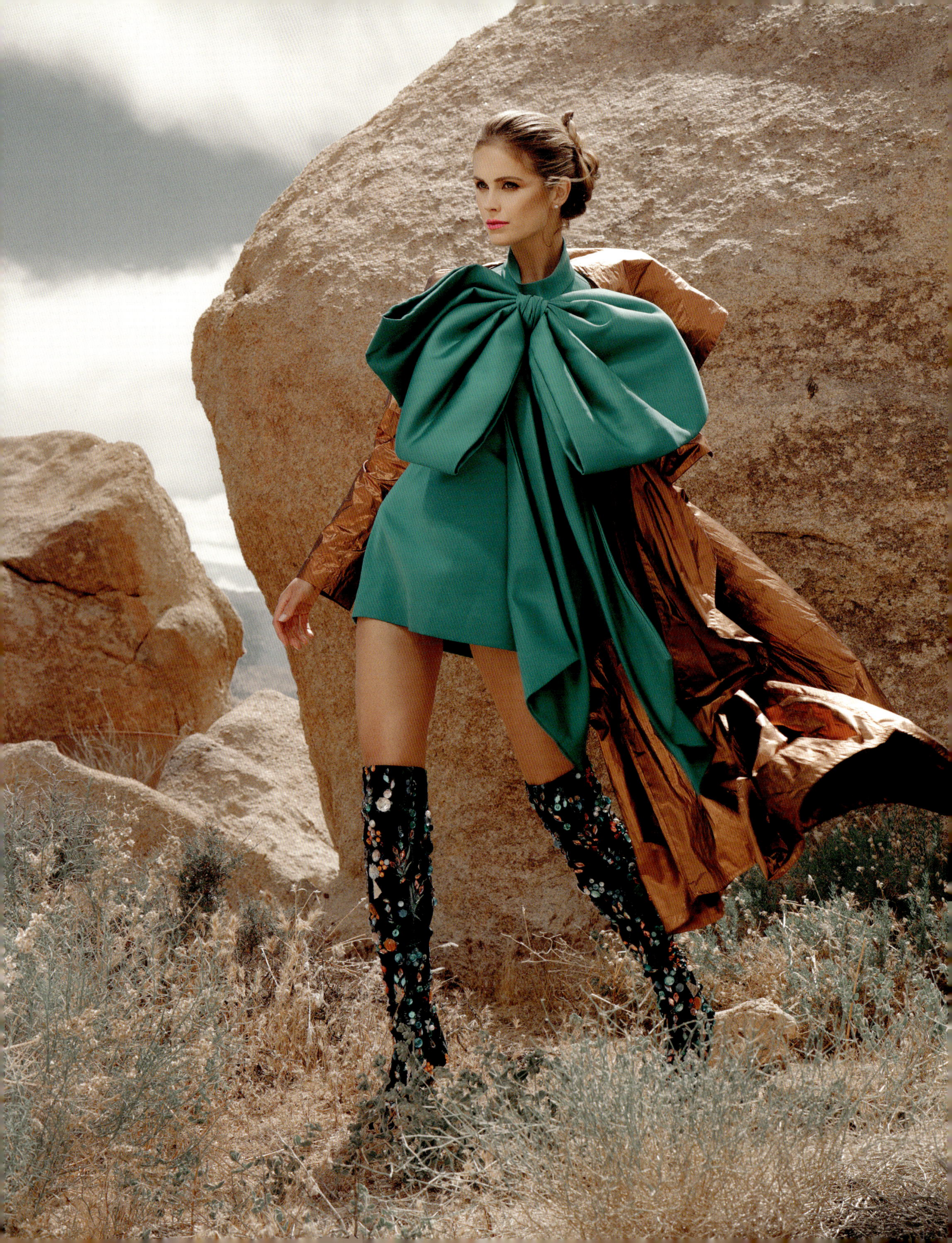

Chapter 9

Manual Mode

Hands down, Manual mode is the easiest mode to understand and enjoy when using flashes or portable strobes. All portable strobes and flashes have Manual mode, but not all portable strobes and flashes have TTL mode. Manual mode and TTL mode are the two main modes to choose from when using artificial light.

When you buy a flash and take it out of the box, the flash will most likely be in TTL mode. But I wish the flashes were set to Manual mode as their default setting, because everyone can understand Manual mode. Even my six-year-old son Lucas can understand it. It is that simple.

In Manual mode, if the flash is too bright, you turn the power down, and if the flash is too weak, you turn the power up. There are no computers guessing what the main subject is, no metering modes to think about, and no focus point making a difference. In Manual mode, the flash simply behaves like the volume control on a radio. If you want more volume, turn it up; if you want less volume, turn it down. I believe that if Manual mode were the only available mode to use, more people would quickly understand how flash works, and the fear of introducing flash into their photography would dissipate.

Manual Versus TTL

When a flash is set to TTL mode, the flash will compensate for any settings on your camera to achieve what the flash considers to be a proper exposure. For example, in TTL, if your aperture setting is f/8 and you take a photo, the flash will output whatever power it thinks it needs to provide you with a good exposure. And if you change your aperture to f/16, the flash will output more power to compensate for the change in aperture from f/8 to f/16. No matter what you do with your camera settings, the flash in TTL mode will do its best to always give you a consistent middle gray, or 18% gray, exposure, which in many cases, works well.

However, in Manual mode, every change you make to your camera settings or to the flash power is going to have a visible and noticeable effect on your exposure. That's why it's called "Manual" mode—because you have complete control over how bright or dark you wish the exposure to be. There is a relationship that happens between your camera settings and your flash power that you need to become very familiar with.

Making Exposure Changes Using Flash Power Only

Since this concept can be a little tricky, I'm going to demonstrate the relationship between camera settings and flash/portable strobe in your exposure one section at a time. This will give you the best chance to understand exactly what's happening with minimal confusion. Be patient with these examples. At first, they seem obvious, but there is a method at play, and the examples build upon each other. I highly encourage you to not only read these examples carefully, but to try them for yourself. Yes, it takes time to do them, but you will learn the material three times better than from just reading about it.

To begin, we must assume some basic camera settings. These settings are going to remain constant throughout these images. The settings are ISO 400, f/8, 1/160. The portable strobe head is set to Manual mode, of course.

Figure 9.1: This image was created with the portable strobe at halfway through its power range. If we assume that the strobe head has power levels of 1–10, this photo was taken at power level 5. As you can see, at level 5, we have a perfect exposure.

Figure 9.2: This image was created with the same settings mentioned above, with the only difference being that the power of the flash went up from 5 to 6, or one stop more of light. As you can see, the portrait looks slightly overexposed because we doubled the amount of light from the previous example. Every time you add one stop of light, you are essentially doubling the light.

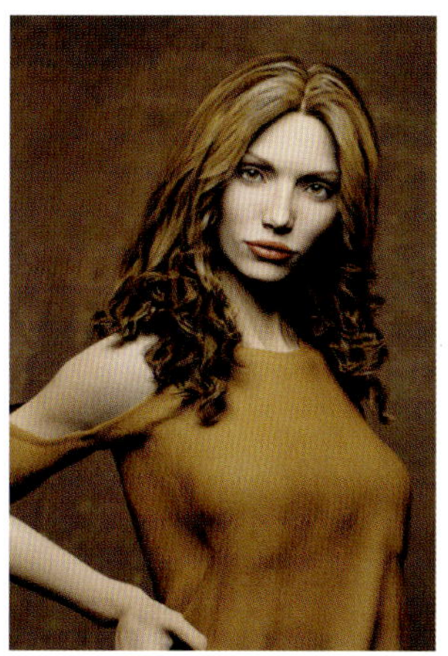

FIGURE 9.1

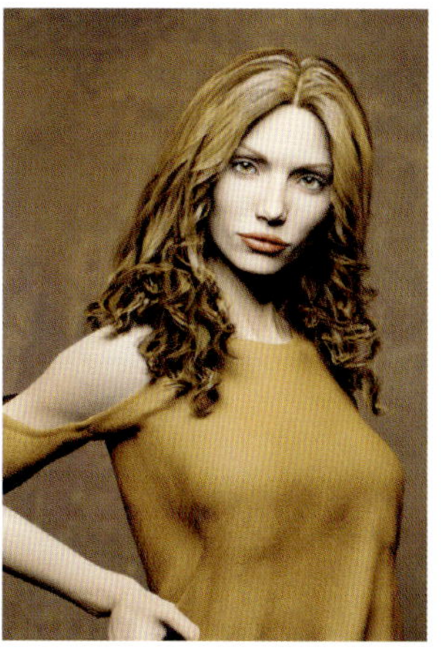

FIGURE 9.2

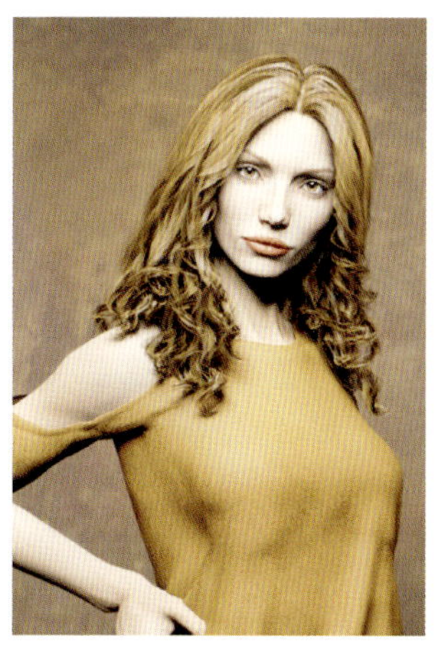

FIGURE 9.3

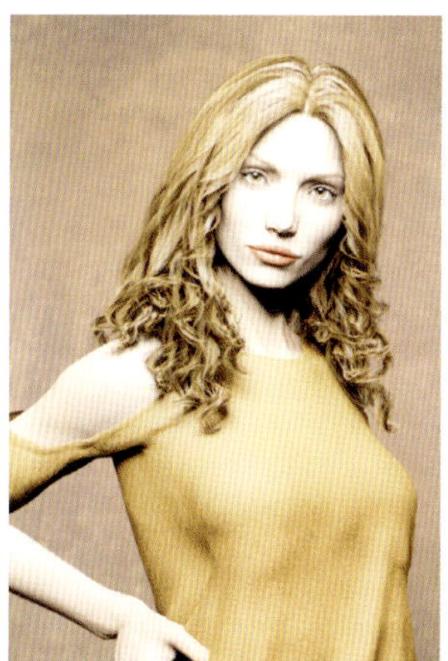

FIGURE 9.4

Figure 9.3: For this image, the power of the flash went up from 6 to 7. This means that the photo is now two stops brighter than the first photo (Figure 9.1).

Figure 9.4: Finally, I adjusted the power of the light from 7 to 8. This is three stops brighter than Figure 9.1. As you can see, the portrait is blown out.

The point of these four images is simple: We kept the camera settings the same for all four photos. The only element that changed was the actual flash power illuminating the model. As the power went up by one stop, the portrait became one stop overexposed. When the power was increased by two stops, the portrait became two stops over-exposed, and so on. The change in exposure is consistent with the change in power. That is what is important to keep in mind.

If You Are Using a Hot Shoe Flash, the Flash Output/Power Is Displayed Differently

Do not let the numbers distract or intimidate you. Read on and you will understand why.

Hot shoe flashes display their power output differently than a portable strobe, such as a Profoto head. As mentioned, for portable strobes, the power setting is displayed using a simple 1–10 scale, 1 being the lowest power and 10 being the maximum power. However, with hot shoe flashes, someone decided to display the power levels using a fraction of the flash's maximum output. For example, a power output reading of 1/1 represents the maximum power. Moving down from there, the next output on a flash is 1/2, which clearly represents exactly what it says: 1/2 of the full power of the flash, or one stop less power than 1/1. The next output from 1/2 is 1/4. This represents—you guessed it—1/4 of the flash's total output, and so on. A power level of 1/4 is one stop less power than 1/2, and two stops less power than 1/1.

<table>
<tr><th colspan="8" style="text-align:center">FLASH OUTPUT SETTINGS</th></tr>
<tr><td>FULL
¹⁄₁</td><td>½</td><td>¼</td><td>⅛</td><td>¹⁄₁₆</td><td>¹⁄₃₂</td><td>¹⁄₆₄</td><td>¹⁄₁₂₈</td></tr>
</table>

FIGURE 9.5

Figure 9.5: This is the way flash output is represented. From one power level to the next, we have a difference of one stop of light. For example, going from 1/2 to 1/4 power would be one stop less of light, which cuts the light in half. Another example: going from 1/64 to 1/16 would mean adding two stops of light: from 1/64 to 1/32 to 1/16.

This is all you really need to know. Don't get caught up or confused by the fractions. They simply represent more or less light output from your flash in one-stop increments. Modern hot shoe flashes, such as the Canon EL-1, can be set all the way down to 1/8192 power! That's amazing! It means that if you set your flash power that low, the flash will output just a tiny kiss of light into your exposure. You could literally put the flash five inches from a person's eye and flash them at that lowest setting. The light would provide beautiful illumination of the eye socket without the danger of overpowering the person's eye with light. Just incredible! Portable strobes cannot be set that low. That is a huge advantage of using hot shoe flashes versus portable strobes.

Making Exposure Changes Using Aperture Only

For the previous example, we made changes to the exposure using the flash power only, without touching any other settings. Now, we will do the same thing, except this time we will make the changes to the exposure using only the aperture setting.

Figure 9.6: Here is a simple, graphic representation of the various apertures and their effects on the background. As you can see in this chart, the aperture of f/1.4 allows the most amount of light to reach the sensor, and it also blurs the background to the maximum level via very shallow depth of field, making your subject stand out the most. By contrast, the aperture f/22 closes the aperture (lens opening) down so much that it only lets a very small amount of light reach the sensor, and at the same time, it brings everything into focus with its deep depth of field.

Clearly, if you were to blast a ray of light into the lens with these aperture settings, the aperture with the largest opening (f/1.4) would let more light in than the aperture with the smallest opening (f/22). This makes sense.

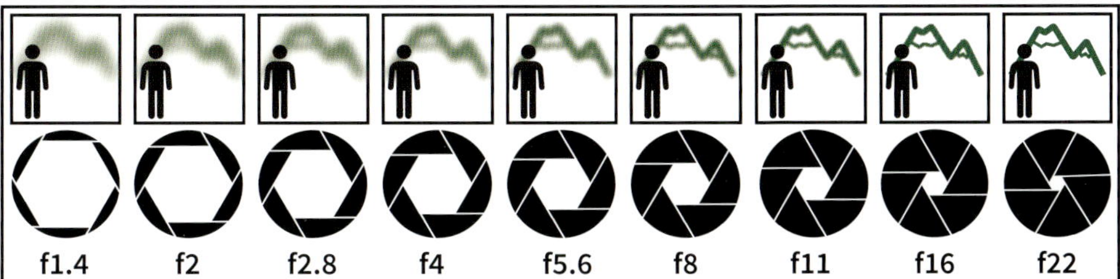

FIGURE 9.6

Let's now put this into practice. For the following examples, again, we will use our starting point settings of ISO 400, f/8, 1/160. The strobe power is set to 5 (midway) and it will *not* be touched throughout these four examples.

Figure 9.7: This image represents the exposure achieved taken at f/8. This aperture of f/8 seems to give us the perfect exposure.

Figure 9.8: For this image, the aperture was changed to f/5.6, which lets in more light than f/8 by one stop (see Figure 9.6). As a result, the exposure is overexposed by one stop.

Figure 9.9: For this image, the aperture was changed to f/4. An aperture of f/4 is two stops to the left of f/8 (see Figure 9.6). This means that it lets in two more stops of light than f/8 because the opening is so much larger. Thus, the portrait is two stops overexposed.

Figure 9.10: Finally, we change the aperture to f/2.8. If you look at the chart, f/2.8 is three stops to the left of f/8. You know the drill now. This means that, at f/2.8, the portrait is three stops overexposed.

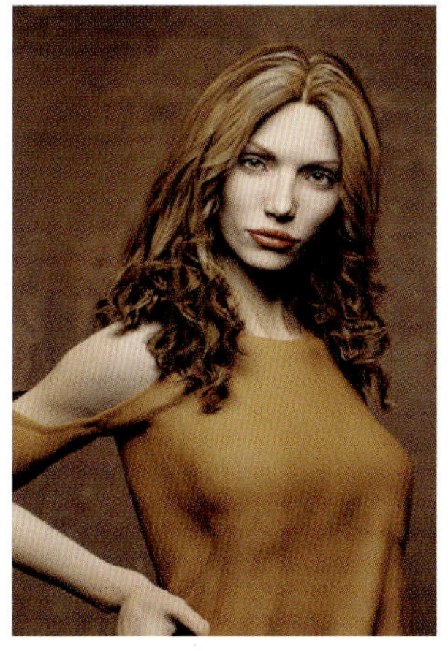

FIGURE 9.7

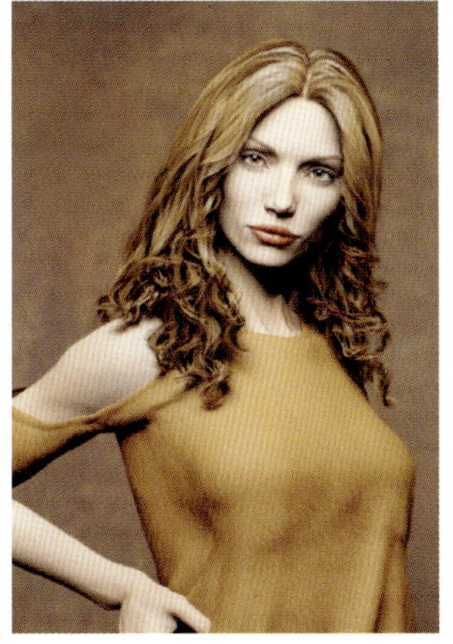

FIGURE 9.8

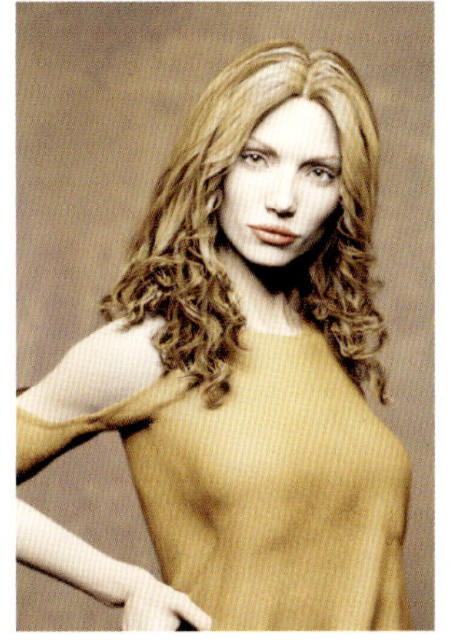

FIGURE 9.9

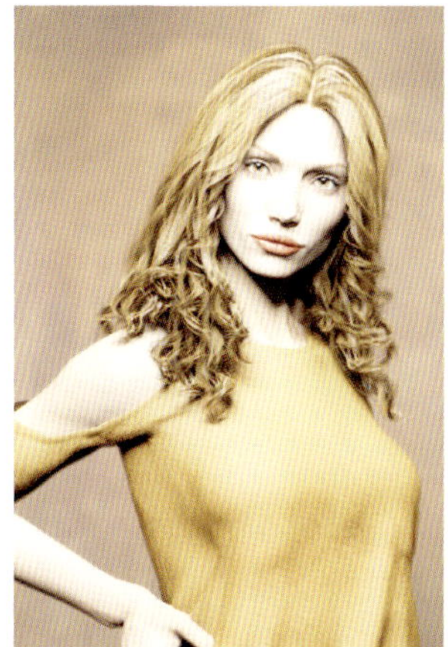

FIGURE 9.10

Do you notice that Figure 9.10 and Figure 9.4 look the same? Both photos are three stops overexposed. The first one was overexposed using only the flash/strobe power. The second was overexposed by the same exact amount by using the aperture and not the power of the flash/strobe. The same applies to the other photos. Both sets of examples look identical, but the method used to overexpose the images was different.

Making Exposure Changes Using ISO Only

Let's move on and make changes to the exposure again, but this time we will not use either the flash/strobe power or the aperture. For these photos, we will use the ISO setting only.

Figure 9.11: This chart shows the various ISO settings you can choose from in most cameras. The lower the ISO setting, the less sensitive to light the sensor will be. This means that the sensor will need more light to achieve a good exposure. Also, the lower the ISO, the less digital noise the image will have. In other words, the lower the ISO, the higher the quality of the file. The exact opposite happens if you choose the higher ISO numbers. Also notice how this chart moves up and down in one-stop increments of light, similar to the aperture chart and the flash power chart.

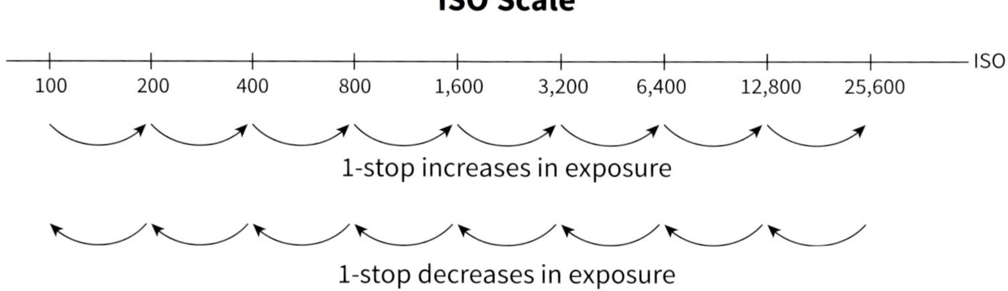

FIGURE 9.11

Figure 9.12: Starting with our agreed-upon camera settings of ISO 400, f/8, 1/160 and our flash/strobe power again at level 5, these settings, once again, give us the perfect exposure.

Figure 9.13: Keeping everything the same, I changed only the ISO from ISO 400 to ISO 800. Looking at the chart (Figure 9.11), ISO 800 is one stop to the right of ISO 400. One stop to the right means double the light.

Figure 9.14: For this image, I changed the ISO from ISO 800 to ISO 1600. This is two stops to the right of ISO 400. Each time you move to the right, you are doubling the amount of light that reaches the sensor from the previous ISO number.

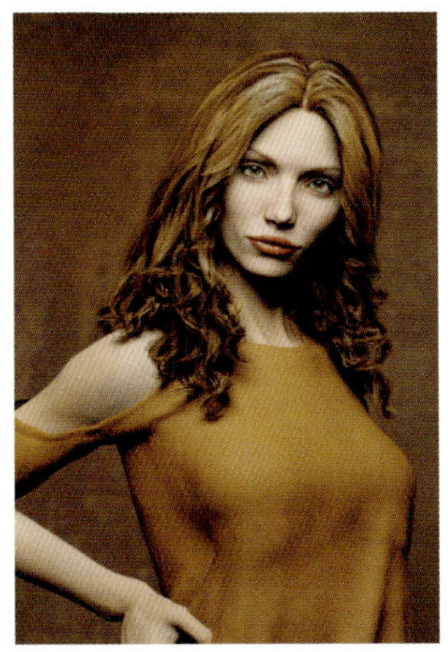

FIGURE 9.12

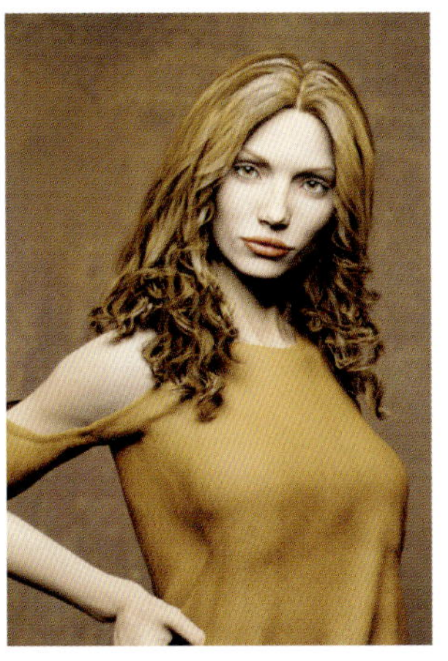

FIGURE 9.13

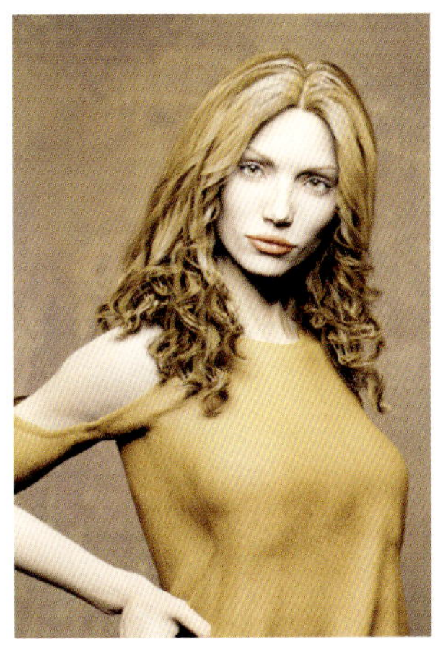

FIGURE 9.14

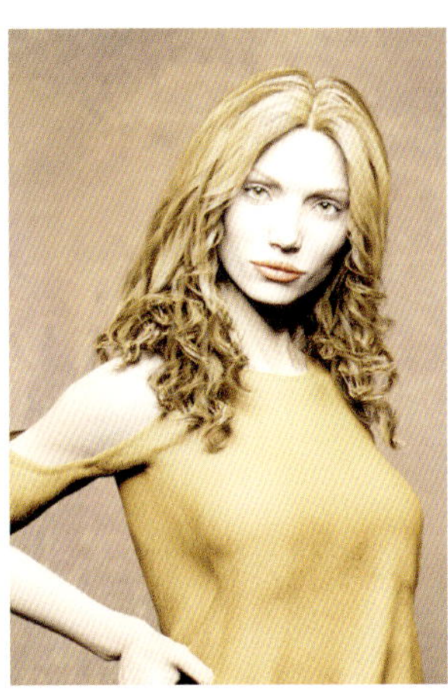

FIGURE 9.15

Figure 9.15: The last image uses an ISO setting of ISO 3200. This is three stops brighter than the original image at ISO 400.

I think by now it's clear: Adding or subtracting one stop of light, or two stops of light, or whatever amount of stops you want can be achieved in different ways with the exact same results. So, if you want to double the amount of light from your current photo, you need to be one stop brighter, correct? This one stop can be achieved by increasing the flash power by one stop—for example, from 5 to 6 on a strobe head or from 1/4 to 1/2 power on a hot shoe flash. You could also choose an aperture with the next larger opening, which would be one stop—from, for example, f/8 to f/5.6. Or you could change the ISO one step to the right on the chart, which would give you one more stop of light— for example, change the ISO from ISO 200 to ISO 400. Regardless of what method you choose, you will obtain what you want: a one-stop increase of light.

F-Stop Compensation Game

It's time to bring everything together and truly understand the relationship between camera settings and flash settings.

Let's say you have an exposure you are happy with, but you want to change the aperture so it's one stop wider in order to blur the background and separate it more from your subject. Let's say you want to go from f/4 to f/2.8. Since you just doubled the light by going up one stop on the aperture scale, you must now compensate for this increase in light by making the flash output one stop darker. With flash, this would be something like 1/16 to 1/32 power. For a portable strobe, you would change the power setting from something like 7 to 6.

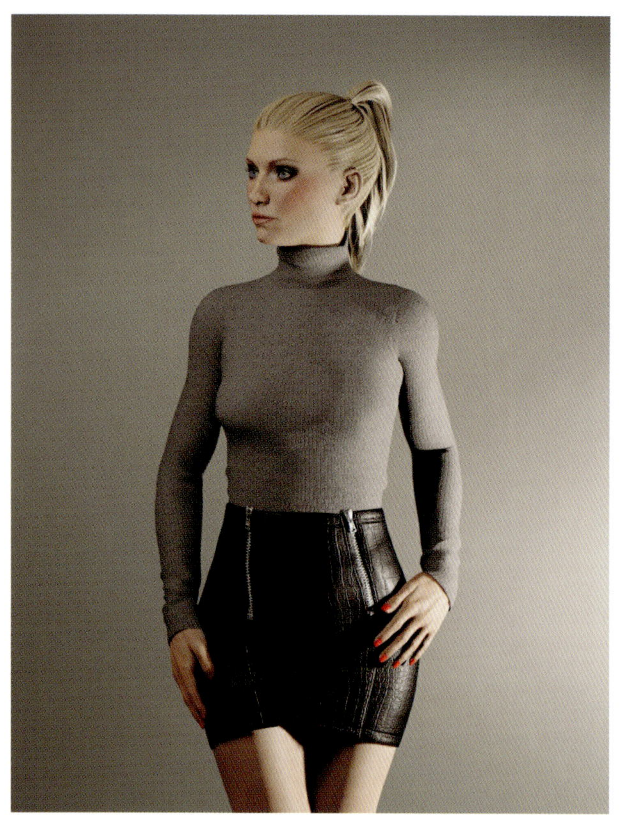

FIGURE 9.16

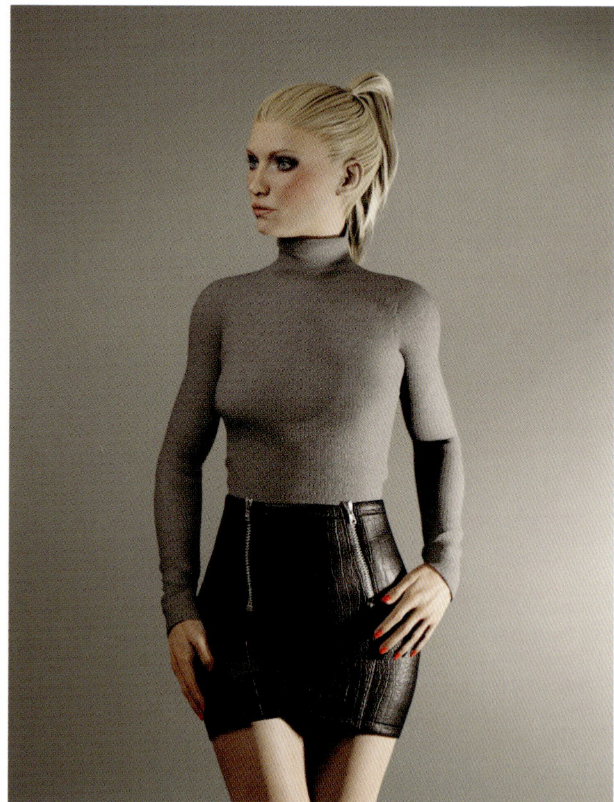

FIGURE 9.17

The key point: If you make the camera settings brighter by one stop, you then must make the flash output darker by one stop so they balance each other out, and the overall exposure remains the same.

Figure 9.16: To make this point clear with a visual, this image was created at ISO 100, f/4, 1/125. Look carefully at the lighting in this image.

Figure 9.17: This image looks identical to Figure 9.16, but it's actually a different image. The settings here are ISO 100, f/2.8, 1/125. The aperture changed and became one stop brighter, from f/4 to f/2.8. However, the lighting on both photos looks identical because I compensated for the brighter aperture by making the strobe output one stop darker, resulting in an identical exposure.

That's how this f-stop game is played. With your flash in Manual mode, anything you change in the camera settings will give you a different result for the exposure. If you want to keep the overall exposure the same but still change the settings in the camera, you must play this F-Stop Compensation game.

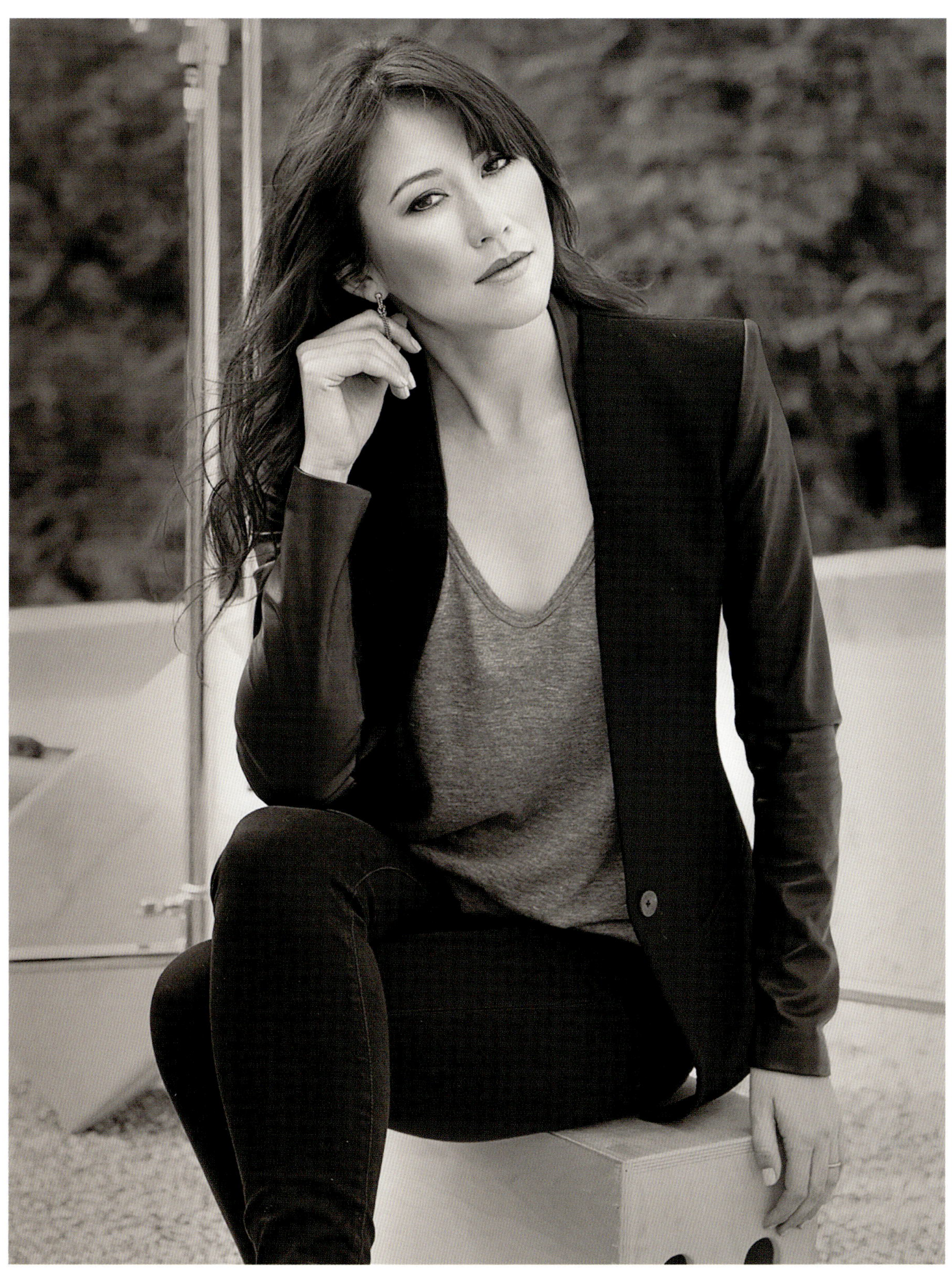

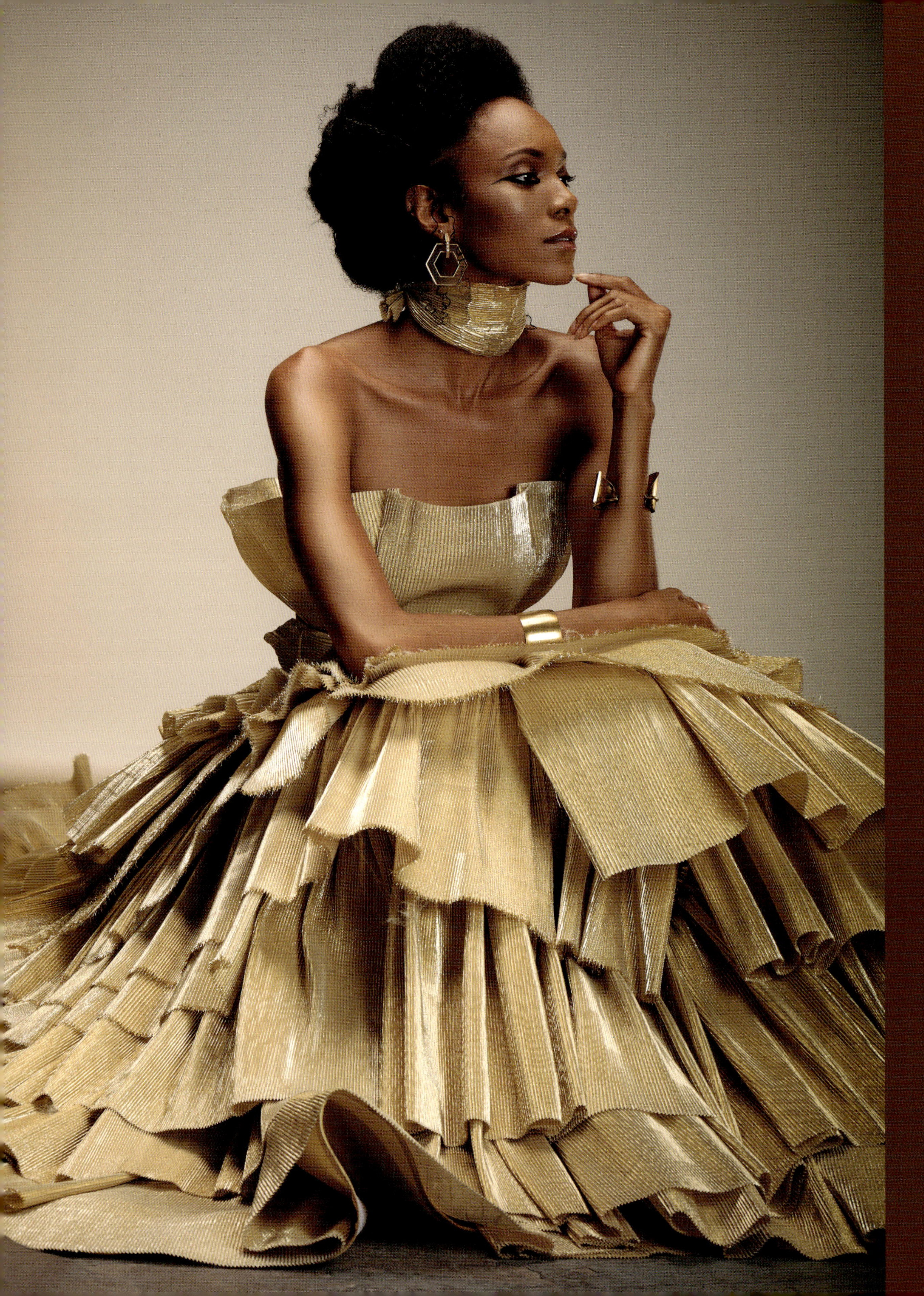

Chapter 10

1st Curtain Sync, 2nd Curtain Sync, and High Speed Sync

I know that you are thinking this all sounds quite strange. "What is a 'curtain' and what is 'curtain sync'? And why do these terms have anything to do with my flashes and strobes?"

Let's keep things simple. This information matters so that you can understand how your flash works. Your camera has two small mechanical curtains that open and close to expose the sensor to light. These curtains make up the camera's shutter, and how quickly they open and close equates to your shutter speed. The curtains (or shutter) can expose the entire sensor to light all at once, or they can accomplish it little by little. The curtains can also open and close across a wide range of time, from an incredibly fast fraction of a second to minutes or an hour or longer.

Since technology keeps moving forward and camera companies keep innovating, we now have the introduction of a purely electronic shutter in mirrorless cameras. An electronic shutter has no physical curtains like a mechanical shutter does. However, before any confusion sets in, just realize that, for now, the effects remain the same with an electronic shutter; the curtains are just replaced by the readout rate of the sensor. It's the same result, just different technology.

Soon, camera manufacturers will completely move away from any physical curtains, and exposures will be determined entirely by electronic shutters. Whether you are dealing with the sensor's readout rate from an electronic shutter or the curtains of a mechanical shutter opening and closing, this affects the method in which the flash syncs with your camera. This is not an exhaustively technical book. If you can understand how the three types of flash sync methods we'll discuss in this chapter affect your results, that is all you really need to know.

1st Curtain Sync

1st Curtain Sync is the default method by which flash syncs with the camera. This terminology really should be changed now, since electronic shutters no longer have curtains. For now, these are the names everyone uses, so let's accept it and move forward.

What you need to know about 1st Curtain Sync is that the flash is programmed to fire at the very beginning of the exposure—as soon as the first curtain opens. The instant your finger touches that shutter button, the flash fires. At faster shutter speeds—such as between 1/100 to 1/200 of a second—the time between the beginning of the exposure and the end of it is almost instantaneous. Therefore, you won't notice much of a difference when the flash fires.

But at slower shutter speeds, it makes *all* the difference. At slower shutter speeds—for example, anything slower than 1/50—the effects of the flash firing at the very beginning of the exposure will be very evident. When a flash fires, it travels at a ridiculously hard-to-comprehend speed. This burst of instantaneous light freezes the motion that it illuminates. This speed of the flash is called the flash duration speed (see Chapter 5). The lower the power of the flash, the faster the duration speed will be, and thus it will have more motion-freezing capability. As you crank your flash's power up to a higher output, the flash duration speed, or motion-freezing power, goes down because the flash burst must stay on longer throughout the exposure in order to build up more light.

Figure 10.1: Even though names like "1st Curtain Sync" can be confusing with new mirrorless technology and the various types of shutters available now, the good news is that the principles for understanding how this affects your flash behavior doesn't change. With 1st Curtain Sync, which is the default flash sync mode, the flash simply fires at the beginning of the exposure, then turns off like a lightning bolt. This happens very quickly. Looking at this figure, from left to right, the black line represents the time the shutter is open. In this case, it is at 1/80 of a second. On the left, the first curtain opens and starts to expose the sensor to light. The black spike is the flash firing at the beginning of the exposure. Notice how fast the flash burst is in relation to the overall shutter speed of 1/80.

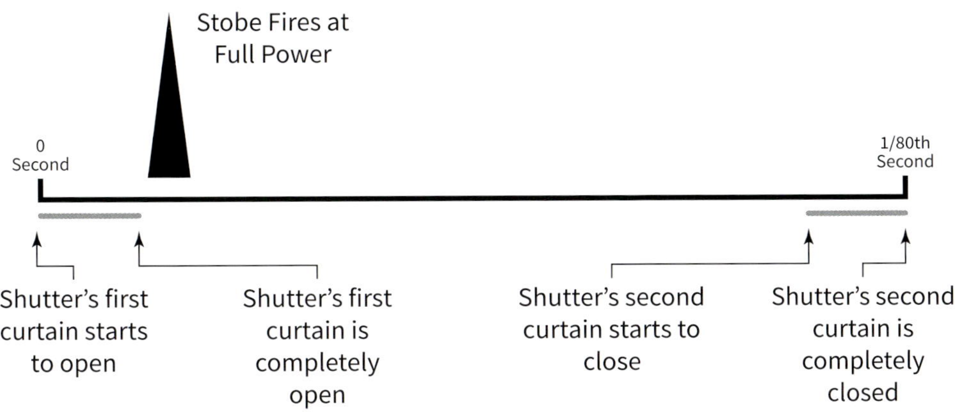

FIGURE 10.1

Note that the flash's power to freeze motion greatly depends on how close the moving subject is to the light emitted by the flash. This is very important. Simply using flash on a subject that is 15 feet away is not going to have any motion-stopping power. However, if the moving subject is illuminated primarily by the burst from a flash or strobe, that moving subject will be frozen—and this happens especially if the moving subject is very close to the light from the flash/strobe.

If your light and the moving subject cannot be too close in distance (for any number of reasons), yet you still wish to freeze the motion of your subject, then you must significantly increase the power of your strobe. A simple hot shoe flash or a common portable strobe probably won't work. For a scenario like this, you would need a powerful strobe that can produce around 1,200 or more Watt seconds of power. Another helpful trick is to use 1st Curtain Sync to freeze the motion at the beginning of the exposure to eliminate any other light source from reaching your sensor.

Figure 10.2: This figure shows 1st Curtain Sync in action. At the very beginning of the exposure, the flash fires and freezes the motion of the runner at full stride. However, as the exposure continues for 1/15 of a second, the runner becomes a blur for the rest of the exposure. This is how the default setting for flash works.

How could a photographer use this combination of slow shutter speed and 1st Curtain Sync creatively? That's an easy question to ask, and a very hard question to answer. If you take the time to think about this question and come up with some ideas, you could make some really unique photographs.

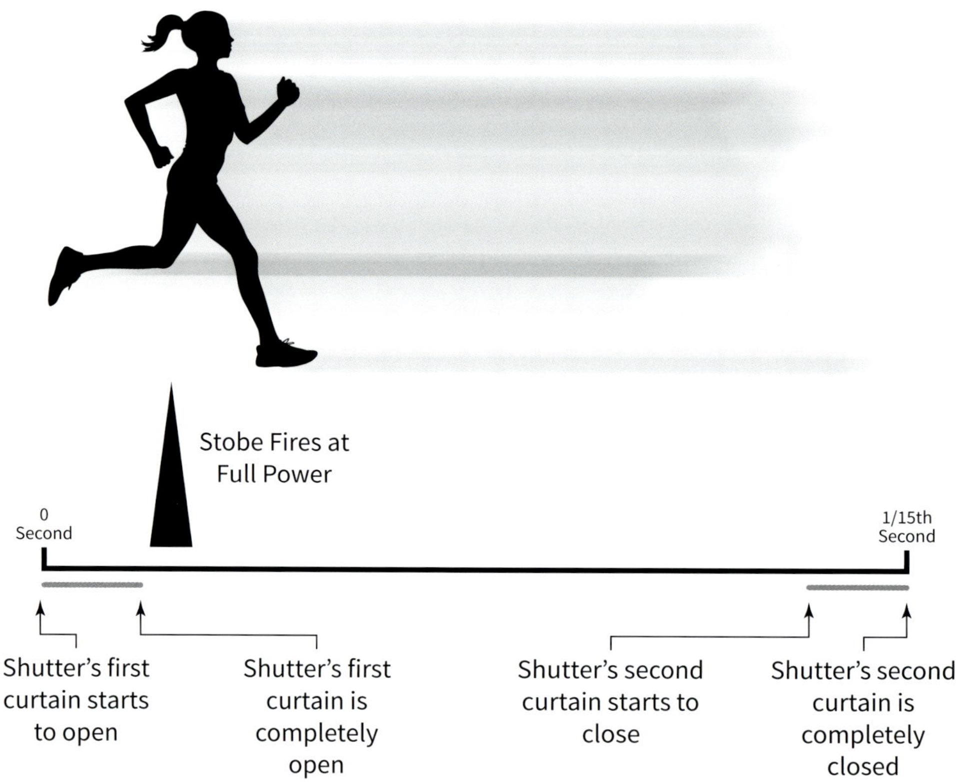

FIGURE 10.2 First curtain sync

2nd Curtain Sync

A very useful feature of flashes and strobes is their ability to fire the flash at the end of the exposure instead of at the beginning. When the flash fires at the end of the exposure, this is called 2nd Curtain Sync, or Rear Curtain Sync. As I mentioned earlier, in the very near future, most, if not all, mirrorless professional cameras will no longer have any physical curtains. Exposing the sensor to light will be accomplished electronically. The good news is that, whether you're using electronic shutters or physical shutters, the principles of 1st and 2nd Curtain Sync do not change.

You need to know that when you choose to fire your flash with 2nd Curtain Sync, it means that no matter how short or long your shutter speed is, the flash will wait until the very last instant before the end of the exposure to fire. Therefore, when using a slow shutter speed, anything moving from the beginning of the exposure to the point just before the flash fires will be a blur. However, the moving subject will be frozen at the end of the exposure when the flash burst illuminates it.

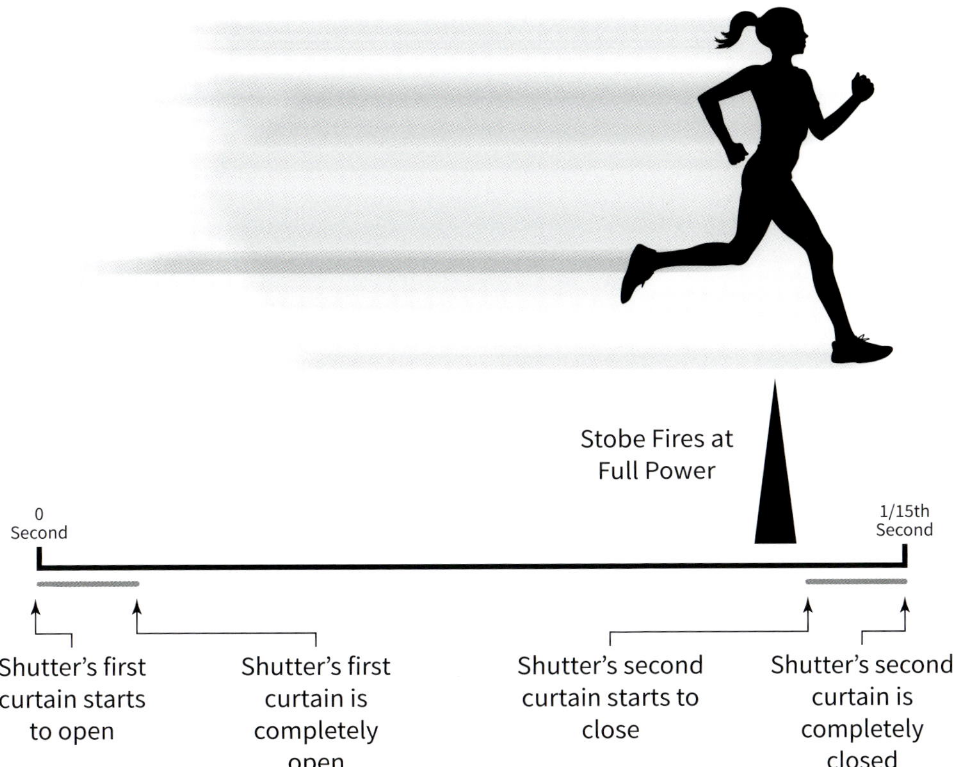

FIGURE 10.3 Second curtain sync

Figure 10.3: Notice how, with a shutter speed of 1/15 of a second, the runner blurs throughout the exposure until the very end, when the flash fires and freezes her. The image looks much more natural to the human eye because it seems as if she is moving so fast that she is leaving a blur behind her. That makes sense.

With 1st Curtain Sync, the blur happens in front of the runner, which doesn't really make sense because it appears as if she is chasing her own blur. For this reason, 2nd Curtain Sync is a much more popular technique to use to freeze motion when using slower shutter speeds. It is important to remember that, for the light to have maximum motion-freezing power, the flash/strobe and the moving subject must be as close to each other as possible.

TIP FOR USING 2ND CURTAIN SYNC

I prefer to leave my flash on 2nd Curtain Sync most of the time. And I make sure it's set to 2nd Curtain Sync as soon as my shutter speed drops below 1/100. I take a higher number of successful photographs this way.

USING A THREE-STOP OR SIX-STOP NEUTRAL DENSITY FILTER TO KEEP YOUR SHUTTER SPEED UNDER THE CAMERA'S FLASH SYNC SPEED LIMIT

One of the most useful techniques I have employed through the years to avoid using High Speed Sync is to use a three-stop or six-stop ND filter when shooting outdoors in broad daylight. If you don't know what an ND filter is, it's basically sunglasses for your lens (see Chapter 5 for more). The problem with using ND filters is that they traditionally get screwed on in front of the lens you are using. This means that you have to buy a new ND filter for every lens you have. That's not only impractical, but very expensive. For this reason, I use ND filters made by a company called Kolari Vision. Their ND filters are placed right in front of the camera's sensor, behind the lens, instead of in front of the lens. By placing the ND filter inside the lens mount, you can use one ND filter for all the lenses you own. That's fantastic!

Figure 10.4: This photo was taken during my Canon campaign for the new Canon RF 100–300mm f/2.8 lens. The location was adjacent to Malibu, California, and it was a bright and sunny day as usual. Canon asked me to make as many photos as I could at f/2.8 to show the capabilities of the lens with this incredible range. But to shoot at f/2.8 I would have had to set my shutter speed much higher than the camera's flash sync speed. The solution was a common one for me: I used a Kolari Vision three-stop ND filter to bring my exposure all the way down to 1/200 of a second at f/2.8 with ISO 100. How cool is that!? At that point, I was within the camera's flash sync speed and I could take advantage of the full power capabilities of my Profoto B1 strobe. This is a huge lifesaver!

Had I not used the ND filter, I would have had to set the Profoto strobe to High Speed Sync, which means I would have lost most of its power. I would have had to use two or even three B1 strobes to make up for the loss of power when using HSS. No thank you!

I recommend trying out this approach. You will notice a big difference in the effectiveness of your flash/strobe when shooting outdoors on location.

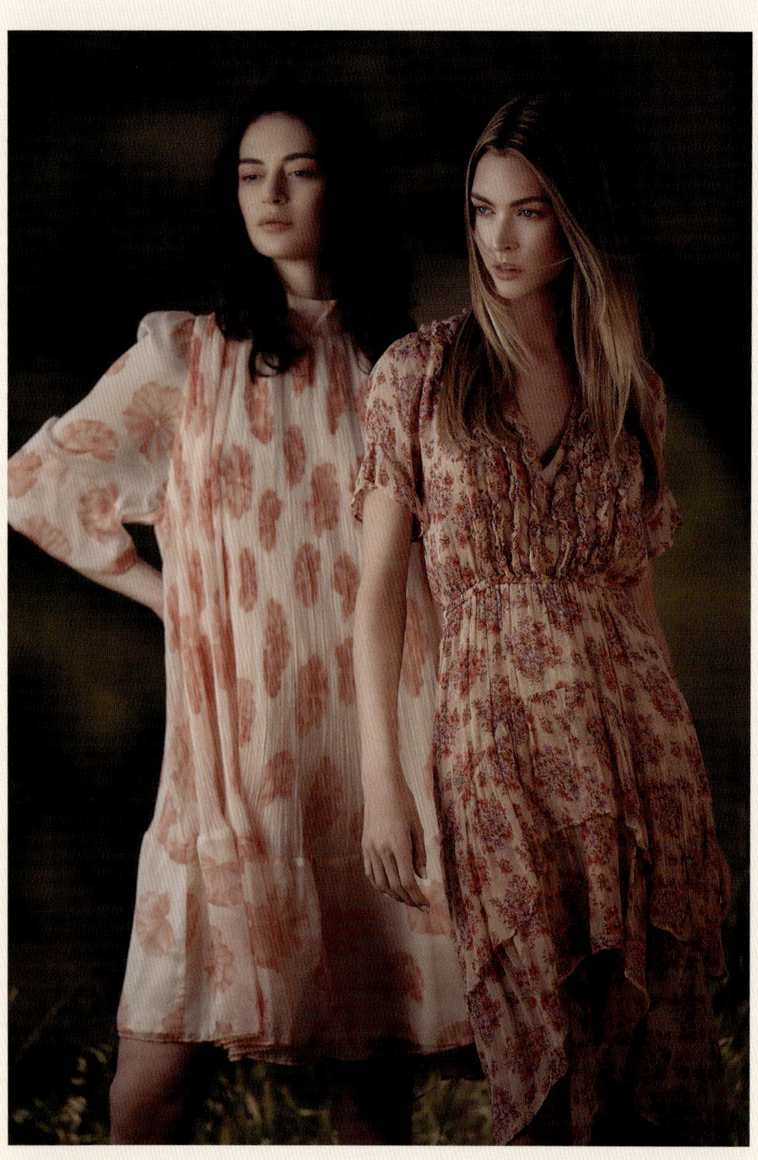

FIGURE 10.4

High Speed Sync (HSS)

High Speed Sync (HSS) is a crucial feature of flashes and most portable strobes. Cameras have limitations on how fast the shutter speed can be while still using flash to influence the exposure. Think about it: The light from your flash/strobe must reach the sensor while it's being exposed to light for just a fraction of a second. At fast shutter speeds, the camera's mechanism must change to be able to open and close fast enough to achieve a high shutter speed. At any shutter speed faster than 1/200 or 1/250 (depending on your camera), the sensor is not exposed to light all at once; it is exposed to light little by little from the top down. While each portion of the sensor is being exposed to light, the flash pulses very fast bursts to illuminate the subject for each portion of the sensor as it is exposed to light. It's really quite remarkable.

But here is the bad news. As with everything else in photography, there is a trade-off for every exposure decision you make. In this case, the benefit of High Speed Sync is that you can use the light from your flash/strobe to influence the exposure at any shutter speed faster than the camera's sync speed of either 1/200 or 1/250. For example, you could go outside and use a fast shutter speed such as 1/2000 or even 1/8000. The trade-off when using flash at such a fast shutter speed is that the flash is highly weakened when you use High Speed Sync. Even if you set your flash at full power, it will be very noticeable how weak "full power" becomes when using HSS. In fact, if you were to compare your flash in normal mode at full power with the same flash at full power when using HSS, you would notice that you lose around 2.5 stops of light! Expressed as a percentage, HSS reduces the power of your flash by 75–85%, depending on various factors.

Figure 10.5: This figure can help you visualize what's happening inside your camera when the shutter speed is set faster than 1/200 or 1/250. At these shutter speeds, the sensor is exposed to light by a thin slit that moves down from the top. The faster the shutter speed, the thinner that slit becomes. You can see how, in High Speed Sync mode, the flash pulses very quickly to keep up with the opening of the thin slit moving down the sensor.

What does this tell you? It tells you that in HSS mode, the flash, with its multiple pulses, takes on the behavior of continuous light. Therefore, if you increase your shutter speed from perhaps 1/2000 to 1/4000, the exposure will darken accordingly, just as the camera would behave with constant light. By using this amazing technology, photographers can go outside and shoot with wide-open apertures such as f/2.8, or even larger, and obtain a beautiful and aesthetically pleasing background bokeh.

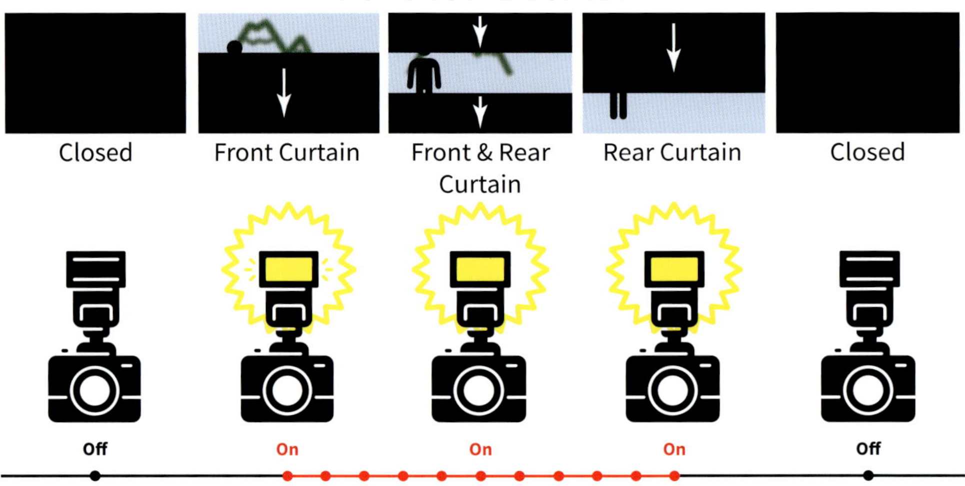

FIGURE 10.5

Earlier in this book, we discussed how to use these features creatively. But here we are just learning more about the techniques that are available and what they can accomplish. It is very hard to be creative if you don't have a solid understanding of each technique and know how it works. The more time you take to truly understand every flash function available to you, the greater ability you will have to think outside the box and use these tools creatively.

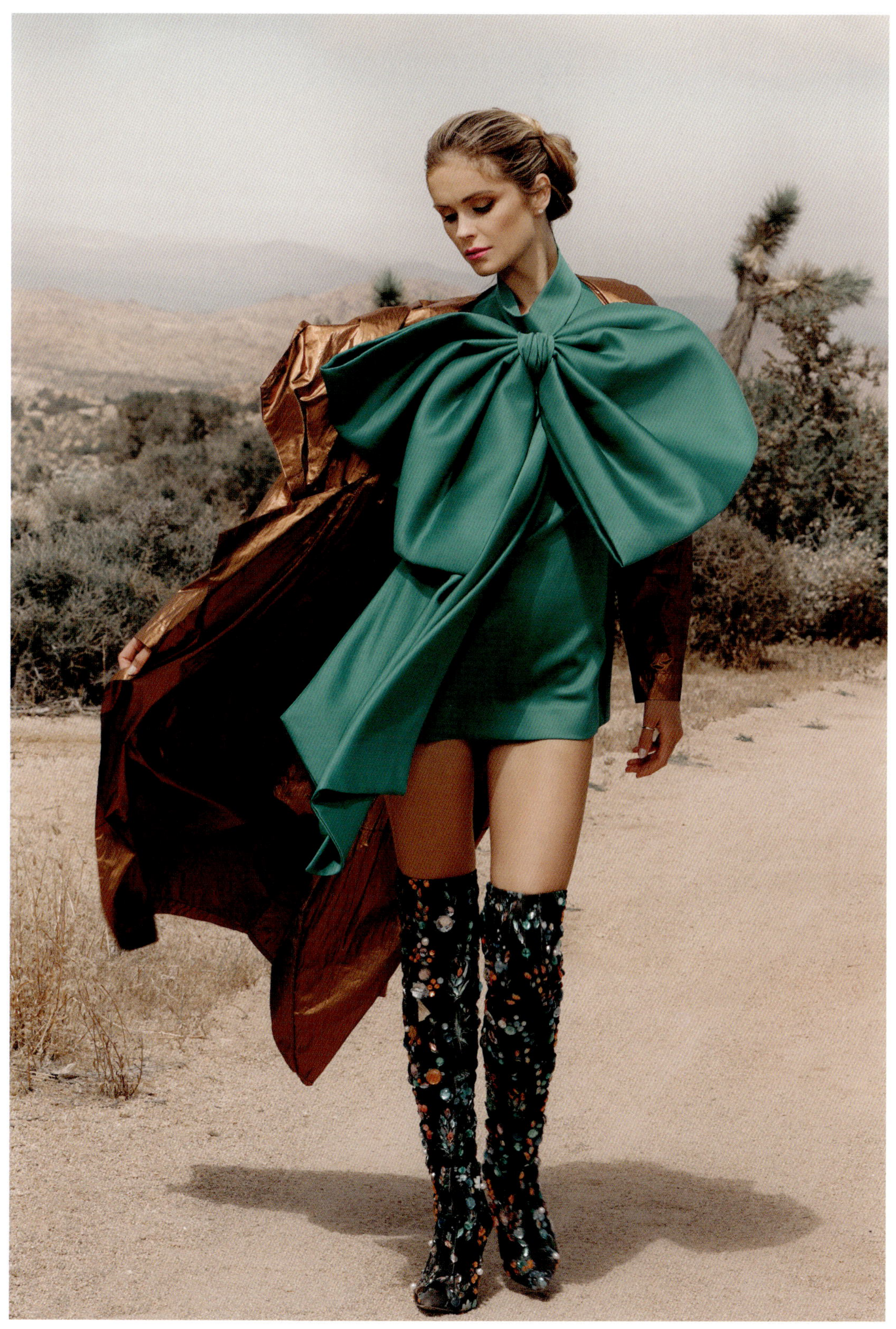

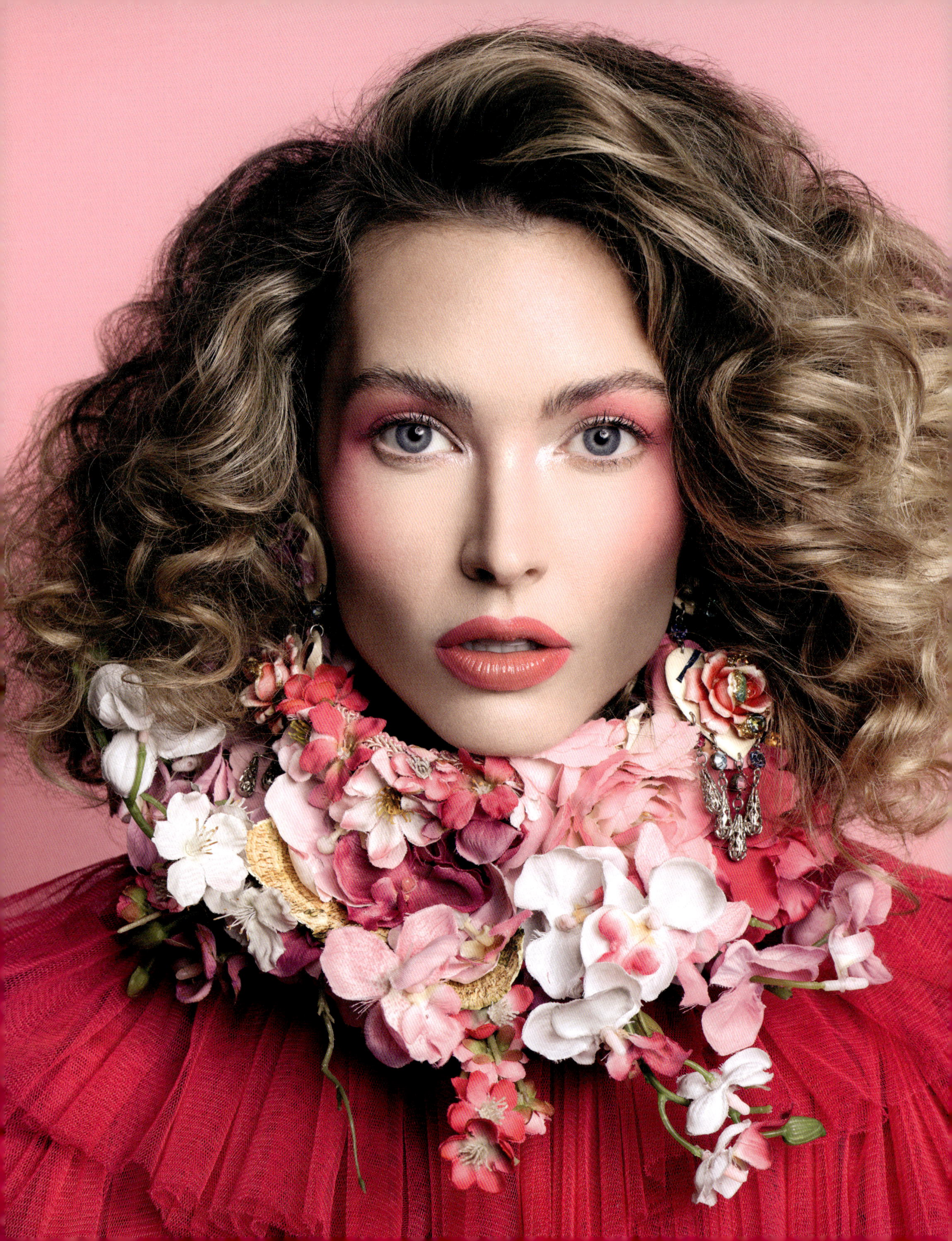

Chapter 11

Channels and Groups

Channels and groups offer a way to organize multiple flash units for off-camera flash setups. Off-camera flash allows the photographer to take the flash off the hot shoe and place it anywhere they want to create any lighting setup. Without off-camera flash capabilities, we would be stuck with the limitation of direct on-camera flash, which is not amusing.

All portable strobes and flashes, regardless of the brand, are organized into channels and groups. This is what makes using flashes/strobes that you may not be too familiar with easy to grasp. Channels and groups are also a lifesaver when you're working with multiple photographers who are using flash in the same proximity, as they allow each photographer to use their own flashes reliably and without firing the other photographers' flashes.

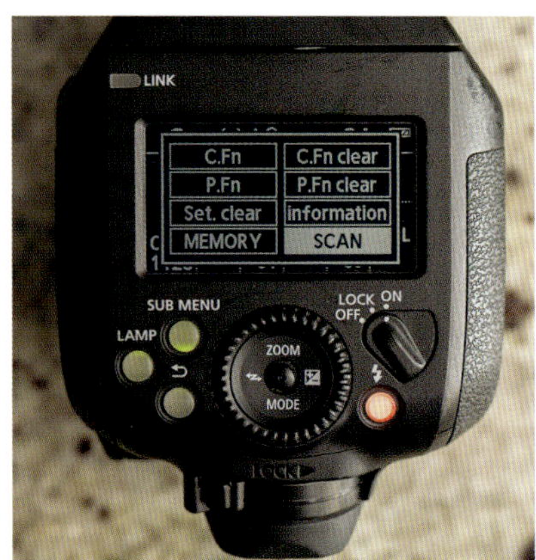

FIGURE 11.1

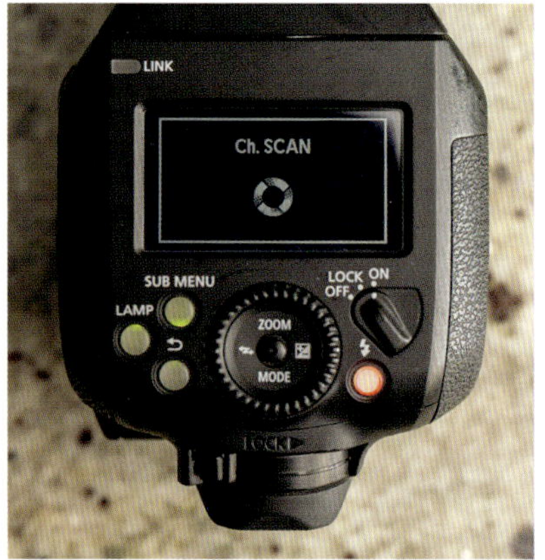

FIGURE 11.2

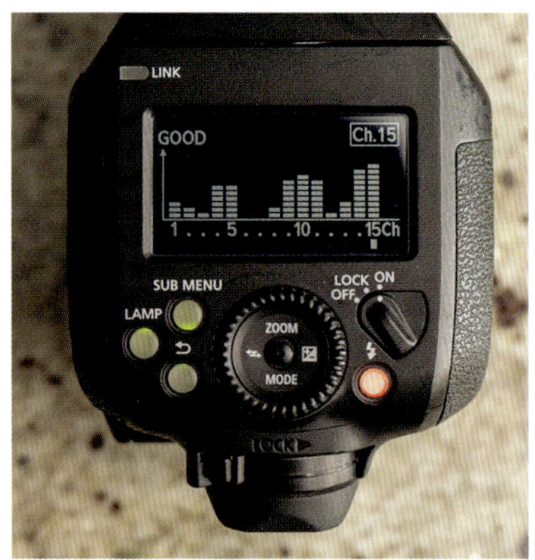

FIGURE 11.3

Channels

Let's begin with the simple concept of channels. Channels are set to a specific radio frequency. This frequency can be strong, or it can be weakened by other electronic devices that are transmitting radio signals through the air, such as mobile phones. If you are working on a channel that has a strong frequency, you will have a cleaner signal communicating with your off-camera flashes. So, how do you find the channel with the best signal?

Figure 11.1: Most modern flashes have the ability to scan the air to determine the signal strength of available channels. This image shows my Canon flash. When I press Sub Menu, this screen shows up with the choice to Scan for channel strength.

Figure 11.2: Selecting the Scan option initiates the process of scanning the air for all channel frequencies and their respective strength.

Figure 11.3: These are the results, showing the strength of all the available channels. If you look carefully at the screen, Channels 1–3 have a very poor signal, which is usually the case. I bet that if you grabbed your flash right now, chances are you would be on Channel 1. Channel 1 is usually a very busy channel, and it's full of interference. Therefore, I stay away from Channel 1 as much as possible. Channels 4 and 5 are better, but not great. Channels 6 and 7 have such poor signal that my flash couldn't even detect any life on those two channels. Channels 9, 10, and 11 have a good signal. However, Channels 14 and 15 have the strongest and cleanest signal. Therefore, I would choose Channel 14 or 15.

What are channels used for in off-camera flash? It's simple. In the very common situation when you are working an event with multiple photographers, each with their own set of flashes, channels allow you to set all your flashes to the same channel, while other photographers each use their own channel.

In fashion runway events, for example, many photographers set up their own flashes along the catwalk to obtain the best possible lighting on the models as they walk by. Just imagine a world without channels. Every photographer would be firing each other's flashes every time they pushed their shutter button. It would be a nightmare!

To clean up this messy situation, you simply set the flashes that belong to you to one channel—for example, Channel 15. Next, you arrange with the other photographer to be on a different channel, perhaps Channel 14. If there are three photographers, then the third photographer can be on Channel 10. Now, when you push the shutter button, only the flashes that are set to your specific channel will fire, leaving the other photographers' flashes alone.

Some portable strobes have upwards of 100 channels available to choose from.

Sharing or Not Sharing Flashes with Channels

Let's say you are working an event, such as a wedding reception or a fashion show. You have your own set of flashes all set up, and you have a second shooter with you covering different angles. Here are some easy-to-follow instructions and diagrams to help you handle these situations without technical issues.

Figure 11.4: In this case, both you and your assistant have your own sender remotes or hot shoe flash (an on-camera flash acting like a remote). You are both on Channel 1, and the receiver flashes are also on Channel 1. Both of you can send signals to the receiver flashes to fire every time each of you pushes the shutter button. This is a very helpful setup because you can set up one set of flashes throughout a room, and simply tell your assistant to set their sender flash on the same channel as you, so both of you can share the flashes.

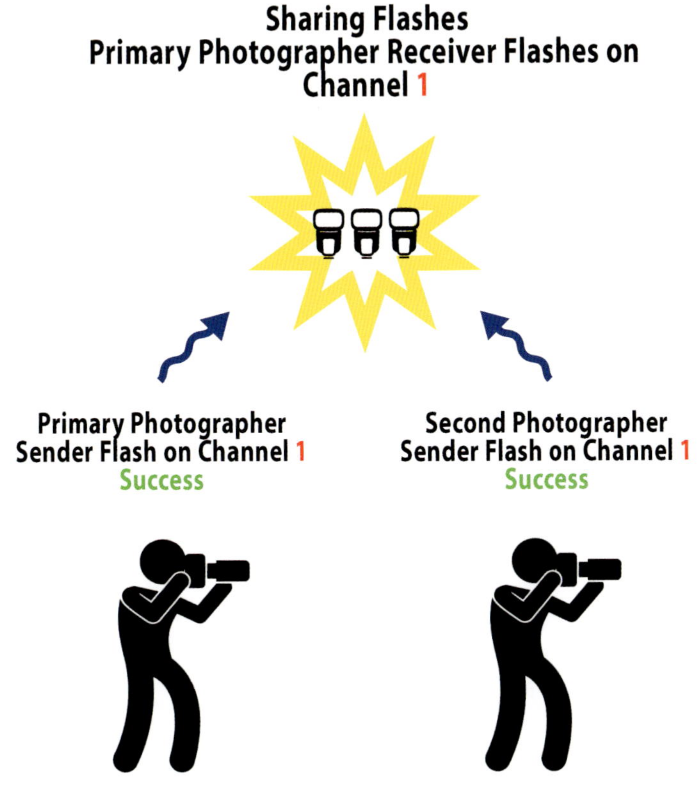

FIGURE 11.4

Figure 11.5: In this scenario, the Primary photographer on the left has his sender remote set to Channel 1, and the receiver flashes are also set to Channel 1. Therefore, the photographer on the left can trigger the flashes. The photographer on the right has her sender remote set to Channel 4. This photographer will not be able to trigger the flashes, because those flashes are set to Channel 1. This is the setup you want when working with other photographers that are not part of your team but are photographing the same event.

Figure 11.6: In this scenario, there are two sets of receiver flashes, so there is no need to share flashes this time. Each photographer has their own set. The photographer on the left has his sender remote set to Channel 1, and his set of flashes is also set to Channel 1. The photographer on the right set her sender remote and receiving flashes to Channel 8. Each photographer will be able to trigger their own set of flashes, but not trigger the other photographer's flashes.

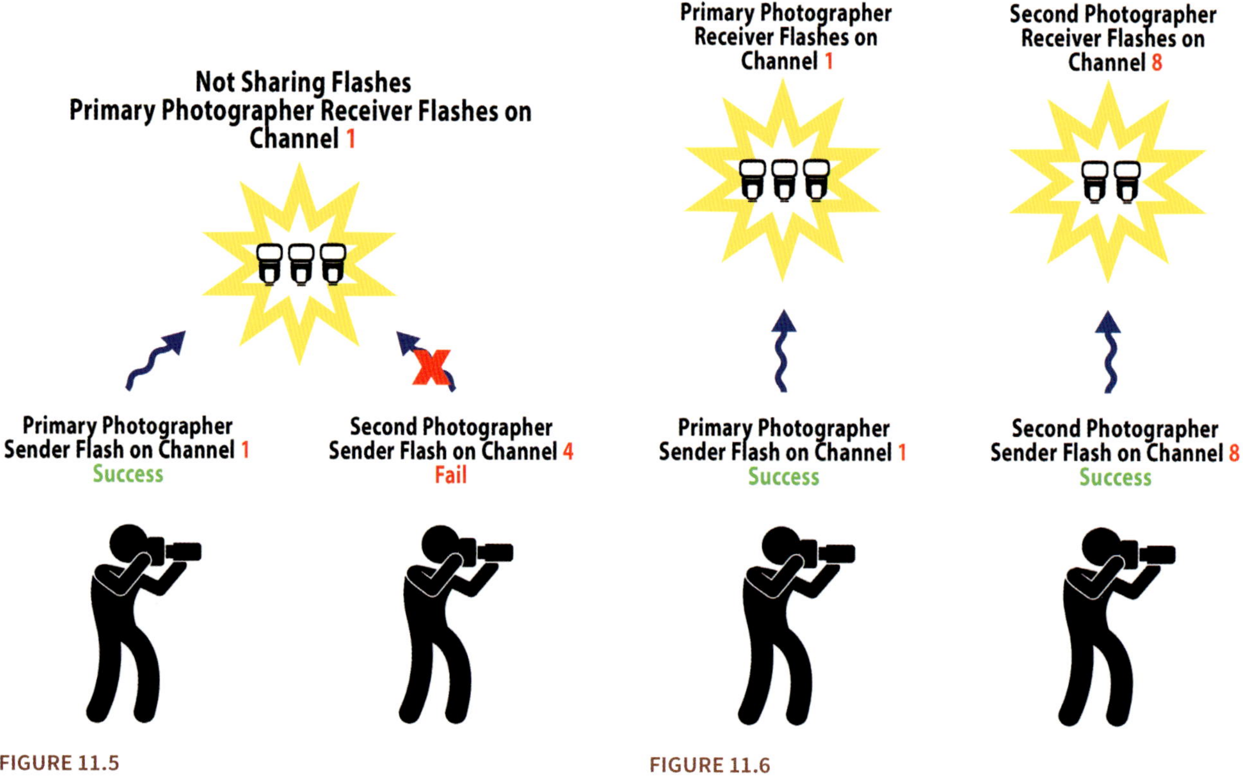

FIGURE 11.5

FIGURE 11.6

Groups

Groups allow the photographer to organize their flashes into sets, or groups. By giving each flash a group name, you can control each group independently from the others. Furthermore, all flashes/strobes that have the same group name will work together as one.

Let's say you need more power than your current flash can provide on its own. In this case, you could grab two or three additional flashes from your bag, put them all together, and give them all the same group name, such as Group B. When you fire the shutter, all the flashes in Group B will fire at the same time and at the same power as if they were one big flash.

Figure 11.7: This example takes place at a studio, but the location doesn't matter. This works the same at any location. In this example of how groups operate, there are five flashes being used. To control the two front flashes (key light and fill light), I set the key light to Group A and the fill light to Group B. Now that this is set, I can use the remote on my camera (provided by the manufacturer of your lights) to control Group A at a certain power, and Group B at a different power, depending upon how much fill I want.

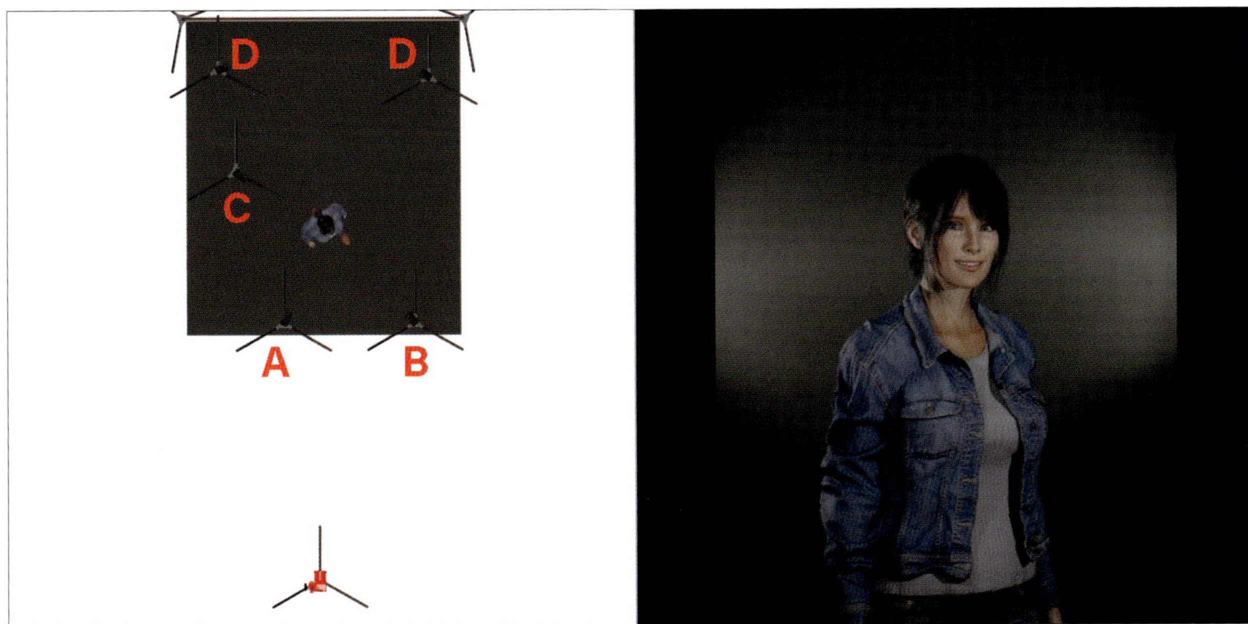

FIGURE 11.7

Next, I added a kicker light at camera left, and I put that flash in Group C. I love using kicker lights in my work because they do a great job of adding dimensionality. If my kicker light is too obvious, I can push "C" on the remote on camera and dial the power down only for that light.

Finally, I positioned two background flashes to equally illuminate the background. The key word is "equally." The reason is that both background flashes are set to Group D. This means that whatever I set for D flash, the other D flash will adopt the same power setting. Both Group D flashes will fire at the same time and at the same power because they are in the same group.

Let's say that I don't want the background lit equally, that I prefer some sort of gradient in the background. In that case, I can grab one of the background flashes and put it in a different group: Group E. Now I can choose different power settings for each of my two background lights, giving me that gradient.

I can't imagine not having access to groups to organize my lights. Not only do groups allow you to have independent control of each light, but they allow you to control every light via the remote on the camera's hot shoe. It's so convenient!

I have one final note. The remote on the camera is referred to as the "sender" because it sends the signal to the flash and tells it what to do. The light receiving the signal is referred to as a "receiver." For many years, these used to be called "master" and "slave," which are horrible names. But thankfully, we have moved on from this nomenclature to a more globally accepted one. "Sender" and "receiver" sound much better!

A Word About Line-of-Sight (Infrared) Flash Triggering

Flashes/strobes have modern radio transmission technology built into them. This technology allows the signal to travel from the sender to the receiver units through walls, rooms, and most other obstacles. You no longer have to rely on the old technology, called line-of-sight or infrared.

With line-of-sight triggering, when one flash fires, the other flashes must be able to "see" the light burst from the initial flash, and then they react and fire themselves. This happens so fast that all flashes essentially fire together and reach the camera's sensor at the same time. Crazy, right? But if the other flashes are too far away, or if they are blinded by the midday sun, or if the other flashes' sensors that are meant to see the initial flash's burst are not pointed at that flash, then they won't fire. It can be very frustrating.

Line-of-sight triggering works best indoors with no walls to block the line of sight from one flash to the other. A studio setting is perfect for line-of-sight triggering. Non-studio settings can give the flashes too much trouble in their effort to see each other. Furthermore, if the sender flash fires a weak amount of light, the receiver units could have a hard time seeing that weak flash output, and simply not fire. Again, very frustrating.

Fortunately, radio transmission technology has taken over. Now, you can pretty much put your sender and receiver units anywhere—under a bed, in another room, behind a wall—and the radio signals will reach the receiver units with no problem.

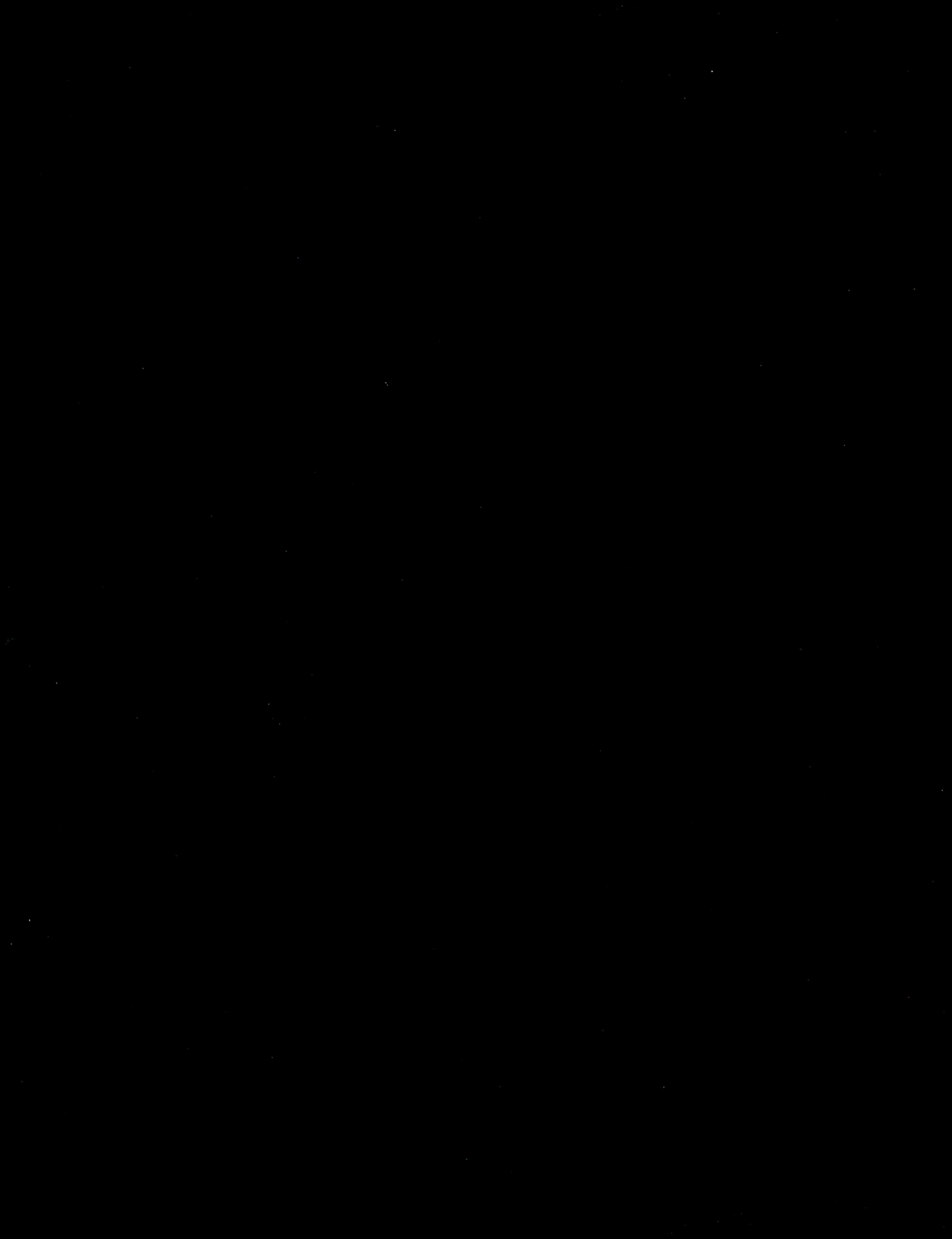

DYNAMIC FLASH EXERCISES

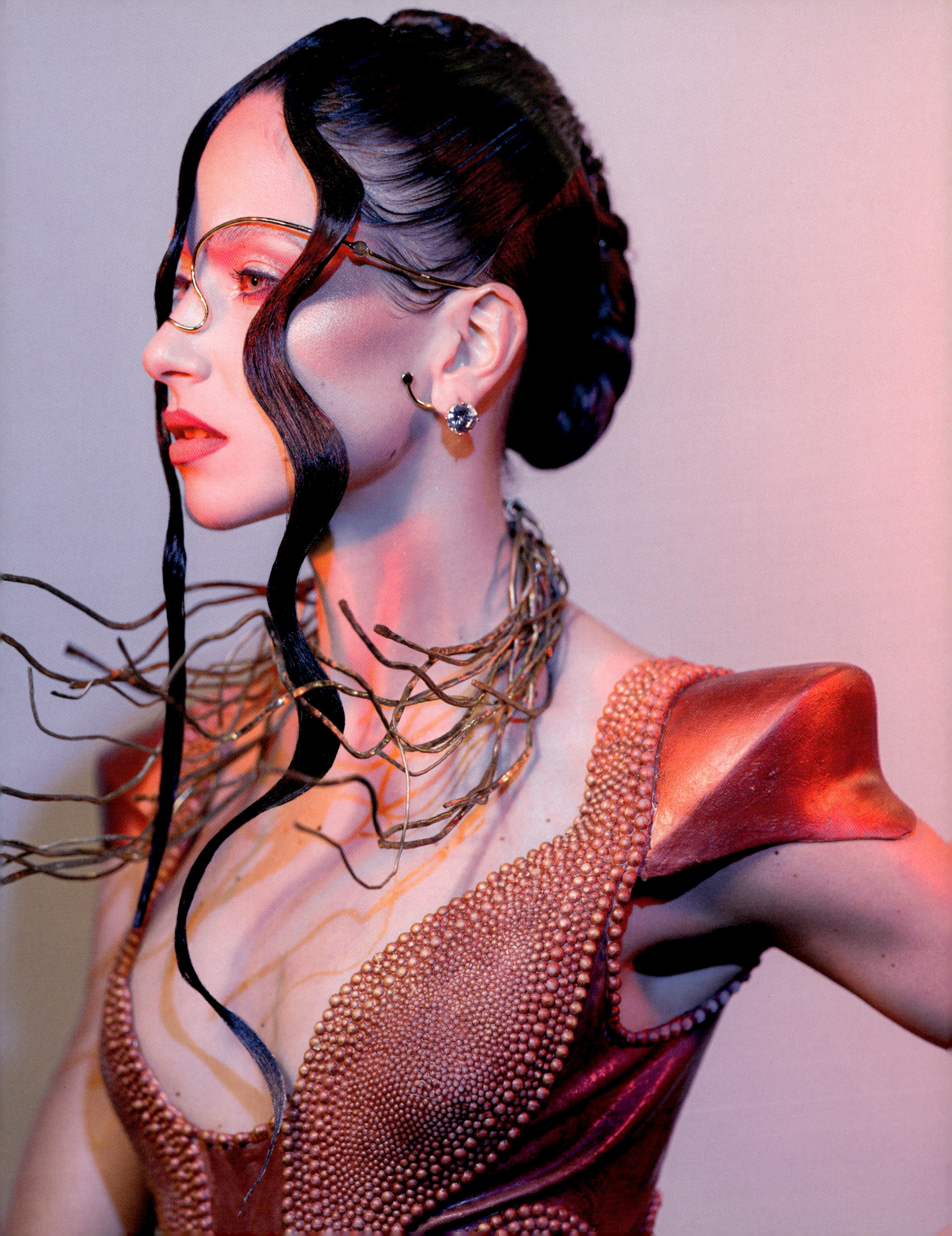

Chapter 12

Lighting Exercises

Bringing everything together, I thought it would be good to end the book with a series of exercises that you can use to sharpen your skills and take your lighting knowledge to the next level. In order to get the most out of these exercises, take your time with them and really think through the entire process from start to finish. Let's get started.

Lighting Exercise #1:
Diffusing Hard Light and Sculpting

Purpose of Exercise

This is a powerful technique because it's so useful in practically any situation. This is meant more for outdoor use, but the software I used to make these figures does not have outdoor sets. I recommend doing this exercise both in a studio and also outside in midday sun.

The purpose of this exercise is to get used to diffusing or fixing the hard light from the sun or a strobe. When you have clean light on your subject, then start sculpting the light with another flash/strobe. In the final setup here, I decided to go with short lighting the male model as my sculpting technique. But you can do broad lighting or butterfly lighting if you wish (later exercises discuss these techniques). The main goal is to clean up hard light by diffusing it, then create the light sculpting you want using flash.

Conditions

For the outside shoot, you want to shoot outdoors in strong midday sun with no clouds. The sun must be harsh on your subject. For the indoor shoot, use a strong light reflector to act as the sun; the rest is the same.

Set your camera to ISO 100 for both indoors and outdoors.

Goals

Goal 1: Start by taking a properly exposed photo of the subject with direct sunlight without diffusion (**Figure 12.1**).

Goal 2: Next, work with someone (or use a C-stand with a grip) to hold a diffuser over the subject's head to diffuse the hard light on your subject, and take another photo. This photo will result in clean light, but not sculpted light (**Figure 12.2**).

Goal 3: Finally, experiment with a sculpting light or an accent light to create dimensionality by forcing shadows on the face. You can try short lighting, broad lighting, and center/butterfly lighting as your sculpting techniques. You will have to change the aperture on your camera to make up for the higher light intensity from your accent light, which is responsible for sculpting the face (**Figure 12.3**).

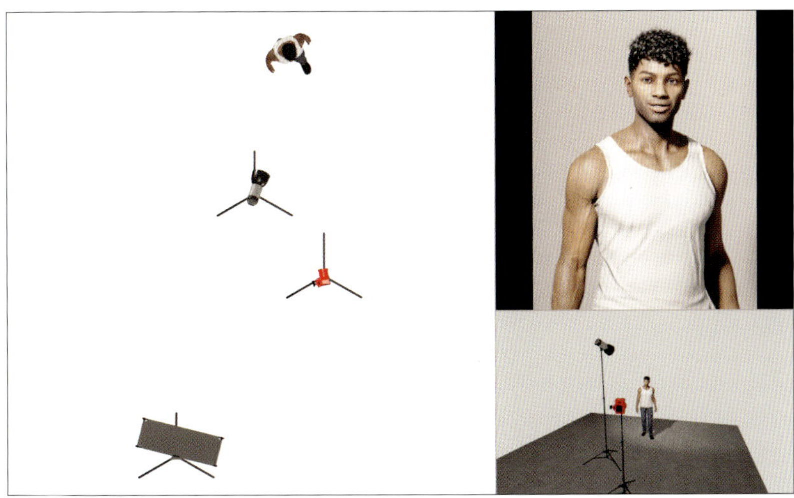

FIGURE 12.1

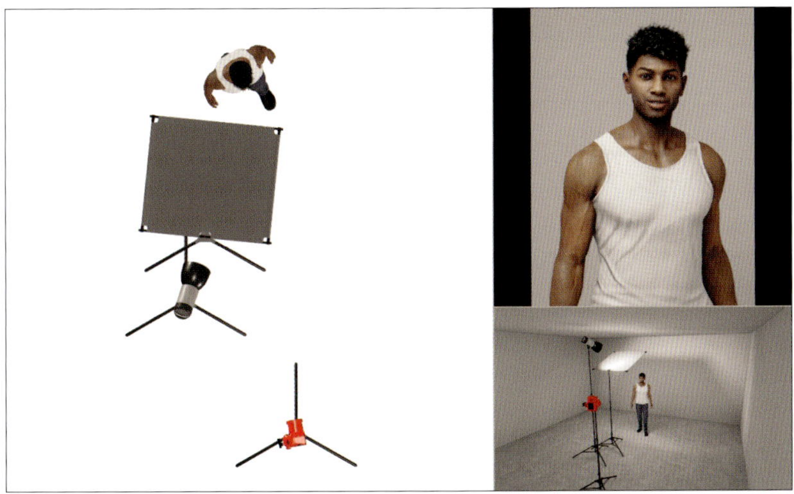

FIGURE 12.2

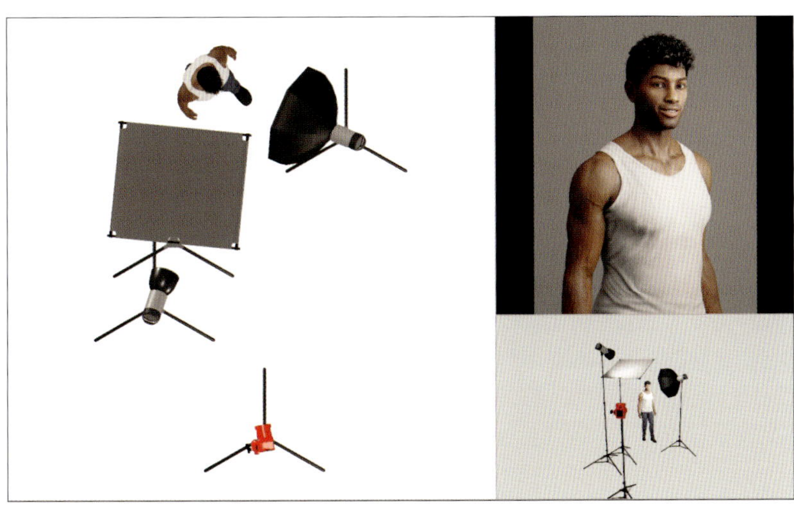

FIGURE 12.3

Lighting Exercise #2: Relationship Between Light Distance and Modifier Point of Failure

Purpose of Exercise

All modifiers are made for a specific look and purpose. The further the modifier is from the subject, the more that look degrades. Which is why it is silly to, for example, use a beauty dish 15 feet from the subject. At that distance, there is no evidence of the look of a beauty dish anymore.

This exercise helps you learn how far you can push your light modifiers indoors or outdoors so that they can still perform the way they were designed to. The lighting characteristics of each modifier changes depending on the distance to the subject. You don't have to memorize the lighting characteristics at every distance using every modifier, but you do want to have at least a basic idea of how the light is changing based on the modifier and its distance to the subject.

Conditions

In a typical studio, you have four walls. These walls create light pollution by bouncing the light around. The further the light is from the subject, the more light pollution will be evident on your subject and in the photo. Use the following modifiers for this exercise:

- Beauty dish

- Snoot

- Larger softbox

Set your camera to ISO 100, f/5.6, 1/200, and use a 50mm focal length.

Take a photo at three different distances: very close to the subject with the modifier just out of camera frame, then with the modifier at a medium distance away, then with it far away. Use the same 45-degree angle from the subject (see **Figures 12.4–12.6**).

Do the same thing outdoors to see how these modifiers behave outside in broad daylight. Outside there will be no walls to create light bounce and spill, so the lighting from the modifiers will look different on your subject. You want to know what that difference is and what it looks like. You will have to adjust the power of your flash or the aperture on your camera to maintain the correct exposure on your subject's face as the modifier's distance increases.

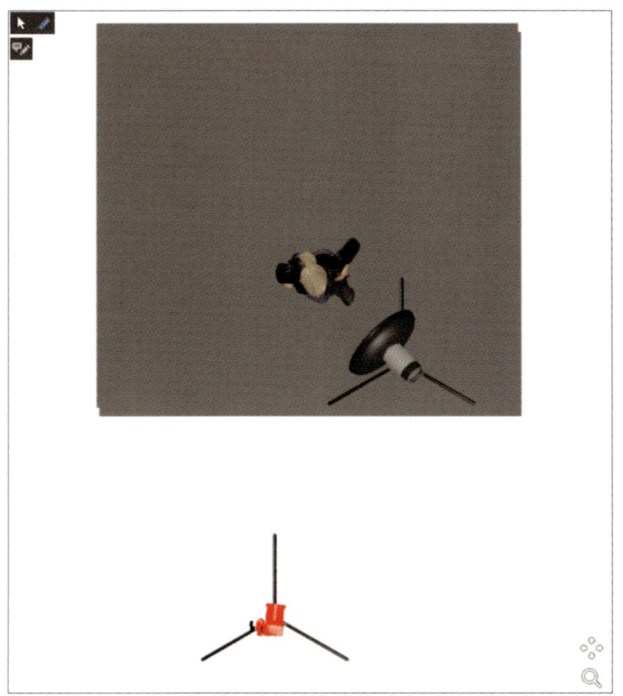

FIGURE 12.4

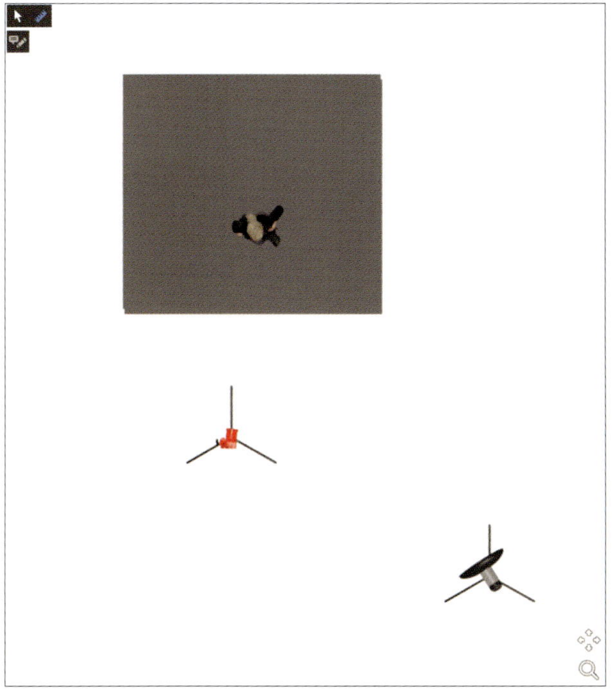

FIGURE 12.6

Goals

Goal 1: At what point does it become evident that the specific look of the modifier is being lost by light bounce/spill?

Goal 2: What happens to the background lighting at different distances for each modifier and at each distance?

Goal 3: What happens to the shadow/light transitions on your subject for each modifier and at each distance?

Goal 4: What could you do to remedy this light bounce/spill problem at the further distances?

Lighting Exercise #3:
Feathering the Light from Modifiers

Purpose of Exercise

Most modifiers are best used by feathering their light. With few exceptions, direct light modifiers create a hot spot in the middle of the modifier. But they create great light when the middle of the modifier is not directly pointed at the subject. In this exercise, you'll get to know how your modifiers behave when they are not pointed directly at your subject. When working through this exercise, ask yourself these questions:

- What does the light look like when the modifier is mostly behind the subject versus mostly in front of the subject?

- How does the light drop off?

- How does it look when the modifier is half-gelled with a color gel?

Conditions

With a non-black background, use these modifiers:

- Beauty dish

- Small softbox (single diffusion)

- Large umbrella

- Larger softbox (single diffusion, no grid)

Set your camera to ISO 100, f/11, 1/200, and use a 50mm focal length.

Take the same photo three times with the same pose. Keep everything the same per set. The only change between each of the three photos will be the angle of the light relative to the subject's face. With the light at a 45-degree angle to your subject's head, take a photo with the middle of the modifier directly pointed at their nose (**Figure 12.7**). Now change the horizontal angle of the light so that 75% of the modifier is pointed behind your subject (**Figure 12.8**). Next, shift the angle again so that 75% of the modifier is in front of your subject (**Figure 12.9**).

Goals

Goal 1: Determine how the various modifiers can be used when their light is feathered by not always pointing the middle of the modifier directly at the subject. Find and know the feathering quality of each modifier.

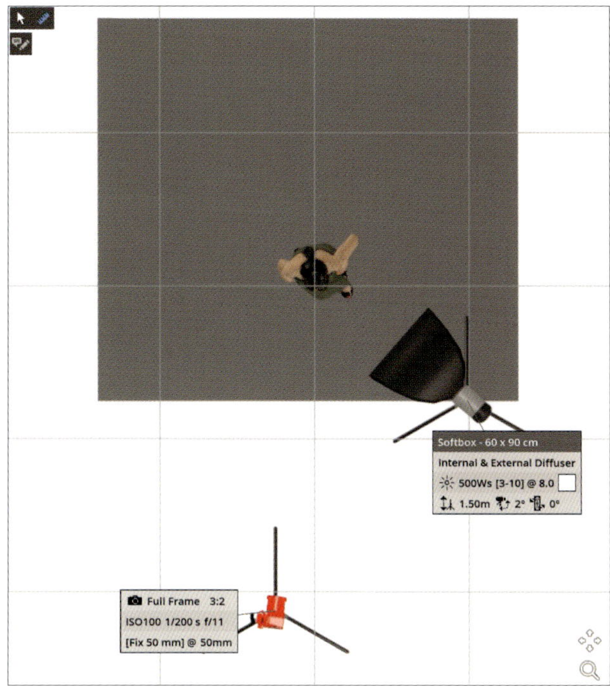

FIGURE 12.7

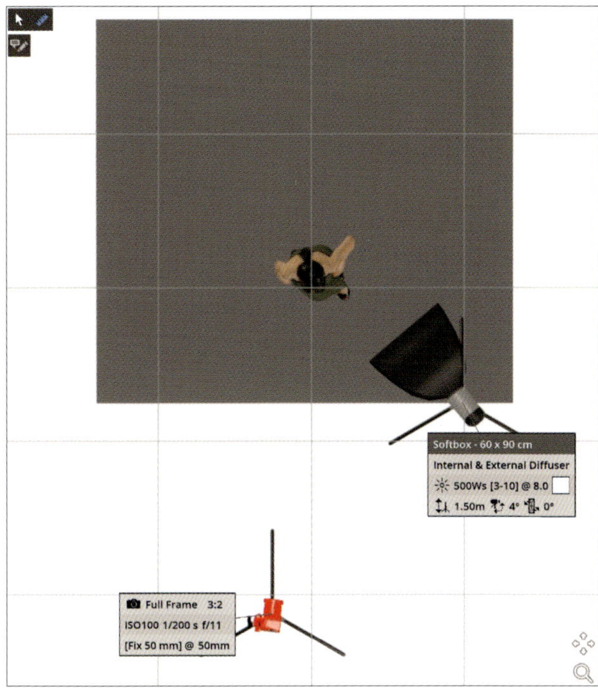

FIGURE 12.8

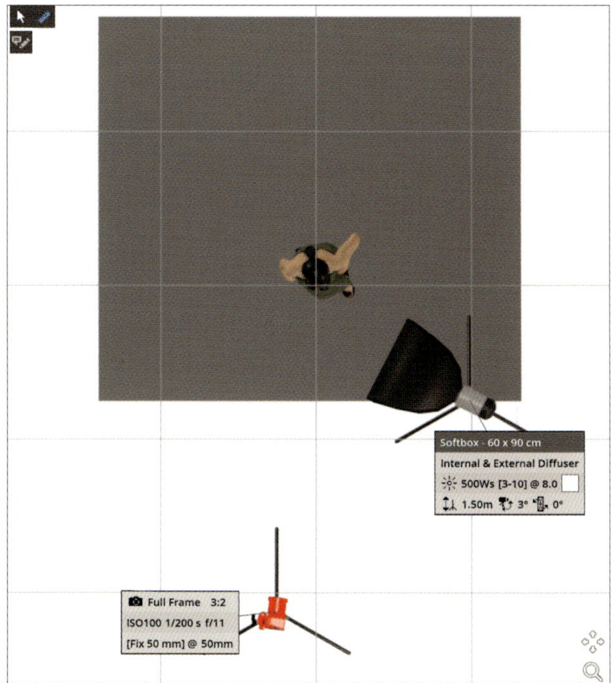

FIGURE 12.9

Goal 2: What happens to the background lighting at the three different lighting positions?

Goal 3: What happens to the shadow/light transitions on your subject for each modifier and at the three different angles?

Goal 4: Experiment with a fill reflector or V-flat to find out how each look can be modified by adding a fill light (**Figure 12.10**).

Goal 5: Use a creative color gel on the small softbox and only cover half of the modifier vertically. What look do you get with this technique?

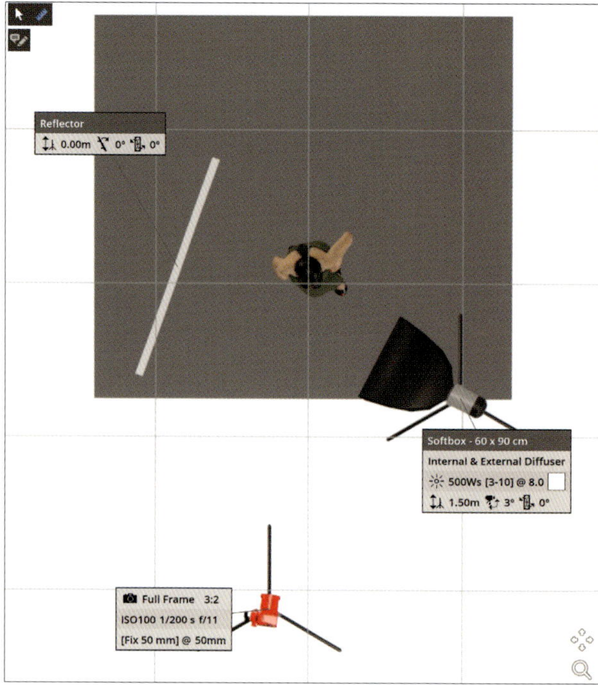

FIGURE 12.10

Lighting Exercise #4: Three-Point Lighting Setup—Combinations and Creativity

Purpose of Exercise

The purpose of this exercise is to become familiar and get creative with a Three-Point Lighting Setup. Mostly, the goal is for you to move the three types of lights around to achieve different looks. For example, you could move the rim light (also called hair light) into a kicker position to give you a slightly different effect. It is important to become aware of the many looks that a Three-Point Lighting Setup can provide because, for most portrait applications, you will most likely use this bulletproof setup. It never fails, and people love it! When things are going wrong, you can always count on the Three-Point Lighting Setup to rescue you. This is also the most popular type of lighting for video shoots.

There are three light positions in a Three-Point Lighting Setup. Notice I said "light positions" instead of lights. That's because you can have more than one light per position. You could have two lights mounted together as a key light, for example, and three lights working together to illuminate the background somehow. So, the Three-Point Lighting Setup is more like the Three Lighting Positions Setup. Don't get caught up on the number of lights, though. Just think about the positions and the role of the lights.

Position 1: Hair Light/Background Light: This position's main job is to create separation between the subject and the background. This light position can be behind the subject and high up, pointing down at the back of the subject's head and shoulders; or it can be pointed toward the background; or it can be moved a little into a kicker position to create soft, feathered light on the side of the subject's face.

Figure 12.11: This example shows the contribution the hair light makes. You can see how the hair and shoulders have a nice rim light that creates separation between the subject and the background.

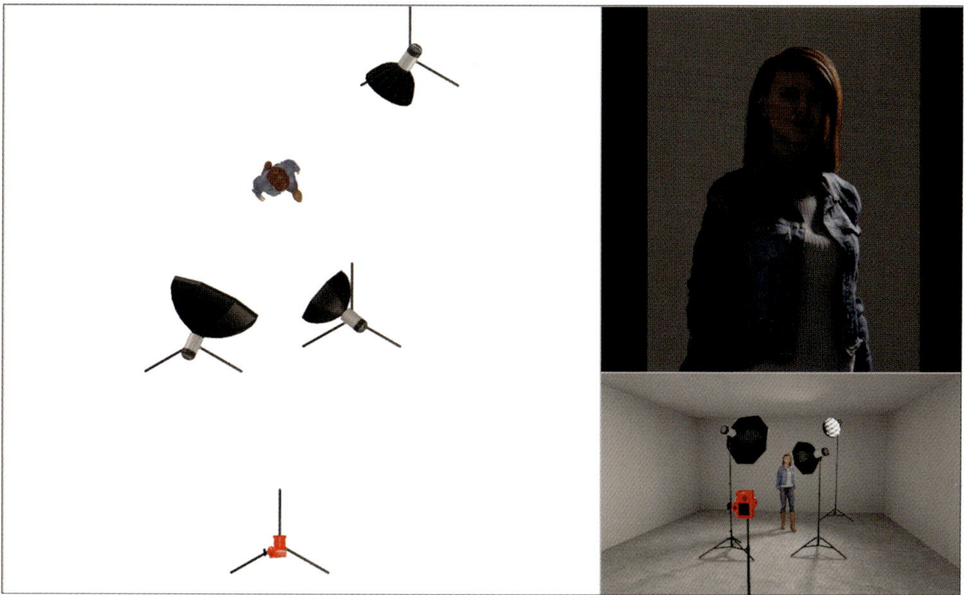

FIGURE 12.11

Position 2: Key Light: This is the key to the entire setup. It's the most important light. This is the light that is responsible for most of the illumination on your subject.

Figure 12.12: In this example, we have both the hair light and the key light working together. The key light is the light in front of the subject at camera left. You can see how the other side (the camera right side) of the subject's face is quite dark. That's why we add the third light position, called the fill light.

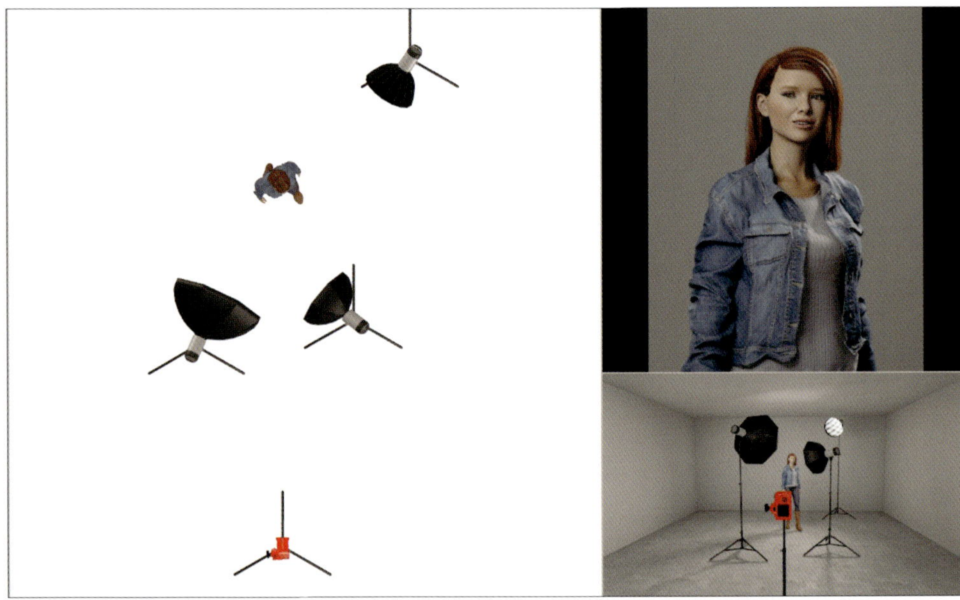

Position 3: Fill Light: A fill light's job is to fill the shadows created by the key light. This light is positioned on the other side of the face from the key light at a lower intensity to fill the shadows to your desired amount.

Figure 12.13: What a difference it makes to have that fill light lifting the shadows on the other side of the key light. Remember that these lights could be replaced by reflectors, walls (if outside), or anything that gets the job done. This photo employs the Three-Point Lighting Setup with all the lights working together to create the final photograph.

Conditions

This exercise should be done in the studio and also outdoors. By doing both, you will gain much more knowledge of how the lighting looks with a Three-Point Lighting Setup both indoors in a controlled environment and outdoors. When shooting outdoors, you could, for example, use a building wall as the fill light, the sun could be positioned behind the subject as the hair light, and a flash/strobe could be used as the key light. Get creative with this!

Goals

The goals for this exercise are creativity and awareness of the different looks you can achieve indoors and outdoors using a Three-Point Lighting Setup. This is an exercise in creativity, not technical ability. Keep that in mind. Move the lights around, use reflectors instead of lights, use gels, turn the hair light and move it to become a kicker light, and try lights on the background. Get creative. It will be a lot of fun!

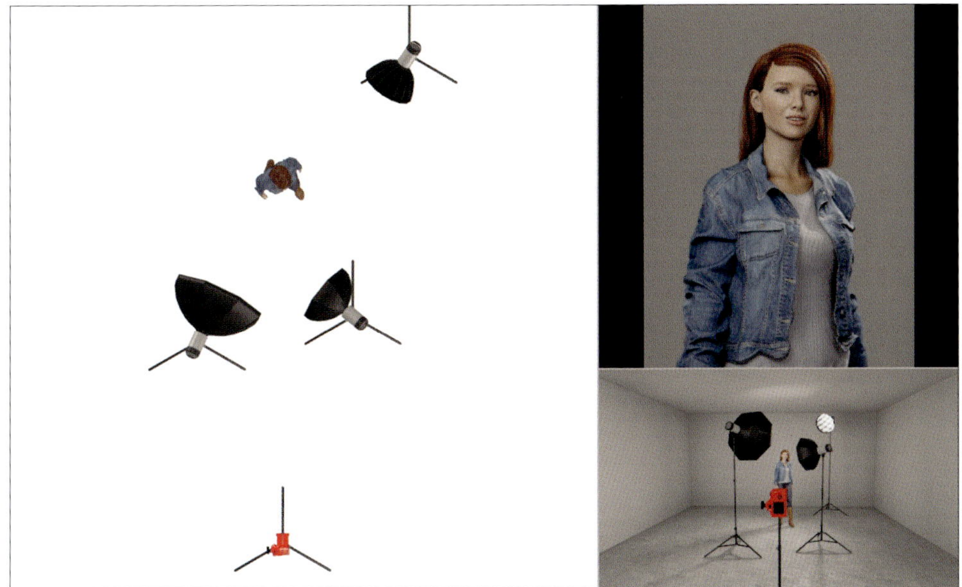

Lighting Exercise #5:
Complementary Colors Using Gels

Purpose of Exercise

Colors play a very important role in psychology. We can determine how we want the viewer of our photograph to feel simply by using the appropriate colors to create the mood and feeling we want in the image. Furthermore, we can add a visual kick to our work by taking advantage of the power of complementary colors.

The purpose of this exercise is to become familiar with the basics of color grading with complementary accent colors using gels.

Conditions

For this exercise, you need to be in a controlled environment such as a studio. This will eliminate any ambient light contamination that will take away from the effects of the color gels.

Goals

Goal 1: Using a white seamless background paper, use gels to color the background. Use ungelled white light on your subject. This is all about coloring the background (**Figure 12.14**).

Goal 2: Using a black seamless background, use gels on your subject to add color from the waist up. Minimize color spill onto the background by using a grid **(Figure 12.15)**.

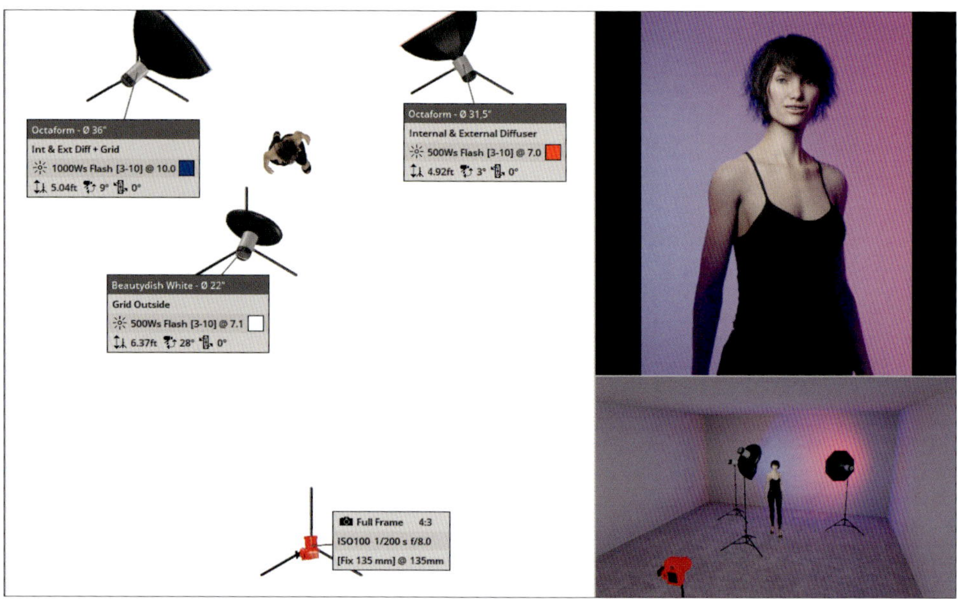

FIGURE 12.14

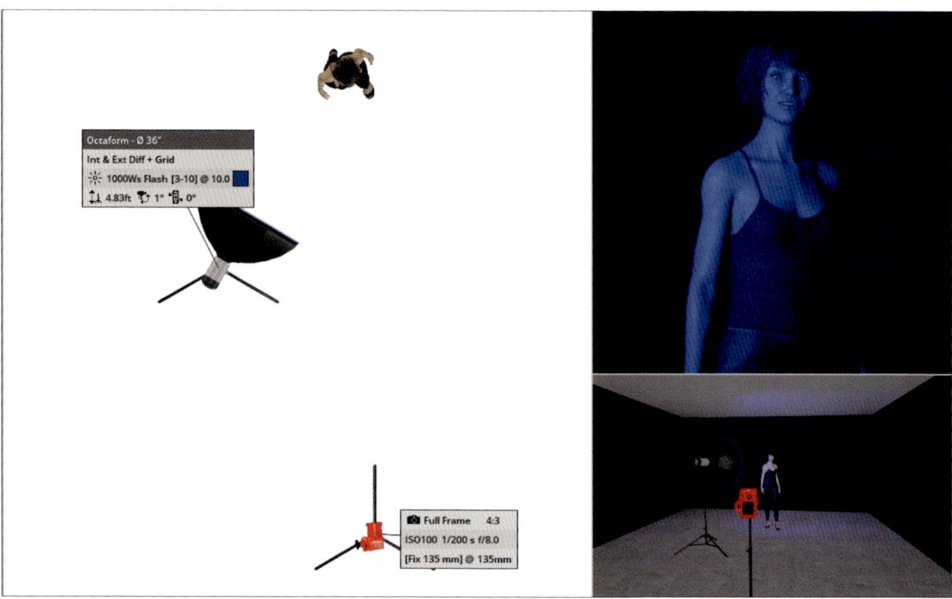

FIGURE 12.15

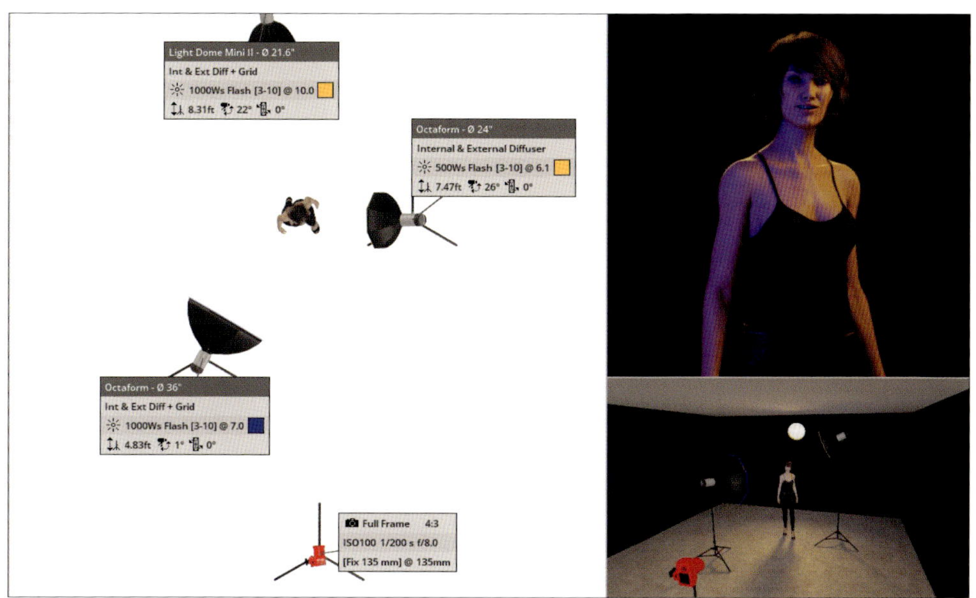

FIGURE 12.16

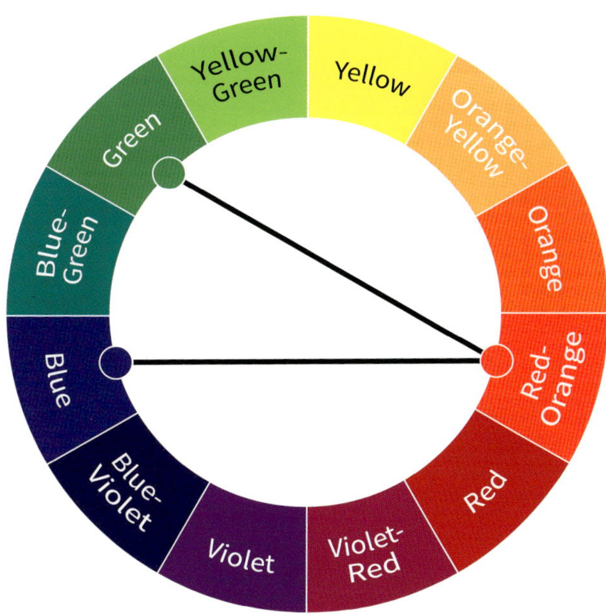

FIGURE 12.17

Goal 3: Continuing from Goal 2, now add a complementary accent color somewhere on your subject (**Figure 12.16**). This could be a rim light or a hair light. For example, you could use blue on your subject, then use one or two accent lights to color the hair yellow, or create a yellow accent outline behind the subject using rim lighting. Refer to the color wheel for ideas on complementary colors (**Figure 12.17**).

Lighting Exercise #6: Creating Accurate and Specific Separation Between Subject and Background Using a Light Meter

Purpose of Exercise

Photographers often simply set up lights with modifiers, place their subject in a typical spot, and start shooting. Whatever the background looks like, they simply accept it. But we can do better. In this exercise, you will use your light meter to get an accurate and specific separation between the subject and the background. We will shoot what we intended to shoot, not just accept whatever the camera gives us.

If you don't have a light meter, I recommend getting one. I understand that these days a light meter seems old-fashioned and unnecessary. However, for training purposes, a light meter can be a huge help! You don't have to get an expensive one, but you should definitely have one if you are serious about mastering flashes/strobes.

Conditions

The entire exercise requires the use of a light meter set to ISO 100. You will need two lights for the background on either side, and one light for the main subject. If you want to make it more challenging, you can use two lights on the main subject. Note, be sure to measure the background directly behind the main subject.

Goals

Create three different exposures with specific parameters between the subject and background. The goal is to understand the basics of flash metering using a light meter, and to be able to choose how bright or dark the background is relative to the subject based on the photographer's vision and desire, instead of by chance.

Goal 1: Photograph the main subject at standard settings (these can be whatever settings you want at ISO 100), but the background must measure the same exposure as the subject (**Figure 12.18**). For example, if you are at ISO 100, f/8, 1/160 on your subject, your background should read the same: ISO 100, f/8, 1/160.

Goal 2: Photograph the main subject at standard settings just like you did with Goal 1, but this time, the background must be one stop darker than the main subject (**Figure 12.19**). For example, if you are at ISO 100, f/8, 1/160 on your subject, your background should be at ISO 100, f/5.6, 1/160.

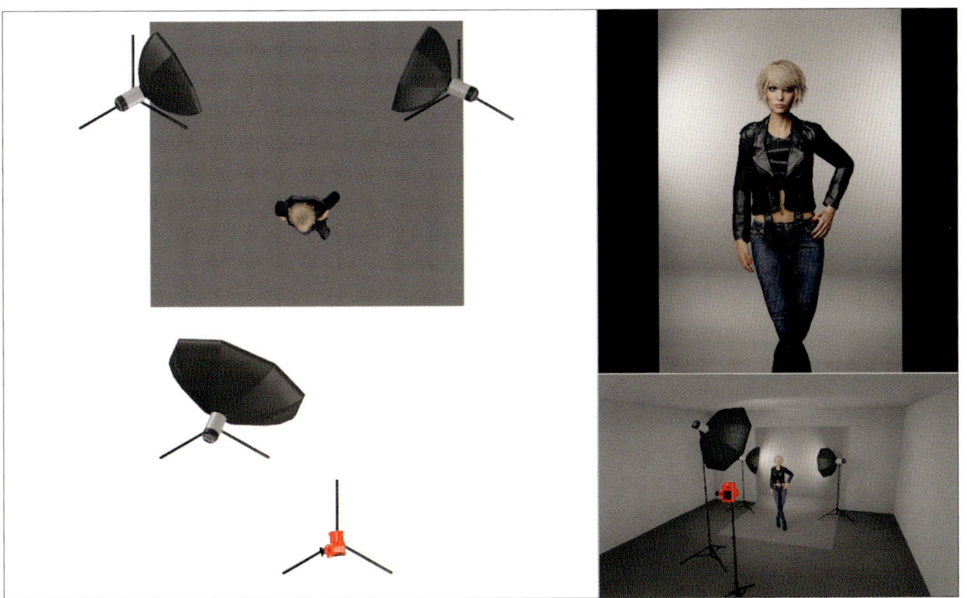

FIGURE 12.18

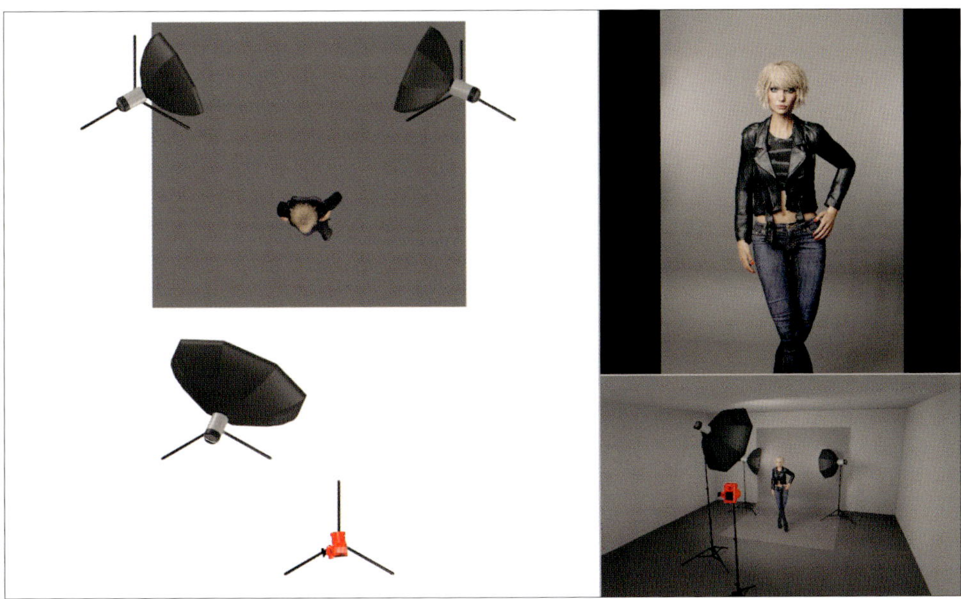

FIGURE 12.19

Goal 3: Photograph the main subject at the same standard settings, but this time, the background must be three stops darker than the main subject (**Figure 12.20**). For example, if you are at ISO 100, f/8, 1/160 on your subject, your background should be at ISO 100, f/2.8, 1/160.

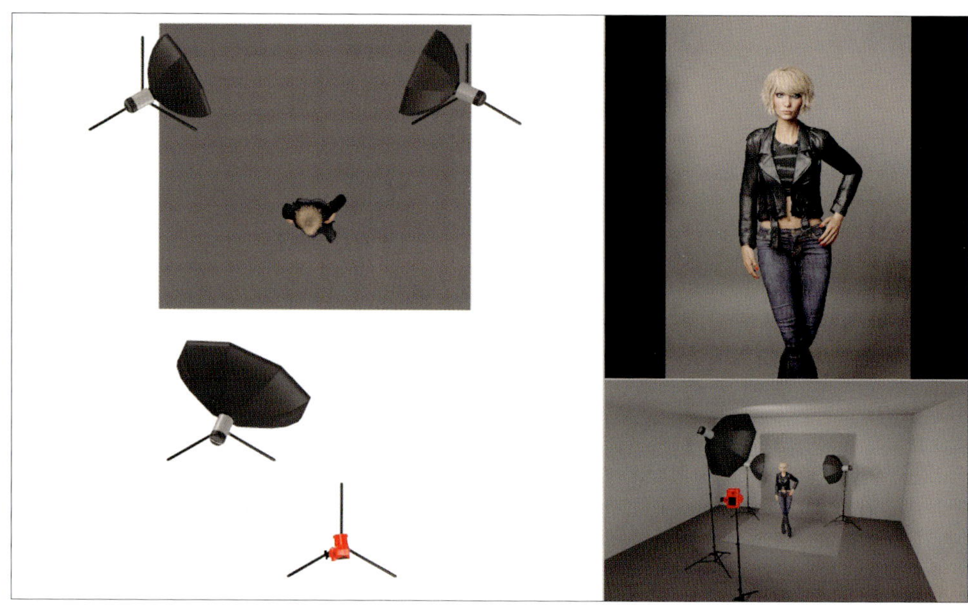

Lighting Exercise #7: Profile Portrait Lighting Using the Inverse Square Law

Purpose of Exercise

The purpose of this exercise is to understand and see the impact of the Inverse Square Law on a portrait. The best way to see the effects of the formula is to create a portrait in profile. With I = light intensity and d = distance, here again is the Inverse Square Law (**Figure 12.21**):

$$I = \frac{1}{d^2}$$

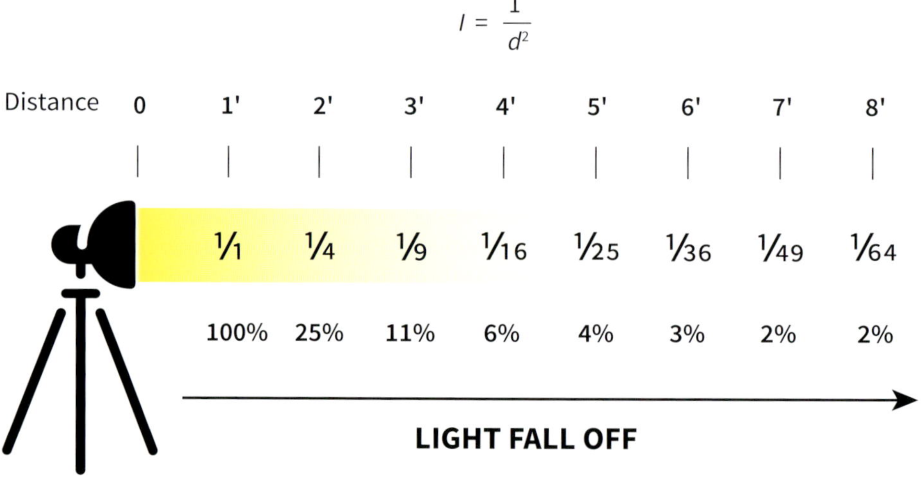

Conditions

As the light gets further away from the subject, you must increase the power of the light to maintain the same exposure on the front of the face.

For this exercise, keep your camera settings consistent. I used ISO 100, f/11, 1/200.

Goals

Take four photos of your subject in profile with varying distances of your light to the subject (**Figures 12.22–12.25**).

Take note of how the light on the face (cheeks) begins to change as the light gets further away.

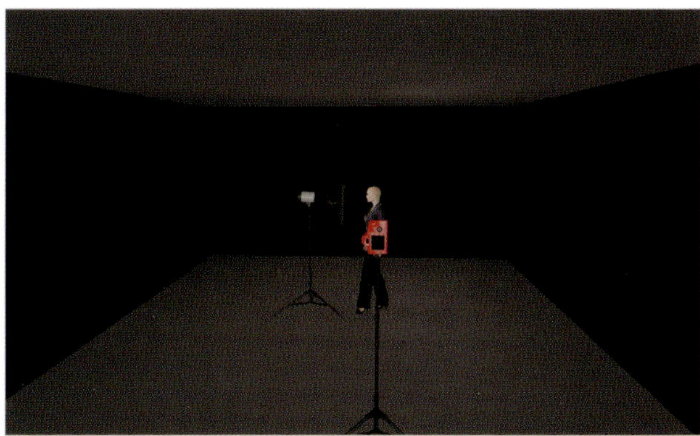

FIGURE 12.22

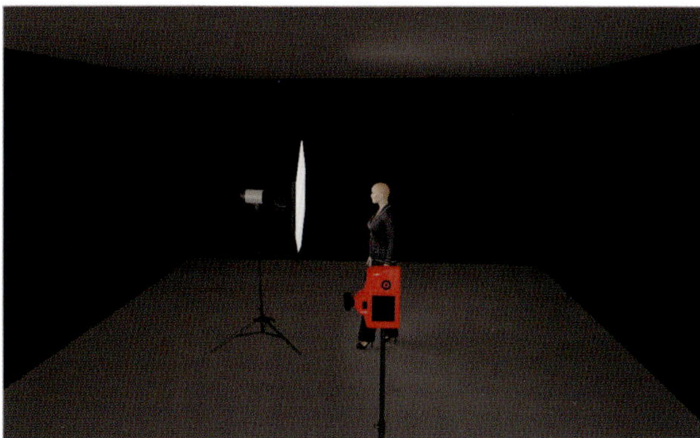

FIGURE 12.23

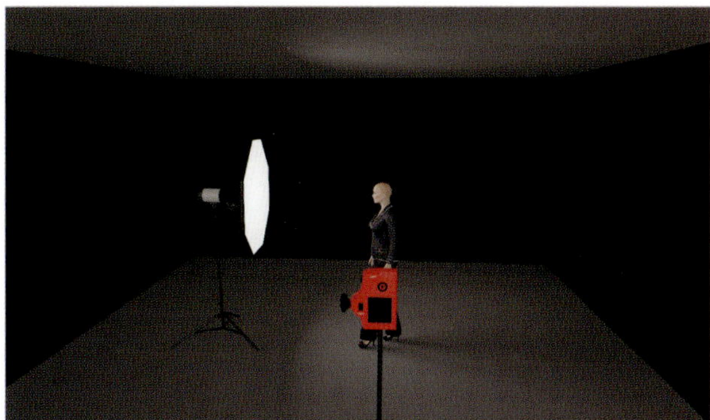

FIGURE 12.24

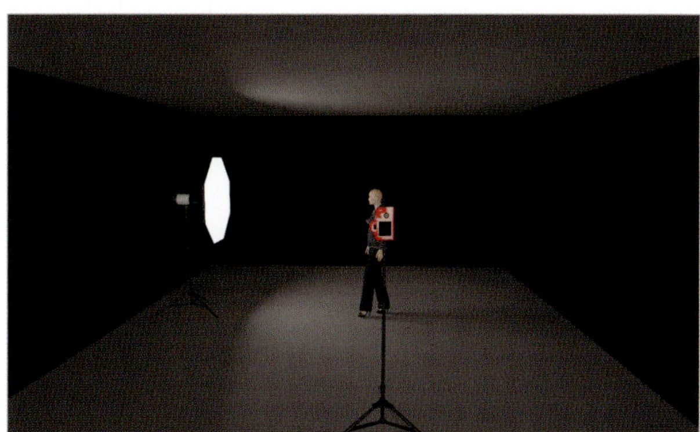

FIGURE 12.25

Lighting Exercise #8: Bounced Light Using the Inverse Square Law

Purpose of Exercise

The purpose of this exercise is to continue exploring the Inverse Square Law and its effect on portraiture. In this exercise, we will take two photos using indirect bounced light and compare the results. One photo will be with the bounced light close to the subject, and the other will be with the bounced light far from the subject.

You want to know the look and light behavior of both. When a subject is standing close to the wall being used to bounce the light from, figure out what kind of light behavior and sculpting capabilities you have. What does the lighting on the background look like relative to the lighting on the subject? Is it much darker or similar in luminosity? Ask yourself the same questions with the subject much further from the wall being used as a bounce.

For your flash settings, start with the most powerful light you have, set to the middle power level.

Conditions

Begin the exercise at ISO 100 and the rest of the camera settings set to obtain a correct exposure on your subject's face. Use the light meter for this. First measure with the light meter, then dial in the settings and shoot. Please don't guess at settings. Use your light meter.

Goals

Take two photos in your studio. For the first photo, place your subject around 5 feet from the white wall with the light right next to them, at head level, and positioned to bounce off the wall and illuminate the subject (**Figure 12.26**).

For the second photo, keep the light in the same place, but move the subject away and toward the back of the studio, around 10–15 feet away if possible (**Figure 12.27**). You will have to increase the power of your flash/strobe in order for the light to reach your subject's face with a correct exposure. You can bounce the flash on a white seamless paper or a white wall. Make sure you use the light meter to obtain a correct exposure for the second photo, as well, with your ISO set to 100. Both photos must be taken with ISO 100 and a correct exposure on the subject's face.

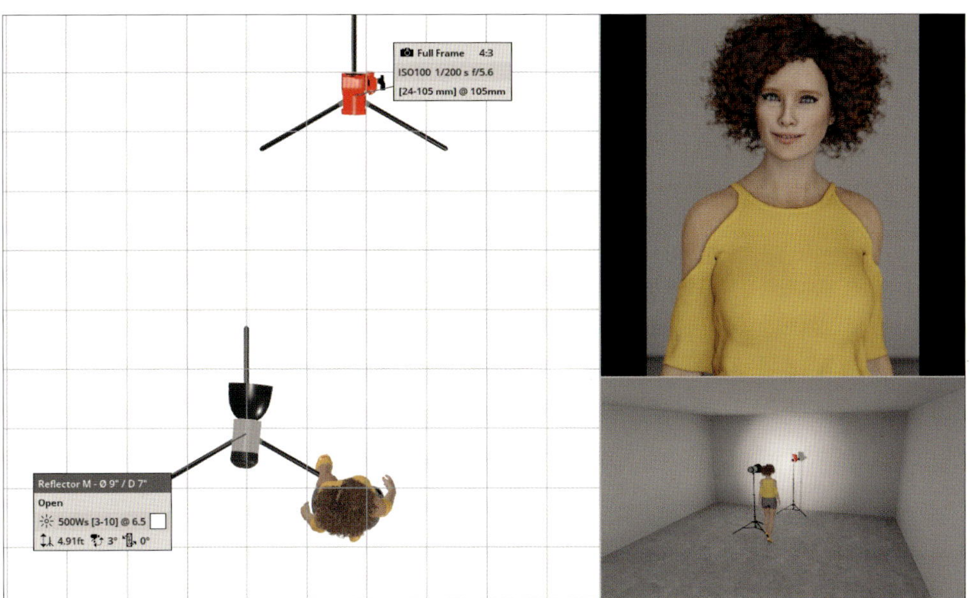

FIGURE 12.26

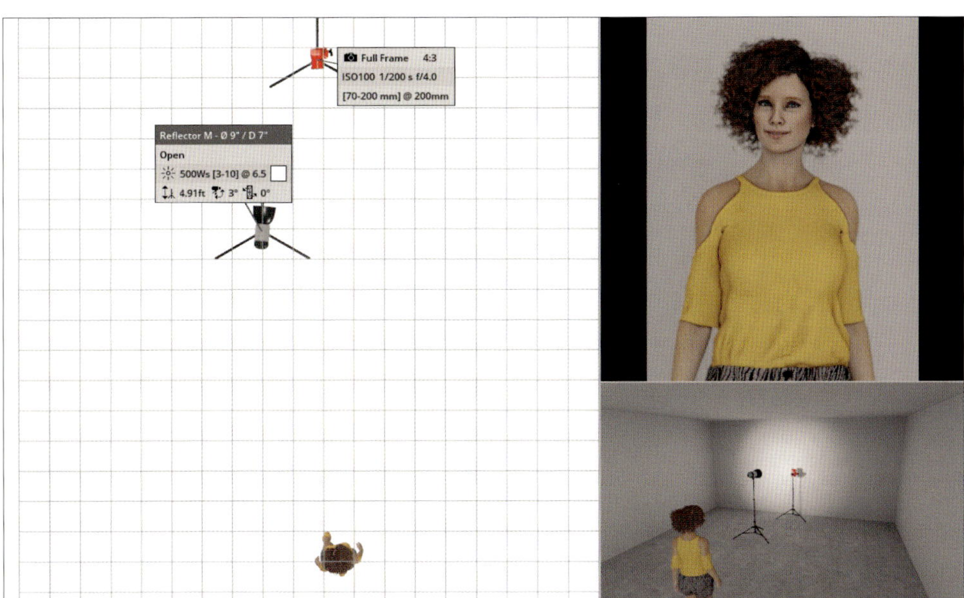

FIGURE 12.27

Lighting Exercise #9: Combining High-Contrast and Low-Contrast Lighting Using the Opposite Spectrums of the Inverse Square Law

Purpose of Exercise

In this exercise, we will explore the opposite sides of the Inverse Square Law in a single photo. The face will be lit by a high-contrast light setup. The clothes and rest of the body will be lit by a big and soft low-contrast lighting. This is one of my favorite and most used techniques for most of my fashion work.

Conditions

You will need two lights for this. One light needs to be a small light source such as a beauty dish with a grid set to a high power setting. The goal for the small light is to use the Inverse Square Law to yield the correct exposure on the key features of the face (nose and eyes), and as the light moves through the face (cheeks and ears), it quickly falls into dark shadows. The strong shadows throughout the face are key for this exercise.

The second light should be the biggest light source you have, set to the necessary power to give you a proper exposure (use a light meter). You could also bounce the light off a wall to make the light even bigger. The goal for the second big light is to illuminate the clothes without much contrast or shadows. This second light will also act as a fill light to control the high-contrast lighting on the face, in addition to illuminating the clothing to your desired level.

For your camera settings, use ISO 100 and a shutter speed of 1/125. For the aperture, choose the appropriate setting by using a light meter.

Goals

You only need to take one photo for this exercise. But to get to the final photo, you will have to experiment with different light settings on your strobes until you find the perfect balance (**Figure 12.28**).

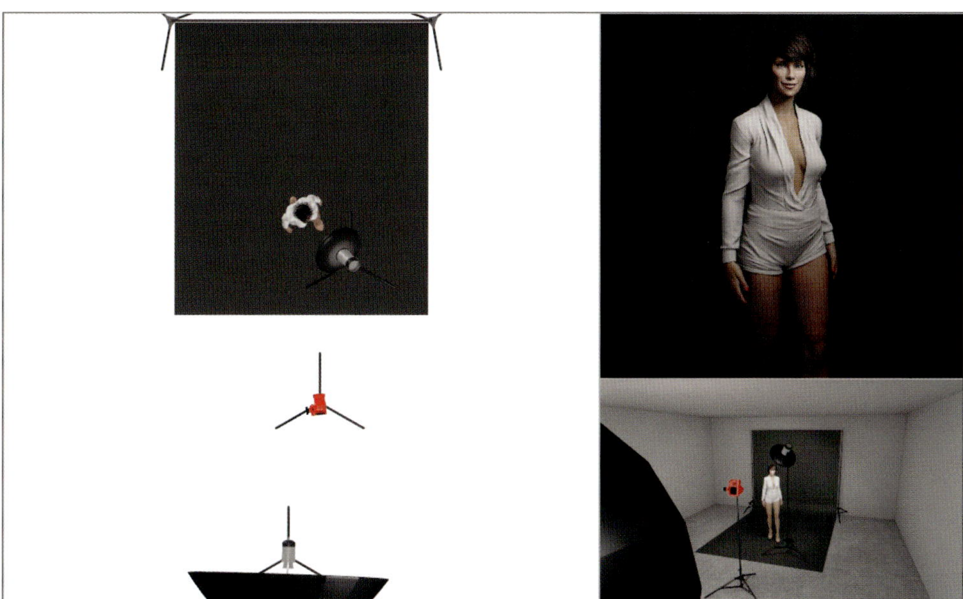

Lighting Exercise #10: In-Camera Skin Softening Using a Slow Shutter Speed and 2nd Curtain Sync

Purpose of Exercise

Let's explore in-camera skin softening. I use this technique often to create a different look in studio for beauty and fine-art portraiture. This technique combines the use of a very slow shutter speed with a very high-powered strobe set to 2nd Curtain Sync. The slow shutter will create a skin softening effect, and the powerful light firing at the end of the exposure will act as a "secondary shutter speed" due to the fast flash duration time, which will freeze the subject at the end of the exposure.

Conditions

Your strobe should be set to near its highest power. Use a big modifier to create a bigger lit area from head to toe. For a three-quarter body shot, use a smaller modifier.

Set your camera to ISO 100, 1/2 of a second to a full second for the shutter speed, and choose the correct aperture by using a light meter.

Goals

Have the subject stay still for the duration of the exposure. You can experiment with a little movement to create additional creative effects. But make sure their eyes are sharp regardless of what you do. If you have some fabric to play with, you can experiment with a little fabric movement. But try to keep the subject relatively still.

The photo examples in **Figures 12.29** and **12.30** are straight out of camera.

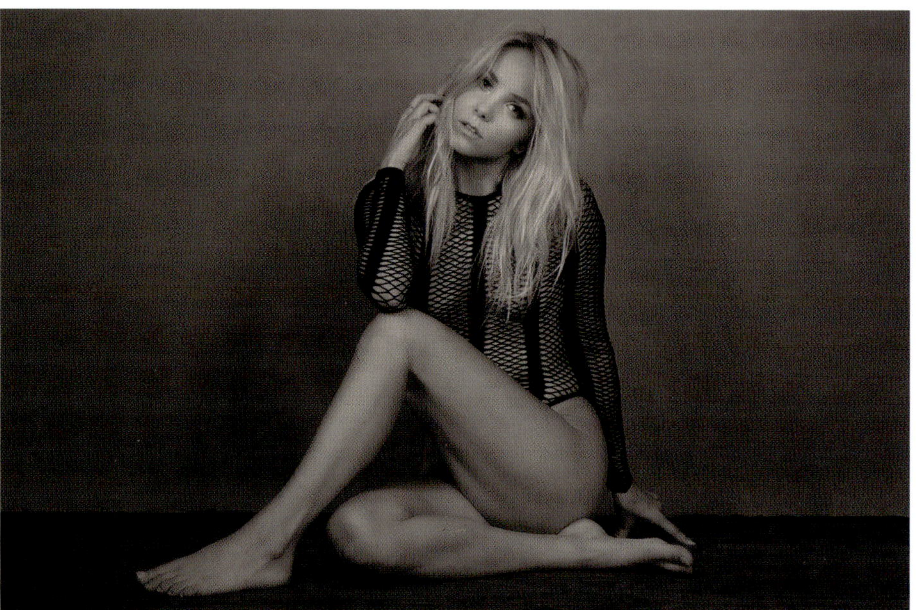

FIGURE 12.29

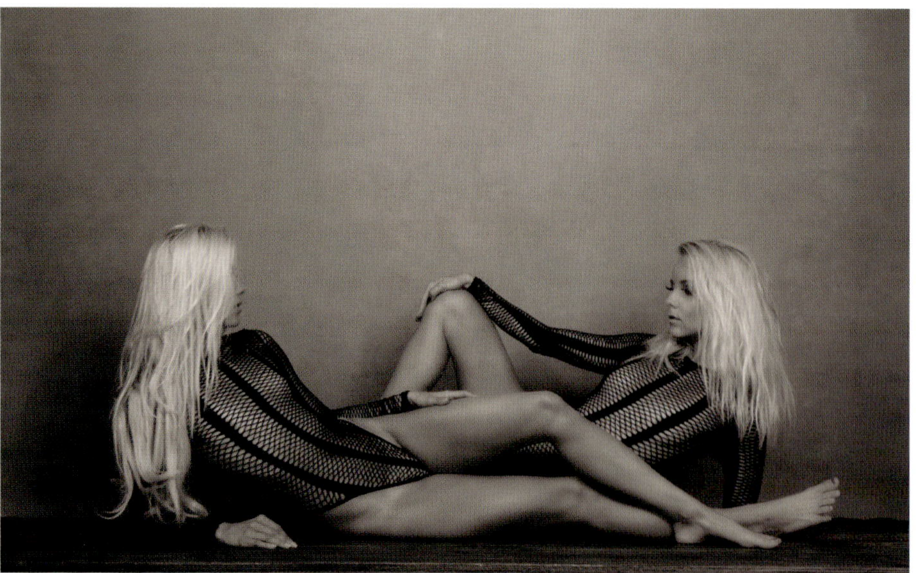

FIGURE 12.30

Lighting Exercise #11:
Short Versus Broad Lighting

Purpose of Exercise

The purpose of this exercise is to become familiar with the look of short lighting and broad lighting. Broad and short lighting are two of the most common lighting approaches in portraiture that you will encounter. Here are a couple quick definitions of each type of lighting.

Short lighting: Short lighting is when the side of the face that is farther from the camera is brighter than the near side.

Broad lighting: Broad lighting is when the side of the face that is closest to the camera is brighter than the far side.

When working through these exercises, think about the strengths and weaknesses of each approach.

Strengths: Ask yourself what each type of lighting is best at. What does it achieve? What are the benefits of this type of lighting? Who is this type of lighting good for? What do short lighting and broad lighting convey on male and female subjects?

Weaknesses: What are the weak points of these two types of lighting approaches? This is hard to answer, but try to determine any weaknesses you encounter through your experimentation.

Goals

Use different sized modifiers, and change the angle and proximity to the subject little by little to determine what gives you the very best rendition of short lighting and broad lighting. Make sure to try different intensities of light on the face for both lighting types.

Figure 12.31: Broad lighting the near side of the face to the camera.

Figure 12.32: Short lighting the far side of the face to the camera.

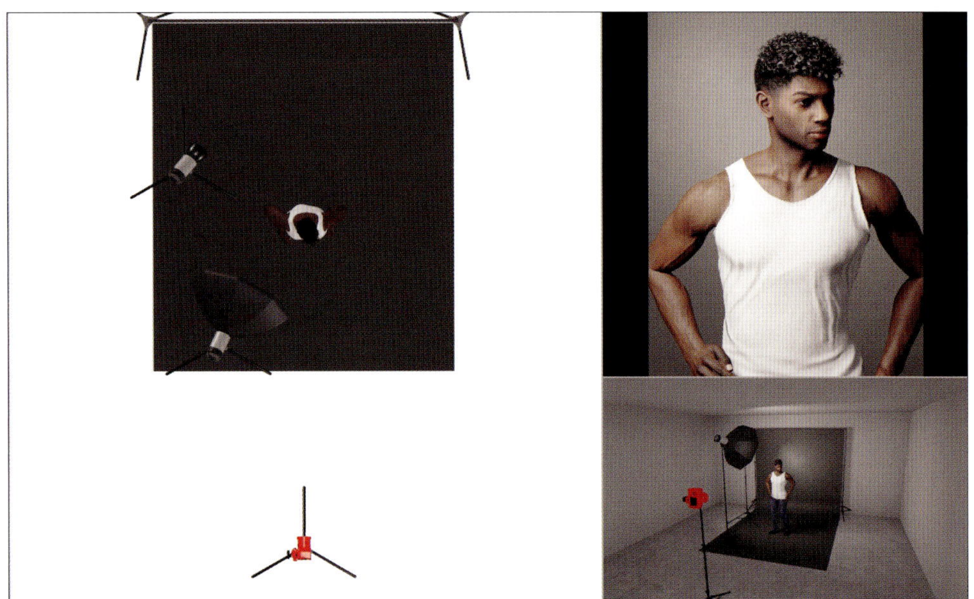

FIGURE 12.31

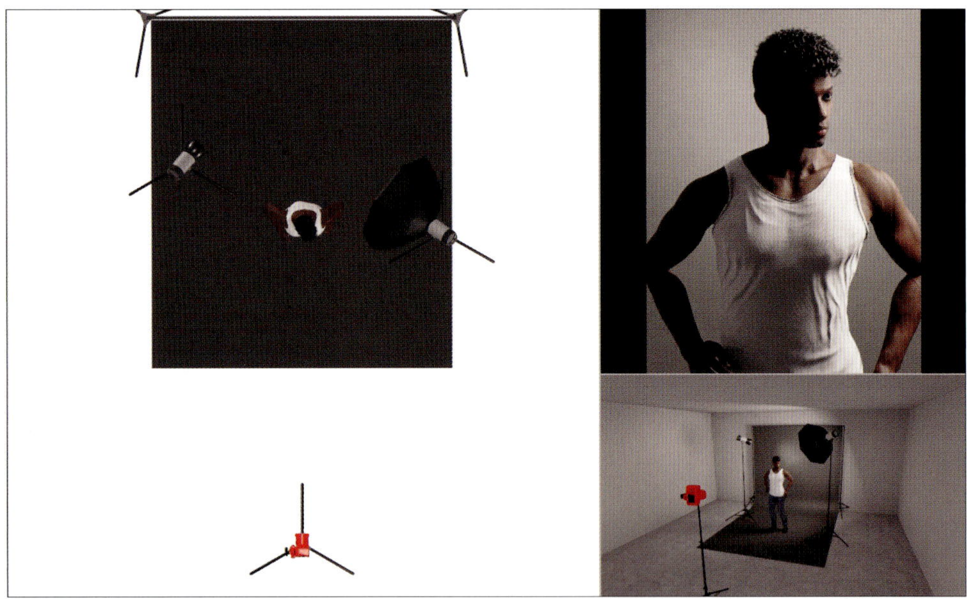

FIGURE 12.32

Lighting Exercise #12:
Butterfly Lighting Analysis

Purpose of Exercise

There are many types of portrait lighting patterns that have, over time, been categorized and given names. Even though I don't stick to these exact formulas all the time, I do use derivatives of these proven lighting types.

But one thing is for sure: knowing the strengths and weaknesses of each of the most important portrait lighting patterns can greatly influence how you work, how fast you work, and how creative you can be. In this exercise, we will examine butterfly lighting. But instead of adding more exercises for each of the most popular lighting patterns, I can just tell you that this exercise should be repeated for:

- Flat lighting

- Loop lighting

- Rembrandt lighting

- Split lighting

As you did in the previous lighting exercise, for each lighting pattern, assess its strengths and weaknesses on its own and compared to the others.

Strengths: What is this type of lighting best at? What does it achieve? What are the benefits of this type of light? What does this type of lighting do to different skin textures and colors?

Weaknesses: What are the weak points of this type of lighting? Try to note any weak points that you can think of.

Definition of Butterfly Lighting

Butterfly lighting is considered one of the key lighting patterns, and it's often used for beauty. Butterfly lighting is created by putting a light source, such as a beauty dish, directly above the subject's head and aligned exactly in the middle of their face.

If done correctly, you will see shaping of the cheekbones, a symmetrical shadow under the nose that resembles a butterfly, and a catchlight in both eyes from the light (**Figure 12.33**). If you don't see a catchlight in the eyes, your light is too high and most of the modifier is angled more toward the top of the subject's head instead of the face. Make adjustments as necessary.

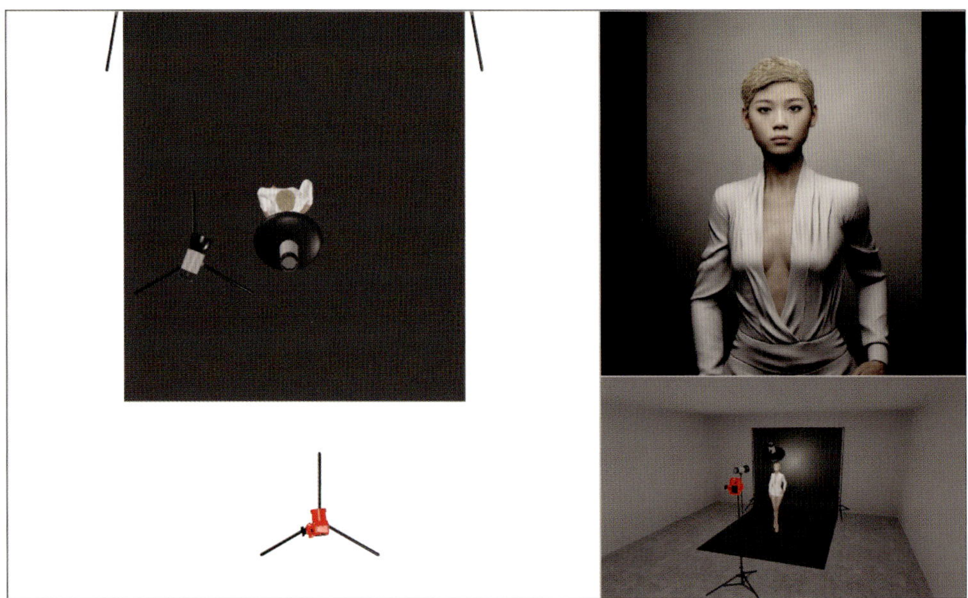

Goals

Use different sized modifiers and change the angle little by little to determine what gives you the very best rendition of butterfly lighting with catchlights in both eyes. The most common modifier for butterfly lighting is a beauty dish. If you have one, use it. If you don't, use a small- or medium-sized softbox or octabox.

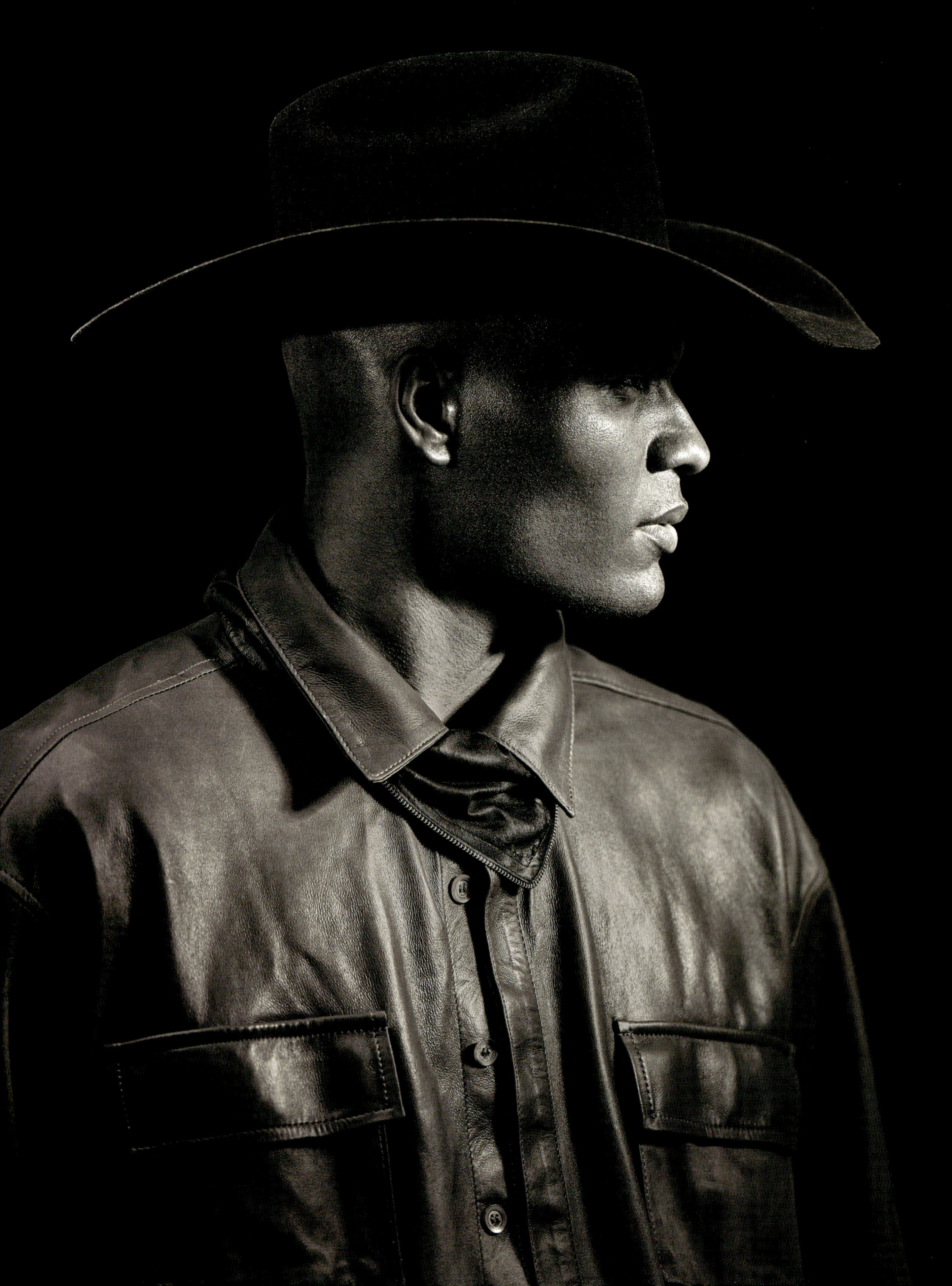

Index

blown-out light problem, 38–45
    adapting the pose to the sun technique for, 45
    diffuser overhead technique for, 41–42
    fill flash technique for, 43–44
    shadow direction technique for, 38–41, 43–44
blue gels, 100, 106, 108, 130
bounced light
    controlling contrast using, 79–80
    Inverse Square Law and, 236–237
    lifting shadows using, 70
bridal portraits, 36, 162, 163
Bright blending method, 128
broad lighting, 241–242
butterfly lighting, 243–244

C

cameras
    hot shoe flash on, 8, 211
    light meter of, 178–182
    mirrorless, 119, 199, 200, 202
    skin softening in, 239–240
Capture One, 35, 49, 51, 91, 93
case studies on NAME, 166–173
catchlight in eyes, 243, 244
Center Weighted metering mode, 181
channels, 157, 210–212
    how they work, 210–211
    sharing/not sharing flashes with, 211–212
children, high-key images of, 95
circumstantial light modifiers, 164
clashing moods problem, 55–56
clean white light, 52, 106
collapsible diffuser, 41, 64
color cast problems, 51–52
color grading, 106, 229
color relationships, 106
color wheel, 231
colored gels
    adding light with, 64
    angle of light and, 161
    color relationships and, 106–107

complementary colors using, 106, 229–231
    flash flaring effect with, 102–103, 134
    illuminating backgrounds with, 73, 103, 105
    moods created with, 19, 56, 97–109
    selective placement of, 108
    steps for shooting with, 97
complementary colors, 106, 229–231
contrast
    controlling with light, 75–80
    creating by adding light, 67–69
    Inverse Square Law and, 238–239
Cowboy Joe, 60–61
crafting the light, 31–32
creating a mood. *See* mood creation
CTO gels, 19, 56, 64, 100, 101, 102, 169

D

Dark blending method, 128, 129
diffuser overhead technique
    blown-out light and, 41–42
    splotchy light and, 47
diffusing hard light, 220–221
direct lighting, 156–160
direction of light problem, 53–54
distance from light source
    Inverse Square Law and, 140–141, 234–235
    modifier point of failure and, 222–223
dragged shutter effect, 20, 125–128
    1st and 2nd Curtain Sync and, 125–128
    panning technique and, 125
drama, creating with light, 67–69
Duran, Ivan, 15

E

effects with flash, 20–21, 115–135
    dragged shutter, 20, 125–128
    flash flaring, 133–135
    freezing motion, 116–120
    light painting, 34, 35
    Multi/Stroboscopic, 21, 33, 121–124
    multiple exposure, 128–133

electronic shutters, 199–200
energy of lights. *See* flash power
Evaluative metering mode, 180
exposure
    aperture for changing, 192–194
    flash power for changing, 190–192
    f-stop compensation game for, 195–196
    ISO for changing, 194–195
    not enough light problems with, 26–37
    too much light problems with, 37–48
eyes
    catchlight in, 243, 244
    heavy squinting of, 48
    importance of seeing, 62

F

FACES techniques, 6–7, 10–23
    add light, 13–15, 59–83
    create a mood, 16–19, 85–113
    descriptive overview of, 10
    effects with flash, 20–21, 115–135
    fix the light, 10–12, 25–57
    sculpt the light, 22–23, 137–153
    See also NAME process
facial expressions
    matching poses to, 45
    too much light and, 48
feathered lighting, 156–157, 159, 160, 224–225
Fernando case study, 167–168
fill light
    feathered lighting and, 159
    filling shadows using, 228
    flash group for, 213
    high-contrast lighting and, 238
    hot shoe flash used as, 173
    shadow direction technique and, 43–44
filters, neutral density, 125, 204
fixing the light, 10–12, 25–57
    clashing moods problem, 55–56
    exposure based problems, 26–48
    not enough light problems, 26–37
    poor quality of light problem, 49–51

too much light problems, 37–48
unflattering light problems, 26, 48–56
unwanted color cast problem, 51–52
wrong direction and size of light
    problem, 53–54
flags, 108–109, 150
flare effect. *See* flash flaring effect
flash
    angle of, 156–163
    bouncing, 70, 79–80, 236–237
    channels, 157, 210–212
    duration speed, 116–120, 200
    effects with, 20–21, 115–135
    fill light from, 43–44, 159
    groups, 156, 157, 213–214
    hot shoe, 8, 191–192
    Manual mode, 189–197
    metering modes, 179, 180–182
    natural light and, xv, xviii
    number of lights, 156
    stroboscopic, 21, 33, 121–124
    terminology for, 8
    triggering, 214–215
    TTL mode, 177–187
    See also lighting
flash duration speed, 116–120, 200
    freezing motion using, 118, 200
    measurements for describing, 116–117
    power setting related to, 118–120, 200
Flash Exposure Compensation (FEC), 185, 186–187
flash flaring effect
    examples of creating, 133–135
    gels used with, 102–103, 134
Flash ID setting, 157
flash power
    balancing lights using, 165, 173
    case studies on using, 167, 168, 170, 171, 173
    exposure adjustments and, 190–192
    flash duration speed and, 118–120, 200
    f-stop compensation and, 195–196
    Multi/Stroboscopic mode and, 121

flash sync
    1st Curtain Sync, 200–202
    2nd Curtain Sync, 126–127,
        202–203, 239
    High Speed Sync, 119, 204, 205–206
    typical speed of, 119
flat lighting, 67, 243
focusing attention with light, 80–83
freezing motion
    1st Curtain Sync for, 201
    2nd Curtain Sync for, 202–203
    flash duration speed for, 116–120, 200
f-stop compensation game, 195–196

G

Gabriel, R'Bonney Nola, xiv, 23, 32, 64–66,
    67–69, 111, 169–170
gels. *See* colored gels
GOBOs, 113, 164
gradient backgrounds, 214
grids
    function of, 164
    low-key photos and, 92
    minimizing color spill with, 230
    sculpting light with, 98, 145, 151
groups, flash, 156, 157, 213–214

H

hair
    freezing motion of, 120
    illuminating dark, 72, 96
hair light, 226, 227, 228, 231
Hanoi portrait case study, 170–171
hard light
    diffusing, 220–221
    moods created with, 88–90
hard modifiers, 164
Hertz (Hz) setting, 121
High Speed Sync (HSS), 205–206
    avoiding with ND filters, 204
    shutter speed and, 119, 205
high-contrast lighting, 238–239

high-key portraits, 91, 94–96
highlight feature, 83
hot shoe flashes, 8
    fill light using, 173
    flash output/power for, 191–192
    Multi/Stroboscopic mode on, 121–124
    remote function on, 211, 214

I

illuminating subjects, 28–30
indirect lighting, 156–160
infrared flash triggering, 214–215
intensity of light, 139–141
    explanation of, 139
    Inverse Square Law and, 140–141,
        234–235
Inverse Square Law of Light
    bounced light and, 236–237
    formula and illustrations, 140, 141
    high- vs. low-contrast lighting and,
        238–239
    light distance and, 140–141, 146, 150
    portrait profile lighting using, 234–235
ISO settings
    changing exposure using, 194–195
    creative use of gels and, 97
    problems with higher, 27

K

key light, 162, 213, 227
kicker lights, 214
Kolari Vision ND filters, 125, 204
Krause, Mandy, 60

L

Leibovitz, Annie, 59
light
    adding, 10, 13–15, 59–83
    angle of, 156–163
    blown-out, 38–45
    bounced, 70, 79–80, 236–237